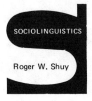

SERIES IN
SOCIOLINGUISTICS

Roger W. Shuy, *Series Editor*
Georgetown University and
Center for Applied Linguistics

The term *sociolinguistics* has been used since approximately the mid-1960s to designate the complex intersection of the fields of language and society. Sociologists have used linguistic data, often referring to the expression, *the sociology of language,* to describe and explain social behavior. Linguists, on the other hand, have tended to make use of social behavior to interpret linguistic variation. Still others have conceived of sociolinguistics in a more practical or applied sense, usually related to social dialects in an educational setting or language teaching. These three perspectives, sociological, linguistic and educational, are all legitimate, for it would be difficult to claim that any one group has an exclusive right to the term. It has become apparent increasingly that those who are interested in the ethnography of speaking, language planning, linguistic variation, the dynamics of language change, language attitudes, pragmatics, multi-lingualism and applied sociolinguistics are all concerned with sociolinguistics in one sense or another. As might be expected in any field, some scholars prefer the more linguistically dominating aspects, some the social or ethnographic, and some the applied or relational. Thus sociolinguistics may be studied in a number of different contexts.

This new series of books will cover a broad spectrum of topics which bear on important and changing issues in language and in society. The significance of social, linguistic, and psychological factors as they relate to the understanding of human speech and writing will be emphasized. In the past most language analyses have not taken these factors into account. The most exciting development of recent linguistic theory and research has been the recognition of the roles of context, variability, the continuum, and cross-disciplinary understanding.

To our mothers,

Alison Comish Thorne and Estella Ziegenhein Main,

in sisterhood

NEWBURY HOUSE PUBLISHERS, Inc.

Language Science
Language Teaching
Language Learning

68 Middle Road, Rowley, Massachusetts 01969

ISBN: 88377-043-1

Printed in the U.S.A.   First printing: August, 1975

LANGUAGE AND SEX:
Difference and Dominance

Edited by

Barrie Thorne
Michigan State University

and

Nancy Henley
University of Lowell, Massachusetts

NEWBURY HOUSE PUBLISHERS INC., ROWLEY, MASSACHUSETTS

FOREWORD

Current studies in sociolinguistics are being carried out from several linguistic and social perspectives. The "linguistics of sociolinguistics" has approached variability in language from the accesses of phonology, lexicon semantics and language acquisition. The "sociology and ethnography of sociolinguistics" has approached variability from the viewpoint of stereotyping, power structure, status, interaction and role development. In addition to an annotated bibliography, editors Thorne and Henley have used care in their selection of papers to represent examples of current sociolinguistic interest. Included here are the recent papers of linguists, sociologists, psychologists, and educators, all addressing the topic of language and sex from one of these perspectives. Any perspective could be expanded to book length, as the editors would gladly admit. It is hoped, in fact, that this book will stimulate such efforts.

Whenever a new or recurring theme develops in sociolinguistics, scholars face the problem of finding adequate materials to serve as a basis for research, practical action programs, and teaching. No theme gives a better example of this than the current discussions about language and sex. An immediate need is a practical bibliography—one which tells the reader more about the citations than simply their titles and authors' names. Researchers who want to build on past experiences can be saved hours of false starts and blind alleys in literature reviews; developers of action programs can get a quick assessment of available resources; teachers can select effectively from among rapidly developing literature for student readings or personal classroom preparation. With the bibliography in this book, editors Thorne and Henley have provided such a reference tool.

With pride, then, this new series opens treating a subject which is of immediate social and political concern, and one which has already attracted the attention of such competent scholars as those whose articles are included.

Roger W. Shuy

Georgetown University and
Center for Applied Linguistics
July 1, 1975

PREFACE

"Speech and sex are linked in obvious ways," wrote the anthropologist Edward T. Hall in 1959. "Let the reader if he [sic] doubts this, start talking like a member of the opposite sex for a while and see how long people let him [sic] get away with it." Unfortunately for those of us to whom those "obvious ways" were less than obvious, Hall wrote little more on the topic. Fifteen years later, a range of investigators (mostly women) are finally beginning to explore the myriad and complex—and far from obvious—ways in which language and sex are linked.

This book rides in on the first crest of what we expect to be an ocean of interest in the topic. The articles it includes are exciting as only important new discoveries can be. All the facts are by no means in for a full understanding of sex differences in language, but enough hard facts *are* in to lay a foundation for a wide-ranging program of research in years to come. And from the facts that are in, theoreticians have begun to provide important analyses and provocative speculations. We, like many others directly or peripherally involved in studying the sexual differentiation of language, are thrilled to be caught up in this developing field.

But more than that, it's a field whose implications strike to the core of our lives. The social consequences of a language—in daily use by hundreds of millions of people—which tends to deprecate or ignore a whole class of human beings, and to set them apart by their usage, are devastating. Enough hard facts on gender and language are also in to lay a foundation for a wide-ranging program of action, in addition to research. As women committed to equality and liberation, we hope this book will serve as a resource that will lead to the understanding that is a necessity for change. By definition, social science cannot possibly exist in an ivory tower. Nor can linguistics; it is the study of the human language which voices our hopes and tragedies, loves, hates, fears, strivings, and failures. To divorce such study from life, from social and political reality, is to have a mockery of a science studying a mockery of human beings.

This book, which we hope will further both systematic inquiry and social change, is divided into two parts. The first is a selection of articles which cover some of the range of questions, methods, and disciplines which converge in this area. The second is a comprehensive annotated bibliography on sex differences in language, speech, and nonverbal communication. Because they come from a variety of fields and sources, the articles at times duplicate each other, particularly in reviewing the field. This occasional repetition, however, is enlightening with regard to different researchers' approaches and interpretations.

The bibliography is a revision of one that we have been circulating, upon request, since June 1973. (We would like to acknowledge assistance from the Department of Sociology, Michigan State University, which made such circulation physically possible.) The bibliography has already gone through three previous editions; this latest is as up-to-date as we could make it at the time of writing, summer 1974. The bibliography owes a great debt to women, and some men, all over the country, who have kindly called our attention to articles we had missed, sent us copies of their papers, shared information with us, and generally been most supportive. We thank them in a glow of pride in developing sisterhood. A special word of thanks to Mary Ritchie Key and Cheris Kramer.

Bringing together the articles for this book has also brought us into contact with scholars with whom it has been a pleasure to work, either in person or through the mails. We are particularly grateful to those who prepared or revised articles especially for this book, and we thank them for their patience in working with two editors half a continent apart.

We do not wish to lose sight of the fact that it was the women's liberation movement that pushed this field of study into prominence, and created the atmosphere for its acceptance and legitimation. We cannot begin to thank all the women whose unknown acts of courage, in direct and indirect ways, have made this book possible; but as the women's liberation movement forwarded the book, we hope that the book in turn may forward the movement.

Finally, we wish to thank those around us, especially Craig, Peter, and Andrew, for their positive support and substantive contributions in our months of work on the bibliography and book.

Barrie   Thorne
July   1975   Nancy   M.   Henley

CONTENTS

**SEX DIFFERENCES IN LANGUAGE, SPEECH,
AND NONVERBAL COMMUNICATION: AN
ANNOTATED BIBLIOGRAPHY**

Language and Sex:

DIFFERENCE AND DOMINANCE

Selected Papers

INTRODUCTION

The following papers have been selected to represent current inquiry into the relationship of language and sex. Seven of the papers are being published here for the first time; the other five were first published elsewhere. The first two papers (by Thorne and Henley and by Kramer) and the last paper (by Henley) are comprehensive, laying out and interpreting the state of this general field of research, and suggesting questions which warrant further study. The other papers, which in each case provide new empirical data (or, in Bodine's case, a reinterpretation of data), are arranged roughly in the order of the bibliography topics.

The papers by Graham, based on analysis of children's schoolbooks, and by Schulz, which examines the historical development of pejorative terms relating to women, both explore facets of sexism in language. Swacker's experimental study of the speech of males and females indicates sex differences in word choice and language style. Brend's brief paper documents sex differences in intonation patterns, and Trudgill analyzes data about sex differences in choice of phonetic variants. The paper by Zimmerman and West is an ingenious analysis of conversational patterns between the sexes, especially of interruption and control of topics. Under the general theme of cross-cultural research on women's and men's "languages," Bodine provides a comprehensive review and reanalysis of an old body of literature, much of it about societies which no longer exist. There are two papers which fall under the general rubric of language acquisition: the one by Sachs shows the importance of cultural learning in shaping the voice patterns of prepubertal boys and girls, and Cherry examines the effect of sex of child on the verbal interaction between teachers and children in preschools.

The wide variety of disciplines and research methods encompassed in these papers is typical of this field as a whole. The area of inquiry has not grown in a centralized or unitary fashion, but rather by parallel development and by a convergence of interest coming from widely dispersed places. The authors of these papers come from linguistics (Brend; Trudgill); lexicography (Graham); anthropological linguistics (Bodine); psycholinguistics (Henley); sociolinguistics (Zimmerman, West, and Thorne); speech communication (Kramer); speech physiology (Sachs); child development (Cherry); and English (Schulz; Swacker).

There is a similar range of methods of research, including analyses of the content of language (Graham; Schulz), linguistic analysis of corpuses of speech (Trudgill; Brend); structural analysis of speech gathered in naturalistic settings (Cherry; Zimmerman and West); and experiments (Swacker; Sachs).

Our hope is that this juxtaposition of methods, topics, and frameworks of study will serve to stimulate further research and interest in language and sex. The topic is just coming into its own; we hope that the publication of this volume will help bring it to fruition.

3

DIFFERENCE AND DOMINANCE:
AN OVERVIEW OF LANGUAGE, GENDER, AND SOCIETY*

Barrie Thorne and Nancy Henley

Interest in the different relations of the sexes to their language dates back at least to 1664, the year of the publication of a report which cites different women's and men's forms in the speech of the Carib people (Jespersen, 1922). Throughout the history of this area of study, the issues of difference and dominance have remained at the heart of the field. While the cataloguing of sex *difference* in language has seemed the primary task to most investigators (preliminary to any analysis), and the whole task to some, the social context of male *dominance* has nevertheless found occasional recognition. And when it has not, it has remained an unobserved influence, affecting the interpretation and presentation of data. In the recent spurt of growth in this developing field, this context is generally taken for granted as a necessary background for discussion and interpretation of data.

This overview, which will explore the themes of difference and dominance in some detail, begins with a brief history of research on the sexual differentiation of language. It then turns to the *language* side of the intersection between language, gender, and society, emphasizing sociolinguistic frameworks and distinctions. Next it examines the *social context,* relating sex differences in language and speech to the social differentiation of the sexes, the structure of male dominance, and the division of labor by sex. The paper concludes with a discussion of language and social change, and with attention to some of the many speculations, questions, and untested hypotheses which await further research.

*We would like to thank Cheris Kramer for critical comments on an earlier version of this paper.

A DEVELOPING FIELD

The study of sex differences in English is now coming into its own. Mary Ritchie Key has been teaching a course on "Linguistic Behavior of Male and Female" at the University of California, Irvine since 1969, and scores of similar courses have since been taught at colleges and universities across the country. The authors of this paper began distributing an annotated bibliography on sex differences in language, speech, and nonverbal communication in July 1973; the bibliography found great demand and went through three revisions within a year. In the edition of the bibliography which appears in this book, in the area of language differences there are 81 items dated after 1970, compared with 34 items dated in the years 1961-70, 12 from 1951-60, and a total of 20 items from the first fifty years of the century. This count indicates the relatively sparse attention to this subject in earlier years, and the rapid spread of interest more recently.

In the early part of this century anthropologists wrote about "men's and women's languages" in other societies, all far removed from Western cultures (which were generally imagined to be linguistically androgynous). Over the years, as linguistics matured as an independent discipline, this topic has remained one of the esoteric cubbyholes of language study, notwithstanding a small spurt of interest in sex-based language variation in the 1940's (Bodine, 1975). In the 1960's sociolinguistics emerged as an interdisciplinary field of interest, bringing systematic attention to language as a social phenomenon. Here was a specialty that should certainly have turned its attention to the relationship of sex and language—it looked at the linguistic consequences of such nonlinguistic phenomena as class, race, social setting, and political relations. Nevertheless, sex differentiation in language did not become a focus of study.

And the little that was written about sex difference in English often defined it as a curiosity, a source of some amusement, hardly worth serious study. Jespersen's influential *Language: Its Nature, Development and Origin* (1922) cited women's supposed preference for refined, euphemistic, and hyperbolic expression, and men's alleged greater use of slang and innovations—those examples both reflecting and reinforcing traditional sex stereotypes.

It may seem puzzling that linguists who observed variations by sex in other languages and the use of gender in their own and in other languages, failed to note any correspondence between the two phenomena (cf. Bodine, 1975) or to examine their own languages for sex-based variation. It may seem even stranger that sociolinguistics, which documented great social and linguistic consequences from accidents of birth, failed to note the consequences of being born female, especially when we consider that the identification of sex is probably the primary organizing variable in thinking about ("processing information" about) other human beings.

However, as Kuhn's (1962) study of the development of scientific paradigms has shown us, knowledge does not progress entirely linearly, or "rationally," according to some internal dynamic; its progress is determined more by the dynamics of forces external to itself, especially those forces we would term "social." Such is the case in linguistics and other disciplines dealing with language. Often disciplines have been pushed by social movements into interests they long avoided. In this case, it took the impetus of the women's movement in the late '60's and early '70's to spur the study of sex differences in English.

Being part of a social movement doesn't make the going easy. When women both in and out of linguistics argued the importance of such study, or questioned the logic of certain linguistic givens, or recommended deliberate efforts to change the language, they were met with ridicule, particularly from academicians. However, this field of study grows stronger daily, and it won't be transitory or superficial. The questions of the women's movement are fundamental, raising doubts about those very basics of life we unconsciously take for granted. These basics form the "unconscious patterning of behavior in society" which Sapir (1927) wrote is best appreciated when left unexamined—except, he added, when its examination is necessary for the purpose of social change.

The questions raised cast doubts on our habits, our knowledge, and our theory, as well as point to the gaps in our knowledge: Can the "generic *he*" be justified? Are women really more talkative than men? Are there separate women's and men's languages, and if so, do they constitute merely a gender-marking convention, or an act of political supremacy? Is there a women's language which both sexes learn when young, and a men's language to which boys must later switch? (cf. Lakoff, 1973).

DISCIPLINES, FRAMEWORKS, AND METHODS

One reason for the vitality of this field of study, in addition to its newness and promise, is the variety of backgrounds from which its students hail, a variety which offers intriguing juxtapositions of data and perspective. Analysis, findings, and commentaries on the sexual differentiation of language have come from linguists, lexicographers, speech physiologists, anthropologists, psychologists, sociologists, novelists; people in speech communication, English literature, literary criticism, education; and feminists writing for women's liberation publications. This convergence of disciplines, with possibilities for future additions, promises a continuing vigor and, perhaps, bold breakthroughs.

The variety of backgrounds naturally leads to diverse frameworks for investigation, beyond the usual array of methodologies which linguistics itself has to offer. There are, first, the classic linguistic methods of using *informants:* the old ethnographic studies (e.g., Haas, 1944; Flannery, 1946) best exemplify this approach. Labov (1972*b*), Swacker (1975), and Winitz (1959) all used *elicitation* to obtain speech samples from their English-speaking informants. Lakoff (1973) follows the tradition of using oneself as an informant in one's own language; and Lakoff, Jespersen (1922), Kramer (1974b), Miller and Swift (1972), and Varda One (1971) all use *anecdotal material* to support their claims. *Observation* is another favored method, with the observers recording speech either by hand transcription or by tape recorders; Barron (1971), Cherry (1975), Coser (1960), Gleason (1973), Soskin and John (1963), Strodtbeck and Mann (1956), and Zimmerman and West (1975) are some who have used this method. Many writers have made some sort of *structural analysis* of a language: e.g., Bodine (in press) of the sex-indefinite pronoun; Schulz (1975), of the pejorative quality of female-marked terms; Nilsen (1973) correlating gender marking and other semantic features; Conners (1971), of feminine agentives; Stanley (1973), of terms for prostitutes; Key (1972), of contexts for female-marked words. Some of the structural analyses are based on a search of the dictionary, which may be one sort of *textual analysis;* others are offered by Burr *et al.* (1972), Shuster (1973), and Ellman (1968), who have examined literary sources. Legman (1968) and Kramer (1974*a*) have made *content analyses* of dirty jokes and cartoons, respectively. Graham (1973) has, with the aid of a computer, obtained a *numerical analysis* providing information such as frequency and types of contexts for various target words. In a similar spirit, Lieberson (1965) examined *census data* to study bilingualism. Numerous investigators have used the *experiment:* Gilley and Summers (1970), Hilpert *et al.* (1975), Rosenfeld (1966), and Wood (1966) are all examples. And finally, the use of *tests* has been reported by a number of researchers, particularly students of child development, and by Warshay (1972).

No one of these methods can be called the one right way; they all have their various strengths and shortcomings, which can be found outlined in many texts. However, we might point out here the particular consequences of some methodologies for the study of sex differentiation in language. The methods of past study and/or commentary, as of linguistics in general, have been largely the use of informants, anecdotes, and observations, all highly susceptible to influence by preconceptions. Cherry (1975) notes that in the observational method, the simple act of transcribing provides the opportunity for such an unconscious value judgment as what constitutes an utterance and what doesn't (leading to what is to be transcribed and what isn't). This judgment in turn may be the vehicle for expressing an unconscious expectation that one sex produces more utterances, or utterances of a different type, than the other. Bodine (1975) notes the questionable accuracy of the system by which anthropologists, usually male, typically queried male informants: not only is much possible information never found out, and other information grossly distorted, but the male forms are inevitably taken as "the" language, and the female forms regarded as a deviant afterthought.

Other present-day writers in this area have seen this point—the assumption of male speech as the norm—as a fundamental issue. It shows up everywhere in linguistic study, as it does in the other social sciences; often females are not studied at all! Conklin (1973), for example, calls attention to Labov's practice (e.g., 1972a) of studying only male adolescent peer groups. At one point he even claims that "males are the chief exemplars of the vernacular culture" (Labov *et al.*, 1968: 41). But, Conklin replies, "no conclusive evidence has been presented that females do not participate fully in the vernacular culture. Sociolinguistic data do *not* show that women are less 'nonstandard' in casual, relaxed, natural speech, only that they are less likely to exhibit their most relaxed speech styles in front of a linguistic investigator, especially a male investigator . . . " (p. 11). And, as she further remarks, the female-only group has rarely been investigated. Male speech has simply been studied more than female speech; not only that, it has been reported as if it is the speech of *both* sexes.

Lieberson's (1965) interpretation of census data reveals another source of bias: women are defined out of the data in the first place. For making one particular calculation, he writes, "we standardized on the basis of males rather than females because ethnic origin in the case of mixed offspring is traced through the male lineage in the Canadian census enumerations" (p. 19). In this particular calculation, an effort to predict the native tongue distribution of children under five, the *mother's* ethnic origin might well have been a better predictor. Lieberson adds his own bias to the already skewed census data: he reports male figures on bilingualism, but for female bilingualism rates, he states only that "Equally lopsided differences are found for females, although they are of a lower magnitude" (p. 17). This is one of many cases where males are treated as the norm.

SUBSTANTIVE ISSUES AND STARTING POINTS

Diverse disciplines, methods, and frameworks have been used for exploring the sexual differentiation of language. This overview seeks to draw together these varied strands in order to clarify underlying themes, assumptions, and explanatory frameworks. One starting point is to begin with *language;* this, for example, is the approach taken by Jespersen (1922), Key (1972), and the annotated bibliography in this volume (Henley and Thorne, 1975). One can move, in almost checklist fashion, through traditional linguistic distinctions, noting sex differences in phonology (e.g., pronunciation, intonation patterns, pitch); in morphology and grammar (e.g., sex differences in choice of adverbs and in syntactic usage); in semantics (e.g., sex as a dimension in pronominal referents, and in the elaboration and content of lexicons. One can also trace the effect of gender[1] on the structuring of speech events (e.g., allocation of speaking turns, patterns of interruption, and the choice and development of conversational topics).

We will briefly focus on the language part of the juncture of language, gender, and society, noting especially the way in which sociolinguistic distinctions (such as the notion of "verbal repertoire") may be useful in guiding future research. However, the other starting point of analysis—sexual differentiation of language as a *social* phenomenon—will be our primary emphasis. In asking *why* there are sex differences in language and speech—including why the differences take certain forms and not others, and why popular stereotypes of female and male speech don't always match empirical reality—one must reach far beyond linguistics and directly examine the social context. Speech, we will seek to demonstrate, is intimately bound up with the social differentiation of the sexes ("gender display"), with the structure of male dominance (expressed and maintained through language *about* women and men, as well as in the ways men and women *use* speech), and with the division of labor by sex.

DIMENSIONS OF LANGUAGE AND SPEECH

As a number of writers have amply demonstrated (Schulz, 1975; Nilsen, 1972, 1973; Feminist Writers Workshop, 1973), one needs nothing more than a dictionary to prove that sex is a variable central to language. Words themselves—probed for denotative and connotative meanings, for derivations and histories, for suffixes and prefixes—are infused with messages about the sexes. Written materials other than dictionaries have also proven fruitful for analysis of language and sex, e.g., children's schoolbooks (Graham, 1973); folklore (Legman, 1968); newspapers (Miller and Swift, 1972); novels (Kramer, 1974*a*; Shuster, 1973).

At the level of *spoken* language, sex is one of many sources of linguistic variation. Sociolinguists (e.g., Labov, 1972*b*; Hymes, 1974; Ervin-Tripp, 1972) have shown that communication systems are heterogeneous and multilayered. Social class, region, ethnicity, age, occupation, and sex all affect speech behavior; speakers may also shift speech styles depending on situation, topic, and roles.

The notion of *verbal repertoire* (Fishman, 1972; Hymes, 1974) suggests one way of organizing the diversity of language use. Verbal repertoire refers both to the language varieties from which an individual may choose, and to language alternatives present in a community of speakers. Verbal repertoire implies the possibility of *choice* among forms of speech, an implication especially apt in the case of sex differences in English. While, to draw on Bodine's (1975) analysis, there are "sex exclusive" linguistic distinctions in some languages, most differentiation in English is "sex preferential," a matter of *frequency* of occurrence. Both female and male speakers, for example, use the *-ing* and *-in* variants in pronouncing words like *running,* but men, more often than women, use the less formal *-in* (Fischer, 1958; Shuy *et al.,* 1967; Labov, 1972*b;* Trudgill, 1972). Analogously, while both sexes may use the intensifiers *so* and *such* in an expressive way ("we had such a good time"), these forms are thought to appear more often in the speech of females (Jespersen, 1922; Key, 1972). Finally, to draw an example from the patterning of conversations, the phenomenon of interruption is not unique to either sex, but in mixed-sex conversations, men are more likely to interrupt women than vice versa (Zimmerman and West, 1975).

One may argue that the various features associated with male or with female speech add up to two distinct *styles* or *varieties* of spoken English.[2] This, in effect, is Kramer's (1974*b*: 14) argument when she suggests that there are "systems of co-occurring, sex-linked linguistic signals" or "genderlects" in the United States; it is also Lakoff's (1973) claim when she writes in a general way of "women's language."

The term *style* refers to "the co-occurrent changes at various levels of linguistic structure within one language" (Ervin-Tripp, 1972: 235). Thus, the female style of speech may involve the *co-occurrence* of certain phonological features (e.g., *-ing* and other more formal phonetic variants); certain intonation patterns rarely used by men (Brend, 1972); less frequent use of swearing (Kramer, 1974*b*), joking (Coser, 1960), and hostile verbs (Gilley and Summers, 1970); more frequent use of psychological state verbs (Barron, 1971; Gleser *et al.,* 1959), expressive intensifiers like *so* and *such,* certain adjectives like *adorable* and *lovely* (Lakoff, 1973), the words *mm hmm* (Hirschman, 1974), and tag questions (Lakoff, 1973); the use of conjunctions rather than interjections to mark topic shifts (Swacker, 1975); preference for certain conversational topics and speech genres (see Henley and Thorne, 1975: sec. IV), etc. These details are drawn from diverse sources, samples, and methods of study; such co-occurrence, as well as the relative frequency of many of these features in female vs. male speech, remains to be demonstrated in a systematic and empirical way. We know very little about the rules and restrictions inherent in the sexual differentiation of speech, nor about the interrelations of different levels of linguistic structure involved in male and female styles.

Sex, of course, is one of many social factors that impinge on language use. As in most research, the literature on the sexual differentiation of speech deals largely with the white, middle- and upper-middle-class segment of the population. There has been sparse attention to sex differences in speech across social classes (although the work of Labov [1972*a*; 1972*b*]; Shuy, Wolfram, and Riley [1967]; and Trudgill [1972] is sensitive in this regard). There is also little research on sexual differentiation (a term which one should always realize includes the possibility of *lack* of differentiation) in the speech of racial minorities, ethnic groups, and different regional dialects. Age is an important factor which no doubt intersects with gender in shaping verbal repertoires; the phonological studies of Labov (1972*b*), Trudgill (1972), and Fischer (1958) indicate the importance of age as well as sex and social class in affecting choice of phonetic variants.

In studying the effect of sex (and other social factors) on speech, many studies take a correlational approach; for example, Crystal (1971) suggests that certain types of voice quality correlate with sex, age, status, and occupation; and Lieberson (1965) shows a correlation between sex and patterns of bilingualism in Montreal. However, this "correlational drive to bring in ever new social attributes as determinants of speech behavior" (Goffman, 1964: 133) neglects the element of *situation*—the social context in which particular verbal and nonverbal gestures are used.

> Is the speaker talking to same or opposite sex, subordinate or superordinate, one listener or many, someone right there or on the phone; is he reading a script or talking spontaneously; is the occasion formal or informal, routine or emergency? Note that it is not the attributes of social structure that are here considered, such as age and sex, but rather the value placed on these attributes as they are acknowledged in the situation current and at hand (Goffman, 1964: 134).

Social situations, Goffman emphasizes, have their own structure and properties, which are not intrinsically linguistic in character, although they may be expressed through a linguistic medium.

Hymes (1974: 5) also stresses the importance of "situations, exchanges, and events," of approaching language "neither as abstracted from nor as an abstract correlate of a community, but as situated in the flux and patterns of communicative events." Hymes' (1964: 10) list of the components of communicative events suggests dimensions which may all prove relevant to understanding the sexual differentiation of language: (1) The various *participants* in communicative events (senders, receivers, addressors, addressees, audience, etc.). Bodine's (1975) reminder that sex of speaker, sex of spoken to, and sex of spoken about may each (or in combination) be a basis of language difference is relevant here. The speech used in situations where both sexes are present may be quite different from the speech of single-sex occasions; other social attributes of the participants (roles, age, social class) may interact with sex in complicated ways. (2) The available *channels* and their modes of use. Do the sexes use written language, spoken language, and nonverbal communication in different ways? How do these channels, and their sexual differentiation, interrelate? For example, some research (Argyle *et al.*, 1970; Rosenthal *et al.*, 1974) indicates that women are more sensitive than men to nonverbal cues; a number of researchers (e.g., Hilpert *et al.*, 1975; Soskin and John, 1963;

Strodtbeck and Mann, 1956) have found that in mixed gatherings (of different types, most experimental), men talk more than women, indicating differential use of a channel. (3) The range of *codes* (linguistic, paralinguistic, kinesic, musical, interpretive, interactional) shared by various of the participants. In a bilingual setting, as in Montreal, how does the fact of the greater bilingualism of males (Lieberson, 1965) affect relationships between the sexes? (4) The *settings.* Existing research on the sexual differentiation of speech covers only a few types of settings. Many studies have been done in experimental, laboratory, or contrived situations (e.g., Hirschman, 1973, 1974; Markel *et al.,* 1972; Swacker, 1975; Wood, 1966); the few that use data gathered from natural settings include a summer resort (Soskin and John, 1963), preschools (Cherry, 1975), a classroom (Barron, 1971), hospital staff meetings (Coser, 1960), and work situations in a telephone company (Langer, 1970). There is extensive ethnographic work waiting to be done on the effect of different social settings on the speech of females and males. (5) The *forms of messages,* and their *genres.* There is evidence, for example, that males more often engage in verbal dueling (Mitchell-Kernan, 1973), and in certain kinds of joking (Coser, 1960; Legman, 1968). (6) The *attitudes and contents* that a message may be about and convey. Do men and women speak differently if the topic, for example, is sports as compared with child-rearing? Hirschman (1974) suggests that having experimental subjects discuss human relations may produce different results from discussion of alternative topics. The sexism implicit in the English language is also relevant to the issue of message content. (7) The *events* themselves, taken as a whole.

THE SOCIAL CONTEXT

Hymes' framework suggests various social dimensions relevant to understanding the sexual differentiation of language. To understand the social context of these differences, however, requires analysis which extends beyond the immediate structure of communicative events. Many reports of sex differences in communication leave the reader with a lingering sense of *why.* Why, for example, do men and women pronounce words differently? Why are some adjectives and qualifiers more frequently found in the speech of one sex or the other? Why might men be less sensitive than women to nonverbal cues? Some studies do not try to account for the findings; for example, Brend (1972) describes male and female intonation patterns in English, but does not speculate about their social functions. Others make only a minimal effort at interpretation and explanation; for example, Wood (1966) and Strodtbeck and Mann (1956) account for sex differences in speaking styles by drawing on the distinction sociologists have drawn between the "expressive" role, imputed to women, and the "instrumental" role, associated with men.

To more fully account for the sexual differentiation of language, one must shift perspective. Society, rather than language, becomes a theoretical starting point, and the growing literature on the sociology, psychology, and anthropology of gender becomes directly relevant. This sort of focus is not simply, however, a matter of matching up ready-made social science theories, interpretations, and findings with data about female and male language and speech. As recent writers have demonstrated, many sociological, anthropological, and psychological theories embody unexamined assumptions and stereotypes about women and men.[3] Research into sex differences in communication is no exception, and one must proceed carefully, being alert to theoretical and methodological biases.

With this shift in perspective, gender becomes not just a variable which correlates with various linguistic details, but rather a complicated social and cultural phenomenon. At the same time, speech is seen in broader focus—as one kind of action, as an intimate part of the fabric of social life. Three major themes seem essential in accounting for the sexual differentiation of language: the social elaboration of gender, the structure of male dominance, and the division of labor by sex (the interests, activities, and position of women and men in society, including the socialization of children, and forms of social bonding).

GENDER DIFFERENTIATION AND DISPLAY

The fact of sex *differences*—postulated, documented, sometimes not discovered where expected—is a preoccupation in the literature on gender and language, as well as in the literature, for example, on the sociology and psychology of gender. Although some writers imply that speech differences have a biological base (e.g., Jespersen's [1922: 246] claim that women "instinctively" shrink from "coarse and gross expressions"), the clear weight of evidence is that few of the differences are rooted in biology. Even pitch, which is related to size of vocal tract, apparently has a learned component; according to several studies, acoustic differences among speakers of English are greater than can be accounted for by anatomical differences between adult men and women (Mattingly, 1966; Sachs *et al.,* 1973).

Birdwhistell (1970; also see Henley, 1973-74) indicates that humans, compared with other species, are weakly sexually dimorphic; they organize learned characteristics, such as posture, gesture, facial expression—and, we would add, speech—to enhance sexual dimorphism. The sexual differentiation of speech can thus be conceptualized as part of human gender display, as one way in which sex differences are *socially* marked, emphasized, and enacted.

How extensive are the differences in male and female speech? Other cultures have had more extreme sexual differentiation of language than is apparent in contemporary American culture (Bodine, 1975). It is possible that there is more overall sexual differentiation of speech in some groups (e.g., socioeconomic, age, occupational, religious) than in others,[4] and in some contexts than in others (e.g., in dating situations vs. classrooms). The relationship of degree of verbal differentiation between the sexes to other types of cultural differentiation—in activities, tasks, rights, and, at the symbolic level, nonverbal gestures, dress, and ornamentation—remains to be explored.

Finally, it should be noted that popular stereotypes of female and male speech (as shown, for example, in cartoons, etiquette books, and people's statements) apparently assume more differentiation than is, in fact, the case (Kramer, 1974a; in press). Some empirical studies which hypothesized sex differences in speech did not find them (Kramer, 1974a; Hirschman, 1974). This is significant knowledge, and one must be wary of a general tendency to exaggerate differences and underestimate similarities between the sexes.

LANGUAGE AND MALE DOMINANCE

Many studies seem content to suggest or document one more type of difference between women and men. Difference, however, is only part of the picture; the fact of male dominance—built into the economic, family, political, and legal structures of society—is also central to language and speech. Language helps enact and transmit every type of inequality, including that between the sexes; it is part of the "micropolitical structure" (Henley, 1973-74) that helps maintain the larger political-economic structure.

Dominance in Language About the Sexes

Male dominance is strikingly apparent in the content of words, in language *about* women and men.[5] If words are regarded as verbal artifacts of a culture, a sort of verbal archeological exploration, like Nilsen's (1972, 1973) could be made by thumbing through a dictionary. Such exploration would quickly substantiate the point that, in the culture of English speakers, men are more highly regarded than women. The male is associated with the universal, the general, the subsuming; the female is more often excluded or is the special case. Words associated with males more often have positive connotations; they convey notions of power, prestige, and leadership. In contrast, female words are more often negative, conveying weakness, inferiority, immaturity, a sense of the trivial. Terms applied to women are narrower in reference than those applied to men, and they are more likely to assume derogatory sexual connotations which overshadow other meanings (Schulz, 1975; Lakoff, 1973). This derogation and overgeneralization, Schulz observes, is related to the process of stereotyping and is also present in other situations of dominance, e.g., racial and ethnic situations.

Verbal Gestures of Dominance and Submission

When one turns from the way language defines the sexes to the everyday uses of talk, as well as nonverbal gestures, sexism is also apparent. As Henley (1973-74) has demonstrated, there is a micropolitical structure of everyday details—patterns of touching, smiling, eye contact, intonation, interruption—which help establish, express, and maintain power relationships. A wide range of verbal and nonverbal cues function as gestures of dominance and submission—in work hierarchies, between adults and children, between social classes, and between men and women.

These gestures often fall into the paradigm of terms of address, where an asymmetric exchange (e.g., person A addresses person B by first name only, while person B addresses person A by title and last name) indicates relationships of status (Brown, 1965). Nonverbal gestures of dominance and submission often follow this asymmetric pattern: males signal dominance through nonreciprocal touch, with women responding passively or by cuddling to the touch; males more freely stare at females, who lower or avert their eyes; males smile less often (as a way of asserting dominance) and women more often (signaling submission; Henley, 1973-74).

This asymmetry—one cue associated with dominance, and the other with subordination—is also present at the verbal level. Nonreciprocal naming patterns are often found in relations between men and women; in many work settings, e.g., businesses, universities, hospitals, more women than men are called by first name only. This reflects, in part, the fact that females are disproportionately found at the bottom and men at the top of work hierarchies. Lakoff (1973) observes that there is a general tendency at work and in media commentary and talk shows to use first names sooner and more often with women than with men. Even where women are equal to men in training and rank, they often do not receive the full repertoire of naming that signifies easy colleagueship.

Other aspects of speech are distributed asymmetrically between the sexes. In mixed conversations, men are more likely to interrupt women than vice versa, and women, indicating submission, are more likely to allow interruption (Zimmerman and West, 1975). The patterns of hesitation (Brend, 1972), qualification (Lakoff, 1973; Kramer, 1974b), and "syntactic looseness" (Jespersen, 1922) which some attribute to female speech may be related to conversational subordination, for example, to the fact that women are more vulnerable to being interrupted. A related phenomenon is the repeated, although not always consistent, finding (see Henley and Thorne, 1975: sec. IV-D) that in mixed gatherings, men talk more than women. (Strodtbeck [1951] found that a greater rate of talking was related to greater "influence," which is one aspect of power.) In general, the female style of speech seems to be characterized by less obtrusiveness; for example, by less speech intensity (Markel *et al.*, 1972); by the use of head nods and *mm hmm* (rather than the more obtrusive and emphatic, *yeah* or *right*) to indicate agreement and attention (Hirschman, 1974); by more frequent use of tag questions and compound request forms (Lakoff, 1973).

Finally, some speech genres embody patterns of dominance. In an ethnographic study of staff meetings in a mental hospital, Coser (1960) found that higher status people, such as senior psychiatrists, more often took the initiative to use humor, and that the target of a witticism was never higher in authority than the initiator. Even though women were amply represented at the meetings, including two female psychiatrists, men made 99 out of the 103 witticisms, "but women often laughed harder" (p. 85). In this situation, status was signaled by making witticisms, and subordination by laughing; women, even those with high occupational status, more often took the subordinate role. Goffman (1956) also indicates that patterns of deference may be conveyed through asymmetric teasing. Legman (1968) observes that women have no place in dirty jokes except as the butt of humor. Power differences may also be expressed in the way in which conversational topics are raised, developed, changed, and dropped (see Henley and Thorne, 1975: sec. IV-G).

Why Is Women's Speech More Polite and "Correct"?

One stereotype with empirical support is that women's speech is more polite, "correct," and "proper" than the speech of men. (One version of the stereotype, "Miss Fidditch," has become a symbol of those upholding "correct grammar" [Joos, 1961; Farb, 1973] ; since hypothetical people are usually male, e.g., John Q. Public and the Man-in-the-Street, it's significant when a female joins the ranks.)

Lakoff (1973) describes women's language as generally more "polite" than that of males; Brend (1972) points to "polite, cheerful" patterns of intonation used only by women; women do not swear as much as men, and may be less likely to use slang (Jespersen, 1922; Flexner, 1960). However, the most detailed evidence that women use more correct speech forms is at the phonological level. This difference is also the best documented of all the linguistic differences between the sexes. Where there are phonological variants (e.g., *-ing* vs. *-in*; or pronunciation or absence of the postvocalic *r*), women, compared with men of the same social class, age, and level of education, more often choose the form closer to the prestige, or "correct" way of talking. This pattern has been found for whites and blacks in the Detroit Dialect Study (Shuy, Wolfram, and Riley, 1967; Fasold, 1968; Wolfram, 1969); among blacks and whites in North Carolina (Levine and Crocket, 1966; Anshen, 1969), among children in a New England village (Fischer, 1958); among speakers in New York City and Chicago (Labov, 1972*b*), and among speakers of urban British English in Norwich (Trudgill, 1972). Haugen (1974) reports that studies of local dialects in Norway have found greater "carefulness" in the speech of women.

At first glance, the fact that women use the more standard, prestige linguistic forms (which are also more prevalent in higher social classes and in formal situations) seems to contradict their position of subordination. This notion of prestige, however, is not equivalent to power; in fact, greater circumspection in behavior often accompanies subordination. Goffman (1956:490) observed that in hospital staff meetings, the doctors "had the privilege of swearing, changing the topic of conversation, and sitting in undignified positions," while attendants were more careful and less relaxed in demeanor. Coser's (1960) observations about joking, mentioned earlier, carry out this theme: those lower in the hospital staff hierarchy were less likely to make witticisms. Explaining why women are less likely to engage in verbal dueling in black culture, Mitchell-Kernan (1973:328) suggests that verbal dueling permits "a great deal of license," and "women cannot be suitably competitive because other social norms require more circumspection in their verbal behavior." The notion that women should be "nice" and "ladies," that is, that they should carefully monitor their behavior, functions as a strong mechanism of social control (Fox, 1973).

Trudgill (1972) offers a related explanation for the tendency of women to use more standard forms; he suggests that women try to compensate for their subordination by signaling status linguistically. He claims this will be "particularly true of women who are not working," a speculation which could be empirically checked, although one would have to specify this variable more carefully. Trudgill also notes that appearances are more important for women than for men; lacking occupational status, women rely more on symbols of status, including the symbolic import of speech.

Why do men, to look at the other side of the coin, seem to prefer the less prestigeful, more stigmatized phonetic variants? It seems to be more than a matter of males being secure in status and hence able to relax; Trudgill offers evidence that in his Norwich sample, working-class, nonstandard speech has positive connotations for male speakers of all social classes. On the one hand, males expressed the greater value attached to more correct forms (e.g., making comments such as "I talk horrible"), but on the other hand, they indicated in various ways that they were favorably disposed to nonstandard speech, which has strong connotations of masculinity, and may signal male solidarity. "Privately and subconsciously, a large number of male speakers are more concerned with acquiring prestige of the covert sort and with signaling group solidarity than with obtaining social status, as this is more usually defined" (Trudgill, 1972:182).

This observation suggests an interesting intersection of sex and class: male working-class forms seem to symbolize masculinity, or at least stereotyped masculinity, for men of other social classes as well. This seems to be the case for phonetic variants, swearing, nasality as a vocal modifier (Austin, 1965), and, in general, for images of roughness, toughness, and violence.[6] The greater segregation of the sexes in the working class (Komarovsky, 1962; Klein, 1965; Bott, 1957) may enhance the value of these symbols as indicating male solidarity and masculinity in general. Labov (1973) found that deviants from all-male peer groups tended to use more standard speech forms; "lames," that is, individuals isolated from black male street culture, are more likely to pronounce the postvocalic *r* and to use other nonvernacular forms. (The relationship of the vernacular to male bonding and the issue of female bonding will be discussed later.)

Crossing the Sex Barrier

Under what conditions, and with what consequences, do women and men use the speech style associated with the opposite sex? There are obvious constraints against such behavior—women who use forms associated with men may be put down as aggressive and "unfeminine"; men who "talk like women" are called "effeminate" and regarded with disdain. (It is interesting to note the degree to which speech is integrated into basic notions of "masculinity" and "femininity.")

Although both women and men are constrained to keep on their respective sides of the sex barrier, women can more freely use both forms; that is, men who use female forms seem to be more stigmatized than women who use male forms.[7] Women, in fact, receive certain social rewards for using a more male speech style; for one thing, they may be taken more seriously (Lakoff, 1973).[8]

Lakoff (1973) argues that certain groups of men—homosexuals, hippies, and academic men, who have in common a rejection of the American masculine image, including the search for power and money—are more likely to use speech forms generally associated with females. Legman (1968: 337) claims that where men are in "dominated situations, as in armies or on college faculties, very hedged and repressed ways of speech become habitual." He also observes that "the Milquetoast or Dagwood has, traditionally, a weakly faint or absurdly screeching voice" (a voice designed to indicate, perhaps, that these are men who have too much association with the female domestic sphere and with subordination). Certain tasks or situations may make it more acceptable for men to use forms typed as female; in care-giving situations, e.g., in talking to babies or to pets, both sexes may make exaggerated use of traits, such as higher pitch and variable intonation, which are associated with women (Sachs *et al.,* 1973).[9]

Why is it more of a stigma for men to use women's speech, than for women to use men's speech? One obvious reason is that switching styles means downward mobility for men; it entails use of a less socially valued form, while for women, there is some upward mobility involved in using male speech. But this does not seem to fully account for the sense of contamination, the strong aura of stigma attached to male use of female forms (including female modes of dress and styles of walking and sitting). Other types of stratification do not seem fully parallel; there is no parallel stigma attached to upper-class people imitating lower-class mores, nor to whites adopting cultural forms (e.g., certain forms of speech, dress, and music) created by blacks. The fact that women and men live in closer contact than do whites and blacks, or different social classes—the fact that there is no female equivalent to the residential ghetto—may make symbolic stratification more important in maintaining sexual dominance. There also seems to be a psychological dimension: where children of both sexes are raised primarily by a woman (as is the case under the traditional division of labor), they both begin life by identifying with a female, including female culture and ways of speaking. To establish male identity, males go through what Margaret Mead (1949) calls "the second weaning"; at some point, often around five or six, they break a close bond with the mother, begin to identify with the father and male culture, and at the same time, one may speculate, switch speech patterns.[10] The need to prove masculinity, to assert one's self as *not* feminine, seems central to male identity. Maintaining masculine symbols (and rigidly avoiding female forms) may be part of this drive. In contrast, female identification and speech learning, at least in the early years, may be more continuous, and women may have no parallel drive to prove femininity or that they are not masculine.[11]

THE DIVISION OF LABOR BY SEX

The third basic theme evident in the sexual differentiation of language has to do with the division of labor between women and men. Every society uses sex, to one degree or another, in allocating tasks, activities, rights, and responsibilities. In some societies (e.g., traditional Moslem culture) the division of labor along gender lines is more rigid and polarized than in others (e.g., hunting and gathering bands); it might be expected, although this remains to be demonstrated, that in the former case, sex-related language differences will also be more extreme. The relationship of degree of difference between the sexes (in behavior, activities, and popular conceptions) to the extent of male dominance also remains to be explored. Anthropologists have found no societies in which women are publicly recognized as equal to or more powerful than men; "everywhere men have some authority over women," with "a culturally legitimated right to [female] subordination and compliance" (Rosaldo, 1974: 21). But women do have relatively higher status in some societies than in others (Sanday, 1974).

In Western, industrialized societies, even with birth control and advanced technology, a strong sexual division of labor persists. Women and men are found in very different positions in the world of work: the majority of occupations are sex-typed, that is, predominantly male or female in composition (Epstein, 1970), and housework and child care are still considered largely the responsibility of women. Even though almost half of all American women are employed full-time outside the home, the belief persists that woman's place is mainly, and primarily, in the roles of wife and mother. And although men also have family roles, they are defined primarily by their economic or occupational position.

This strong ideology or "cultural mandate" (Coser and Rokoff, 1971), which actually contradicts much of the reality of both female and male lives, can be documented at the level of language. Women, even within non-family settings, are defined mainly by their relationships to men, for example, by being titled *Mrs.* or *Miss.* In a computerized analysis of five million words drawn from children's schoolbooks, it was found that, although there are seven times as many men as women in the books, the word *mother* occurs more frequently than *father,* and *wife* three times as often as *husband*—when women are referred to, it is mainly in relationship to men and children (Graham, 1973; see also Nilsen, 1972, 1973). Language also reflects the association of men with occupations: examining dictionary items marked for gender, Nilsen (1973) found more masculine items marked for occupations, and Conners (1971) observes that feminine agentives, especially for occupational terms, (e.g., *aviatrix* and *stewardess*) behave as the marked, or deviant, category, while generic terms are taken for masculine. Furthermore, individual feminine agentives and suffixes (e.g., *-ette*) have repeatedly taken on derogatory or facetious connotations.

What do women and men talk about? Studies reveal a division of labor in conversational topics which parallels much of the social, including the ideological, division of labor. Harding (1975) found such a parallel in speech in a Spanish village: men (whose domain is work in agriculture, livestock, and in some shops and trades) talked of the land, crops, weather, prices, wages, inheritance, work animals, and machinery. The primary work of women is at home; their talk focused on people and their personal lives, and the needs and concerns of household members. Komarovsky (1962) describes the extensive sex segregation in the lives of blue-collar couples in America, a segregation that also affects patterns of talk. In her study, each sex felt it had little to say to the other, and even in social situations involving couples, the sexes split up for conversation. The women talked to other women about family and interpersonal matters; the men talked to male friends about cars, sports, work, motorcycles, carpentry, and local politics. The men ridiculed female conversation ("dirty diapers stuff," one called it), a derogation the women were aware of, but did not apparently reciprocate, although they did complain about lack of communication in their marriages. Klein (1965) found a similar sex segregation in speech topics in a mining community in England. It is significant that in all these studies, most of the women did not have employment outside the home. This raises the question of how is the growing fact of female employment affecting sex differences in speech?

Given that the sexes have different spheres of activity, do they also have different vocabularies? Are there sex-typed areas of lexical elaboration? This line of inquiry is familiar in studies of language and culture; for example, a matter of environmental and ecological importance to a culture (such as snow, yams, or cattle) is often elaborated at the level of vocabulary, although the pattern does not always hold, and it is more complicated than language simply reflecting culture (see Whorf, 1940; Brown, 1965; Hymes, 1964). Lakoff (1973) claims that women differentiate colors more than men (e.g., using words like *mauve* and *lavender*).[12] Conklin (1974: 59) suggests that women are more likely to know the terminology of sewing, fabric, cooking methods and utensils, and child care, while men more frequently use and understand the vocabulary of sports and auto mechanics. She goes on to observe:

> Since men may be professionals in any field, it is quite conceivable that men who command the vocabulary of what are generally women's subjects may be taken for professional (rather than "amateur," like the housewives) practitioners of that subject matter area (i.e., chefs, child psychologists, designers). Because women are more rarely professionals of any sort and almost never achieve professional status in areas which are viewed as "male," they are less likely to be given the benefit of the doubt (i.e., assumed to be trained mechanics, sportscasters, or even chemists, lawyers, or film directors, the "neutral" areas).

Kramer's (1974a; in press) analysis of the speech of the sexes in magazine cartoons raises another theoretical issue. She found that in the world of the cartoons—which she emphasizes is a stereotyped world, but does indicate something of popular conceptions—women and men discuss different topics. Men, wherever they are pictured, are shown in control of language, while women, especially if they step outside largely domestic and human relations topics (venturing, for example, into discussion of politics) often seem incapable of handling the language appropriate to the new location. Cartoon women are pictured speaking in fewer places. Is it possible that female speech styles are also more situationally restricted than those of males? That is, are speech forms associated with men considered appropriate in a wider number of behavioral settings? This would go along with the general pattern of confinement of women, in territory and time. That is, there are places where females are not supposed to venture; in television shows and advertisements, men control more space than women. Lee (1974) found in a large sample of advertisements that the home is the setting for females 71% of the time, but for males, only 34% of the time; more males are pictured in far-away places, such as "Marlboro Country." There has traditionally been greater control over the hours women keep, e.g., college dormitory parietal hours (see Fox, 1973). It is also a fact that, proportionate to their representation in the labor foce, women are concentrated in *fewer* total occupations than men (U.S. Bureau of the Census, 1970). One linguistic reflection of females' territorial restriction is a pattern often found in multilingual societies: men are more likely to be bilingual than are women (e.g., in French Canada [Lieberson, 1965], and in Oaxaca, Mexico [Diebold, 1964]). This is due to the greater mobility of men, who come into contact with the other language through employment and other extradomestic activities. Male and female speech could be further compared for range, extent, and locales of use.

How Is Sex-Typed Language Learned?

Universally, women are largely responsible for early child care (Chodorow, 1974). This aspect of the sexual division of labor has important linguistic consequences: women play a central role in the transmission of language across generations.[13] Little is known about the ways in which males and females learn the speech styles associated with their respective sexes, although there are a few speculations (McCarthy, 1953; Lakoff, 1973; Garcia-Zamor, 1973). Nor is much known about how sex-typed language acquisition fits in with the overall learning of gender-related roles and behavior. Lakoff (1973: 47) suggests that both sexes first learn "women's language" from mothers and other female figures, e.g., nursery school teachers, who are primarily female. As they grow older, girls retain this first way of talking, but boys begin to shift to more male forms, for example, by going through a stage of rough talk which is discouraged in girls. By around age ten, she suggests, both sexes are involved in same-sex peer groups, and the two types of speech are present.

Peer groups may exert a strong influence on the learning of sexually differentiated speech styles (as well as on other aspects of language acquisition), yet linguists have traditionally emphasized mainly mother-child interaction as the social context of language learning. Labov (1972b: 304) observes that there is evidence, e.g., from dialect studies, that "children follow the pattern of their peers." He has strengthened this evidence with detailed studies of single-sex peer groups, e.g., 11-year-old boys in a suburb of Philadelphia (Labov, 1972b: 305), and black, male, preadolescent peer groups in South Central Harlem (Labov, 1972a; 1973). It is significant, however, that all Labov's studies are of *male* peer groups. As mentioned earlier, Conklin (1973) has criticized Labov's assertion that "males are the chief exemplars of vernacular culture," a claim with weak empirical support since females have been so little studied.

It is possible—but there is no strong proof of this—that peer groups *are* more central to male, as opposed to female, language behavior. Stewart (1964: 16-17) observes of lower-class black children in Washington, D.C., that males shift dialects when they move from the status of "small boy" to "big boy" in the informal social structure of the local peer group. Girls do not show such a rapid dialect shift; they have less rigid age grading, and their speech is more affected by formal education. Stewart, who relegates his brief discussion of females to a footnote, says nothing specifically about the peer behavior of girls.

Theorists of male bonding can point to aspects of male speech which facilitate group ties. Swearing often functions to exclude women, and is used as a justification for such exclusion—"We'd like to hire you, but there's too much foul language." Slang, which Flexner (1960) claims is the exclusive property of males, is largely restricted to those with a close relationship. Verbal dueling, although aggressive, also has strong group functions. It is significant that the content of verbal dueling in Turkish culture (Dundes *et al.,* 1972) and in black American culture (Mitchell-Kernan, 1972; Abrahams, 1970; Labov, 1972*a*) often has to do with comments about the other's sexual status as a male, e.g., accusations of being effeminate and insulting comments about female relatives. Sexist language in general may build a certain kind of solidarity, as males share aggression against and domination of women.

Do females, then, not bond with one another to the extent that males do? There is no strong proof of this, mainly because all-female groups have been nearly invisible to investigators (most of whom are male). Thus Tiger (1969), who celebrates male bonding, does not review the anthropological literature on female groups (in contrast with the attention which Leis [1974] and Lamphere [1974] pay to female bonding). Movies and literature portray male friendships much more than friendships among women; the socialization and personality literature neglects mother-daughter relationships (Chodorow, 1974). And, one can add, the sociolinguistic literature is heavily weighted toward the study of males, and of females mainly in relationship to males. Women, as Conklin (1974) argues, may well have their own vernacular, their own kinds of slang, their own verbal rituals and ways of bonding. Many female language phenomena await documentation.

Hirschman (1973, 1974), who has analyzed the speech of single-sex pairs, tentatively suggests that women may talk more easily to each other than to men. In her studies, female-female speech often had fewer hesitations (indicating greater ease); it had more *mm hmm*'s (acknowledging the speech of the other person) and more elaborations on each other's utterances (while men talking with men tended to argue with each other, a contrast which Bernard [1972] also describes). This pattern of acknowledging the other's speech, of building upon, rather than disputing the other person's utterance, implies a pattern of bonding, although a very different type of bonding than is realized, for example, through verbal dueling.

LANGUAGE AND MALE DOMINANCE REVISITED

Is Men's Speech Superior?

Popular stereotypes and beliefs, Kramer (1974*a*: 82) notes, characterize women's speech as "weaker and less effective than the speech of men"; the female style is supposed to be "emotional, vague, euphemistic, sweetly proper, mindless, endless, high-pitched, and silly." These generalizations, she emphasizes, "are not based on carefully controlled research." But they do reflect the lower status often associated with female speech.

Lakoff (1973) argues that "women's language," in actuality and not just according to stereotype, is inferior to that of men: it contains patterns of "weakness" and "uncertainty" (e.g., tag questions; compound request forms); it focuses on the "trivial," the frivolous, the unserious (e.g., by elaborating color terminology); it stresses personal emotional reactions. In contrast, Lakoff claims, male speech allows for "stronger" and more "forceful" statements; it "reinforces men's position of strength in the real world" (p. 51). Women, she argues, are denied equality "partially for linguistic reasons" (p. 51), and they "prejudice the case against themselves by their use of language" (p. 57). In short, women's speech forms are taken as proof that they are not capable of holding power.

In their quest for equality, should women, then, abandon the female style and adopt forms of speech associated with men? This seems to be the implication of Lakoff's argument. She says that this *is* the current direction of change; as women enter the public sphere of occupations and professions, they tend to adopt male forms, and there is no parallel movement of men adopting women's speech. And, although stressing the primacy of social rather than linguistic change, Lakoff seems to argue that equality *should* entail women using the "stronger" forms now associated with men.

Other writers disagree. They question whether males should be taken as setting the norm of desirable speech,[14] and they argue that women's speech has certain strengths—that men, in fact, might benefit from sharing. Rather than emulating men in the search for equality, women (and men) should create new directions of change which go beyond current hierarchies. This is the perspective of Ellen Morgan of the Feminist Writers Workshop (1973: viii):

> A new style is emerging. As Mary Ellman points out, the linguistic mode characteristic of many men is the authoritative and declarative. Because neo-feminists tend to reject elitism and authoritarianism, and base their politics on personal experience, their style is more descriptive and, if not more tentative, more relative, more inclined to the many-faceted, less structured by the desire to assert one idea to the exclusion of others than to convey the multiple and personal character of experience.[15]

Conklin (1974) also contends that patterns traditionally associated with women, and hence devalued, should be reexamined. For example, she argues that women are more sensitive linguistically than men. Phonological studies, e.g., Labov [1972b] and Trudgill [1972] indicate that women are more likely to shift style, to hypercorrect, and to be sensitive to stigmatized forms than men of their respective ethnic or socioeconomic group.[16] Although this trait has been devalued by society, women can turn it to their own advantage: "in dealing with the power structure, and in dealing with other women, an awareness of the ebb and flow below the surface of the interaction is a useful tool and also a valuable weapon" (Conklin, 1974: 69).

Men who are discontented with traditional notions of masculinity often refer enviously to the greater ability of women to express emotions and to engage in personal self-disclosure (e.g., Bradley *et al.*, 1971; Jourard, 1971). Mark Fasteau (1972) writes of "the personal communication," the easy expression of feelings, that women have developed among themselves, but which is relatively absent among men. Some language studies can be fitted into this theme. Brend (1972) found that women have a wider range of intonation, using a high level of pitch that men usually avoid. This fourth level of pitch may be associated with emotional expressiveness, as may tag questions, which Lakoff (1973) says are more frequent in female than in male speech.[17] Gleser *et al.* (1959) analyzed samples of speech and found that females used significantly more words implying feeling, emotion, or motivation. The findings and speculations of Wood (1966), Barron (1971), and Bernard (1970) are also relevant to the claim that women's speech is more emotionally expressive than that of men.

While self-disclosure and emotional expressiveness seem to be desirable attributes, it depends on the context. As Henley (1973-74: 8) suggests, there is a general pattern by which "personal information flows opposite to the flow of authority"; that is, subordinates generally disclose more personal information than those over them (information which may be used for purposes of control). "The cultures of most poor and 'ethnic' peoples in our societies, and those of women and children, allow for a broader and deeper range of emotional display than that of adult white males, and members of these cultures are commonly depicted as 'uncontrolled' emotionally" (Henley, 1973-74: 8-9). If self-disclosure is involuntary (as it often seems to be for the powerless), it may be another way in which power differences are maintained.

The issue of sex differences in emotional expressiveness easily shades into a dichotomy which has long been a mainstay of sociologists in theorizing about the sexes: the distinction, originally formulated from the study of small groups (Bales, 1950), between "instrumental" (or "task-oriented") functions and "expressive" (or "social-emotional") functions.[18] This distinction carried over into family sociology (Parsons and Bales, 1955), and a presumed division of labor between the sexes, with the husband as the "instrumental leader" (involved in the world outside the family, especially his occupation), and the wife as the "social-emotional" leader (providing emotional support, and boosting the morale of family members). As critics have shown (e.g., Laws. 1971) this framework has been used to legitimize conservative ideologies, such as the notion that it is "dysfunctional" for women to be employed, or at least to have work equal or superordinate to that of their husbands. Furthermore, as Slater (1961) argues, there is evidence that one spouse may be *both* more "expressive" and more "instrumental" than the other, i.e., that these qualities are not mutually exclusive.

There is a general tendency for people ("experts" included) to think in an either/or pattern when they seek to describe or interpret the behavior of men and women. This sort of dichotomous thinking—positing two mutually exclusive traits, one associated with women, the other with men—needs to be reexamined for hidden stereotypes, ideologies, and assumptions[19] Traits posited as opposites may, in fact, be independent of each other, or be combined. Hirschman (1974), in what seems a useful approach, abandons an either/or notion of female/male speech style (with one style more obviously valued than the other) and suggests the distinction between "assertive" behavior, more associated with men, and "supportive behavior," traditionally associated with women, although "supportiveness and assertiveness are not to be understood as opposites in any sense; ideally it would be possible to be simultaneously assertive and supportive" (p. 2).

The Importance of Social Context

There is another pitfall to be avoided: the assumption that given speech forms are intrinsically strong or weak, valued or less valued. As Kramer (1974*a*: 85) writes:

> Words, phrases, and sentence patterns are not inherently strong or weak. They acquire these attributes only in a particular cultural context. If our society views female speech as inferior, it is because of the subordinate role assigned to women. Our culture is biased to interpret sex differences in favor of men.

There are many examples that bear out this point, showing that the same communication gesture may be interpreted one way if used by a man, and another way if used by a woman. One example is found in the evidence, mentioned earlier, that men talk more than women in mixed gatherings. (There is also some contrary data; see review in Henley and Thorne (1975: sec. IV-D). In an experimental study of decision making, Strodtbeck (1951) found that a greater rate of talking was related to greater influence for both male and female subjects. But in a similar study of the relation of amount of talk to influence, Kenkel (1963) found that high influence was related to amount of talking for males, but *not* for females.[20] Verbal fluency may also be evaluated differently according to sex of speaker. Gall *et al.* (1969) found that for women, verbal fluency had a negative correlation with "good impression," but for men, the correlation was consistently positive. Analogously, a study of the effect of voice differences on personality perception found that the same paralinguistic feature received differential response if the speaker was male or female (Addington, 1968: 502).

Another way of phrasing the issue of context is to ask what happens if women use gestures of dominance in relationship to men.[21] If a woman aggressively stares at a man, he is likely to intensify his dominance gestures, and to interpret her gesture as a sexual advance, or perhaps label her a lesbian (O'Connor, 1970; Henley, 1973-74: 18; Battle-Sister, 1971b: 596). "Why should these concomitants of status lose these connotations, and in addition, take on sexual connotations, when used by the wrong sex? It is because the implication of power is unacceptable when the actor is a woman, and therefore must be denied" (Henley, 1973-74: 18). In short, the significance of gestures changes when they are used by men or women; no matter what women do, their behavior may be taken to symbolize inferiority.

CAN SEXIST LANGUAGE BE CHANGED?

A final area in which social and linguistic issues merge is the question of change. Is it possible to change sexist language? Which parts of language can and should be changed? These issues have occasioned considerable debate both in the popular media and in scholarly places.[22] Much of the debate has centered around two types of change: the coining of new terms (such as *Ms.* to replace *Miss/Mrs.*, and *chairperson* to replace *chairman* and *chairwoman*), and various proposals to replace *he* as the generic third person singular pronoun.[23] Although some writers, such as Lakoff (1973), claim that the new lexical items advocated by feminists will be a long time in gaining acceptance, popular language already indicates that headway has been made. Words like *Ms., spokesperson,* and *sexist*—which were virtually unknown a decade ago—have, under pressure from the women's movement, become relatively common parlance.

It is generally agreed, however, that the introduction of new lexical items is easier than changing the pronoun system, which is more basic to language structure. Some linguists suggest that change from the use of *he* as the generic pronoun will be virtually impossible. For example, Lakoff (1973: 75) argues that since pronouns are so thoroughly embedded in language and are relatively unavailable to the speaker's conscious analysis, "an attempt to change pronominal usage will be futile." Bodine (in press) offers a strong counter-argument, based on evidence from the history of pronominal usage in English. Although prescriptive grammarians have, since the eighteenth century, pressed for *he (his, him)* as the only correct third person singular pronoun for sex-indefinite antecedents (as in the sentence, "Everyone must take his place"), there have always been other usages, especially *they (their, them)* ("Everyone must take their place"). *They* persists in ordinary conversation; the continuing attack of teachers and textbook writers on the singular *they* and on *he or she*, also indicates that both forms are still much a part of American English. The earlier elimination of *thou-thee* as a second person pronoun in English is evidence that pronominal systems are susceptible to change, and Bodine thinks that the feminist attack on the sex-indefinite *he* will have an effect.

> As English pronominal usage is increasingly affected by [the feminist movement], it will afford an ideal opportunity to study differences in language change among those who make a conscious decision and deliberate effort to change, among those who are aware that the change is taking place but have no particular interest in the issue, among those who are oblivious to the change, and among those who are consciously resisting the change (Bodine, in press).

Opponents of feminist proposals for language change often claim that the new forms, e.g., *spokesperson* and *he or she,* are awkward and clumsy. Yet parallel constructions—*salesperson,* and phrases like *one or more*—have long been accepted by English teachers, textbook writers, and other keepers of the language status quo, as well as by ordinary speakers. As Bodine suggests, grammarians have stressed pronominal agreement in number (arguing that *they* is incorrect for singular antecedents), but, rather inconsistently, they have not stressed agreement in gender (advocating *he* to encompass both sexes). In a survey of twenty-eight junior and senior high school grammars, Bodine found, "Without exception, all of these books condemn both *he or she* and singular *they,* the former because it is clumsy and the latter because it is inaccurate. And then the pupils are taught to achieve both elegance of expression and accuracy by referring to women as *he!*"[24]

The more general issue behind this controversy is often phrased as the relationship between linguistic and social change. Lakoff (1973) argues that language change and social change are different processes, that sexist language is an external "symptom" of the underlying "disease" of social inequality between men and women, and that linguistic change follows social change. Thus, she claims, only if *society* changes "so that the distinction between married and unmarried women is as unimportant in terms of their social position as that between married and unmarried men" will *Ms.* have a chance of gaining general acceptance (p. 73).

We would argue that language and society cannot be so easily separated. Speech is a form of action, not simply a reflection of underlying social processes. To call people *Mrs.* or *Miss* is to help maintain a definition of women which relegates them primarily to family roles. To use *he or she,* rather than *he,* for sex-indefinite antecedents is a tangible gesture of including, rather than excluding women from consciousness. Males who consistently interrupt females in conversation are engaging in acts of social domination. In short, verbal and nonverbal communication patterns are not simply epiphenomena; they help establish, transmit, and maintain male dominance. Language change is obviously not the whole story, but it is certainly a part of social change.

CONCLUSION: THIS IS ONLY A BEGINNING . . . .

By now the contours of this area of study should be visible. Although interest in this area is spreading like wildflower, we would stress that this is only a beginning. There are numerous speculations, untested hypotheses, and anecdotal observations which await systematic inquiry. Jespersen's (1922) chapter on women's speech has been around for 50 years, but most of his notions remain in the realm of speculation. Kramer (1974b) offers a variety of leads and insights which await systematic inquiry, including the suggestion that popular stereotypes can be used as a source of hypotheses, leading to research which may, in some cases, disprove the stereotypes. Conklin (1973; 1974) and Bernard (1972) also offer a range of ideas which are ripe for further study. As mentioned earlier, Hymes' (1964) paradigm of communicative events suggests a variety of issues bearing on an understanding of the sexual differentiation of language.

There are whole areas of study which have been virtually untouched, for example, the communication patterns of all-female groups, and of populations other than the white, middle class. We know very little about the interrelations of sex, social class, ethnicity, race, and age as they affect the use of language. Nor has there been analysis of the pervasive heterosexual bias which no doubt exists in language as it does in the rest of the culture. Although there is an early anthropological literature about the sexual differentiation of language, there is little recent cross-cultural study along these lines (an interesting exception is Keenan [in press]). Data about verbal behavior would be helpful in building a general comparative understanding of the place of the sexes in different societies.

Attention to the sexual differentiation of language may prove fruitful for those pursuing more general issues, for example, the relationship of verbal to nonverbal communication. Those studying language acquisition cannot afford to ignore the variable of sex, which apparently enters socialization patterns earlier than any other social category. The learning, and perhaps unlearning, of language continues throughout the life cycle, yet few have studied this process beyond acquisition of the first language (Grimshaw, 1973: 584). Do boys, as earlier suggested, switch language styles after initially learning female speech patterns? Do adult women switch to more "male" speech when they enter male-dominated occupations? What are the continuities and discontinuities of language use and learning for each sex throughout the life cycle?

Language change is another general topic which intersects with the study of sex differences in language and speech. Labov (1972a) has shown that men and women play different roles in the process of phonological change; what about other aspects of linguistic change? As Bodine (in press) emphasizes, the effort of feminists to eliminate sexist language provides a fascinating, first-hand example of the process of change and resistance to change. Students of social movements and of language planning will also find much of interest in the current controversy over sexist language.

Sociologists with an interest in social stratification are finally beginning to acknowledge sex as a dimension worthy of as serious attention as class or race. Inequality is not just a matter of differential income or education; it also shapes everyday experience, and patterns of verbal and nonverbal communication can provide substantial information about the nature of male (as well as class, racial, and ethnic) dominance. Sexual inequality is one of a variety of sociological issues which could be usefully explored through attention to verbal behavior as a "social indicator" giving subtle information about social structure.

A variety of psycholinguistic questions may also be raised. For one, what is the connection between language usage, e.g., female and male speech styles, and the speaker's and hearer's attitudes and behavior? How does sexist language shape our perception of others? After mapping out all the subtle forms of derogation applied to women, can we determine their immediate effects on female response? That is, might specific putdowns evoke gestures of submission, or deter women from a particular action? In the cognitive process of sentence construction, at what point is the decision made about pronoun gender for sex-indefinite antecedents (e.g., *everyone*, the *doctor*)? Different structural models for gender may be tested by psycholinguistic experiment to give us both linguistic and psychological information. Key (1972) looked at word groupings to locate those in which *woman* appears; this approach could be expanded, for example, to examine groupings of adjectives applied to women (e.g., "big dumb blonde," "brainy but beautiful") and whether they can be classified into a few themes, such as looks, intelligence, aggressiveness, etc.

The questions are endless; the answers are few, but the search for them is expanding. The important thing about this field (whether all of its scholars recognize it or not) is that here is socially useful study, study that will shape our future, even as it interprets our past. Language exists not in a social vacuum but at the very core of human interaction. As the study of gender and language uncovers the answers to old questions, not only will new questions emerge, but the very situation itself, at the nexus of language, gender, and society, will be changed. Here the dynamics of scholarly progress and social progress may be observed in interaction, with the scholar and subject at the heart of the action, one and the same.

NOTES

[1] The term *gender* seems preferable to *sex roles* which, although it has wide usage, is in many ways misleading. One's sex is not a *role* in the way that being a parent, piano teacher, or plumber is a role; sex is less changeable and changing, and it is central to identity and infuses all other roles that one plays. This is shown by language, e.g., the prevalence of terms like *female doctor,* and also by the differential pay and status received by women and men performing the same work roles. The term *role* also, rather euphemistically, tends to gloss over power differences between men and women. It is significant that role terminology, which tends to imply "different but equal," is not applied to other cases of power differentials, e.g., we do not speak of *racial roles* or *class roles* (Battle-Sister, 1971b; Benson, 1973). A more accurate and flexible vocabulary for referring to the social and cultural differentiation of the sexes is needed. *Gender* (a social term, while *sex* is a biological term) is coming into more widespread use in the social sciences, although—an important difficulty in this particular area of study—in writing about language, there is some possibility of confusion with the specific linguistic meaning of *gender.*

[2] The terminology for referring to the sexual differentiation of language is often ambiguous. Although Lakoff (1973) refers to "women's language," she seems to be using the term *language* in a loose sense (no one claims that women and men use mutually unintelligible codes in English, or in any other language). Ervin-Tripp's (1972) term *style,* which suggests the co-occurrence of linguistic features, seems to be a more appropriate designation for the speech patterns associated with men and with women. Another relevant term is *variety* (Fishman, 1972: 15-18), which refers to "a kind of language," and includes, for example, dialects (both social and regional), distinctive forms associated with ethnic or religious groups, and the specialized language of occupational groups. In Fishman's terminology, *variety* designates "a member of a verbal repertoire."

[3] Several general points reappear in critiques of sexism in social science: researchers, who are usually male, have tended to ignore women, as informants, as subjects, as a focus of study and theorizing. Theories and interpretations often involve a pervasive male bias, an elevation of stereotypes to scientific fact, and have the effect of justifying, rather than questioning the status quo. Feminist critiques of sociology include Bart (1971), Bernard (1973), and Laws (1971); of psychology, Carlson (1972), Henley (1973), Silveira (1973), and Weisstein (1970); of anthropology, Linton (1971), and Rosaldo and Lamphere (1974).

[4] There are some indications that this is the case. In his study of speech patterns in Norwich, England, Trudgill (1973) found that the young of both sexes converged in preference for nonstandard phonetic variants, while there was more sexual differentiation in the speech of older people. Gleser *et al.* (1959) found that there were fewer sex differences in speech content (e.g., use of words implying time, space, quantity, and destructive action) among those with more education.

[5] For a review of the growing literature on sexism in English, see Henley and Thorne, 1975: sec. II-A.

[6] Discussing the black patois and its origins, Grier and Cobbs (1968) have observed that black men revert to the patois as a technique of seduction, as part of making "sexual

conquests." This may be another example of the association of masculinity with less standard speech.

[7]Austin (1965) observes that one of the strongest means of verbal insult is to imitate a male with derogatory female imitation; this is much more insulting than the reverse: imitating a woman in a male way.

[8]The reward may even be occupational advancement: a low-pitched female voice is almost a prerequisite for a woman becoming a radio or TV broadcaster (Hennessee, 1974; Kramer, 1974b).

[9]One of us (Thorne) has informally observed that men are more likely than women to use noises and sound effects in communicating with infants (for related observations, see Gleason [1973]). Are men embarrassed by high pitch and other female characteristics of stereotyped talk to babies?

[10]We will come back to this point in a later discussion of the effect of peer groups on language learning. However, it should be briefly noted that Lakoff (1973) speculates along these lines, suggesting that boys first learn female language and later switch to the speech associated with men.

[11]For a more detailed elaboration of this theory, see Chodorow (1974). McCarthy (1953) argues along related, although somewhat different, lines, suggesting that girls have the edge in early language development partly because they can identify with and imitate the mother's speech, while boys, who need to identify with the father, have less possibility for echo-reaction with the deeper adult male voice.

[12]Females have been found to be superior to males at speed of color naming, i.e., correctly identifying presented colors (Ligon, 1932; DuBoix, 1939) and in consistency of assigning color names to a wide array of colors (Chapanis, 1965).

[13]Labov (1972b: 303) observes that since women talk to young children more than men do, they have special influence on the rate and direction of linguistic change.

[14]We are indebted to an unpublished paper by Virginia Valian which helped clarify our understanding of the way in which theorists may assume male values in judging men's and women's speech. As mentioned earlier, the methodologies employed to study sex differences in language tend to assume "the male as norm."

[15]This raises an interesting empirical and political question: how *do* feminists speak? On the one hand, as Morgan suggests, feminists may assert traditionally female forms, in a manner not unlike cultural nationalism among blacks or chicanos. (Battle-Sister [1971] argues that this response is a reaction to oppression, and that rather than creating an independent culture, women should try to capture existing power bases.) On the other hand, Conklin (1974: 56) claims that the use of *shit, fuck,* and other words traditionally tabooed for women (and now chosen not just for their shock value but because they are "strong language") is "one of the marks of the feminist in American society."

[16]The evidence about sex differences in linguistic sensitivity seems mixed; see, for example, Hilpert *et al.* (1975); Frieze (1974); Rosenthal *et al.* (1974); Soskin and John (1960); Thompson (1968); and Trudgill (1972).

[17]Some female intonation patterns, as Eble (1972) suggests, may be of the "whining, questioning, helpless" type which are due to the subordination of women, just as tag questions may partly have to do with submission, as Lakoff (1973) argues. Verbal gestures of submission seem to be bound up with patterns of self-disclosure and emotional expressiveness. In reevaluating women's speech, these intricacies need sorting out. Can women move to positions of equality, while retaining emotional expressiveness? Need wide-ranging intonation and tag questions—which may have positive as well as negative value—be left behind?

[18]The instrumental/expressive distinction appears in the literature on the sexual differentiation of speech, e.g., in Wood (1966), and in Bernard (1972), who uses the framework somewhat critically.

[19]Conceptual dichotomies which go along with sexual stereotypes may persist in spite of lack of solid empirical support; for example, the field dependence/independence distinction in psychology (Silveira, 1973). Sometimes limited, speculative findings get re-cited without qualification or careful documentation, until they emerge as authoritative fact. This is a general hazard of research, but it is probably more likely where the data appear to support stereotypes. Ruch and Zimbardo (1971: 12-13) traced down an assertion in the popular press that "leading psychologists" had found a general increase in the use of obscene language by women of all social classes. The statement, it turned out, was based entirely on Zimbardo's anecdotal observation about schizophrenic patients in two mental hospitals, years earlier.

[20]Komarovsky (1962) suggests that experimental settings may encourage an association of talk with dominance; in contrast, in an intensive interview study of 58 blue-collar couples, she found that in some couples, the dominant partner (of either sex) was the less talkative.

[21]The parallel question, which also needs more study, is what happens when men use gestures of submission to women. More attention should also be paid to dominance/submission patterns among men, as well as among women.

[22]Such debates, which have occurred not only in written form, but also in many conferences and private conversations, provide fascinating material about reaction to a social movement (women's liberation), about folk attitudes toward language, and about the ongoing process of language change (see Henley and Thorne, 1975: sec. II-A).

[23]The earlier discussion of whether male speech is superior—the issue with which some women are grappling so that they can decide whether they should adopt male forms or revalue their own speech—is also relevant to questions of change.

[24]Readers might ask themselves: is this book—which contains no instances of the generic *he* or other sexist language—any more awkwardly written or unreadable than others of its type?

REFERENCES

Abrahams, R. (1970). *Deep down in the jungle.* Chicago: Aldine.

Addington, D.W. (1968). The relationship of selected vocal characteristics to personality perception. *Speech Monographs,* 35, 492-503.

Anshen, F. (1969). Speech variation among Negroes in a small southern community. Unpublished Ph.D. dissertation, New York Univ.

Argyle, M., Salter, V., Nicholson, H., Williams, M., & Burgess, P. (1970). The communication of inferior and superior attitudes by verbal and nonverbal signals. *British Journal of Social and Clinical Psychology,* 9, 222-31.

Austin, W.M. (1965). Some social aspects of paralanguage. *Canadian Journal of Linguistics,* 11, 31-39.

Bales, R.F. (1950). *Interaction process analysis.* Cambridge, Mass.: Addison-Wesley.

Barron, N. (1971). Sex-typed language: the production of grammatical cases. *Acta Sociologica,* 14, 24-72.

Bart, P.B. (1971). Sexism and social science: from the gilded cage to the iron cage, or, the perils of Pauline. *Journal of Marriage and the Family,* 33, 734-45.

Battle-Sister, A. (1971*a*). Conjectures on the female culture question. *Journal of Marriage and the Family,* 33, 411-20.

———. (1971*b*). Review of "A tyrant's plea," *Dominated Man, Born Female,* and *Sisterhood is Powerful. Journal of Marriage and the Family,* 33, 592-97.

Benson, E. (1972). Dual-career families: alternative research approaches. Unpublished paper, Michigan State Univ.

Bernard, J. (1972). *The sex game.* New York: Atheneum.

———. (1973). My four revolutions: an autobiographical history of the ASA. *American Journal of Sociology,* 78, 773-91.

Birdwhistell, R. (1970). Masculinity and femininity as display. In *Kinesics and context.* Philadelphia: Univ. of Penn. Press.

Bodine, A. (in press). Androcentrism in prescriptive grammar. *Language in Society.*

———. (1975). Sex differentiation in language. In B. Thorne & N. Henley (eds.), *Language and sex: difference and dominance.* Rowley, Mass.: Newbury House.

Bott, E. (1957). *Family and social network.* London: Tavistock.

Bradley, M., Danchik, L., Fager, M., & Wodetzki, T. (1971). *Unbecoming men.* New York: Times Change.

Brend, R.M. (1972). Male-female intonation patterns in American English. *Proceedings of the Seventh International Congress of Phonetic Sciences, 1971*. The Hague: Mouton, 1972. Reprinted in B. Thorne & N. Henley (eds.) (1975), *Language and sex: difference and dominance*. Rowley, Mass.: Newbury House.

Brown, R. (1965). *Social psychology*. New York: Free Press.

Burr, E., Dunn, S., & Farquhar, N. (1972). Women and the language of inequality. *Social Education, 36*, 841-45.

Carlson, R. (1972). Understanding women: implications for personality theory and research. *Journal of Social Issues, 28* (2), 17-32.

Chapanis, A. (1965). Color names for color space. *American Scientist, 53*, 327-46.

Chodorow, N. (1974). Family structure and feminine personality. In M.Z. Rosaldo & L. Lamphere (eds.), *Woman, culture, and society*. Stanford, Calif.: Stanford Univ. Press.

Cherry, L. (1975). Teacher-child verbal interaction: an approach to the study of sex differences. In B. Thorne & N. Henley (eds.), *Language and sex: difference and dominance*. Rowley, Mass.: Newbury House.

Conklin, N.F. (1973). Perspectives on the dialects of women. Paper presented at American Dialect Society.

———. (1974). Toward a feminist analysis of linguistic behavior. *The University of Michigan Papers in Women's Studies, 1* (1), 51-73.

Conners, K. (1971). Studies in feminine agentives in selected European languages. *Romance Philology, 24*, 573-98.

Coser, R.L. (1960). Laughter among colleagues. *Psychiatry, 23*, 81-95.

Coser, R.L. & Rokoff, G. (1971). Women in the occupational world: social disruption and conflict. *Social Problems, 18*, 535-54.

Crystal, D. (1971). Prosodic and paralinguistic correlates of social categories. In E. Ardener (ed.), *Social anthropology and language*. London: Tavistock.

Diebold, A.R. (1961). Incipient bilingualism, *Language, 37*, 97-112. Reprinted in D. Hymes (ed.) (1964), *Language in culture and society*. New York: Harper & Row.

DuBois, P.H. (1939). The sex difference on the color-naming test. *American Journal of Psychology, 52*, 380-82.

Dundes, A., Leach, J.W., & Ozkok, B. (1972). The strategy of Turkish boys' verbal dueling rhymes. In J.J. Gumperz & D. Hymes (eds.), *Directions in sociolinguistics*. New York: Holt, Rinehart & Winston.

Eble, C.C. (1972). How the speech of some is more equal than others. Paper presented at Southeastern Conference on Linguistics.

Ellman, M. (1968). *Thinking about women.* New York: Harcourt Brace Jovanovich.

Epstein, C.F. (1970). *Woman's place: options and limits in professional careers.* Berkeley: Univ. of Calif. Press.

Ervin-Tripp, S. (1972). On sociolinguistic rules: alternation and co-occurrence. In J.J. Gumperz & D. Hymes (eds.), *Directions in sociolinguistics.* New York: Holt, Rinehart & Winston.

Farb, P. (1973). *Word play: what happens when people talk.* New York: Alfred A. Knopf.

Fasold, R.W. (1968). A sociolinguistic study of the pronunciation of three vowels in Detroit speech. Washington, D.C.: Center for Applied Linguistics, mimeo.

Fasteau, M. (1972). Why aren't we talking? *Ms.,* 1 (July), 16.

Feminist Writers Workshop. (1973). *The feminist English dictionary, vol. one.* Chicago: Loop Center Y.W.C.A.

Fischer, J.L. (1958). Social influences on the choice of a linguistic variant. *Word,* 14, 47-56. Reprinted in D. Hymes (ed.) (1964), *Language in culture and society.* New York: Harper & Row.

Fishman, J. (1972). *The sociology of language.* Rowley, Mass.: Newbury House.

Flannery, R. (1946). Men's and women's speech in Gros Ventre. *International Journal of American Linguistics,* 12, 133-35.

Flexner, S. (1960). Preface to H. Wentworth & S. Flexner (eds.), *Dictionary of American slang.* New York: Thomas Y. Crowell.

Fox, G.L. (1973). 'Nice girl': the behavioral legacy of a value construct. Paper presented at National Council on Family Relations.

Frieze, I.H. (1974). Nonverbal aspects of femininity and masculinity which perpetuate sex-role stereotypes. Paper presented at Eastern Psychological Association.

Gall, M.D., Hobby, A.K., & Craik, D.H. (1969). Non-linguistic factors in oral language productivity. *Perceptual and Motor Skills,* 29, 871-74.

Garcia-Zamor, M.A. (1973). Child awareness of sex role distinction in language use. Paper presented at Linguistic Society of America.

Gilley, H.M. & Summers, C.S. (1970). Sex differences in the use of hostile verbs. *Journal of Psychology,* 76, 33-37.

Gleason, J.B. (1973). Code switching in children's language. In T.E. Moore (ed.), *Cognitive development and the acquisition of language.* New York: Academic Press.

Gleser, G.C., Gottschalk, L.A., & Watkins, J. (1959). The relationship of sex and intelligence to choice of words: a normative study of verbal behavior. *Journal of Clinical Psychology,* 15, 182-91.

Goffman, E. (1956). The nature of deference and demeanor. *American Anthropologist,* 58, 473-502. Reprinted in E. Goffman (1967). *Interaction ritual.* New York: Anchor.

———. (1964). The neglected situation. *American Anthropologist,* 66 (6), Part 2, 133-36.

Graham, A. (1973). The making of a nonsexist dictionary. *Ms.,* 2 (Dec.), 12-16. Reprinted in B. Thorne & N. Henley (eds.) (1975). *Language and sex: difference and dominance.* Rowley, Mass.: Newbury House.

Grier, W.H. & Cobbs, P.M. (1968). *Black rage.* New York: Basic Books.

Grimshaw, A.D. (1973). Survey essay: on language in society: part 1. *Contemporary Sociology,* 2, 575-85.

Haas, M.R. (1944). Men's and women's speech in Koasati. *Language,* 20, 142-49. Reprinted in D. Hymes (ed.) (1964), *Language in culture and society.* New York: Harper & Row.

Harding, S. (1975). Women and words in a Spanish village. To appear in R. Reiter (ed.), *Towards an anthropology of women.* New York: Monthly Review Press.

Haugen, E. (1974). 'Sexism' and the Norwegian language. Paper presented at Society for the Advancement of Scandinavian Study.

Henley, N. (1973-74). Power, sex, and nonverbal communication. *Berkeley Journal of Sociology,* 18, 1-26. Reprinted in B. Thorne & N. Henley (eds.) (1975), *Language and sex: difference and dominance.* Rowley, Mass.: Newbury House.

———. (1973). Tracking the elusive female psyche: books on psychology and women. *Radical Therapist,* 3 (Feb.-March), 15-17; (April-May), 8-10.

Henley, N. & Thorne, B. (1975). She said/he said: an annotated bibliography of language and sex including nonverbal communication. In B. Thorne & N. Henley (eds.), *Language and sex: difference and dominance.* Rowley, Mass.: Newbury House.

Hennessee, J. (1974). Some news is good news. *Ms.,* 3 (July), 25-29.

Hilpert, F., Kramer, C., & Clark, R.A. (1975). Participants' perceptions of self and partner in mixed-sex dyads. *Central States Speech Journal.*

Hirschman, L. (1973). Female-male differences in conversational interaction. Paper presented at Linguistic Society of America.

———. (1974). Analysis of supportive and assertive behavior in conversations. Paper presented at Linguistic Society of America.

Hymes, D. (ed.). (1964). *Language in culture and society.* New York: Harper & Row.

———. (1974). *Foundations in sociolinguistics.* Philadelphia: Univ. of Penn. Press.

Jespersen, O. (1922). *Language: its nature, development and origin.* London: Allen & Unwin.

Joos, M. (1961). *The five clocks.* New York: Harcourt, Brace & World.

Jourard, S. (1971). *The transparent self.* New York: Van Nostrand Reinhold.

Keenan, E. (in press). Norm-makers, norm-breakers: uses of speech by men and women in a Malagasy community. In J.F. Sherzer & R. Baumann (eds.), *Explorations in the ethnography of speaking.* New York: Cambridge Univ. Press.

Kenkel, W.F. (1963). Observational studies of husband-wife interaction in family decision-making. In M. Sussman (ed.), *Sourcebook in marriage and the family.* Boston: Houghton Mifflin.

Key, M.R. (1972). Linguistic behavior of male and female. *Linguistics,* 88 (Aug. 15), 15-31.

Klein, J. (1965). *Samples from English culture,* Vol. 1. London: Routledge & Kegan Paul.

Komarovsky, M. (1962). *Blue-collar marriage.* New York: Random House.

Kramer, C. (1974a). Folklinguistics. *Psychology Today,* 8 (June), 82-85.

———. (1974b). Women's speech: separate but unequal? *Quarterly Journal of Speech,* 60, 14-24. Reprinted in B. Thorne & N. Henley (eds.) (1975), *Language and sex: difference and dominance.* Rowley, Mass.: Newbury House.

———. (in press). Stereotypes of women's speech: the word from cartoons. *Journal of Popular Culture.*

Kuhn, T.S. (1962). *The structure of scientific revolutions.* Chicago: Univ. of Chicago Press.

Labov, W. (1972a). *Language in the inner city: studies in the Black English vernacular.* Philadelphia: Univ. of Penn. Press.

———. (1972b). *Sociolinguistic patterns.* Philadelphia: Univ. of Penn. Press.

———. (1973). The linguistic consequences of being a lame. *Language in Society,* 2: 81-115.

Labov, W., Cohen, P., Robins, C., & Lewis, J. (1968). A study of the non-standard English of Negro and Puerto Rican speakers in New York City. U.S. Office of Education, Cooperative Research Project 3288, Vol. 1.

Lakoff, R. (1973). Language and woman's place. *Language in Society,* 2, 45-79.

Lamphere, L. (1974). Strategies, cooperation, and conflict among women in domestic groups. In M.Z. Rosaldo & L. Lamphere (eds.), *Woman, culture, and society.* Stanford, Calif.: Stanford Univ. Press.

Langer, E. (1970). The women of the telephone company. *New York Review of Books,* 14 (March 12), 16-24; (March 26), 14-22.

Laws, J.L. (1971). A feminist review of marital adjustment literature: the rape of the Locke. *Journal of Marriage and the Family,* 33, 483-516.

Lee, D.R. (1974). Spatial setting of advertisements: some sexist observations. Unpublished paper, Florida Atlantic Univ.

Legman, D. (1968). *Rationale of the dirty joke: an analysis of sexual humor.* Castle Books.

Leis, N.B. (1974). Women in groups: Ijaw women's associations. In M.Z. Rosaldo & L. Lamphere (eds.), *Woman, culture, and society.* Stanford, Calif.: Stanford Univ. Press.

Levine, L. & Crockett, H.J. (1966). Speech variation in a Piedmont community: postvocalic *r.* In S. Lieberson (ed.), *Explorations in sociolinguistics.* The Hague: Mouton.

Lieberson, S. (1965). Bilingualism in Montreal: a demographic analysis. *American Journal of Sociology,* 71, 10-25.

Ligon, E.M. (1932). A genetic study of color naming and word reading. *American Journal of Psychology,* 44, 103-22.

Linton, S. (1971). Woman the gatherer: male bias in anthropology. In S. Jacobs (ed.), *Women in cross-cultural perspective.* Urbana, Ill.: Univ. of Ill. Dept. of Urban and Regional Planning.

Markel, N.N., Prebor, L.D., & Brandt, J.F. (1972). Bio-social factors in dyadic communication: sex and speaking intensity. *Journal of Personality and Social Psychology,* 23, 11-13.

Mattingly, I.G. (1966). Speaker variation and vocal-tract size. Paper presented at Acoustical Society of America. Abstract in *Journal of the Acoustical Society of America,* 39, 1219.

Mead, M. (1949). *Male and female.* New York: Morrow.

Miller, C. & Swift, K. (1972). One small step for genkind. *New York Times Magazine* (April 16), 36+.

Mitchell-Kernan, C. (1973). Signifying. In A. Dundes (ed.), *Mother wit from the laughing barrel.* Englewood Cliffs, N.J.: Prentice-Hall.

Morgan, E. (1973). Sexism in language. In Feminist Writers Workshop, *The feminist English dictionary, vol. one.* Chicago: Loop Center Y.W.C.A.

Nilsen, A.P. (1972). Sexism in English: a feminist view. In N. Hoffman, C. Secor, & A. Tinsley (eds.) *Female studies VI.* Old Westbury, N.Y.: The Feminist Press.

———. (1973). The correlation between gender and other semantic features in American English. Paper presented at Linguistic Society of America.

O'Connor, L. (1970). Male dominance: the nitty gritty of oppression. *It Ain't Me Babe* (June 11-July 1), 9-11.

Parsons, T. & Bales, R.F. (1955). *Family, socialization, and interaction process.* New York: Free Press.

Rosaldo, M.Z. (1974). Woman, culture, and society: a theoretical overview. In M.Z. Rosaldo & L. Lamphere (eds.), *Woman, culture, and society.* Stanford, Calif.: Stanford Univ. Press.

Rosaldo, M.Z. & Lamphere, L. (eds.). (1974). *Woman, culture, and society.* Stanford, Calif.: Stanford Univ. Press.

Rosenfeld, H.M. (1966). Approval-seeking and approval-inducing functions of verbal and nonverbal responses in the dyad. *Journal of Personality and Social Psychology,* 4, 597-605.

Rosenthal, R., Archer, D., DiMatteo, R., Koivumaki, J.H., & Rogers, P.L. (1974). Body talk and tone of voice: the language without words. *Psychology Today,* 8 (Sept.), 64-68.

Ruch, F.L. & Zimbardo, P.G. (1971). *Psychology and life.* Glenview, Ill.: Scott, Foresman.

Sachs, J., Lieberman, P., & Erickson, D. (1973). Anatomical and cultural determinants of male and female speech. In R.W. Shuy & R.W. Fasold (eds.), *Language Attitudes.* Washington, D.C.: Georgetown Univ. Press.

Sanday, P.R. (1974). Female status in the public domain. In M.Z. Rosaldo and L. Lamphere (eds.), *Woman, culture, and society.* Stanford, Calif.: Stanford Univ. Press.

Sapir, E. (1927). The unconscious patterning of behavior in society. In E.S. Dummer (ed.), *The unconscious: a symposium.* New York: Knopf. Reprinted in D.G. Mandelbaum (ed.) (1949), *Selected writings of Edward Sapir.* Berkeley: Univ. of Calif. Press.

Schulz, M.R. (1975). The semantic derogation of woman. In B. Thorne & N. Henley (eds.), *Language and sex: difference and dominance.* Rowley, Mass.: Newbury House.

Shuster, J. (1973). Grammatical forms marked for male and female in English. Unpublished paper, Univ. of Chicago.

Shuy, R.W., Wolfram, W.A., & Riley, W.K. (1967). *Linguistic correlates of social stratification in Detroit speech.* Final Report, Project 6-1347. Washington, D.C.: U.S. Office of Education.

Silveira, J. (1973). Male bias in psychology. In J.R. Leppaluoto (ed.), *Women on the move.* Pittsburgh: KNOW, Inc.

Slater, P. (1961). Parental role differentiation. *American Journal of Sociology,* 67, 296-311.

Soskin, W.F. & John, V.P. (1963). The study of spontaneous talk. In R. Barker (ed.), *The stream of behavior.* New York: Appleton-Century-Crofts.

Stanley, J.P. (1973). Paradigmatic woman: the prostitute. Unpublished paper.

Stewart, W. (1964). Urban Negro speech. In R.W. Shuy (ed.), *Social dialects and language learning.* Bloomington, Indiana: Indiana Univ. Press.

Strodtbeck, F.L. (1951). Husband-wife interaction over revealed differences. *American Sociological Review,* 16, 468-73.

Strodtbeck, F.L. & Mann, R.D. (1956). Sex role differentiation in jury deliberations. *Sociometry,* 19, 3-11.

Swacker, M. (1975). The sex of the speaker as a sociolinguistic variable. In B. Thorne & N. Henley (eds.), *Language and sex: difference and dominance.* Rowley, Mass.: Newbury House.

Thompson, W.N. (1967). *Quantitative research in public address and communication.* New York: Random House.

Tiger, L. (1969). *Men in groups.* New York: Random House.

Trudgill, P. (1972). Sex, covert prestige, and linguistic change in the urban British English of Norwich. *Language in Society,* 1, 179-95. Reprinted in B. Thorne & N. Henley, (eds.), *Language and sex: difference and dominance.* Rowley, Mass.: Newbury House.

U.S. Bureau of the Census (1970). *Occupations by industry report.* Washington, D.C.: U.S. Gov. Printing Office.

Varda One. (1971). Manglish. Pittsburgh: KNOW, Inc. (reprint).

Warshay, D.W. (1972). Sex differences in language style. In C. Safilios-Rothschild (ed.), *Toward a sociology of women.* Lexington, Mass.: Xerox College Pub.

Weisstein, N. (1970). 'Kinder, Kuche, Kirche' as scientific law: psychology constructs the female. In R. Morgan (ed.), *Sisterhood is powerful.* New York: Vintage.

Whorf, B.L. (1940). Science and linguistics. *Technological Review,* 42, 229-31; 247-48. Reprinted in J.B. Carroll (ed.) (1956), *Language, thought, and reality.* Cambridge, Mass.: MIT Press.

Winitz, H. (1959). Language skills of male and female kindergarten children. *Journal of Speech and Hearing Research,* 2, 377-86.

Wolfram, W.A. (1969). *A sociolinguistic description of Detroit Negro speech.* Washington, D.C.: Center for Applied Linguistics.

Wood, M.M. (1966). The influence of sex and knowledge of communication effectiveness on spontaneous speech. *Word,* 22, 112-37.

Zimmerman, D.H. & West, C. (1975). Sex roles, interruptions and silences in conversation. In B. Thorne & N. Henley (eds.) *Language and sex: difference and dominance.* Rowley, Mass.: Newbury House.

WOMEN'S SPEECH: SEPARATE BUT UNEQUAL?*

Cheris Kramer

In generalizing about sex differences, Margaret Mead (1949) says that although societies differ in the way traits are assigned to men and women, all cultures set up societal norms for the sexes which go beyond the biological differences. There continues to be disagreement, of course, on which behavioral differences are caused by cultural influence and which by biological characteristics. For researchers in speech and linguistics, however, the first task is to search for possible differences in the ways men and women speak.

Although there have recently been published a number of articles dealing with sexism in the English language (for example, the use of the dominant "he" meaning either male or female), there has been relatively little concern about the ways men and women use the English language differently. The sex role differences, so important to our culture, seem to have been largely ignored in communication research.

We need to consider not only the possibility of differences in grammatical, phonological, and semantic aspects, but also possible differences in the verbal skills, instrumental use of language, and the relationship of nonverbal uses to verbal behavior. We need to ask if there are differences between the sexes in their linguistic competence. Do women control some speech structures or vocabulary that men lack or vice versa? We need to ask if there are differences in linguistic performance. Are there syntactic structures, vocabulary, phonological rules that, say, women might know but not use while men both know and use?

*Reprinted with permission from the *Quarterly Journal of Speech,* February 1974, 60, 14-24.

This paper will consider the evidence for there being systems of co-occurring, sex-linked, linguistic signals in the United States.[1] There are, of course, very important implications of such a finding for future linguistic research. Discussion of possible reasons for sex-related differences in speech will be limited; the emphasis will be on, first, what type of research in linguistic sex contrasts has been done and then on relevant material in folk-linguistics (with suggestions of further areas of study).

It has been easier to see the differences of language between the sexes in other cultures than in our own. For example, Furfey (1944) says that sex contrasts in language usage are common among primitive tribes (though such contrasts are, he says, "barely discernible in the familiar languages of Europe"). He reports differences in phonetics, grammar, and vocabulary found in tribes in Siberia, Bengal, Bolivia, the United States (Indians), and the Lesser Antilles. There is, he writes, "linguistic evidence that in at least some scattered instances, the existence of these distinctions is associated with an assertion of masculine superiority." Haas (1944) indicates that differences in the language spoken by men and women are common to many cultures. Although differences in grammar have been noticed, most differences seem to be either of vocabulary or of pronunciation.

Frazer (1900, I: 404-41) writes about the special speech used by the women of the Caffres of South Africa. A Caffre wife must not pronounce the names of her father-in-law or the names of her mate's male relations in the ascending line, or words which contain a syllable of any of those names. In the case of the Caffres, avoiding the emphatic syllable contained in many male names means that many words used by the women have a syllable changed and at times the entire words. Frazer's source states that the Caffres call this language "Ukuteta Kwabafazi" ("women's speech"). Restrictions are evidently often imposed on the males of a tribe also.

Jespersen (1922) warns that differing lists of words restricted to either men or women do not necessarily make different languages. In his chapter "The Woman," he quotes Rochefort speaking of his experiences in the seventeenth century among the Caribbeans: "The men have a great many expressions peculiar to them, which the women understand but never pronounce themselves. On the other hand, the women have words and phrases which the men never use, or they would be laughed to scorn. Thus it happens that in their conversations it often seems as if women had another language than the men." Rochefort is saying that these systems are exclusive. There are categorical differences. Women have words which the men *never* use. However, in the United States many differences appear to be a matter of context and frequency; for example: women perhaps know but do not use swear or curse words in the same context or with the same frequency as men. By the same token, women seem to use such words as "pretty," "cute," "lovely," and "oh dear" in contexts and in frequencies that differ from men.

In a 1969 article Shuy reviewed some of the small amount of research which had been done on women's speech in the United States. He mentions a Detroit study by Shuy himself, Wolfram, and Riley, that found clear sex differences in frequency of a linguistic feature. For example, males used "-in" (in place of "-ing") 62.2 per cent of the time compared to only 28.9 per cent of the time by females. (In a New England study, Fischer [1964] found that girls used "-ing" more frequently, while boys used "-in" more frequently.) Shuy also reported that Wolfram in his work with Black English found that black females "have fewer *f, t* or ∅ realizations of *th.* . . . Females come closer than males at approximating the norm." Black females show greater tendency toward norms in their grammar, also, especially black females of the lower middle class.

Labov (1966: 310-14) also found that lower middle class New York women have a more extreme pattern of hypercorrection than men in the same class. Levine and Crockett (1966) found in a study of one American community that it was primarily the middle class women who led the community toward the national speech norms. Trudgill (1972) found the same type of sex differentiation for speakers of urban British English. His study demonstrated that "women informants . . . use forms associated with the prestige standard more frequently than men." His study also discovered that male speakers place a high value on working class nonstandard speech. He offers several possible reasons for the finding that the women are more likely to use forms considered correct: (1) The subordinate position of women in English and American societies makes it "more necessary for women to secure their social status linguistically"; and (2) While men can be rated socially on what they *do*, women may be rated primarily on how they *appear*—so their speech is more important.

Another study, by Sachs, Lieberman and Erickson (1973) discovered, in tests involving boys and girls, that even when there is no difference in articulatory mechanism size, the sex of the speaker can be accurately identified from his or her speech. The researchers offered some possible reasons for this finding, one of which was:

> If there is no average difference in articulatory mechanism size, the differences we have observed could arise from differential use of the anatomy. The children could be learning culturally determined patterns that are viewed as appropriate for each sex. Within the limit of his anatomy, a speaker could change the format pattern by pronouncing vowels with phonetic variations, or by changing the configuration of the lips. . . . Spreading the lips will shorten the vocal tract, and raise the formants. The characteristic way some women have of talking and smiling at the same time would have just this effect (pp. 80-81).

Goldberg (1968) conducted an experiment which found that women college students are predisposed to value the scholarly writings of men in their professional fields over the writing of women in the same fields.

Kester found that in a mixed group of people it is the men who talk much more than the women. She found that men interrupt women more often than women interrupt men.[2] In a study involving a verbal task, Wood (1966) concluded that men tended to use more words than women in responding to a given stimulus.

Another study, done by Shuy, Baratz, and Wolfram in 1969, tested men's and women's subjective reactions to language performance, and found only an insignificant difference in men's and women's ability to identify the race of speakers heard on tape. Considering that his earlier study (that I have mentioned) had shown clear sex contrasts in language use, with women using the prestige forms more often than men, Shuy found the results of this later study surprising. He gives several possible reasons for the evidence that subjective reactions and performance in speech are asymmetrical, including the disappointing final one that "women continue to be one of the mysteries of the universe" (Shuy, 1969, pp. 12-14). This reaction in itself offers a possible reason that so little research has been done. Firestone (1970) calls such a reaction part of an "exaggeration process" that provides for stereotyping of women as a peculiar type of human being that cannot be understood or treated by the laws that govern mankind, i.e., males (p. 100).

I could find few other studies dealing with linguistic sex contrasts in English. There have been some published papers on the ratio of male to female stutterers. There is general agreement that there are more male stutterers than female. Here again, there is disagreement about whether biological or social factors are working. Some scholars have found evidence that stuttering is a hereditary trait but recent studies indicate that a male is more likely to stutter than a female because our culture places more importance on speech fluency in males than speech fluency in females. Conscious of the pressure on him to speak well, the male feels more insecure about his speech (see Goldman, 1967).

A number of publications deal with sex-related differences in comprehension and retention of oral messages. Although early studies found that males comprehend more than females in tests using oral messages, a recent study did not find this result. The authors, Kibler, Barker, and Cegala (1970) conclude that the inconsistent findings of this type of research "demonstrate that the role of sex in communication has not been clearly defined. Further research should provide added insight into the role of sex in influencing communication effects, a problem which no researcher employing both males and females in communication research can ignore" (p. 292).

Experiments dealing with possible sex-related differences in comprehension of compressed speech and in persuasibility show the same conflict in results (McCracken, 1969, and Bostrom and Kemp, 1969). There is evidently some factor or factors which have not been controlled in these tests.

I have mentioned, then, some of the few types of research projects which have been designed to find sex-related differences in speech. This is not to say that there has been no other word on the subject. The next section of my paper will try to pull together what can be called the folk-linguistics (using Hoenigswald's [1966] term) of women's speech. Much can be said about the popular beliefs of what constitutes women's speech. These beliefs are not always articulated as beliefs, but from a reading of etiquette manuals, speech books, cartoons, and novels, a stereotype of the woman as having particular characteristics of speech will emerge. Sometimes belief is confused with fact. While researching this paper I became aware that there seems to be a conflict not only between what women's speech really is like and what people think women's speech really is like, but also between what people think women's speech is like and what they think it should be like.

Females are cautioned against talking too much. *The New Seventeen Book of Etiquette and Young Living* described in a 1972 *New Yorker* advertisement as "AN IDEAL GRADUATION GIFT" ("social confidence for girls starts here") gives the "basic rules of conduct" for young girls who are interested in learning to "fit in." The book (Haupt, 1970) makes reference to a "survey of opinions" collected from boys. Some of these opinions, given as support for guidelines for girls, mention speech: "I hate girls who can't stop talking." "I like a girl who talks—but not a whole lot." "I like girls who listen to me without interrupting and who pay attention." The editor adds some comments in support of the boys' opinions: "Concentrate on the other person. Ask questions to draw him out. He'll love talking about himself." "Everybody loves to hear praise, and boys in particular." "Any male is happy to be the source of information" (pp. 101-102).

Girls are not *supposed* to talk as much as men. Perhaps a "talkative" woman is one who does talk as much as a man. A number of experiments suggest themselves. The total amount of talking time could be measured for men and women in a variety of situations. (In a study by Gall, Hobby and Craik, 1969, women were found to have a higher word count than men when giving descriptions of verbal displays. The experiment tested only one subject at a time; there were no interruptions.) Here are several focal ideas for other possible experiments: Does the ratio of men to women in a group make a difference in the relative verbosity of members of the two sexes? Is there a difference in the rate at which men and women produce words and sentences? Is there a difference in the number of times men and women in a group speak? And corresponding to this, is there a difference in the time of individual speeches?

How much talking can a woman do before she is labelled "talkative"? This last question might involve a study of the types of sentence construction used, the volume of the voice, and the topics of speech.

Jespersen (1922) cites proof from literature to support his discussion of the way women frequently leave sentences, especially exclamatory sentences, unfinished. "Well, I never"; "I must say!" (p. 251).

It may be that women ask more questions. In an article on the role of men and women as represented in children's books, Marjorie U'Ren (Key, 1971) is quoted on the fictional mother. "She enters a scene only to place a cake on the table and then disappears. Or she plays foil to her husband by setting him up for his line. It is mother who asks, 'What shall we do?' and by doing so invites a speech from father" (p. 170). Do women indeed use more questions and fewer declarative sentences than men? Is this one way of showing subordination, submission to men?

Lakoff (1973) thinks women do use the tag-question formation more than men. A tag, in Lakoff's words, is "midway between an outright statement and a yes-no question: it is less assertive than the former, but more confident than the latter." It is used when a speaker does not have full confidence in his or her statement. Instead of a firm declaration, the speaker asks for confirmation, and by being less decisive the speaker leaves himself or herself an out. He or she is willing to be persuaded otherwise. "This speech convention is terrible, isn't it?" "That law was poorly drafted, don't you think?"

Lakoff hears another question that has much the same effect. Even if the woman is asked a question for which she alone holds the information, she can turn her answer into a question. Lakoff gives this example: "(A) When will dinner be ready? (B) Oh . . . around six o'clock . . . ?" (p. 56). Here, intonation rather than sentence structure has the woman indicate subordination and uncertainty.

I have heard other ways that women, perhaps more than men, have of avoiding stating an opinion directly. "I kinda like that house." If someone points out to her the garage is too small and the fireplace mislocated, she can change her mind without too much difficulty or fear of embarrassment. "That dress is rather pretty." The qualifier gives her an out. Do women actually use tag-questions more than men? Do their declarative sentences contain more qualifiers? In what situations? On what topics?

Lakoff finds a relationship between the tag-question and the tag-order. Women, she says, are more likely to compound a request (pp. 56-57). "Will you help me with these groceries, please?" is more polite than "Come help me" (and politeness, Lakoff believes, is a characteristic of women's speech); and the longer request stated as a question leaves a stronger possibility of a negative response. I have seen no empirical studies which deal with this possible difference in men's and women's speech.

Another technique women might use to talk without seeming to do much talking is to lower the volume and pitch of their speech. We all know that at least in cartoons and novels whenever a number of women gather the resulting talk will be loud and high-pitched. In fact, such gatherings are often called "hen sessions" and the speech is then called a "cackle." Do women change volume and pitch, depending on the situation and the ratio of men and women present?

Pitch level depends upon the length, tension, and weight of the vocal cords. Women's cords are, in general, shorter, lighter, and stretched more tightly than men's. Pitch level is higher. Again, there seems to be a discrepancy between what really is and what is prescribed. The very fact that etiquette books warn women to avoid loud, high-pitched speaking indicates that performance does not always match the stated norms.[3]

In an article entitled "Down With Sexist Upbringing," Pogrebin (1972) recognizes high pitch as a stereotyped attribute of females, closely associated with other undesirable, but feminine, traits. She writes, "Even Sesame Street, despite its noble educational intentions, teaches role rigidity along with the letters of the alphabet. . . . Boy monsters are brave and gruff. Girl monsters are high-pitched and timid" (p. 28). The pitch of the female voice, which is usually higher because of the given physical traits of the vocal cords, is associated with the undesirable trait of timidness.

The higher-pitched voice is not associated in people's minds with serious topics. Mannes (1969) quotes a broadcaster giving a reason why in the United States so few women are employed as reporters by television networks: "As a whole, people don't like to hear women's voices telling them serious things." Qualities other than pitch alone are evidently involved here; a handbook for announcers states that although women were employed by stations during the war, they were not retained once men were once again available, because "often the higher-pitched female voices could not hold listeners' attention for any length of time, while the lower-pitched voices were frequently vehicles for an overly polished, ultrasophisticated delivery that sounded phoney." According to the handbook, "Women's delivery . . . is lacking in the authority needed for a convincing newscast" (quoted by Key, 1972).

Serious news, then, is not expected from females. It would be interesting to discover if women dislike having women's voices over radio and television to the same degree that men dislike hearing women's voices. Do the relatively few women who do have broadcasting jobs change their pitch and volume for their performances on the air to a greater degree than do male broadcasters? What kind of female voices are hired for broadcasting jobs? At what age does this preference for the male voice begin? And in what situations other than broadcasting? Dillard (1972) in writing about the use of peer recordings on speech to teach Standard English to speakers of Black English states: "Sex-grading has to be taken into account: will little boys be willing to learn seriously from records made by little girls, or by boys who impress them as being 'sissies'?" (p. 42). Note that he is not worried about girls being willing to learn "seriously" from records made by boys.

It would be interesting to see if female speech patterns once found in a variety of situations in which women are in the subordinate positions are found in situations in which a woman speaks from some base of power. Perhaps the male-female division remains the most important consideration. One woman executive "in a top governmental position" has been quoted as saying, "I always try to remember that ... this is a man's world, and when I have big problems to discuss I work with them in such a manner that the first thing I know they're telling *me* their ideas, which are just exactly what I've been talking about ... but in a roundabout way through the backdoor ... it's *their* idea" (in Cussler, 1958, p. 67).

This quotation is not of recent date. It would be interesting to try to discover the present speech habits of female executives. If, as our literature suggests, women learn to control their speech to help convey an impression that they are living in the background, does the woman who has obtained a position of some power alongside or over men have these techniques perfected? Or, alternatively, has she other characteristics of speaking which have aided her in obtaining a position of power?

The material presented on the preceding pages indicates that there are many experiments to be run using the larger hypothesis that women's speech reflects the stereotyped roles of male and female in our society, i.e., women in a subservient, nurturing position in a male-dominated world. The tag-question, the relatively large number of questions asked, the intonation which makes a declarative sentence a question, the compounding of requests, the concern with unobtrusive pitch and volume, the triviality of subjects discussed over the air, the roundabout way of declaring ideas—all aspects of female speech, if they do indeed exist (for what I have been reporting is largely folk-linguistics) for a significant segment of the female population, would indicate one way in which the sex roles are maintained.

There appear to be a number of other differences in the speech of men and women that do not seem as neatly categorized according to dominant-dominated characteristics.

Women are said to have a greater intonational range. "It is generally thought that women have more extremes of high and low intonation than do men and that there are some intonation patterns, impressionistically the 'whining, questioning, helpless' patterns, which are used predominantly by women" (Eble, p. 10).

There is some evidence—at least in jokes and novels—of a syntactic looseness in women's speech. (This is of course in comparison with men's speech.)

Jespersen (1922) writes of the "greater rapidity of female thought" and of the "superior readiness of speech of women"—indicating that the talk is done without much thought. (He offers material from a number of novels written by men as partial proof.) Sentences are not completed, he attests, and women are prone to jump from one idea to another (pp. 250-53). Ellmann (1968) writes of the stereotyped formlessness of women's speech as it is represented in the writing of such men as Joyce, Sartre, Mailer, and Hemingway. Molly Bloom and so many women who followed her in literary history have just let it all flow out. The same looseness is illustrated in a *Saturday Review* cartoon (30 Oct., 1971, p. 56) in which a mini-skirted co-ed is saying in class to her professor (male):

> If we don't know how big the whole universe is, then I don't see how we could be sure how big anything in it is either, like the whole thing might not be any bigger than maybe an orange would be if it weren't in the universe. I mean, so I don't think we ought to get too uptight about any of it because it might be really sort of small and unimportant after all, and until we find out that everything isn't just some kind of specks and things, why maybe who needs it?

Jespersen states that the women can answer and talk more quickly because their vocabulary is more limited and more central—that is, women share a common vocabulary while men show more individuality in word choice. If Jespersen's book of 1922 seems to be referred to here an inordinately large number of times it is because he was a prolific and respected writer on language (selections from his books are still anthologized) and because he wrote one of the very few studies available on women's speech. The statements that he makes about women's speech have not been proved or disproved. The support he uses is largely taken from literature.

"Everyone knows that the vocabulary of women differs considerably from that of men," wrote Greenough and Kittredge back in 1901. Yet one finds very little mention of this supposedly obvious difference. There is surprisingly little interest in linguistic literature even about the use of curse words. Jespersen declares that "there can be no doubt that women exercise a great and universal influence on linguistic development through their instinctive shrinking from coarse and gross expressions and their preference for refined and (in certain spheres) veiled and indirect expressions" (p. 246). Instinctive, he says. Firestone (1970) offers another explanation for this particular difference in the vocabulary of men and women: "As for the double standard about cursing: A man is allowed to blaspheme the world because it belongs to him to damn—but the same curse out of the mouth of a woman or a minor, i.e., an incomplete 'man' to whom the world does not yet belong, is considered presumptuous, and thus an impropriety or worse" (p. 100).

Men have a further claim to slang words in general. Flexner (1960) writes, in the preface to the *Dictionary of American Slang:*

> In my work on this dictionary, I was constantly aware that most American slang is created and used by males. Many types of slang words—including the taboo and strongly derogatory ones, those referring to sex, women, work, money, whiskey, politics, transportation, sports, and the like—refer primarily to male endeavor and interest. The majority of entries in this dictionary could be labeled "primarily masculine use . . . " Men also tend to avoid words that sound feminine or weak. Thus there are sexual differences in even the standard vocabularies of men and women (p. xii).

In her paradigm of terms for "prostitute," Stanley analyzed two hundred words ("not by many means an exhaustive list") used by men to refer to women who sell themselves or who give themselves away.[4]

This creation and use of slang is considered a healthy activity. According to Jespersen (1922), "Men will certainly with great justice object that there is a danger of the language becoming languid and insipid if we are to content ourselves with women's expressions, and that vigour and vividness count for something" (p. 247). Eric Partridge writes about the "vivid expressiveness" and "vigorous ingenuity" expressed by the creation of the more than 1,200 English synonyms for the word "fuck." He says the words "bear witness to the fertility of English and to the enthuiastic English participation in the universal fascination of the creative act" (Stanley, p. 6).

The fascination of the act may be universal, but in this country it is not to be spoken about by girls. Here is *The New Seventeen* on people who use "those four letter words": "Boys find it especially repugnant when girls use these words. One boy described girls who use profanity as having nothing better to say" (p. 106).

This material indicates that there is at least one major restriction on what women are supposed to say. Of course, women often object to the slang used by men. But, after all, "Boys will be boys." (Have you ever heard "Girls will be girls"?) There does seem to be a feeling that there is something instinctive—or should be something instinctive—about the way men use coarse expressions and the way women avoid them.

Reik (1954) mentions what he thinks are differences in the ways men and women use the *same* words. A word such as "sex," "love," or "home" might have different connotations for the two sexes. These differences could conceivably be found by the use of semantic differential tests.

A number of sources I consulted for this paper indicated that women do not use the same adjectives as men do, or they are used in different contexts or with different frequency. Native speakers will recognize "nice," "pretty," "darling," "charming," "sweet," "lovely," "cute," and "precious," as being words of approval used more frequently by women. As one male student in my speech class said, "If I heard a guy say something was 'cute,' I'd wonder about him." That is, his masculinity would be in question.

I found little mention of the use of adverbs in women's speech, although Jespersen (1922) says there are greater differences in the way the sexes use the adverb—and he quotes Lord Chesterfield to prove it (p. 249). (Chesterfield objected to the extensive use of "vastly," which he said women used to mean anything.) Several sources, including Jespersen, mentioned the use of hyperbole in women's speech, especially the intensive *"so."* Lakoff suggests that the heavily stressed *"so"* can be used like the tag-question to avoid full commitment to a statement. She feels that men use the intensive *"so"* most easily when the sentence is unemotional or nonsubjective (p. 3n), as in "That car is so beautiful." Since being emphatic is not seemingly a characteristic of women's speech, it would be useful to determine in what situations and with what topics women do use the intensive *"so."* It might be that it is used in cases where agreement with another speaker is being made. Or where disagreement is unlikely.

Hyperbole perhaps is not a characteristic peculiar to women's speech. Flexner (p. xii) writes that men enjoy using hyperbole in slang. He continues: "Under many situations, men do not see or care to express fine shades of meaning: a girl is either a knockout or a dog." (At the end of this paragraph Flexner says that men like to make themselves the active doer, to use the transitive verb. Here is another syntax pattern to check.)

What I have discussed thus far has been primarily concerned with spoken words. There is some evidence that there are thought to be parallel differences in the written work of men and women. I have already mentioned a study involving the way scholarly writing by women is viewed by college women. Ellmann, in writing about fiction, states the stereotyped dichotomy: the masculine mode of writing contains the properties of reason and knowledge, the feminine mode of writing states feelings and intuitions (p. 158). Ellmann calls this dichotomy "unreal." Reason and knowledge, feelings and intuitions are difficult things to test for, based as they are on a culture's idea of what is real. But perhaps there are lesser tests to run. For example, is the dialogue different for the sexes in the novels? And do women writers treat the dialogue differently? Much of the support Jespersen used for his chapter on the speech of women consisted of dialogue taken from novels by male writers. Does this dialogue correspond with what is actually said by women and men? A female novelist, George Eliot, used Dorothea's speech (in *Middlemarch*) to indicate changes in Dorothea's feeling of self-assurance as she falls under the dominance of her husband. Her use of intensifying adverbs, for example, persists, but she loses her ability to use figurative speech—or she refrains from using it. As she is unable to get positive responses from her husband, she stops trying to gain agreement by means of her former method of using negatives ("Will you not now do . . . " [which seems a feminine, that is, a submissive construction to begin with]), and starts asking rhetorical questions for which no agreement is required. In her loneliness she uses much hyperbole—to herself. This analysis, by Derek Oldfield (1967), provides an interesting look at the ways a female novelist made a woman use her speech to indicate subordination—so that she was able to still use speech as an outlet.

Poetry, letter-writing, and reporting in the media would be other areas of communications to study. Can the written work of women be recognized by subject, sentence structure, or word choice, or by a combination of these features of formal communication?

This paper has stressed the fact that women as speakers have been largely ignored in communication research, but that there is a sizable amount of information that can be called folk-view: how people think women speak or how people think women should speak. Although these beliefs will make useful bases for hypotheses for research, it must be realized that women are individuals. Researchers interested in studying the speech of women as women (not as part of the category termed "man"—said to be an inclusive term but all too often actually meaning "male") must be careful not to make the error of grouping all women together. Labov and Basil Bernstein have made linguistics conscious of the necessity of recognizing the socio-economic status of speakers. The origin and race of women speakers might be important factors which bring diversity into the larger category of "women's speech." Age may be another important interacting factor—as religion might be.[5]

Margaret Mead (1949) has suggested that we need to try to disabuse our minds of assuming stereotypes to be fact and rather to begin asking some "open-ended exploratory questions" about males and females in our society (pp. 135-36). This paper suggests that some of these questions might be derived from those very stereotypes, the folk-linguistics of speech that exist in our society.

NOTES

[1]Wayne Dickerson has suggested that the term "genderlects" be used to describe such systems. Braj Kachru has suggested "sexlects."

[2]Judy Kester, mentioned in "In Other Words," *Chicago Sun-Times*, 7 May 1972. Another comment on this subject is made by Connie E. Eble. "How the Speech of Some Is More Equal than Others," Univ. of North Carolina (mimeographed).

[3]See Emily Post, *Etiquette* (New York: Funk & Wagnalls, 1960), pp. 39-40; and Haupt, p. 104.

[4]Julia Stanley, "The Semantic Features of the Machismo Ethic in English," University of Georgia, 1972 (mimeographed).

[5]This suggestion was made by Fred Hilpert.

REFERENCES

Bostrom, Robert N., and Kemp, Alan P. (1969). Type of speech, sex of speaker, and sex of subject as factors influencing persuasion. *Central States Speech Journal,* 28 (Winter), 245-51.

Cussler, Margaret. (1958). *The woman executive.* New York: Harcourt, Brace & World.

Dillard, J.L. (1972). The validity of black English. *Intellectual Digest,* December, 35-42.

Ellmann, Mary. (1968). *Thinking about women.* New York: Harcourt, Brace & World.

Firestone, Shulamith. (1970). *The dialectic of sex.* New York: William Morrow.

Fischer, John. (1964). Social influence in the choice of a linguistic variant. In Dell Hymes (ed.), *Language in culture and society.* New York: Harper & Row, 483-88.

Flexner, Stuart. (1960). Preface to Harold Wentworth and Stuart Flexner (eds.), *Dictionary of American slang.* New York: Thomas Y. Crowell.

Frazer, J.G. (1900). *The Golden Bough.* London: Macmillan and Co.

Furfey, Paul Hanly. (1944). Men's and women's languages. *American Catholic Sociological Review,* 5, 218-23.

Gall, Meredith D., Hobby, Amos K., & Craik, Kenneth H. (1969). Non-linguistic factors in oral language productivity. *Perceptual and Motor Skills,* 29, 871-74.

Goldberg, Philip. (1968). Are women prejudiced against women? *Trans-action,* April, 28-30.

Goldman, Ronald. (1967). Cultural influences on the sex ratio in the incidence of stuttering. *American Anthropologist,* 69, 78-81.

Greenough, James B., & Kittredge, George L. (1901, 1914). *Words and their ways in English speech.* New York: Macmillan.

Haas, Mary R. (1944). Men's and women's speech in Koasati. *Language,* 20, 142-49.

Haupt, Enid. (1970). *The new Seventeen book of etiquette and young living.* New York: David McKay.

Hoenigswald, Henry M. (1966). A proposal for the study of folk-linguistics. In William Bright, (ed.), *Sociolinguistics.* The Hague: Mouton, pp. 16-20.

Jespersen, Otto. (1922). *Language: its nature, development and origin.* London: Allen & Unwin.

Key, Mary Ritchie. (1972). Linguistic behavior of male and female. *Linguistics,* 88 (15 Aug.), 15-31.

―――. (1971). The role of male and female in children's books―dispelling all doubt. *Wilson Library Bulletin,* 46 (October), 167-76.

Kibler, Robert, Barker, Larry, & Cegala, Donald. (1970). Effect of sex on comprehension and retention. *Speech Monographs, 37,* 287-92.

Labov, William. (1966). *The social stratification of English in New York City.* Washington, D.C.: Center for Applied Linguistics.

Lakoff, Robin. (1973). Language and woman's place. *Language in Society,* 2 (Apr.), 45-79.

Levine, Lewis, & Crockett, Harry. (1966). Speech variation in a Piedmont community: postvocalic *r.* In Stanley Lieberson (ed.), *Explorations in sociolinguistics.* The Hague: Mouton.

McCracken, Sally R. (1969). Comprehension for immediate recall of time-compressed speech as a function of the sex and level of activation of the listener. *Speech Monographs,* 36 (Aug.), 308-9.

Mannes, Marya. (1969). Women are equal but―. In Joseph M. Bachelor, Ralph L. Henry, & Rachel Salisbury (eds.), *Current thinking and writing.* New York: Appleton-Century-Crofts.

Mead, Margaret. (1949). *Male and female.* New York: William Morrow.

Oldfield, Derek. (1967). The language of the novel. In Barbara Hardy (ed.), *Middlemarch: critical approaches to the novel.* New York: Oxford University Press.

Pogrebin, Letty Cottin. (1972). Down with sexist upbringing. *Ms.,* Spring, 18+.

Reik, Theodor. (1954). Men and women speak different languages. *Psychoanalysis,* 2, No. 4, 3-15.

Sachs, Jacqueline, Lieberman, Philip, & Erickson, Donna. (1973). Anatomical and cultural determinants of male and female speech. In Roger Shuy & Ralph Fasold (eds.), *Language attitudes: current trends and prospects.* Washington, D.C.: Georgetown Univ. Press.

Shuy, Roger W. (1969). Sex as a factor in sociolinguistic research. Paper presented at Anthropological Society of Washington. Available from Educational Resources Information Clearinghouse, No. ED 027 522.

Trudgill, Peter. (1972). Sex, covert prestige, and linguistic change in the urban British English of Norwich. *Language in Society,* 1, 179-95.

Wood, Marion. (1966). The influence of sex and knowledge of communication effectiveness on spontaneous speech. *Word,* 22 (Apr.-Aug.-Dec.), 112-37.

THE MAKING OF A NONSEXIST DICTIONARY*

Alma Graham

The first dictionary to define *sexism,* to include the phrase *liberated women,* and to recognize *Ms.* was a wordbook for children published in 1972 by American Heritage Publishing Company.

The American Heritage School Dictionary contains 35,000 entries, which were selected after an unprecedented analysis of 5 million words encountered by American children in their schoolbooks.

When the task of compilation began in 1969, we could not predict that the dictionary would be the first ever published in which lexicographers made a conscious effort to correct the sex biases that exist in English as it is commonly used. But the computer revealed a pattern that we who were editing the dictionary could not ignore: in schoolbooks, whether the subject is reading, mathematics, social studies, art, or science, males command center stage. Boys and girls may go to school in equal numbers; they may be graded for equal achievements; but the computer had tipped the scales on the side of male supremacy.

In some ways the American Heritage computer was no different from any other. It was stupid. Though it devoured reams of printed matter—10,000 passages of 500 words each culled from 1,000 books and magazines—it couldn't read. To the computer the "lead" in flaking paint was no different from the "lead" in a play, and a "row" of cabbages was the same as a "row" between lovers. Fortunately, this lack of discrimination was unimportant, for in addition to alphabetizing all its words and ranking them by the frequency of their usage, the computer's unprecedented contribution was to deliver 700,000 citation slips,

*Reprinted with permission from *Ms.* magazine, December, 1973, 12-14, 16.

each of which showed a word in three lines of context. By using these slips, the editors could see each word as it is used in sentences that schoolchildren read, and we could in turn write definitions that schoolchildren could comprehend.

The original objective in using a computer was this obvious one of gaining access to primary sources. Peter Davies, the editor in chief of the school dictionary, was the first to recognize what else the computer had delivered. To Davies, the vast body of words was a reflection of the culture talking to its children. He suspected that if imaginatively used, the computer could also supply a profile of what was being said between the lines.

For example, Davies noticed that when adults write for one another, they refer to young people as *children,* almost as often as they call them *boys* and *girls.* When writing books and stories for children, however, adults use the gender words *boy* and *girl* twice as often as the neutral words *child* and *children.* When the culture talks *to* its children, it is careful to distinguish them by sex. Moreover, no matter what the subject being taught, girls and women are always in a minority. Overall, the ratio in schoolbooks of *he* to *she, him* to *her,* and *his* to *hers* was almost four to one. Even in home economics, the traditional preserve of the female, the pronoun *he* predominated by nearly two to one.

It was suggested that some of those excess *he's* might apply not to boys and men but to the unspecified singular subject, as in: a person . . . he; a student . . . his; someone . . . him. To check this out I made a survey of pronoun citations from an earlier, experimental sampling of 100,000 words. Out of 940 citations for *he,* 744 were applied to male human beings, 128 to male animals, and 36 to persons such as farmers and sailors who were assumed to be male. Only 32 referred to the unspecified singular subject. The conclusion was inescapable: the reason most of the pronouns in schoolbooks were male in gender was because most of the subjects being written about were men and boys.

In the real world, there are 100 women for every 95 men. Yet in the books read by schoolchildren, there are over seven times as many men as women and over twice as many boys as girls.

Then another oddity came to light. Despite the preponderance of the words *man* and *boy* in textbooks, the word *mother* occurs more frequently than the word *father,* and the word *wife* is used three times as often as the word *husband.* Women, it would seem, are typecast in the supporting roles that refer to their relationships to men and children.

Might this fact simply imply that in the world of the elementary school the mother is seen as the chief parent? The situation changes when the subject words analyzed are not *mother* and *father* but *daughter* and *son.* An examination of citation slips showed that four times as many sons and daughters are referred to as the children of a male parent (Jim's son; the landlord's daughter) as of a female parent (her son; Mrs. Greenwood's daughter).

Other kinship-term citations revealed still more about this schoolbook never-never land. Two out of every three mothers are mentioned in relation to male children. Father references are even more extreme: four out of every five fathers are fathers of a male. And there's more bald bias: twice as many uncles as aunts, and of those aunts, four times as many have nephews (Charley's aunt) as have nieces (Nelly's aunt); sons outnumber daughters by better than two to one, and every single firstborn child is a son.

Where have all the young girls gone?

It seems clear that they have grown up and have been given (or taken) in marriage—because in schoolbooks wives are three times as numerous as husbands, showing that the speakers or main characters are males. Furthermore, many other words besides *husband* serve as counterparts of *wife*. Farmers' wives and farm wives (but no farm husbands) appear in citations, as do diplomats' wives and Cabinet wives.

Obviously, the basic imbalance in male/female pairs was far more than simply a numbers game. The 700,000 computer citation slips contained the evidence that boys and girls were also being taught separate sets of values, different expectations, and divergent goals. Boys in the schoolbooks ran races, rode bicycles, drove fast cars, and took off in spaceships for Mars. Girls, on the other hand, were less concerned with doing than with being. After reading, "He was the manliest of his sex and she was the loveliest of hers," a child would say that the word comparable to *manly* was *lovely,* not *womanly.* In the sentence, "The men are strong, virile, and graceful, and the girls often beauties," we note that girls, not women, are paired with men and that *virile* is parallel to *beautiful.* A feminine figure, a feminine voice, and a feminine laugh are no match for masculine prerogatives, masculine egos, and masculine drives. The "mannish uniform" of a female general in the Chinese Army is condemned by the very adjective that describes it, but three modifiers commend "a very feminine dream gown."

If this new dictionary were to serve elementary students without showing favoritism to one sex or the other, an effort would have to be made to restore the gender balance. We would need more examples featuring females, and the examples would have to ascribe to girls and women the active, inventive, and adventurous human traits traditionally reserved for men and boys.

Our new archetypal woman took form gradually. Each of the dozen editors writing and reviewing word entries had special moments of insight and decision when we recognized her presence among us. Mine came at the word *brain,* where a computer citation asserted "he has *brains* and courage." In what seemed at the time an act of audacity, I changed the pronoun. "She has *brains* and courage."

As the number of word entries grew, the new woman made her way from example to example, establishing her priorities, aspirations, and tastes. She was "a woman of dedicated political *principles.*" She "made a *name* for herself" and "everyone *praised* her good sense and learning." When she "*plunged* into her work, her mind began to *percolate*" (not her coffee), and "she *prided* herself on her eloquence" (not on the sheen of her freshly waxed floors).

Her appearances in the dictionary were widely separated, of course. Her brothers and traditional sisters continued to surround and outnumber her, example for example. But she had arrived, and from A, where at *abridge* she quoted the 19th Amendment, to Z, when "she *zipped* down the hill on her sled," her spirit, character, and credentials were never in doubt.

As the femininists—male and female—who had brought her into the lexicon cheered her on, "her *determination* to win" was bolstered by our "*devout* wish for her success."

Men in the dictionary examples continued to be active and daring, competitive and combative; but the liberated man could be vulnerable, too. He might be "striving to attain *mastery* over his emotions," but he was not disgraced if "his resolve began to *waver*" or if "tears *welled* up in his eyes." Like the new woman, he had a freer choice of careers than heretofore: "He *teaches* kindergarten" and "he *studies* typing at night."

Ms. was the new word we watched with the greatest degree of interest. Some of us favored adopting it right away, but a problem arose over its pronunciation: it was an abbreviation that anyone could write but that no one could say. Arguments over "miz" or "mis" or "em es" continued through the summer. Then, in October, Bruce Bohle, our usage editor, urged that we enter *Ms.* in the dictionary as an abbreviation whether or not the title could be pronounced with ease. Thus supported, I wrote the definition and Peter Davies provided a note explaining the parallel with *Mr.,* the derivation from *mistress,* and the pronunciation possibilities.

Ms. or *Ms* An abbreviation used as a title of courtesy before a woman's last name or before her given name and last name, whether she is married or not.

At the same time that womanpower in the dictionary was beginning to be felt, consciousness of woman's powerlessness in the language was rising. As a lexicographer and feminist, I had started a notebook on sexism in language, collecting examples of ways in which men and women were classified as human beings by being labeled with male or female words.

One method used in this socializing process is a tactic I called "my virtue-is-your-vice." Since men and women are supposed to be polar opposites, what is considered admirable in one has to be contemptible in the other. If a woman is commended for the gentle qualities that make her *feminine,* then a man must be condemned for any similar show of softness with the epithet *effeminate.* A man's tears are *womanish;* a woman's uniform *mannish.* The lessons to be learned by both male and female are clear: biology is not only destiny; it is character and personality.

Another trick of socialization is to label what we consider to be the exception to the rule: the *woman* doctor, the *male* nurse, the career *girl* (the phrase *career man* is restricted to government service). The term "feminine logic" illustrates the most negatively sexist use of the modifier tactic since it implies non-logic or lack of logic. Because *logic* unmodified is assumed by men to apply to men, a woman who thinks logically is said to have "a masculine mind" (a supposed compliment that serves as a questionable exception to the my-virtue-is-your-vice rule).

Then there is the "trivializing tactic." This tactic operates through female gender forms, such as *poetess* and *usherette,* and through the put-down process that turns *liberationist* into *libber,* just as it once turned *suffragist* into *suffragette.*

The tendency in the language that I called "praise him/blame her" is still another device. From Eve and Pandora on, the female has been held responsible for evil and assigned to a semantic house of ill fame. Titles of honor illustrate the point particularly well. *Queen, madam, mistress,* and *dame* have all acquired degraded meanings, whereas *prince, king, lord,* and *father* are exalted and applied to God—for even God is thought of as a male and is called Him.

Most pervasive of all is the phenomenon I called the "exclusionary tactic." Here the possibility is simply not considered that the person or persons being addressed or discussed might be female. A typical example is the loan application that reads: "Full Name. Wife's First Name and Middle Initial. Your Present Employer. Wife's Employer. Your Monthly Salary. Wife's Income (if any)." But the exclusionary tactic employed most tellingly is the constant, careless overuse of the word *man* in its extended senses. When the speakers refer to "the leading man in the field," to "the man whose book sells half a million copies," or to "the man they would most like to see as President," they effectively rule out the possibility of a female authority, author, or candidate.

To fight these sexist habits of language, the school dictionary had to avoid gender assumptions that other dictionaries imposed more through custom than necessity. *Youth,* one dictionary said, is "the part of life between childhood and manhood." *Youth,* we said, is "the time of life before one is an adult." *Sex,* itself, we defined straightforwardly, with impersonal examples, avoiding a rival dictionary's use of "the fair, gentle, or weaker sex" and "the sterner or stronger sex" dichotomy.

While we were working our way through the alphabet, other word watchers were already speaking out. In Venice, California, Varda One (formerly Varda Murrell) was analyzing and commenting on a phenomenon she called

"Manglish." We could not counter her criticism that dictionaries give less space to *woman* than to *man*. This is not the fault of the dictionary makers, but of a language in which the same word denotes both the human species as a whole and those of its members who are male. In English, contradictory propositions are true: a woman is a man; a woman is not a man.

If a woman is swept off a ship into the water, the cry is "Man overboard!" If she is killed by a hit-and-run driver, the charge is "manslaughter." If she is injured on the job, the coverage is "workmen's compensation." But if she arrives at a threshold marked "Men Only," she knows the admonition is not intended to bar animals or plants or inanimate objects. It is meant for her.

In practice, the sexist assumption that man is a species of males becomes the fact. Erich Fromm certainly seemed to think so when he wrote that man's "vital interests" were "life, food, access to females, etc." Loren Eiseley implied it when he wrote of man that "his back aches, he ruptures easily, his women have difficulties in childbirth. . . . " If these writers had been using *man* in the sense of human species rather than male, they would have written that man's vital interests are life, food, and access to the opposite sex, and that man suffers backaches, ruptures easily, and has difficulties in giving birth.

At every level of achievement and activity—from primitive man to the man of the hour—woman is not taken into account.

Consider the congressman. He is a man of the people. To prove that he's the best man for the job, he takes his case to the man in the street. He is a champion of the workingman. He speaks up for the little man. He has not forgotten the forgotten man. And he firmly believes: one man, one vote.

Consider the policeman or fireman, the postman or milkman, the clergyman or businessman. Whatever else he may be, he is by title a man, and if his employer feels that he is "our kind of man," he may become "our man in the home office" or "our man in Algiers."

From Wordsworth's line "The Child is father of the Man" to the recent New York subway poster "Give a kid a job and help mold a man," a woman is a possibility everyone tends to forget.

When a culture makes adulthood synonymous with manhood, a girl can never reach adulthood at all. There is a clear demarcation between the words *boy* and *man* that does not exist between *girl* and *woman*. A boy greatly increases his stature when he becomes a man, but a girl loses status and bargaining power when she loses youth. So females are in effect encouraged to cling to girlhood as long as possible. Nor is this reluctance to grow up surprising when one considers the largely negative connotations attached to the word *woman*. To take defeat like a man is to accept it stoically, like a good sport. To take defeat like a woman is usually understood as meaning to weep.

The American Heritage School Dictionary defines sexism as "discrimination by members of one sex against the other, especially by males against females." In order to avoid sexism in language that has come to sound "natural," we devised logical sex-blind substitutes. When referring to the human species, the dictionary employs the term *human beings,* not *man* or *men.*

In our efforts to reduce the superabundance of words referring to the male, we found it was possible to use the word *person* or a more specific substitute instead of *man.* The best man for the job is the best person or candidate; a 12-man jury is a 12-member jury; a real-estate man is a real-estate agent; and machines are used for work formerly done by people or by human beings—not by men.

To avoid unnecessary use of the pronoun *he,* we frequently shifted from the singular to the plural. Instead of saying "insofar as he can, the scientist excludes bias from his thinking," it is easy to change to *they, scientists,* and *their.* Plural pronouns desex themselves. The use of *one* is also convenient. A breadwinner, for example, can be "one who supports a family or household by his or her earnings."

Because of our conscious efforts, the nonsexist dictionary is as free of discrimination against either sex as the reformist editors could make it. But as proud as we are of our lexicographers' revolution, writing a nonsexist school dictionary is only the barest beginning. Most schoolbooks still reflect the assumptions of our sexist society. As writers and teachers and parents, we have an obligation now to weigh our words, to examine them, and to use them with greater care. Children of both sexes deserve equal treatment, in life and in language, and we should not offer them anything less.

THE SEMANTIC DEROGATION OF WOMAN

Muriel R. Schulz

The question of whether or not language affects the thought and culture of the people who use it remains to be answered. Even if we were to agree that it does, we would have difficulty calculating the extent to which the language we use influences our society. There is no doubt, on the other hand, that a language reflects the thoughts, attitudes, and culture of the people who make it and use it. A rich vocabulary on a given subject reveals an area of concern of the society whose language is being studied. The choice between positive and negative terms for any given concept (as, for example, in the choice between *freedom fighter* and *terrorist*) reveals the presence or absence of prejudicial feelings toward the subject. The presence of taboo reveals underlying fears and superstitions of a society. The occurrence of euphemism *(passed away)* or dysphemism *(croaked)* reveals areas which the society finds distasteful or alarming. To this extent, at least, analysis of a language tells us a great deal about the interests, achievements, obsessions, hopes, fears, and prejudices of the people who created the language.

Who are the people who created English? Largely men—at least until the present generation. Stuart Flexner (1960: xii) points out that it is mostly males who create and use slang, and he explains why. A woman's life has been largely restricted to the home and family, while men have lived in a larger world, belonged to many sub-groups, and had acquaintances who belonged to many other sub-groups. That men are the primary creators and users of the English language generally follows from the primary role they have traditionally played in English-speaking cultures. They have created our art, literature, science, philosophy, and education, as well as the language which describes and manipulates these areas of culture.

An analysis of the language used by men to discuss and describe women reveals something about male attitudes, fears, and prejudices concerning the female sex. Again and again in the history of the language, one finds that a perfectly innocent term designating a girl or woman may begin with totally neutral or even positive connotations, but that gradually it acquires negative implications, at first perhaps only slightly disparaging, but after a period of time becoming abusive and ending as a sexual slur.

That disparagement gravitates more toward terms for women than for men is evident from some matched pairs designating males and females. Compare, for example, the connotations of *bachelor* with those of *spinster* or *old maid*. Or compare the innocuousness of *warlock* with the insinuations of *witch*. *Geezer* "an eccentric, queer old man"[1] and *codger* "a mildly derogatory, affectionate term for an old man" carry little of the opprobrium of such corresponding terms for old women as *trot, hen, heifer, warhorse, crone, hag, beldam,* and *frump*. Furthermore, if terms designating men are used to denote a woman, there is usually no affront. On the other hand, use a term generally applied to women to designate a man, and you have probably delivered an insult. You may call a woman a *bachelor* without implying abuse, but if you call a man a *spinster* or an *old maid*, you are saying that he is "a prim, nervous person who frets over inconsequential details." If you speak of a woman as being a *warlock*, you may be corrected; if you say a man is a *witch*, he is presumed to have a vile temper. Or call a woman an *old man* and you have simply made an error of identification. Call a man an *old woman* or a *granny* and you have insulted him.

The term used to denote a semantic change whereby a word acquires debased or obscene reference is *pejoration*, and its opposite is *amelioration*. It is the purpose of this paper to study the pejoration of terms designating women in English and to trace the pattern whereby virtually every originally neutral word for women has at some point in its existence acquired debased connotations or obscene reference, or both.

The mildest form of debasement is a democratic leveling, whereby a word once reserved for persons in high places is generalized to refer to people in all levels of society. Even this mild form of derogation is more likely to occur with titles of women than with titles of men. *Lord,* for example, is still reserved as a title for deities and certain Englishmen, but any woman may call herself a *lady*. Only a few are entitled to be called *Baronet* and only a few wish to be called *Dame,* since as a general term, *dame* is opprobrious. Although *governor* degenerated briefly in nineteenth century Cockney slang, the term still refers to men who "exercise a sovereign authority in a colony, territory, or state." A *governess,* on the other hand, is chiefly "a nursemaid," operating in a realm much diminished from that of Queen Elizabeth I, who was acknowledged to be "the supreme majesty and governess of all persons" (OED). We might conceivably, and without affront, call the Queen's Equerry a *courtier,* but would we dare refer to her lady-in-waiting as a *courtesan? Sir* and *Master* seem to have come down through time as titles of courtesy without taint. However, *Madam, Miss,* and *Mistress* have all derogated, becoming euphemisms respectively for "a mistress of a brothel," "a prostitute," and "a woman with whom a man habitually fornicates."

The latter titles illustrate the most frequent course followed by pejorated terms designating women. In their downhill slide, they slip past respectable women and settle upon prostitutes and mistresses. When *abbey, academy,* and *nunnery* became euphemisms for "brothel," *abbess* acquired the meaning "keeper of a brothel," *academician,* "a harlot," and *nun,* "a courtesan." (Here, at last, one male title also pejorated. *Abbott* at the same time came to mean "the husband, or preferred male of a brothel keeper.") Although technically *queen* has withstood pejoration in English (*princess* has not), a thinly veiled homonym has existed side-by-side with it since Anglo-Saxon times. The *queen* is "the consort of the king" or "a female sovereign," whereas *quean* means "prostitute." Spelling has kept the two terms apart visually (both derived from the same Old English root, *cwen* "woman"), but as homonyms they have long provided writers with material for puns. Thus, in *Piers Plowman* (IX, 46) we are told that in the grave one cannot tell "a knight from a knave, or a quean from a queen," and Byron calls Catherine the Great "the Queen of queans" (*Don Juan,* Canto 6, Stanza xcvi).

Female kinship terms have also been subject to a kind of derogation which leaves the corresponding male terms untouched. *Wife* was used as a euphemism for "a mistress" in the fifteenth century, as was *squaw* in America during World War II. *Niece* has been used as a euphemism for "a priest's illegitimate daughter or concubine," and surely Humbert Humbert was not the first man to hide his mistress behind the locution, *daughter.* Browning uses *cousin* as an evasive term for Lucrezia's lover in "Andrea del Sarto" (1. 200). As a term for a woman, it was cant for "a strumpet or trull" in the nineteenth century. And *aunt* was generalized first to mean "an old woman" and then "a bawd or a prostitute." It is the latter meaning which Shakespeare draws upon in the lines: "Summer songs for me and my aunts/As we lie tumbling in the hay." (*Winter's Tale,* IV, 3, 11-12). Even *mother* was used as a term for "a bawd" and *sister* as a term for "a disguised whore" in the seventeenth century.

Terms for domestics are also more subject to pejoration if they denote females. *Hussy* derives from Old English *huswif* "housewife" and at one time meant simply "the female head of the house." Its degeneration was gradual. It declined in reference to mean "a rustic, rude woman"; then it was used as an opprobrious epithet for women in general; and finally it referred to "a lewd, brazen woman or a prostitute." In their original employment, a *laundress* made beds, a *needlewoman* came in to sew, a *spinster* tended the spinning wheel, and a *nurse* cared for the sick. But all apparently acquired secondary duties in some households, because all became euphemisms for "a mistress" or "a prostitute" at some time during their existence.

One generally looks in vain for the operation of a similar pejoration of terms referring to men. *King, prince, father, brother, uncle, nephew, footman, yeoman,* or *squire,* for example, have failed to undergo the derogation found in the history of their corresponding feminine designations. Words indicating the station, relationship, or occupation of men have remained untainted over the years. Those identifying women have repeatedly suffered the indignity of degeneration, many of them becoming sexually abusive. It is clearly not the women themselves who have coined and used these terms as epithets for each other. One sees today that it is men who describe and discuss women in sexual terms and insult them with sexual slurs, and the wealth of derogatory terms for women reveals something of their hostility.

If the derogation of terms denoting women marks out an area of our culture found contemptible by men, the terms they use as endearments should tell us who or what they esteem. Strangely enough, in English the endearments men use for women have been just as susceptible to pejoration as have the terms identifying the supposedly beloved object itself.[2] *Dolly, Kitty, Biddy, Gill* (or *Jill*), and *Polly* all began as pet names derived from nicknames. All underwent derogation and eventually acquired the meaning of "a slattern," "a mistress," or "a prostitute." *Jug* and *Pug,* both originally terms of endearment, degenerated to apply contemptuously to "a mistress or a whore." *Mopsy,* a term of endearment still found in Beatrix Potter's *Peter Rabbit,* for centuries also meant "a slatternly, untidy woman," as well. *Mouse* began as a playful endearment, but came to mean "a harlot, especially one arrested for brawling or assault." Even *sweetheart* meant "one loved illicitly" in the seventeenth century, although it has ameliorated since. Duncan MacDougald (1961: 594) describes the course all of these endearments seem to have followed: " 'Tart,' referring to a small pie or pastry, was first applied to a young woman as a term of endearment, next to young women who were sexually desirable, then to women who were careless in their morals, and finally—more recently—to women of the street."

If endearments for young girls have undergone pejoration, so have terms denoting girls and young women. *Doll* "a small-scale figure of a human being" referred first to "a young woman with a pretty babyish face," then became an insulting epithet for women generally, and finally acquired the meaning of "a paramour." *Minx* originally meant "a pert, young girl," and this meaning exists today, despite its pejoration to "a lewd or wanton woman; a harlot." *Nymph* and *nymphet* both referred to beautiful young girls, or women. *Nymph* became a euphemism in such phrases as "nymph of the pave" and "nymph of darkness," while *nymphet* acquired the derogated meaning of "a sexually precocious girl; a loose young woman." *Peach* is an enduring metaphor for "a luscious, attractive girl or woman," but around 1900 it, too, degenerated to mean "a promiscuous woman." *Broad* was originally used with no offensive connotations for "a young woman or a girl" (Wentworth and Flexner, 1960), but it acquired the suggestion of "a promiscuous woman" or "a prostitute." *Floozie,* first "an attractive but uncultivated girl," pejorated to mean "an undisciplined, promiscuous, flirtatious young woman; cynical, calculating." *Girl,* itself, has a long history of specialization and pejoration. It meant originally "a child of either sex"; then it was specialized to mean "a female child"; later it meant "a serving girl or maidservant"; and eventually it acquired the meanings "a prostitute," "a mistress," or "the female sex—or that part of it given to unchastity." Today *girl* has ameliorated (but *girlie* has sexual undertones), and we can call a female child, a *sweetheart,* or even a woman a *girl* without insult (although the emcee who jollies along the middle-aged "girls" in the audience is plainly talking down to them).

That emcee has a problem, though. There just aren't many terms in English for middle-aged or older women,[3] and those which have occurred have inevitably taken on unpleasant connotations. Even a relatively innocuous term like *dowager* is stigmatized. *Beldam* is worse. Formed by combining the English usage of *dam* "mother" with *bel* indicating the relationship of a grandparent, it simply meant "grandmother" in its earliest usage. It was later generalized to refer to any "woman of advanced age," and, as so frequently happens with words indicating "old woman," it pejorated to signify "a loathsome old woman; a hag." *Hag,* itself, originally meant simply "a witch" and was later generalized as a derisive term for "an ugly old woman," often with the implication of viciousness or maliciousness. Julia Stanley (1973) records it as a synonym for "a prostitute." *Bat* followed the opposite course. Originally a metaphor for "prostitute" (a "night bird"), it has become a generalized form of abuse meaning simply "an unpleasant woman, unattractive." It still bears the taint of its earlier metaphoric use, however, and is banned on TV as an epithet for a woman (Wentworth and Flexner, 1960). *Bag* meant "a middle-aged or elderly slattern" or "a pregnant woman" before it came to mean "a slatternly prostitute" or "a part-time prostitute" in the late nineteenth century. In the U. S. it has ameliorated slightly and refers (still derisively) to "an unattractive, ugly girl; an old shrew."

To be fat and sloppy is just as unforgivable in a woman as is being old, and the language has many terms designating such a person (are there any designating slovenly men?)—terms which have undergone pejoration and acquired sexual overtones at one time or another.[4] A *cow* "a clumsy, obese, coarse, or otherwise unpleasant person" became specialized to refer chiefly to women and then acquired the additional sense of "a degraded woman" and eventually "a prostitute." *Drab* (also occurring as *drap*) originally referred to "a dirty, untidy woman," but was further pejorated to refer to "a harlot or prostitute." Both *slut* and *slattern* were first used to designate "a person, especially a woman, who is negligent of his appearance." Both acquired the more derogatory meaning "a woman of loose character or a prostitute," and both are currently polysemantic, meaning concurrently "a sloppy woman" or "a prostitute." *Trollop,* another word for "an unkempt woman," extended to mean "a loose woman," and eventually, "a hedge whore," *Mab,* first "a slattern" and then "a woman of loose character" seems to have withstood the third logical step of degeneration in England. In the U. S., however, it is used as an epithet for "a prostitute," as well.

Horse metaphors used to denote women have also undergone sexual derogation. *Harridan* "a worn-out horse" seems to have originally been used as a metaphor for "a gaunt woman," then "a disagreeable old woman," and later "a decayed strumpet" or "a half-whore, half-bawd." A *jade* was originally "a broken-down, vicious or worthless horse," or else such a man, as is illustrated in the lines from *The Taming of the Shrew:* "Gremio: What! This gentleman will outtalk us all./ Lucentio: Sir. Give him head. I know he'll prove a jade" (I, 2, 249). It became a contemptuous epithet for women, however, and was eventually another synonym for "whore." A *hackney* (or *hack*) was first "a common riding horse, often available for hire." Its meaning was extended to encompass, with derogatory connotations, anyone who hires himself out (hence *hack writer*), but when used for women it acquired sexual overtones as a metaphor for "a woman who hires out as a prostitute" or for "a bawd." A *tit* referred either to "a small horse" or "a small girl," but degenerated to mean "a harlot." There is in all of these horse metaphors, perhaps, the sense of a woman as being a *mount,* a term used indifferently for "a wife" or "a mistress" in the nineteenth century.[5]

All these terms originated as positive designations for women and gradually degenerated to become negative in the milder instances and abusive in the extremes. A degeneration of endearments into insulting terms for men has not occurred. Words denoting boys and young men have failed to undergo the pejoration so common with terms for women. *Boy, youth, stripling, lad, fellow, puppy,* and *whelp,* for example, have been spared denigration. As for terms for slovenly, obese, or elderly men, the language has managed with very few of them. A similar sexual difference is evident in terms which originated as words denoting either sex. Often, when they began to undergo pejoration they specialized to refer solely to women in derogatory terms. Later they frequently underwent further degeneration and became sexual terms of abuse. *Whore* is a well-known example of the process. Latin *carus* "dear" is a derivative of the same Indo-European root. It was probably at one time a polite term (Bloomfield, 1933: 401). Originally it seems to have referred to "a lover of either sex," but eventually it specialized to refer solely to women. Later it degenerated to meaning "a prostitute," and it became a term occurring only in "coarse, abusive speech" (OED). A *harlot* was originally "a fellow of either sex," referring more to men than to women in Middle English and characterizing them as "riffraff." It degenerated further, and Shakespeare's *harlot King (Winter's Tale* II, 3, 4) was characterized as "lewd." However, after Elizabethan times the word was specialized for women only, meaning first "a disreputable woman" and later, specifically, "a prostitute." *Bawd,* similarly, originally referred to a "go-between or panderer of either sex," but after 1700 it was used only for women, either as "a keeper of a brothel" or "a prostitute." *Wench,* "a child of either sex," had sufficient prestige to appear in *Piers Plowman* in the phrase *Goddes Wench* "the Virgin Mary" (1. 336). Later it was specialized to refer to "a rustic or working woman." As do so many terms referring to rustics, male or female (compare *villain, boor, peasant, churl,* for example), the term degenerated. Then it acquired sexual undertones, coming to refer first to "a lewd woman" and finally to "a wanton." *Wench* has been rehabilitated and has lost its stigma. Today it can be used to refer to a woman without suggesting wantonness. Another term which specialized to refer to women, then degenerated to the point of abusiveness, and later ameliorated is *cat.* Originally it was a term of contempt for "any human being who scratches like a cat." Later it was specialized to refer to "a spiteful, backbiting woman" (a usage which survives). For a period it meant "a prostitute," but this sexual taint was lost in the nineteenth century, and only the less denigrating (but still pejorative) sense of "spiteful woman" remains.

A comparison of the metaphors *cat* and *dog* illustrates the difference evident in many terms designating male and female humans. The term for the female is more likely to become pejorative, more likely to acquire sexual suggestions, and less likely to be transferrable to a male. *Cat* originally meant "any spiteful person," but specialized to refer only to women. It remains an abusive term for women. *Dog* is only "sometimes used contemptuously for males." More frequently it is used "in half-serious chiding" (Farmer and Henley, 1965) as in *He's a sly dog,* or to mean "a gay, jovial, gallant fellow" (OED), as in *Oh, you're a clever dog!* However, *dog* has recently been transferred to women, and it occurs in totally negative contexts, meaning either "a woman inferior in looks, character, or accomplishments" or "a prostitute." Or compare the use of *bitch.* It is an abusive term when applied to a woman, meaning either "a malicious, spiteful, domineering woman" or "a lewd or immoral woman." When applied to a man it is "less opprobrious and somewhat whimsical—like the modern use of *dog*" (OED). *Pig,* applied contemptuously to men, means "a person who in some way behaves like a pig." When applied to a woman, it means "a woman who has sloppy morals." *Sow* is not transferrable to men. It is an abusive metaphor for "a fat, slovenly woman," which in the U. S. has acquired the additional sense of "a promiscuous young woman or a prostitute."

Robin Lakoff (1973) has pointed out that metaphors and labels are likely to have wide reference when applied to men, whereas metaphors for women are likely to be narrower and to include sexual reference. She uses as an example the term *professional.* If you say that a man is a *professional,* you suggest that he is a member of one of the respected professions. If you call a woman a *professional,* you imply that she follows "the oldest profession." In a similar way, if you call a man a *tramp* you simply communicate that he is "a drifter." Call a woman a *tramp* and you imply that she is "a prostitute." Historically, terms like *game, natural, jay, plover,* and *Jude* have meant merely "simpleton or dupe" when applied to men, but "loose woman or prostitute" when applied to women. A male *pirate* is "one who infringes on the rights of others or commits robbery on the high seas," whereas a female *pirate* is "an adultress who chases other women's men."[6]

What is the cause of the degeneration of terms designating women? Stephen Ullman (1967: 231-32) suggests three origins for pejoration: association with a contaminating concept, euphemism, and prejudice. As for the first possibility, there is some evidence that contamination is a factor. Men tend to think of women in sexual terms whatever the context, and consequently any term denoting women carries sexual suggestiveness to the male speaker. The subtle operation of this kind of contamination is seen in the fortunes of such words as *female, lady,* and *woman. Woman* was avoided in the last century, probably as a Victorian sexual taboo, since it had acquired the meaning "paramour or mistress" or the sense of intercourse with women when used in plural, as in *Wine, Women, and Song.* It was replaced by *female,* but this term also came to be considered degrading and indelicate. Freyer (1963: 69) tells that "When the Vassar Female College was founded in 1861, Mrs. Sarah Josepha Hale, editor of *Godey's Lady's Book,* spent six years in securing the removal of the offending adjective from the college sign." The OED recorded *female* as a synonym "avoided by writers," and the Third identifies it as a disparaging term when used for women. It was replaced in the 19th century by *lady,* which Mencken (1963: 350) called "the English euphemism-of-all-work." *Lady* also vulgarized, however, and by the time Mencken wrote, it was already being replaced by *woman,* newly rehabilitated. Even so neutral a term as *person,* when it was used as a substitute for *woman,* suffered contamination which Greenough and Kittredge found amusing (1901: 326): "It has been more or less employed as a substitute for *woman* by those who did not wish to countenance the vulgar abuse of *lady* and yet shrank from giving offense. The result has been to give a comically slighting connotation to one of the most innocent words imaginable."

Despite this repeated contamination of terms designating women, we cannot accept the belief that there is a quality inherent in the concept of *woman* which taints any word associated with it. Indeed, the facts argue against this interpretation. Women are generally acknowledged to be—for whatever reasons—the more continent of the two sexes, the least promiscuous, and the more monogamous. Nevertheless, the largest category of words designating humans in sexual terms are those for women—especially for loose women. I have located roughly a thousand words and phrases describing women in sexually derogatory ways.[7] There is nothing approaching this multitude for describing men. Farmer and Henley (1965), for example, have over five hundred terms (in English alone) which are synonyms for *prostitute*. They have only sixty-five synonyms for *whoremonger*.

As for the second possibility, one must acknowledge that many terms for "women of the night" have arisen from euphemism—a reluctance to name the profession outright. The majority of terms, however, are dysphemistic, not euphemistic. For example, the bulk of terms cited by Farmer and Henley (1965) as synonyms for *prostitute* are clearly derogatory: *broadtail, carrion, cleaver, cocktail, flagger, guttersnipe, mutton, moonlighter, omnibus, pinchprick, tail trader, tickletail, twofer,* and *underwear* are just a few.

The third possibility—prejudice—is the most likely source for pejorative terms for women. They illustrate what Gordon Allport calls (1954: 179) "the labels of primary potency" with which an in-group stereotypes an out-group. Certain symbols, identifying a member of an out-group, blind the prejudiced speaker to any qualities the minority person may have which contradict the stereotype. "Most people are unaware of this basic law of language—that every label applied to a given person refers properly only to one aspect of his nature. You may correctly say that a certain person is *human, a philanthropist, a Chinese, a physician, an athlete*. A given person may be all of these but the chances are that *Chinese* stands out in your mind as the symbol of primary potency. Yet neither this nor any other classificatory label can refer to the whole of a man's nature." Antifeminism, he points out, contains the two basic ingredients of prejudice: denigration and gross overgeneralization (p. 34).

Derogatory terms for women illustrate both qualities which Allport attributes to prejudice. And what is the source or cause of the prejudice? Several writers have suggested that it is fear, based on a supposed threat to the power of the male. Fry (1972: 131) says of male humor: "In man's jokes about sex can be found an answer as to why man is willing to forego to a large extent the satisfactions of a reality and equality relationship with his fellow mortal, woman. Part of this answer has to do with the question of control or power." He theorizes that power becomes a question because the male is biologically inferior to the female in several respects. Girls mature earlier than boys physically, sexually, and intellectually. Boys are biologically frailer in their first years of life than girls. At the other end of their life span, they also prove to be weaker. More men have heart attacks, gout, lung cancer, diabetes, and other degenerative diseases than women. Finally, they deteriorate biologically and die earlier than women. Fry (1972: 133) continues: "The jokes men tell about the relationships between the sexes—especially the frankly sexual jokes—reveal awareness and concern, even anxiety, about the general presence of these biologic disadvantages and frailties."[8] Grotjahn (1972: 53) concurs that anxiety prompts man's hostility, but he believes the source is fear of sexual inadequacy. A woman knows the truth about his potency; he cannot lie to her. Yet her own performance remains a secret, a mystery to him. Thus, man's fear of woman is basically sexual, which is perhaps the reason why so many of the derogatory terms for women take on sexual connotations.

I began with the acknowledgment that we cannot tell the extent to which any language influences the people who use it. This is certainly true for most of what we call *language*. However, words which are highly charged with emotion, taboo, or distaste do not only reflect the culture which uses them. They teach and perpetuate the attitudes which created them. To make the name of God taboo is to perpetuate the mystery, power, and awesomeness of the divine. To surround a concept with euphemisms, as Americans have done with the idea of death, is to render the reality of the concept virtually invisible. And to brand a class of persons as obscene is to taint them to the users of the language. As Mariana Birnbaum (1971: 248) points out, prejudicial language "always mirror[s] generalized tabloid thinking which contains prejudices and thus perpetuates discrimination." This circularity in itself is justification for bringing such linguistic denigration of women to a conscious level. The semantic change discussed here, by which terms designating women routinely undergo pejoration, both reflects and perpetuates derogatory attitudes toward women. They should be abjured.

NOTES

[1]Citations are based upon, but are not necessarily direct quotations from, the *Oxford English dictionary,* cited henceforth as (OED), *Webster's third international* (Third), the *Dictionary of American slang* (Wentworth and Flexner, 1960), *Slang and its analogues* (Farmer and Henley, 1965), *A dictionary of slang and unconventional English* (Partridge, 1961), and the *American thesaurus of slang* (Berrey and Van den Bark, 1952). Sources are only indicated if the source is other than one of the above, or if the citation contains unusual information.

[2]Endearments and terms for young women have undergone a similar pejoration in other languages, as well. Thass-Thienemann (1967: 336) cites *Metze* and *Dirne* from German, *fille* or *fille de joie* from French, *hētaira* and *pallakis* or *pallakē* from Greek, and *puttana* from Italian as endearments which degenerated and became sexual slurs.

[3]There are few terms for old people of either sex in English, "senior citizen" being our current favorite euphemism. However, the few terms available to denote old men *(elder, oldster, codger, geezer, duffer)* are, as was mentioned above, less vituperative than are those denoting women.

[4]C. S. Lewis (1961), in discussing four-letter words, makes a point which is perhaps applicable to the tendency these words have to acquire sexual implications. He argues, with evidence from Sheffield and Montaigne, that four-letter words are not used in order to provoke desire. In fact, they have little to do with sexual arousal. They are used rather to express force and vituperation.

[5]Several bird names originating as metaphors for young girls have also become abusive epithets for them. *Columbine, quail, flapper, bird, chicken, hen,* and in this country *sea gull* all began affectionately but acquired the meaning "a prostitute."

[6]Several terms which originally applied to thieves, beggars, and their female accomplices have specialized and pejorated as terms for women: *badger, doxy, moll* (from *Mary*), *mollisher,* and *bulker,* for example, *Blowse* reversed the process. Denoting first "a prostitute," and then "a beggar's trull," it finally ameliorated slightly to mean "a slattern or a shrew." Other terms which originally designated either sex but came to refer only to women with the sense of "a prostitute" are *filth, morsel* (perhaps with the present sense of *piece*), *canary, rig,* and *rep.* The reverse has happened in a strange way with *fagot* (or *faggot*). It was first a term of abuse for women (sixteenth to nineteenth century) or a term for "a dummy soldier." Today it has transferred as an abusive term for "a male homosexual." Not all the terms specializing to women acquired sexual implications. *Potato* "ugly face," *prig, prude, termagant,* and *vixen* were all used in a general sense first and only later narrowed to refer specifically to women.

[7]I have restricted myself in this paper to terms which have undergone the process of pejoration or amelioration—terms which have not always been abusive. The majority of derogatory words for women, of course, were coined as dysphemisms and are, hence, outside the scope of my study. In Farmer and Henley (1965), the chief entry containing synonyms for "prostitute" is *tart,* while for "whoremonger" it is *mutton-monger.* There are, in addition to the English synonyms, over 200 French phrases used to refer to women in a derogatory and sexual way, and another extended listing occurs under the entry *barrack-hack.* Stanley (1973) lists 200, and I found another 100, culled chiefly from Fryer (1963), Sagarin (1962), Berrey and Van den Bark (1952), Partridge (1961), and Wentworth and Flexner (1960).

[8]Bettelheim and Janowitz (1950: 54-55) also cite anxiety as the source of prejudice. They argue that the prejudiced person "seeks relief through prejudice, which serves to reduce anxiety because prejudice facilitates the discharge of hostility, and if hostility is discharged anxiety is reduced. Prejudice reduces anxiety because it suggests to the person that he is better than others, hence does not need to feel so anxious."

REFERENCES

Allport, Gordon W. (1954). *The nature of prejudice.* Cambridge, Mass.: Addison-Wesley.

Berrey, Lester V. & Van den Bark, Melvin. (1952). *The American thesaurus of slang.* New York: Thomas Y. Crowell.

Bettelheim, Bruno & Janowitz, Morris. (1950). *Dynamics of prejudice.* New York: Harper & Row.

Birnbaum, Mariana D. (1971). On the language of prejudice. *Western Folklore,* 30, 247-68.

Bloomfield, Leonard. (1933). *Language.* New York: Henry Holt.

Farmer, J. S., & Henley, W. E. (1965). *Slang and its analogues.* Repr. of 7 vols. publ. 1890-1904. New York: Kraus Reprint Corp.

Flexner, Stuart. (1960). Preface to Harold Wentworth and Stuart Flexner (eds.), *Dictionary of American slang.* New York: Thomas Y. Crowell.

Fry, William P. (1972). Psychodynamics of sexual humor: man's view of sex. *Medical Aspects of Human Sexuality,* 6,128-34.

Fryer, Peter. (1963). *Mrs. Grundy: studies in English prudery.* London: Dennis Dobson.

Gove, Philip (ed.). (1971). *Webster's third new international dictionary.* Springfield, Mass.: G. & C. Merriam.

Greenough, James Bradstreet & Kittredge, George Lyman. (1901). *Words and their ways in English speech.* New York: Macmillan.

Grotjahn, Martin. (1972). Sexuality and humor. Don't laugh! *Psychology Today,* 6, 51-53.

Lakoff, Robin. (1973). Language and woman's place. *Language in Society,* 2, 45-80.

Lewis, C. S. (1961). Four-letter words. *Critical Quarterly,* 3, 118-22.

MacDougald, Duncan, Jr. (1961). Language and sex. In Albert Ellis & Albert Abarbanel (eds.), *The encyclopedia of sexual behavior.* London: Hawthorne Books, Vol. II.

Mencken, H. L. (1963). *The American language. The fourth edition and the two supplements.* Abridged and ed. by Raven I. McDavid, Jr. New York: Knopf.

Oxford English Dictionary. (1933). Oxford: Clarendon Press.

Partridge, Eric. (ed.). (1961). *A dictionary of slang and unconventional English.* 5th ed. New York: Macmillan.

Sagarin, Edward. (1962). *The anatomy of dirty words.* New York: Lyle Stuart.

Stanley, Julia. (1973). The metaphors some people live by. Unpublished mimeo.

Thass-Thienemann, Theodore. (1967). *The subconscious language.* New York: Washington Square Press.

Ullman, Stephen. (1967). *Semantics. An introduction to the science of meaning.* New York: Barnes & Noble.

Wentworth, Harold & Flexner, Stuart Berg. (eds.). (1960). *Dictionary of American slang.* New York: Thomas Y. Crowell.

THE SEX OF THE SPEAKER AS A
SOCIOLINGUISTIC VARIABLE*

Marjorie Swacker

In Jutland they say, "The North Sea will sooner be found wanting in water than a woman at a loss for words." The English are too quick to stereotype, with "Women's tongues are like lambs' tails—they are never still." But this idea is not merely the voice of Northern Europe. The Chinese mean virtually the same when they say, "The tongue is the sword of a woman, and she never lets it become rusty." Contrast these with sayings about both sexes: "Nothing is so unnatural," say the Scots, "as a talkative man or a quiet woman." Perhaps what they mean to say is the notion that the Spanish have articulated more clearly, "Men speak; women chat [hablar: platicar]."

The one thing clear from these adages is that there is no doubt in the folk mind: the speech of men is assuredly not the same as that of women. This notion of nonandrogynous verbal patterns, however, has yet to be generally accepted by those working in sociolinguistics. Therefore, it will be the specific and explicit purpose of this paper to point out the validity of an oft-ignored sociolinguistic variable—that of speaker sex.

The discipline of sociolinguistics, itself a designated area of research for only slightly more than twenty years, seeks to correlate speech varieties with such variables as geographical region, age, education, ethnic background, or any other societal grouping. As a sociolinguistic variable, then, speaker sex, which refers to the sex of the person speaking, points out that speakers can be productively grouped by the only universally standardized, cross-culturally recognized, and

---

*This is a revised and expanded version of a paper, "Speaker Sex: A Sociolinguistic Variable," presented at the annual meeting of the Linguistic Society of America, December 1973.

biologically predetermined distinction available—that is, by sex. With no comment about the possible physiological or sociological origins of these sex-specific speech patterns, it will be contended that this variable is valid even among native speakers of English whose dialects would not normally be considered in some way or another nonstandard.

Some time ago it was fashionable, in discussing language in general or a specific language, to present a few paragraphs or, perhaps, a chapter on the speech of women. Otto Jespersen's (1922) text, which is still required reading in many linguistics programs, is a good example of this format. The underlying assumption of this sort of organization is, of course, that male speaking patterns have established the norm and that women's language is a deviant form based on it. It should go without saying that there is no linguistic nor, for that matter, statistical foundation for such an assumption.

The areas presented in these "women's language" sections are often a curious mixture of folk wisdom and sophisticated analysis. Specifically, Jespersen's thirteenth chapter, "The Woman," discusses taboo words, female linguistic conservatism, word choice, and adverbs, as well as some general characteristics of female speech. Women, according to Jespersen, use incomplete sentences while men do not; women talk more quickly than men do, and women do not share with men the same semantic values for words, a point echoed by Theodor Reik (1954) some thirty years later. In short, women talk and talk and talk while men are the strong, silent type. This image has survived virtually intact and unchallenged.

By the 1940's American sociologists and anthropologists had noted a wide variety of male and female behavioral distinctions. Swedish sociologist Gunnar Myrdal (1944), in observing American life, dramatized the validity of sex-as-social-class, perhaps for the first time, in "A Parallel to the Negro Problem" which appeared as an appendix to his landmark text, *An American Dilemma.* Over the years and, indeed, up to the present, linguistic studies in all areas not usually considered "standard English" have demonstrated a sensitivity to the implications of speaker sex. Japanese, Koasati, Yana, Chiglit, Chiquito, and Spanish have all been shown to have sex-specific speech patterns, as have Black English and the speech of New England children. Studies have pointed to variation in pronunciation patterns, in word choice, and in grammatical structures according to the sex of the speaker.

Until very, very recently American English—excluding speech which is normally classified as, in some way, outside the mainstream, e.g., Black English—has been routinely studied as an androgynous behavior, a fact commented on as early as 1964 by Joyce O. Hertzler in his book, *Sociology of Language.* At that time, Hertzler optimistically asserted, "with the legal equality of the sexes, the vast employment of women, the fact that the sexes increasingly perform the same kinds of work, and the participation of women coequally with men in all sorts of community and national activities, most of the sharply distinct functional divergences between [the speech] of the sexes ... have grown weaker or disappeared" (pp. 319-20). More recent and less philosophically based research has pointed to the folly of his assumptions about speech as well as his evaluation of the social environment. In fact, many popular, nonscholarly comments on male and female speech appearing at that time or shortly thereafter treated the lessening of sex specific patterns. Swearing by women, for example, has been repeatedly lamented as further female encroachment on yet another male domain. William Zinsser's (1968) article, "Ladies: Why Not Creative Cussing?" is a good example of such an attitude, as is "Girl Talk" which was run that same year in *Newsweek*.

In a 1969 paper, Roger Shuy deplored the lack of speaker-sex-oriented sociolinguistic research and presented several studies which indicated that speaker sex variation is a quantitative linguistic reality. Shuy concluded by stating, "Regardless of why the correlation of linguistic performance to sex has been overlooked in the past, there has been, and is, sufficient reason for examining it carefully" (p. 3).

In recent years, a few studies have been concerned specifically with speaker sex. Let me cite some of these:

Nancy Barron's 1970 dissertation dealt with considerations of sex role and grammatical case based on Fillmore's model. Her research indicated significant male/female variation in case frame patterning. It may therefore be assumed that sex roles pattern case selection. She found that women, in general, express themselves more implicitly than men and further, that men tended to discuss things, particularly things acted on.

Theodor Reik published in 1954 a short article which first surveys a number of languages which co-vary morphemes according to speaker sex and then contends that Western European languages also demonstrate speaker sex selection in terms of some taboo words. He further proposed that the same words sometimes carry different connotations depending on the sex of the speaker, a provocative and not counter-intuitive suggestion which deserves further research.

James O. Whittaker and Robert Meade (1967) published the findings of a study in which the sex of the communicator played an important role in credibility of information. Women were found to be considerably less believable. This study parallels one conducted by Philip Goldberg (1968) in which 140 female college subjects were asked to rate six articles. Two identical booklets of articles were prepared. Some articles were attributed to males, e.g., John T. McKay; the same articles in the second booklet were attributed to females, e.g., Joan T. McKay. Those articles believed to have been written by males were judged "impressive" while those by females were found to be "mediocre."

Mary Ritchie Key's (1972) article, "Linguistic Behavior of Male and Female," began by tracing the history of interest in male and female language behavior. The sex of the listener was examined, as was speaker sex. The main concern, however, was a provocative study in the area of women as part of semantic groupings. Of additional interest are Key's comments on the problems of English nominalization, as well as presupposition and professional designation as they function between the sexes.

One further paper of interest is that by Paul Hanly Furfey (1944), "Men's and Women's Language." He hypothesized that linguistic divergence serves as a sensitive index to social differentiation—an important concept in itself—and further, that speaker sex divergencies sharpen those group differences. He marshalled supportive evidence from a number of languages.

While the foregoing survey of materials is not exhaustive, it should not be taken as only a small fraction of a large body of speaker-sex-oriented research. The fact is that most sociolinguistic, indeed, general, data-based linguistic research fails totally to consider the sex of the informants. As a result, research with an eye to speaker sex is shockingly meager.

My own research was designed to help fill this void. Last spring a study was conducted at California State University, Fresno, using 34 informants: 17 men and 17 women. Special effort was made to have as little variation in background as possible. All the informants were Caucasian, and all had spent most of their lives in the San Juaquien Valley. The median age of male informants was 23:4 years; the median age for women was 22:2; all were between 20 and 28 and were full-time students at the time of the interview. The mean number of academic units completed was comparable for both groups. None of the informants spoke what might be considered a nonstandard dialect and all claimed English as their native language. All were students with majors in speech pathology, education, or English; they had volunteered through their basic linguistics class, a requirement for students in all three majors. The field methods were as follows:

1) Each informant was seated before a tape recorder and a book of black and white graphics by Albrecht Dürer. After being asked their ages, names, and the number of units they had completed, they were told that they were about to see three pictures from about the year 1500—pictures selected because they would be unfamiliar to most people and because they were rich in detail.

2) The informants were asked to look at each picture and to describe what they saw. They were told to take as much time as they needed for their descriptions, to be as thorough as possible, and to try to leave out nothing. The informants

had been told that they would be taking part in a study on "descriptive language."

After the interviews were completed, the total time was calculated for the descriptions of all three pictures and for the description of the middle picture, for each informant. Several variables were hypothesized as significant and a statistical analysis for those was prepared. T-statistics and levels of significance were determined at $\alpha = .05$. Mean scores and standard deviations were calculated for each variable. Three areas pointed to particularly interesting and significant differences between male and female speaking patterns. Indeed, some of the results were quite unexpected.

The first area of distinction was what may be called *verbosity*. As mentioned earlier, each informant was given as much time as he or she deemed necessary and was urged to provide as detailed a description as possible. The female mean time for all three descriptions was about 3.17 minutes, and for males was about 13.0 minutes (see Table 1).

Table 1. TOTAL TIMES FOR MALES AND FEMALES

	Male		Female	
	Total Time in Seconds	Standard Deviation	Total Time in Seconds	Standard Deviation
3 Descriptions	780.29	543.56	221.70	177.81
2nd Description	333.41	106.13	96.00	30.94

It probably should be pointed out that these statistics are not entirely accurate because there were three male informants who simply talked until the cassettes, with unbroken recording times of 30 minutes, ran out. In those cases, the informants were allowed to continue for another five minutes each and then the interviews were tactfully terminated. The times for these three were arbitrarily set at 30 minutes for statistical purposes, even though there is really no way of determining how long they might have continued, had they not been interrupted. Even without these exceptionally verbose males, the mean for men was significantly longer than that for females. The second descriptive passage averaged 333.41 seconds for men and only 96.0 seconds for women. Interestingly, no significant difference in the speed of discourse was found. While women averaged 113.382 words per minute and men, 107.994, this difference in rapidity is well below the level of significance.

Clearly then, when both men and women were given as much time as they deemed necessary to describe a picture, men spoke for considerably longer intervals than did women.

It has been suggested that the standard deviation figures may be especially significant in that they point out that females demonstrate more uniform behavior in terms of discourse length than do males. It is further postulated that this behavior clustering by women might well be caused by females conforming to a set of social expectations which males either do not perceive or do not feel the need to follow. Further research in the area of behavior standardization and deviation as a correlate of sex may well prove fruitful.

Because of the disparity between the quantities of male and female speech, all other statistics were based on occurrences per minute.

The second area in which men and women displayed distinct speaking patterns is *numerals*. Interestingly, but not surprisingly, males tended to use considerably more numerals in their descriptive passages than did women. An examination of the speech context for each numerical reference produced two distinctions in the way that numbers are used. First, four men were found to count while giving their descriptions. For example, in describing the bookshelf one man said:

" ... there are one, two, three, four, five, six books on ... " Another informant described the same shelf: " ... to his left with books on it—one, two, three, four, five, six books on it ... " This counting behavior was nowhere displayed by the female informants. For statistical purposes each counting sequence was counted as a single numeral reference.

A second number pattern distinction between the sexes is the use of estimating elements with numerals. Women were found to have preceded half of their numerals with indicators of approximation. For example, in discussing the bookshelf, women often stated [italics mine] :

... *about* six books. ...
... six *or* seven books. ...
... *around* five *or* six books. ...

While referring to that same six-book shelf, men responded with:

... five books. ...
... six books. ...
... seven books. ...

and even,

... nine books. ...

In fact, even in contexts where the informant is clearly making a guess, there was only one instance of a male using an estimating element compared, as stated earlier, with a full 50% of the female numerical references. It is often asserted that males tend to be much more accurate than females, and their frequent use of numbers is offered as proof. On the basis of this study, however, it might be hypothesized that male preoccupation with the verbal tokens of numerical precision is what is at question and not the precision itself. In other words, male accuracy may well turn out to be an illusion based on a sex-specific verbal pattern.

The third and final area in which proof of nonandrogynous verbal behavior arose was that of the *topic shift marker*. As mentioned earlier, the graphics used were full of unfamiliar items and were rich in detail. When the informant had described one part of the picture, a wall or the foreground for example, and wanted to move on to a different part of the picture, a "topic shift" was required. The shifts were marked by pauses, interjections and conjunctions, or a combination of two or more of these.

While both groups of informants displayed pause patterns to mark their shifts, some distinctions are highly noteworthy. Women, for example, used significantly more conjunctions than did men. Men, on the other hand, used interjections to mark topic shifts—a pattern not exhibited at all by female informants in this study. These were particularly noticeable following expressed uncertainty. For example, in speaking of an hour glass [italics mine] : " . . . sand pouring down—I can't get the word—*OK*—also behind the man, on the shelf is. . . ";[1] or another male informant, " . . . a small shelf with some books piled up on it—*OK*—the man seems to be wearing a great big robe draped over him with no style at all—*OK*—the man himself has a. . . "; and one more, " . . . I can't remember what you call it—*Oh, well*—forget about that—*OK*—up to the right of the podium. . . ." This pattern was found to be unique to men.

In conclusion, then, it is clear that there are sex-specific speech patterns, demonstrated by the descriptions given by those participating in this study. While more comprehensive research into speaker sex distinctions is definitely called for, perhaps with a variety of elicitory devices and varied interviewing situations, areas such as topic shifts, discourse length, and specialized treatment of numerals all point to the fact that men and women simply do not speak English in the same way.

That is, those speakers who would not normally be classified as non-standard do display sex-specific speech patterns. This argues strongly for the adoption of speaker sex as a separate sociolinguistic variable—a variable as important, as methodologically necessary, and as valid as education or region or socioeconomic level. Indeed, any sociolinguistic research which does not, at least, specifically give consideration to the sex of the informant might well be of questionable validity.

NOTE

[1] – indicates pauses

REFERENCES

Barron, Nancy. (1970). Grammatical case and sex role: language differences in interaction. Dissertation, University of Missouri. Abstract, Dissertation Abstracts, 31 (1970), IIA, p. 6155.

Furfey, Paul Hanly. (1944). Men's and women's language. *American Catholic Sociological Review,* 5, 218-23.

Girl Talk. (1968). *Newsweek,* December 16, 104+.

Goldberg, Philip. (1968). Are women prejudiced against women? *Trans-action,* 5, April, 28-30.

Hertzler, Joyce O. (1964). *Sociology of language.* New York: Random House.

Jespersen, Otto. (1922). *Language: its nature, development and origin.* London: Allen & Unwin.

Key, Mary Ritchie. (1972). Linguistic behavior of male and female. *Linguistics,* 88 (August 15), 15-31.

Myrdal, Gunnar. (1944). *An American dilemma.* New York: Harper.

Reik, Theodor. (1954). Men and women speak different languages. *Psychoanalysis,* 2, No. 4, 3-15.

Shuy, Roger. (1969). Sex as a factor in sociolinguistic research. Paper presented at Anthropological Society of Washington. Available from Educational Resources Information Clearinghouse, No. ED 027 522.

Whittaker, James O., & Meade, Robert. (1967). Sex of communicator as a variable in source credibility. *Journal of Social Psychology,* 72, 27-34.

Zinsser, William. (1968). Ladies: why not creative cussing? *Life,* November 22, 12.

MALE-FEMALE INTONATION PATTERNS
IN AMERICAN ENGLISH*

Ruth M. Brend

It is now over twenty-five years since Rulon Wells (1945) and Kenneth L. Pike (1945) published on the pitch and intonation of American English. These authors implied that every adult used all intonation (or pitch) patterns in the situations they described, and publications since that time, which are available to me, do not state otherwise.

Recently, however, while summarizing English phonology for a group of English teachers from the Soviet Union, and providing patterns for them to imitate, I often found myself dissatisfied with the pronunciation of several of them (some of the men, especially) in spite of the fact that they were apparently mimicking my pronunciation correctly. This experience led me to an investigation of the differences in the use of specific intonation patterns in the speech of men and women in the midwestern part of the United States.

Pike, in his 1945 volume, presented a comprehensive listing and discussion of intonation patterns, including their meanings and variations. In a very short section on dialect differences, he tentatively concluded that very little, if any, difference is found in the intonation patterns of American dialects. He minutely discussed the circumstances in which the different patterns were used, but said very little concerning which speakers used the different patterns.

My preliminary studies indicate, however, some very definite preferences in the general usage and avoidance of some of these patterns by men versus women.

Certain patterns which both sexes use in common need only be briefly mentioned—for example, the down-glides which end at the lowest level of pitch in utterance-final and non-final positions as in:

*Reprinted with permission from the *Proceedings of the Seventh International Congress of Phonetic Sciences, 1971,* 866-69 (The Hague: Mouton, 1972).

(1)   I want to/ 'go.
       I/ 'don't \ think it's his.
       He's 'gone.

the upstep patterns (from low to low-mid) or the downstep ones (from high-mid to low-mid) which indicate incompleteness in utterance-medial positions, as in:

(2)   When I 'went down town,   I saw a 'fire.
       When I 'went down town,   I saw a 'fire.

and the upstep in various kinds of interrogative sentences, as in:

(3)   Are you 'going?
       Is it 'there?
       Are you 'coming, or/ not?
       He's coming?

Other patterns which were catalogued by Pike, however, do not seem to be used equally by men and women. Certain ones seem to be completely lacking from men's speech, while others are differently preferred by men and women. For example, men tend to use the incomplete "deliberative" (here and below, Pike's labels are used) pattern, i.e., the small upstep from low, as in:

(4)   'Yes, 'yes, I 'know.

much more often than women, who, contrary to men, prefer the "more polite" incomplete longer upstep as in:

(5)   'Yes, 'yes I 'know.

The "unexpectedness" and "surprise" patterns of high-low down-glides as:

(6)   'Oh 'that's 'awful!

appear to be absent from men's speech (or at least are *much* more often used by women) as are the "request confirmation" patterns such as:

(7)   You 'do!
       You/ 'do!

Although the incomplete and non-final pattern-medial upstep of (2) seems to be used by both sexes, the varying "implication" non-final patterns as in:

(8)   I know he has /'gone.
       He's coming 'when?

and the hesitation pattern:

(9)   Well, I /'studied. . .

tend to be found solely in women's speech. The "polite, cheerful" pattern:

(10)   Are you 'coming?

is used only by women, I believe. The "reverse-glide, incomplete deliberation" pattern is used by both men and women when spread over several words or syllables as in:

(11)   'What \ are you having?

but men seem not to use this pattern on one syllable, as in:

(12)   Oh /'yes.

The "polite and cheerful, incomplete sequence and surprise" forms of:

(13)   Won't you come 'in?
        Come │'on.
        Good │'bye.

are used only by women, in very restricted circumstances (such as when speaking to small children, etc.). Women also seem to be the only users of the "incomplete and unexpected" pattern as in:

(14)   What's my /'name?

Some summarization of the above may now be possible. Men consistently avoid certain intonation levels or patterns: they very rarely, if ever, use the highest level of pitch that women use. That is, it appears probable that most men have only three contrastive levels of intonation, while many women, at least, have four. Men avoid final patterns which do not terminate at the lowest level of pitch, and use a final, short upstep only for special effects (for example, pattern

[2] for deliberativeness), for incomplete sequence, and for certain interrogative sentences. Although they also use short down-glides also, occasionally, they seem in general to avoid the one-syllable, long pitch glides, and completely avoid the reverse glides on one syllable. (Of course it is possible for any speaker to use any pattern if he wishes; I have been referring here to general communication situations.)

Pike (1945) does make some statements which indicate that he may have been aware of some of the materials I have presented. When discussing the sentence-final hesitation pattern (9), for example, he states that occasionally this pattern "especially when used by female speakers, implies *endearment*".[1]

From this brief study it seems clear that there are indeed specific differences in male and female intonation patterns (although some of the specifics herein mentioned may vary to some extent from dialect to dialect and, to a lesser degree, from speaker to speaker within one dialect). I now believe that contrasting male-female speech may be present in many more languages than those for which it has already been reported, and, indeed, may be present in all languages. (Dr. Robin Lakoff recently informed me that she has been studying vocabulary differences in men's and women's speech in American English and it appears that our studies complement and confirm one another.)

The pedagogical importance for teaching English as a foreign language is obvious. Many well-meaning teachers must have been teaching their students to speak culturally unacceptable intonation patterns, and it is hoped that some of the findings presented here will reach the authors of English-language textbooks, so that they may be included.

NOTE

[1] Another of Pike's many far-sighted intuitive comments is the following: "The meaning of incompleteness added by the rising contour can be interpreted to imply (1) the necessity for information from the hearer, or (2) doubt on the part of the speaker." It seems to me that this statement could be directly incorporated into the current discussion on presuppositions.

REFERENCES

Pike, K. L. (1945). *The intonation of American English.* Ann Arbor: Univ. of Michigan Press.

Wells, R. S. (1945). The pitch phonemes of English. *Language,* 21, 27-39.

SEX, COVERT PRESTIGE AND LINGUISTIC CHANGE IN THE URBAN BRITISH ENGLISH OF NORWICH*

Peter Trudgill

It is known to be the case that in some societies linguistic phenomena are involved in covariation, not only with parameters such as social stratification, social context and age, but also with the parameter of sex.[1] The fact that speech of men and women may differ in interesting ways, however, has been noted in only a rather small number of linguistic articles and discussions (see, for example, Haas, 1944; Fischer, 1958; Sapir, 1929),[2] and, until very recently, research on this topic has tended to concentrate either on non-urbanized communities (Haas, 1944) or on relatively peripheral aspects of the subject (Hertzler, 1954).

In the past few years, however, a number of studies have appeared which have begun to present accurate, structured data illustrating the form that sex differentiation takes in the linguistic communities of complex urbanized societies. For the most part, the work that has been published on this topic is based on sociolinguistic investigations that have been carried out into varieties of urban American English. Shuy, Wolfram & Riley (1967), Wolfram (1969), and Fasold (1968), for example, have all discussed sex differentiation in the speech of Detroit, while Labov (1966) and Levine & Crockett (1966) have investigated the same phenomenon in other varieties of American English. This means that, for the first time, we have evidence not only to show that this type of variation actually does occur, if only for a restricted number of varieties of one language, but also to illustrate the exact form that this variation takes.

*Reprinted from *Language in Society,* 1972, 1, 179-95, by permission of Cambridge University Press.

So far, the results of all these studies have one striking feature in common. They are all agreed that women, allowing for other variables such as age, education and social class, consistently produce linguistic forms which more closely approach those of the standard language or have higher prestige than those produced by men, or, alternatively, that they produce forms of this type more frequently. Results of this kind have been obtained only in the study of American English. We are therefore justified in asking: Does the same sort of pattern of differentiation occur in other linguistic communities, including those of Britain, or is it peculiarly a product of the American social structure?

Impressionistically, one would say that sex differentiation of this precise type *does* occur in British English. It is clearly preferable, however, to be able to demonstrate conclusively that this is actually the case. In this paper I propose to present some data which illustrates quite clearly that this type of differentiation does occur in at least one variety of British English. I shall then attempt to discuss what factors may underlie this form of differentiation, and to consider what role it plays both in the propagation and in the study of linguistic change.

The results from which these figures are taken are based on an urban dialect survey of the city of Norwich carried out in the summer of 1968 with a random sample, 60 in number, of the population of the city, and reported in detail in Trudgill (1971). This sociolinguistic research was concerned mainly with correlating phonetic and phonological variables with social class, age, and stylistic context, and with developing a generative phonological diasystem which would in some way account for all varieties of Norwich English. Some work was also done, however, in studying the relationships that obtain between linguistic phenomena and sex.

In order to relate the phonological material to the social class of informants and the other parameters, a number of phonetic and phonological variables were developed, and index scores calculated for individuals and groups in the manner of Labov (1966). The first of these variables that I wish to discuss is the variable (ng). This is the pronunciation of the suffix -*ing* in *walking, laughing,* etc., and is a well-known variable in many types of English. In the case of Norwich English there are two possible pronunciations of this variable: [ɪŋ], which also occurs in the prestige accent, RP, and [ən~n]. The former is labelled (ng)-1 and the latter (ng)-2.

Index scores were developed for this variable by initially awarding 1 for each instance of (ng)-1 and 2 for each instance of (ng)-2. These scores were then summed and divided by the total number of instances, to give the mean score. Indices were finally calculated by subtracting 1 from the mean score and multiplying the result by 100. In this case, this gives an index score of 000 for consistent use of RP (ng)-1, and 100 for consistent use of (ng)-2, and the scores are equivalent to the simple percentage of non-RP forms used. (For variables with more than two variants this simple relationship, of course, does not apply.) Indices were calculated in the first instance for individual informants in each contextual style and subsequently for each group of informants. The four contextual styles:

> Word List Style: WLS
> Reading Passage Style: RPS
> Formal Speech: FS
> Casual Speech: CS

are equivalent to the styles discussed by Labov (1966) and were elicited in a similar manner. Indices for other variables were calculated in the same way.

Table 1 shows the average (ng) index scores for informants in the five social class groups obtained in the survey, in the four contextual styles. The social class divisions are based on an index that was developed using income, education, dwelling type, location of dwelling, occupation, and occupation of father as parameters. The five classes have been labelled:

> Middle Middle Class: MMC
> Lower Middle Class: LMC
> Upper Working Class: UWC
> Middle Working Class: MWC
> Lower Working Class: LWC

The table shows very clearly that (ng) is a linguistic variable in Norwich English. Scores range from a high of 100 per cent non-RP forms by the LWC in CS to a low of 0 per cent by the MMC in RPS and by the MMC and LMC in WLS. The pattern of differentiation is also structured in a very clear manner. For each of the social classes, scores rise consistently from WLS to CS; and for each style scores rise consistently from MMC to LWC.

TABLE 1. *(ng) Index scores by class and style*

Class	Style				
	WLS	RPS	FS	CS	N:
MMC	000	000	003	028	6
LMC	000	010	015	042	8
UWC	005	015	074	087	16
MWC	023	044	088	095	22
LWC	029	066	098	100	8

In his study of this same variable in American English, Fischer (1958) found that males used a higher percentage of non-standard [n] forms than females. Since we have now shown that (ng) is a variable in Norwich English, we would expect, if sex differentiation of the type we have been discussing also occurs in British English, that the same sort of pattern would emerge here. Table 2 shows that this is in fact very largely the case. In 17 cases out of 20, *male* scores are greater than or equal to corresponding *female* scores.[3]

We can therefore state that a high (ng) index is typical not only of WC speakers in Norwich but also of *male* speakers. This pattern, moreover, is repeated for the vast majority of the other nineteen variables studied in Norwich. We can therefore claim to have demonstrated that the type of sex differentiation already illustrated in American English also occurs in urban British English: our initial impression is confirmed.

TABLE 2. *(ng) Index scores by class, style and sex*

Class	Sex	Style			
		WLS	RPS	FS	CS
MMC	M	000	000	004	031
	F	000	000	000	000
LMC	M	000	020	027	017
	F	000	000	003	067
UWC	M	000	018	081	095
	F	011	013	068	077
MWC	M	024	043	091	097
	F	020	046	081	088
LWC	M	060	100	100	100
	F	017	054	097	100

Women informants, then, use forms associated with the prestige standard more frequently than men. How can we explain this phenomenon? What follows is necessarily speculative, but there would appear to be perhaps two interconnected explanatory factors.

1. Women in our society are more status-conscious than men, generally speaking (see Martin 1954), and are therefore more aware of the social significance of linguistic variables. There are two possible reasons for this:

   (i) The social position of women in our society is less secure than that of men, and, usually, subordinate to that of men. It may be, therefore, that it is more necessary for women to secure and signal their social status linguistically and in other ways, and they may for this reason be more aware of the importance of this type of signal. (This will be particularly true of women who are not working.)

   (ii) Men in our society can be rated socially by their occupation, their earning power, and perhaps by their own abilities—in other words by what they *do*. For the most part, however, this is not possible for women. It may be, therefore, that they have instead to be rated on how they *appear*. Since they are not rated by their occupation or by their occupational success, other signals of status, including speech, are correspondingly more important.

2. The second, related, factor is that WC speech, like other aspects of WC culture, appears, at least in some Western societies, to have connotations of masculinity (see Labov 1966a, 495), probably because it is associated with the roughness and toughness supposedly characteristic of WC life which are, to a certain extent, considered to be desirable masculine attributes. They are not, on the other hand, considered to be desirable feminine characteristics. On the contrary, features such as refinement and sophistication are much preferred.

It has also been suggested (Shuy, 1969) that this phenomenon may in part be the result of differential responses to the school situation. Female domination would appear to be the norm in primary schools in Britain, and female values (for example the emphasis traditionally placed on quietness in schools) seem to predominate in the teaching situation generally. It is possible that boys react to this kind of domination in a negative way and reject the standard English that is typically taught in schools, along with other aspects of the value system, to a greater extent than girls.

For the purposes of this paper I want to concentrate on the second factor: the argument that WC speech in our culture has desirable connotations for male speakers. Again, impressionistically speaking, I feel that one would wish to claim that this argument is essentially correct. As it stands at the moment, however, the argument is largely speculative because of the lack of concrete evidence. This lack of evidence has been discussed by Labov (1966b: 108) who states that in New York "the socio-economic structure confers prestige on the middle-class pattern associated with the more formal styles. [But] one can't avoid the implication that in New York City we must have an equal and opposing prestige for informal, working-class speech—a covert prestige enforcing this speech pattern. We must assume that people in New York City want to talk as they do, yet this fact is not at all obvious in any overt response that you can draw from interview subjects."

We suspect, in other words, that there are hidden values associated with non-standard speech, and that, as far as our present argument is concerned, they are particularly important in explaining the sex differentiation of linguistic variables, but so far we have been unable to uncover them or prove that they exist. We can guess that these values are there, but they are values which are not usually overtly expressed. They are not values which speakers readily admit to having, and for that reason they are difficult to study. Happily, the urban dialect survey carried out in Norwich has now provided some evidence which argues very strongly in favour of our hypothesis, and which has managed, as it were, to remove the outer layer of overtly expressed values and penetrate to the hidden values beneath. That is, we now have some objective data which actually demonstrates that for male speakers WC non-standard speech is in a very real sense highly valued and prestigious.

Labov has produced evidence to show that almost all speakers in New York City share a common set of linguistic norms, whatever their actual linguistic performance, and that they hear and report themselves as using these prestigious linguistic forms, rather than the forms they actually do use. This "dishonesty" in reporting what they say is of course not deliberate, but it does suggest that informants, at least so far as their conscious awareness is concerned, are dissatisfied with the way they speak, and would prefer to be able to use more standard forms. This was in fact confirmed by comments New York City informants actually made about their own speech.

Overt comments made by the Norwich informants on their own speech were also of this type. Comments such as "I talk horrible" were typical. It also began to appear, however, that, as suggested above, there were other, deeper motivations for their actual linguistic behavior than these overtly expressed notions of their own "bad speech." For example, many informants who initially stated that they did not speak properly, and would like to do so, admitted, if pressed, that they perhaps would not *really* like to, and that they would almost certainly be considered foolish, arrogant or disloyal by their friends and family if they did. This is our first piece of evidence.

Far more important, however, is the evidence that was obtained by means of the Self-Evaluation Test, in which half of the Norwich informants took part. This is particularly the case when the results of this test are compared to those obtained by a similar test conducted by Labov in New York. In the Norwich Self-Evaluation Test, 12 lexical items were read aloud, to informants, with two or more different pronunciations. For example:

tune   1. [tjʉːn]   2. [tʉːn]

Informants were then asked to indicate, by marking a number on a chart, which of these pronunciations most closely resembled the way in which they normally said this word.

The corresponding Self-Evaluation Test in New York for the variable (r)—presence or absence of post-vocalic /r/ (a prestige feature)—produced the following results. Informants who in FS used over 30 per cent /r/ were, very generously, considered to be (post-vocalic) /r/-users. Seventy per cent of those who, in this sense, were /r/-users reported that they normally used /r/. But 62 per cent of those who were *not* /r/-users *also* reported that they normally used /r/. As Labov says (1966a: 455): "In the conscious report of their own usage. . . New York respondents are very inaccurate." The accuracy, moreover, is overwhelmingly in the direction of reporting themselves as using a form which is *more* statusful than the one they actually use. Labov (1966*a*: 455) claims that "no conscious deceit plays a part in this process" and that "most of the respondents seemed to perceive their own speech in terms of the norms at which they were aiming rather than the sound actually produced."

The full results of this test are shown in Table 3. It shows that 62 per cent of non-/r/-users "over-reported" themselves as using /r/, and 21 per cent of /r/-users "under-reported," although in view of Labov's 30 per cent dividing line, the latter were very probably simply being accurate.

TABLE 3. *Self-Evaluation of (r)—New York*

Used	Percentage Reported		
	/r/	∅	
/r/	79	21	=100
∅	62	38	=100

In the Norwich test, the criteria used were much more rigorous. In comparing the results obtained in the Self-Evaluation Test to forms actually used in Norwich, *casual speech* was used rather than *formal speech*, since CS more closely approximates everyday speech—to how informants normally pronounce words, which is what they were asked to report on. Moreover, informants were allowed *no* latitude in their self-evaluation. It was considered that the form informants used in everyday speech was the variant indicated by the appropriate CS index for that individual informant. For example, an (ng) index of between 050 and 100 was taken as indicating an (ng)-2 user rather than an (ng)-1 user. In other words, the dividing line is 50 per cent rather than Labov's more lenient 30 per cent. If, therefore, the characteristics of the Norwich sample were identical to those of the New York sample, we would expect a significantly *higher* degree of *over-reporting* from the Norwich informants.

The results, in fact, show the exact reverse of this, as can be seen from Table 4.

This table gives the results of the Self-Evaluation Test for the variable (yu), which is the pronunciation of the vowel in items such as *tune, music, queue, huge*. In Norwich English items such as these have two possible pronunciations: (yu)-1 has [j] as in RP-like [kju:~kjʉ:]; (yu)-2 omits [j] as in [kʉ:~k3ʉ], *queue*.

Table 4 provides a very striking contrast to the New York results shown in Table 3 in that only 16 per cent of (yu)-2 users, as compared to the equivalent figure of 62 per cent in New York, over-reported themselves as using the more statusful RP-like variant (yu)-1 when they did not in fact do so. Even more significant, however, is the fact that as many as 40 per cent of (yu)-1 users actually *under*-reported—and the under-reporting is in this case quite genuine.

A further breakdown of the scores given in Table 4 is also very revealing. Of the 16 per cent (yu)-2 users who over-reported, *all* were women. Of the (yu)-1 users who under-reported, half were men and half women. Here we see, for the first time, the emergence of the hidden values that underlie the sex

TABLE 4. *Self-Evaluation of (yu)*

Used	(yu) Percentage Reported		
	1	2	
1	60	40	=100
2	16	84	=100

TABLE 5. *Percentage of informants over- and under-reporting (yu)*

	Total	Male	Female
Over-r	13	0	29
Under-r	7	6	7
Accurate	80	94	64

differentiation described earlier in this paper. If we take the sample as a whole, we have the percentages of speakers under- and over-reporting shown in Table 5. Male informants, it will be noted, are strikingly more accurate in their self-assessment than are female informants.

The hidden values, however, emerge much more clearly from a study of the other variables tested in this way, (er), (ō) and (ā), illustrated in Tables 6, 7 and 8 respectively. The variable (er) is the vowel in *ear, here, idea,* which in Norwich English ranges from [ɪə] to [ɛː]; (ō) is the vowel in *road, nose, moan* (but not in *rowed, knows, mown,* which are distinct) and ranges from [ɵu] through [uː] to [ʊ]; and (ā) is the vowel in the lexical set of *gate, face, name,* which ranges from [eɪ] to [æi].

For each of these variables, it will be seen, there are more male speakers who claim to use a *less* prestigious variant than they actually do than there are who over-report, and for one of the variables (ō), the difference is very striking: 54 per cent to 12 per cent. In two of the cases, moreover, there are more male speakers who under-report than there are who are accurate.

Although there are some notable differences between the four variables illustrated here,[4] it is clear that Norwich informants are much more prone to under-report than New York informants, and that—and this is central to our argument—*male* informants in Norwich are much more likely to *under*-report, *female* informants to *over*-report.

TABLE 6. *Percentage of informants over-
and under-reporting (er)*

	Total	Male	Female
Over-r	43	22	68
Under-r	33	50	14
Accurate	23	28	18

TABLE 7. *Percentage of informants over-
and under-reporting (ō)*

	Total	Male	Female
Over-r	18	12	25
Under-r	36	54	18
Accurate	45	34	57

TABLE 8. *Percentage of informants over-
and under-reporting (ā)*

	Total	Male	Female
Over-r	32	22	43
Under-r	15	28	0
Accurate	53	50	57

This, then, is the objective evidence which demonstrates that male speakers, at least in Norwich, are at a subconscious or perhaps simply private level very favorably disposed towards non-standard speech forms. This is so much the case that as many as 54 per cent of them, in one case, claim to use these forms or hear themselves as using them *even when they do not do so*. If it is true that informants "perceive their own speech in terms of the norms at which they are aiming rather than the sound actually produced" then the norm at which a large number of Norwich males are aiming is *non-standard WC speech.* This favourable attitude is never overtly expressed, but the responses to these tests show that statements about "bad speech" are for public consumption only. Privately and subconsciously, a large number of male speakers are more concerned with acquiring prestige of the covert sort and with signalling group solidarity than with obtaining social status, as this is more usually defined. By means of these figures, therefore, we have been able to demonstrate both that it is possible to obtain evidence of the "covert prestige" associated with non-standard varieties, and that, for Norwich men, working-class speech is statusful and prestigious. The clear contrast with scores obtained by female informants, with as many as 68 per cent of the women over-reporting, in one case, underlines this point and indicates that women are much more favorably disposed towards MC standard forms. This in turn explains why the sex-differentiation pattern of Table 2 takes the form it does.

Why it should have been possible to obtain this sort of evidence of covert prestige from Norwich speakers but not from New York speakers it is difficult to say. This may be due to the fact that WC speakers in this country have not accepted MC values so readily or completely as WC speakers in America. If this is the case, it could be explained by "the conspicuous lack of corporate or militant class consciousness [in America], which is one of the most important contrasts between American and European systems of stratification" (Mayer, 1955: 67) and by the related lack of "embourgoisement" of the British WC (cf. Goldthorpe & Lockwood, 1963).

On the other hand, Tables 9 and 10 show that this cannot be the whole story. These tables illustrate the amount of over- and under-reporting of (er) and ($\bar{o}$) respectively by male speakers as a whole, and then by MC as opposed to WC

TABLE 9. *Percentage male informants over-
and under-reporting (er)*

	Total	MC	WC
Over-r	22	25	21
Under-r	50	50	50
Accurate	28	25	29

male speakers. It can be seen that there is no significant difference in the behaviour of the two classes. The MC, it is true, shows a slightly greater tendency to over-report than the WC, but this is very small. The significant parameter controlling presence or absence of this "covert prestige" is therefore sex rather than social class. Recognition of these hidden values is something that is common to a majority of Norwich males of whatever social class (and something that they do not share with WC female informants). Many MC males appear to share with WC males the characteristic that they have not so completely absorbed the dominant mainstream societal values as have their American counterparts.

Having established that covert prestige does in fact exist, and can be shown to exist, we are now in a position to move on to a discussion of one of the problems that arises from the Norwich data. It was shown in Table 2 that for the variable (ng) men had higher index scores than women. We also stated that the

TABLE 10. *Percentage male informants over- and under-reporting (ō)*

	Total	MC	WC
Over-r	12	15	11
Under-r	54	54	54
Accurate	34	30	35

TABLE 11. *(o) Indices by class, style and sex*

Class	Sex	Style			
		WLS	RPS	FS	CS
MMC	M	000	000	001	003
	F	000	000	000	000
LMC	M	004	014	011	055
	F	000	002	001	008
UWC	M	011	019	044	060
	F	023	027	068	077
MWC	M	029	026	064	078
	F	025	045	071	066
LWC	M	014	050	080	069
	F	037	062	083	090

same pattern occurred for the vast majority of other Norwich variables, and we have since been able to offer at least a partial explanation of why this pattern occurs. There is one Norwich variable, however, which does not conform to this pattern of sex differentiation. This is the variable (o), the pronunciation of the vowel in the lexical set of *top, dog, box*. There are two main variants in Norwich English: (o)-1, a rounded RP-like vowel [ɒ]; and (o)-2, an unrounded vowel [ɑ~a]. Table 11 gives index scores for this variable by social class, contextual style and sex, and shows a pattern of differentiation markedly different from that shown for (ng) in Table 2.

As far as the two MC groups are concerned in all eight cases men again have scores that are higher than or equal to those of women. The striking fact to emerge from this table, however, is that for the three WC groups the normal pattern of sex differentiation is almost completely *reversed*. In ten cases out of twelve, women have higher scores than men. If it is true that for Norwich men WC non-standard speech forms have high covert prestige, then this would appear to be a counter-example which we have to explain. (This is the only Norwich variable for which a reversal of pattern of sex differentiation was found.)

In order to be able to handle this problem we must first turn our attention to the examination of another variable, the variable (e). This is the pronunciation of the vowel in *tell, bell, hell,* for which there are three main variants: (e)-1=[ε]; (e)-2=[3]; (e)-3=[Λ]. Table 12 shows index scores for this variable by class and style.

TABLE 12. *(e) Indices by class and style*

Class	Style			
	WLS	RPS	FS	CS
MMC	003	000	001	002
LMC	007	012	023	042
UWC	027	039	089	127
MWC	030	044	091	087
LWC	009	026	077	077

The figures in this table illustrate quite clearly that the pattern of class differentiation for (e) differs rather strikingly from the normal pattern of differentiation illustrated for (ng) in Table 1. The difference lies in the fact that the bottom group, the LWC, consistently has scores that are *lower* (more nearly standard) than those of both the UWC and MWC. A regular pattern of differentiation could only be obtained by placing the LWC scores between those for the LMC and UWC. It should also be noted that the MWC has a *lower* score than the UWC in CS. In CS, in fact, the class differentiation pattern for the WC is completely the reverse of the normal pattern.

The answer to the problem of why this should be the case lies in some research that was carried out into linguistic change in Norwich English. It was noted several times in the course of this research that the LWC, as a relatively underprivileged group, appeared to be isolated from certain innovating tendencies. Since we have found in the case of (e) that the LWC is differentiated from the UWC and the MWC in an unusual way, we can guess that high scores for this variable (that is, a large amount of non-standard centralization) represent an *innovation* in Norwich English: the variable (e) is involved in linguistic change, in that centralization of this vowel is increasing. We can further hypothesize that in the vanguard of this linguistic change, which would appear to be leading Norwich English in a direction away from the RP standard, are the *upper members* of the WC. The LWC and LMC are also participating in this change, but at a lower level, and the MMC are not participating at all, or very little.

This hypothesis is in fact confirmed by the pattern of age differentiation illustrated in Table 13. This illustrates that younger people in Norwich, those aged under 30 and in particular those aged under 20, have much higher (e) scores than the rest of the population. This is particularly true of the crucial CS scores. Only the youngest two age groups achieve scores of 100 or over. This large amount of age differentiation confirms that a linguistic change is in fact taking place in Norwich.

TABLE 13. *(e) Indices by age and style*

| | Style | | | |
Age	WLS	RPS	FS	CS
10-19	059	070	139	173
20-29	021	034	071	100
30-39	025	031	059	067
40-49	015	026	055	088
50-59	006	013	035	046
60-69	005	018	055	058
70+	005	031	050	081

It is therefore possible to suggest that linguistic changes in a direction away from the standard norm are led in the community by members of the UWC and MWC. In particular, because of the covert prestige non-standard forms have for them, we would expect changes of this type be spear-headed by MWC and UWC *men*. (Correspondingly, standard forms will tend to be introduced by MC women.) This point is confirmed in the case of (e), since the highest (e) index score of all was obtained in CS by *male* MWC 10-19-year-olds, who had a mean index of 200, i.e., they all consistently used (e)-3 in CS.

It is interesting to relate this change in a non-standard direction to the concept of covert prestige. We have already seen that for Norwich men this kind of prestige is associated with non-standard forms. But it also appears to be the case that very high covert prestige is associated with WC speech forms by the young *of both sexes*. Tables 14 and 15 illustrate this point. They compare the figures obtained in the Self-Evaluation Test for (er) and (ō) respectively by male WC speakers as a whole with those obtained by male WC speakers aged under 30. In the case of female speakers, because of the size of the sample at this point, it was not possible to remove class bias from the data, and the figures for female speakers also shown in Tables 14 and 15 simply compare scores obtained by female speakers as a whole with those of the female under-30 group.

In the case of (er) it is clear that younger informants are rather more accurate in their self-evaluation than are older informants. With the female informants this is particularly striking: 40 per cent accuracy as compared to only 18 per cent accuracy from the female sample as a whole. In the case of (ō), the differences are rather more striking. The younger informants are slightly less accurate than the sample as a whole, but this is due to a greater tendency—and in the case of the female informants a *much* greater tendency—to under-report. It is therefore not only male speakers who attach covert prestige to WC speech forms, but also the younger female informants. Whether this is a feature which is

TABLE 14. *Percentage of informants over-*
and under-reporting (er) by age

	Male		Female	
Percentage	Total WC	WC 10-29	Total Female	10-29
Over-r	21	8	68	40
Under-r	50	58	14	20
Accurate	29	33	18	40

TABLE 15. *Percentage of informants over-*
and under-reporting (ō) by age

	Male		Female	
Percentage	Total WC	WC 10-29	Total Female	10-29
Over-r	8	8	25	0
Under-r	50	58	18	50
Accurate	42	33	57	50

repeated in every generation of female speakers, or whether it reflects a genuine and recent change in ideology it is not possible at this stage to say. What is clear, however, is that the linguistic change associated with (e) is being caused, at least in part, by the covert prestige which the WC form [ʌ] has for certain Norwich speakers. Group identification of a kind considered desirable by these speakers is signalled by the usage of the non-standard form, and this leads to its increase and exaggeration. Covert prestige, therefore, leads not only to the differentiation of the linguistic behavior of the sexes, but also to the exaggeration of certain non-standard features, particularly by UWC and MWC men and by the young, which in turn leads to linguistic change.

If we now return once again to the unusual pattern associated with (o) illustrated in Table 11, we might again hypothesize that the deviant configuration of scores obtained for this variable is due, as in the case of (e), to a linguistic change in progress. However, this does not at first sight appear possible, since, if the RP form [ɒ] were being introduced into Norwich English, we would clearly expect this process to be spear-headed by MC women. The answer would appear to lie in the fact that [ɒ] is not *only* an RP form. It is *also* the form that occurs in the speech of the Home Counties and, perhaps more importantly, in Suffolk. Field records made in the 1930s by Lowman,[5] some of which are published in Kurath & McDavid (1961), give the pronunciation of the vowel in items such as *bog* as [ɒ] in Suffolk and this pronunciation is also recorded for the Suffolk localities in Orton & Tilling (1969).

It would therefore seem to be the case that the unusual pattern of sex differentiation of (o) is due to the following processes. The form [ɒ] in items

TABLE 16. *(o) Indices by age and style*

Age	Style			
	WLS	RPS	FS	CS
10-29	017	017	045	055
30-49	020	030	039	063
50-69	021	037	058	067
70+	043	043	091	093

such as *top, dog* is being introduced as a linguistic innovation into Norwich English. This is demonstrated by the scores shown for different age groups in Table 16. The introduction of this innovation, moreover, is taking place in two ways. First, [ɒ] is being introduced into Norwich English from RP by MC women, who are not only orientated towards RP, as the Self-Evaluation Tests show, but also have access to RP forms, in a way that WC women do not, because of their social class position. Secondly, this form is being introduced, as a result of geographical diffusion processes, from the non-standard WC speech forms of the Home Counties and particularly Suffolk by WC men, who not only are favourably disposed towards non-standard forms just as MC men are, but also, because of their social class position, have access to these forms as a result of occupational and other forms of social contact with speakers of [ɒ]-type accents. The variable (o) therefore represents a relatively rare example of two different types of linguistic change (change "from below" and "from above" in the terms of Labov, 1966a: 328) both leading in the same direction, with the result that it is now only WC women who, to any great extent, preserve the unrounded vowel.

We have therefore been able to argue that "covert prestige" can be associated with certain linguistic forms, and that it is possible in some cases to provide evidence to show that this is in fact the case. This covert prestige reflects the value system of our society and of the different sub-cultures within this society, and takes the following form: for male speakers, and for female speakers under 30, non-standard WC speech forms are highly valued, although these values are not usually overtly expressed. These covert values lead to sex differentiation of linguistic variables of a particular type that appears to be common to at least some varieties of urban British and American English. Covert prestige also appears to lead to linguistic changes "from below," with the result, for example, that in Norwich English non-standard variants of (e) are currently on the increase. A study of the actual form the sex differentiation of a particular linguistic variable takes, moreover, can also usefully be employed in an examination of whether or not the variable is involved in linguistic change.

One important conclusion of a practical nature that we can draw from this data is that, if we wish to teach standard English to younger speakers of non-standard English (and the necessity for this has been disputed—see O'Neil 1968; Newmeyer & Edmonds 1971), we should be very careful to take values of the covert prestige type into consideration. Levine & Crockett (1966) have demonstrated that in one American locality "the community's march toward the national norm" is spear-headed in particular by middle-aged MC women (and by the young). In Norwich, at least, there appears to be a considerable number of young WC men marching resolutely in the other direction.

NOTES

[1]I am very grateful to D. Crystal, P.H. Matthews and the editor for the number of helpful comments and suggestions they have made on this paper.

[2]There have also been a number of discussions in general works, cf. Jespersen (1922, Chapter 13). See also the summary of other work in Crystal (1971).

[3]The low score obtained by male LMC speakers in CS requires some comment. The score is clearly unrepresentative, being lower than both the RPS and FS scores and the male MMC score, and is due to the fact that only a very small number of instances of this variable happened to be obtained for this group in CS.

[4]These differences may be due to a skewing effect resulting from the necessity of using only a small number of individual lexical items to stand for each variable in the tests. (Informants' reports of their pronunciation of *tune,* for example, do not *necessarily* mean that they would pronounce or report *Tuesday* or *tube* in the same way.)

[5]I am very grateful to R.I. McDavid who went to a great deal of trouble to enable me to consult these records.

REFERENCES

Crystal, D. (1971). Prosodic and paralinguistic correlates of social categories. In E. Ardener (ed.), *Social anthropology and language.* London: Tavistock.

Fasold, R. W. (1968). A sociolinguistic study of the pronunciation of three vowels in Detroit speech. Unpublished mimeo: Center for Applied Linguistics.

Fischer, J. L. (1958). Social influences on the choice of a linguistic variant. *Word*, 14, 47-56.

Goldthorpe, J. & Lockwood, D. (1963). Affluence and the British class structure. *Sociological Review*, 11, 133-63.

Haas, M. (1944). Men's and women's speech in Koasati. *Language*, 20, 142-49.

Hertzler, J. (1954). *A sociology of language*, New York: Random House.

Jespersen, O. (1922). *Language: its nature, development and origin*. London: Allen and Unwin.

Kurath, H. & McDavid, R. I. (1961). *The pronunciation of English in the Atlantic states*. Ann Arbor: Univ. of Michigan Press.

Labov, W. (1966a). *The social stratification of English in New York City*. Washington, D.C.: Center for Applied Linguistics.

———. (1966b). Hypercorrection by the lower middle class as a factor in linguistic change. In W. Bright (ed.), *Sociolinguistics*. The Hague: Mouton.

Levine, L. & Crockett, H. J. (1966). Speech variation in a Piedmont community: postvocalic *r*. In S. Lieberson (ed.), *Explorations in sociolinguistics*. The Hague: Mouton.

Martin, F. M. (1954). Some subjective aspects of social stratification. In D. V. Glass (ed.), *Social mobility in Britain*. London: Routledge and Kegan Paul.

Mayer, K. B. (1955). *Class and society*. New York: Random House.

O'Neil, W. (1968). Paul Roberts' rules of order: the misuse of linguistics in the classroom. *The Urban Review*, 2, 12-17.

Newmeyer, F. J. & Edmonds, J. (1971). The linguist in American society. *Papers from the 7th regional meeting of the Chicago linguistic society*. Chicago: Chicago Linguistic Society.

Orton, H. & Tilling, P. M. (1969). *Survey of English dialects: volume III East Midlands and East Anglia*. Leeds: Arnold.

Sapir, E. (1929). Male and female forms of speech in Yana. Reprinted in D. Mandelbaum (ed.) (1949), *Selected writings of Edward Sapir in language, culture and personality*. Berkeley and Los Angeles: Univ. of California Press.

Shuy, R. W. (1969). Sociolinguistic research at the Center for Applied Linguistics: the correlation of language and sex. *Giornata internazionali di sociolinguistica*. Rome: Palazzo Baldassini.

Shuy, R. W., Wolfram, W. A. & Riley, W. K. (1967). *Linguistic correlates of social stratification in Detroit speech*. Cooperative Research Project 6-1347. East Lansing: U. S. Office of Education.

Trudgill, P. J. (1971). The social differentiation of English in Norwich. Edinburgh Univ.: Unpublished Ph.D. Thesis.

Wolfram, W. A. (1969). *A sociolinguistic description of Detroit Negro speech*. Washington, D.C.: Center for Applied Linguistics.

SEX ROLES, INTERRUPTIONS AND SILENCES
IN CONVERSATION*

Don H. Zimmerman and Candace West

INTRODUCTION

Power and dominance constitute significant aspects of many recurring interactions such as those between whites and blacks, adults and children, and—of specific interest here—men and women. It should not be surprising, then, that the distribution of power in the occupational structure, the family division of labor, and other institutional contexts where life chances are determined, has its parallel in the dynamics of everyday interaction. The preliminary findings of the research reported here indicate that there are definite and patterned ways in which the power and dominance enjoyed by men in other contexts are exercised in their conversational interaction with women.

Interruptions, lapses in the flow of conversation, and inattentiveness are commonplace occurrences, seemingly far removed from sociological concerns with such things as institutionalized power. Employing recent developments in the study of conversational interaction (Sacks *et al.,* 1974; Sacks, n.d.; Schegloff, 1972*a,b;* Sacks and Schegloff, 1973) as a resource, this paper shows how these events may be related to the enduring problems of power and dominance in social life.

*An earlier version of this paper was presented at the Linguistics Symposium, California State Polytechnic University, Pomona, March, 1973. The paper is based in part on an unpublished master's paper by Candace West, "Sexism and Conversation," Department of Sociology, University of California, Santa Barbara. The authors would like to thank John Baldwin, Robert Poolman, Charles Spaulding, D. Lawrence Wieder and Thomas P. Wilson for their help and comments. We accept all responsibility for any errors found in this paper.

Specifically, we report striking asymmetries between men and women with respect to patterns of interruption, silence, and support for partner in the development of topics. We discuss these observations in this paper and draw implications from them concerning the larger issue of sexism in American society. Prior to presenting our results, we must briefly consider the relationship of our research to the study of language and social interaction.

SEX ROLES, LANGUAGE, AND SOCIAL INTERACTION

The recognition that sex role differences are reflected in language patterns has stimulated a good deal of recent research in this area (cf. Henley and Thorne, 1975). To consider just one example, Robin Lakoff (1973) suggests that a separate "woman's speech" exists, characterized by a greater preponderance of such forms as tag questions, compound requests, and questioning intonational patterns offered in the context of otherwise declarative answers. She also examines the semantics of sexism by focusing on the discrepancies in supposed referential equivalents (e.g., "master" and "mistress"), and typically female euphemisms (e.g., "lady") for which there is no colloquial male equivalent.

Even a cursory review of studies of sex roles and language patterns suggests that various features of language and speech furnish the resources for male dominance (and, for that matter, female submissiveness) in pervasive and often subtle ways (cf. also Bernard, 1968; Brend, 1971; Key, 1972; and Kramer, 1973). There can be little doubt that speech patterns and particular syntactic, semantic, phonological, and intonational structures function to communicate the cultural and social meanings that cluster around sex roles. We, however, wish to stress the role of language and its constituent structures in the *organization* of social interaction in general and from that perspective view the characteristics of interaction between men and women. Conversation is clearly one very basic form of social interaction and it is the analysis of conversational structure in relation to sex roles that concerns us here.

While studies dealing with the exchange of talk between men and women can be found (e.g., Strodtbeck and Mann, 1956; Strodtbeck, James and Hawkins, 1957; and Soskin and John, 1963), they typically lack any explicit model of conversational interaction *per se* in terms of which their findings could be interpreted. An appropriate model can be found, however, in recent work by Sacks, Schegloff and Jefferson (1974), and Sacks (n.d.), which provides a systematic approach to turn-taking or speaker alternation in naturally occurring (i.e., uncontrived) conversation. This model, taken in conjunction with other work on the structure of conversation by Sacks and Schegloff (Sacks, 1972*a,* 1972*b;* Sacks and Schegloff, 1974; Schegloff, 1972*a;* Schegloff, 1972*b*) furnishes a general approach to the study of conversational interaction strongly rooted in meticulous empirical examination of audiotaped natural conversations.[1]

In this paper, we attempt to adapt relevant portions of this turn-taking model and other work in conversational analysis to the concerns already announced. We wish to make it clear that we do not view our efforts as a contribution to conversational analysis *per se* but rather as an attempt to apply it to a particular problem. In order to carry through this application, it is necessary to spell out the relevant aspects of the model in a brief and simplified form. The first part of this paper is, therefore, an exposition of Sacks, Schegloff, and Jefferson (1974).

THE MODEL

Sacks *et al.* (1974) suggest that speech exchange systems in general are organized to ensure that (1) one party speaks at a time and (2) speaker change recurs. These features are said to hold for casual conversation as well as for formal debate and even high ceremony. Thus it appears that the range of speech exchange systems found in our society (and possibly all societies) is constrained by some form of turn-taking mechanism.

What distinguishes conversation from debate and ceremony is the variability of the distribution of turns, turn size, and turn content. In debate, there is pre-allocation of turns, and standardization of turn size; in ceremony, the content of speech is predetermined as well.

The model Sacks *et al.* (1974) offer describes the properties of the turn-taking mechanism for conversation. A turn consists of not merely the temporal duration of an utterance but of the right (and obligation) to speak which is allocated to a particular speaker. The turn is spoken of as something valued and sought (or sometimes avoided) and allusion is made to the distribution of turns as a kind of economy. This analogy will prove useful to the purposes of this paper in subsequent discussion.

A turn is constructed by the speaker out of what Sacks *et al.* (1974) call "unit-types" which can consist of single words, phrases, clauses or sentences. Each speaker, upon being allocated a turn, has an initial right to produce one such unit. In general, the terminal boundary of a unit-type, e.g., the end of a sentence, is a possible transition place, and the transfer of a turn from one speaker to another properly occurs at that place.

Unit-types are generally projective; that is, the beginning portion of the unit frequently furnishes a basis for anticipating when it will be concluded and hence signals the upcoming transition place for purposes of speaker change. This property of unit-types assumes that the listener performs a syntactic (and/or intonational) analysis of the unit in the course of its production—the internal structure of the sentence, for example, indicating its possible completion point. Elsewhere, Sacks (n.d.) suggests that the phenomenon of sentence completion furnishes evidence for this "on line" analysis. For example, in the following segment,[2] a young man attempting to arrange a date with a young woman he has just met appears to anticipate her objection by completing her sentence for her (lines 4 and 5):

	1	A:	How would'ja like to go to a movie later on tonight?
(3.2)	2	B:	Huh?=
	3	A:	A <u>movie</u> y'know like a like (x) a <u>flick</u>?
(3.4)	4	B:	Yeah I uh <u>know</u> what a movie is (.8) It's just that=
	5	A:	You don't know me well enough?

With appropriate transformation of the pronouns, the sentence reads: "It's just that I don't know you well enough," a syntactically and semantically coherent utterance jointly produced by two speakers. It should also be pointed out that the completion is done with precise timing, i.e., no gap or overlap between the two speakers.

With regard to the timing of transitions between utterances, Sacks *et al.* (1974) observe that much of the time the alternation of speakers is achieved with little or no gap, suggesting a considerable degree of next-speaker readiness to commence a turn upon the occurrence of a possible transition place. These considerations establish the ground for what is undoubtedly presupposed by parties to conversations, namely, that a conversation involves both active speakership and active listenership, with these roles alternating between persons.

Minimal Responses: A Brief Digression

Active hearership is a fundamental prerequisite for the production of instances of a particular class of utterances which may not be considered as unit-types, and hence may not count as filling turns. Such items as "um hmm," "uh huh," and "yeah," when interspersed through a current speaker's ongoing utterance, are not seen as interrupting the current speaker (cf. Schegloff, 1972*b*), but instead serve to display continuing interest and co-participation in topic development. Fishman (1973) continues along these lines to point out the agility with which speakers are able to insert such comments—rarely do they overlap a current speaker's utterance, being interjected virtually between breaths. Characteristically, the current speaker will continue her turn after insertion of a "yeah" or "um hmm" with little if any discernible pause. Fishman (1973) suggests that these phenomena serve to do "support work," functioning as indicators that the listener is carefully attending to the stream of talk.

These "minimal responses" which monitor a speaker's utterance may of course be coupled with energetic nonverbal cues such as nodding of the head, and such gestures often replace the verbal comments when conversationalists are face-to-face. Although the purposes at hand prohibit examination of this matter in detail, it is interesting to note that parties to talk are likely to time these nonverbal signals to coincide with pauses in a current speaker's utterance. Thus,

items like "um hmm," "uh huh," and "yeah" may be viewed as a kind of positive reinforcement for continued talk where the provider of such cues must do
active listening work to determine proper placement.

The Operation of the Rule-Set

The specific mechanism for speaker alternation is furnished by an ordered set
of rules which are applied recursively to generate the distribution of turns and
turn sizes for any actual conversation. In order to simplify this presentation the
operation of the rule-set is represented in Figure 1 as a flow diagram of the
sequence of "decisions" involved.[3] The rule-set is represented by a vertical array
of decision points, with the highest priority decision point at the top.

Inspecting Figure 1 we see that for a given transition place within a turn, the
highest priority decision is whether or not current speaker has selected next
speaker. Current speaker selects next speaker by such techniques as addressing
her by name (or title) or by directing a question to her, or both, where the term
of address or question is constructed as part of the unit-type the terminal
boundary of which marks the next transition place. If next speaker has been
selected by current speaker at this point, the rule-set recycles to the beginning
(I) in preparation for the occurrence of the next transition place, the speaker
just selected having the exclusive right (and obligation) to speak next.

In the event that next speaker has not been selected by current speaker, the
next decision point (II) presents the *option* to potential speakers other than
current speaker to self-select. (Self-selection is an option available to each
potential next speaker; thus, more than one speaker could start to speak, the
right to the turn belonging to the first starter.) The rule-set recycles to (I) if
self-selection occurs; if it does not, the third decision point (III) is reached.

In the absence of self-selection by other parties, the current speaker may (but
is not obligated to) continue speaking. The exercise of this option recycles the
rule set to (I), the process repeating itself until speaker change occurs. If current
speaker does not speak, the rule-set recycles to (II), the first decision point
(current speaker selects next speaker) being obviously inapplicable.

This model of turn-taking, Sacks *et al.* propose, accounts for a number of
regularly occurring features of observed conversations—including the alternation
of speakers in a variable order with brief (if any) gaps or overlaps between turns,
as well as variable length of turns. That is, the model provides for the systematic
initiation, continuation and alternation of turns in everyday conversation.

Sacks *et al.* (1974) characterize their model as a "locally managed" system
by which they mean that over a series of turns the rule-set operates to effect
transitions between successive pairs of adjacent turns, one turn at a time, the
focus of the system being the next turn and the next transition. Turn size is also
locally managed since the concatenation of unit-types to construct longer turns
is also provided for by the system's organization.

Figure 1

Flow diagram of the "decision" process in Sacks' *et al.* (1974) model of turn-taking in naturally occurring conversation

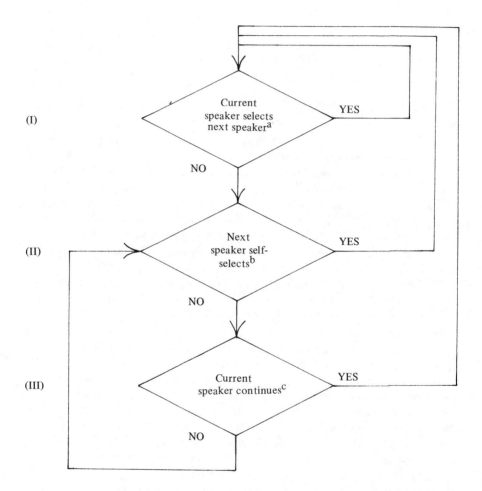

Notes:

[a]The person selected by current speaker has the exclusive right (and obligation) to speak next.

[b]Next speaker other than current speaker.

[c]Current speaker is not obligated to continue speaking.

Moreover, the system is said to be "party administered," i.e., turn order and turn size are under the control of parties to the conversation who exercise the options provided. The system is also characterized as "interactionally managed," turn order and turn size being determined turn by turn by conversationalists, each of whom exercises options which are contingent upon, and undertaken with the awareness of, options available to the other. The point of immediate concern here is that the turn-taking system described by Sacks *et al.* (1974) can be viewed as a representation of speakers' methods for achieving a preferred organization of their conversational interaction, i.e., the intended conversational order from the point of view of speakers. (Violations of this intended order can and do occur, of course, and should be observable as such by virtue of the rules for turn-taking.)

Sacks *et al.* (1974) suggest that this model approaches the status of a context-free mechanism which is, moreover, finely context-sensitive in its application. Here, "context-free" means analytically independent of a wide range of features exhibited by actual conversations, e.g., topics, settings, number of parties, and social identities (which could be subject to analysis in their own right). This independence establishes the basis for the context-sensitivity of the system since, by virtue of its indifference to the particulars of any given conversation, it can accommodate the changing circumstances of talk posed by variation in topic, setting, number of parties, and identity of participants. The model generates an infinite set of possible turn-taking sequences varying in terms of turn order, turn size, and number of speakers, by recourse to a limited set of organizational principles usable on any occasion of conversation.[4]

Our task in this paper is to bring relevant aspects of this model to bear on conversational interaction between men and women. The next section deals with the collection, transcription, and analysis of our data and is followed by the presentation of our findings.

METHODS

Recording Conversations

Three-quarters of the 31 conversational segments analyzed in this paper were two-party interactions recorded in coffee shops, drug stores, and other public places in a university community. Such places were viewed as routine settings in which everyday "chit chat" takes place—the kind of talking we all do, even when others are likely to overhear us.

The tape recorder was carried by one or the other author, and what they could hear by virtue of their routine and unquestioned access to public areas was deemed eligible for taping. Whenever possible, conversationalists were subsequently informed of our recording and their consent obtained. In some of these cases however, the abrupt departure of parties to the talk precluded such debriefing. In the process of transcription, identifying references were disguised and the tape erased after the transcript was completed and checked, thus protecting the anonymity of the persons involved. Some recording was done in private residences to which the authors normally had casual access. In these cases (which comprise the remaining fourth of the data), consent was uniformly obtained after recording, and no refusals to permit the use of the tape or complaints about the covert procedure were encountered. Data collection, moreover, was designed to collect equal numbers of male-male, female-female, and male-female conversations for comparative purposes.[5]

Of the conversations among same-sex pairs (equally divided between 10 male-male and 10 female-female pairs), all parties were white, apparently middle-class persons from approximately twenty to thirty-five years of age with relationships varying from close friendship to that between nurse and patient. The eleven cross-sex pairs were also apparently middle class, under thirty, and white. All but one were university students. Relationships varied from intimacy to first-time acquaintanceship, with one instance of a formal status relationship (see footnote 5). The topics of these exchanges varied widely, touching on everyday concerns. Close friends and lovers quarreled and confessed insecurities to one another, and people meeting for the first time exchanged social amenities.

Classifying Overlaps and Interruptions

Each author inspected the transcripts for instances of simultaneous speech and employed the definitions of overlap and interruption specified below to produce an initial classification of these events. The results of this independent classification were then compared. Of 86 instances of simultaneous speech classified, there was agreement between the authors on 80 (93%). The disagreements were resolved by discussion of the particular utterance.

Two-Party Conversations

The selection of two-party conversations was not accidental. The model outlined above applies, in principle, to any number of participants in a given conversation, although Sacks et al. (1974) suggest that for larger groups (e.g., four or more) there is a tendency for talk to divide into two or more distinct conversations. Our reason for choosing two-party talk was that it is a simpler case to analyze.

In conversations with three or more participants, who speaks next is problematic; this is not the case in two-party talk where the alternation of speakers follows an ABAB ... pattern. Moreover, certain phenomena will be observed only infrequently in two-party talk, e.g., simultaneous starts by two speakers. Simultaneous starts in two-party conversation can be observed after what appear to be lapses, i.e., where current speaker stops for an interval and then elects to continue, and next speaker self-selects.

These considerations notwithstanding, *when* a next speaker commences her utterance remains an interesting problem. A next speaker needn't concern herself that some other next speaker will commence speaking if she doesn't start first, thus eliminating the systemic pressure toward early starts characteristic of multi-party conversations. Thus, two-party conversations are perhaps the best case to inspect for the purposes at hand.

Transcription

Transcription was done by the authors according to a set of conventions modeled after those suggested by Gail Jefferson (see Appendix). Silences between utterances were timed by stop watch twice and averaged. Those portions of our tapes actually transcribed were selected by the criteria that a segment exhibit a pattern (more than two instances) of (a) noticeable silence between speaker turns and/or (b) instances of simultaneous speech, without regard to other features present, e.g., who overlapped whom. Portions of our tapes which were not transcribed included many stretches of talk containing neither noticeable silences nor instances of simultaneous speech (for both same-sex and cross-sex pairs). However, no segment of two-party conversation excluded from transcription by our selection criteria contained any instance of simultaneous speech initiated by a female in a cross-sex pair. Insofar as was possible, the topical coherence of each segment was preserved.

Generality

This collection of conversations does not, of course, constitute a probability sample of conversationalists or conversations. Hence, simple projections from findings based on this collection to conversationalists or conversations at large cannot be justified by the usual logic of statistical inference. The stability of any empirical finding cannot, in any event, be established by a single study. The present research serves to illustrate the utility of Sacks' *et al.* (1974) model as a means of locating significant problems in the area of language and interaction and as a point of departure for further study. Further, more systematic research should settle the question of the stability and generality of our findings concerning sex role differences in conversation. With this note of caution entered, we proceed to the examination of our data.

USING THE MODEL: SIMULTANEOUS SPEECH

The turn-taking mechanism described by Sacks *et al.* (1974) is so constructed that under ideal conditions conversations generated via its use would exhibit, among other features, a minimum of perceptible gaps between speaker turns and no instances of simultaneous talk (e.g., "overlaps"). Parties to such conversations would be observed to alternate their turns at speaking precisely on cue.

As noted earlier, clean and prompt transitions between speaker turns are conditional in part on the competent listenership of the potential next speaker, i.e., the current speaker's utterance must be analyzed in the course of its development in order for the listener to be prepared to commence a turn at a transition place, either by virtue of being selected to speak next or on the basis of self-selection. Indeed, the provision that the self-selector who speaks first gains the turn encourages the intended next speaker in a multi-party conversation to begin at the earliest point of a transition place. This leads to the systematic possibility of briefly overlapping the current speaker. The likelihood of an overlap is also increased if the current speaker varies the articulation of the last syllable or syllables of a unit-type:

A1: I know what you thought I know you://
A2: [Ya] still see her anymore (?)

or adds a tag question:

A2: Oh I did too::: it just doesn't sit well with them not being specialized enough//right (?)
A1: [Or] empirically grounded enough ha (!).

A speaker who has been allocated a turn has the initial right to one unit-type, e.g., a sentence. A sentence, in the course of its development, may project a possible completion point (i.e., the end of a sentence):

B: Well::: my appointment was for two o'clock.

However, this sentence (and hence, the unit-type) can be extended by the speaker:

B: Well::: my appointment was for two o'clock 'n (x) I have a class at three.

A listener, presumably performing an on-going analysis of this sentence, may exercise a legitimate option to self-select as next speaker:

B1: ... 'n I have a class at three//so
B2: [I'm] sure you'll be in by then dear. . . .

In our view, overlaps are instances of simultaneous speech where a speaker other than the current speaker begins to speak at or very close to a possible transition place in a current speaker's utterance (i.e., within the boundaries of the last word). It is this proximity to a legitimate point of speaker alternation that leads us to distinguish overlaps from interruptions.[6]

An interruption in this context, then, is seen as penetrating the boundaries of a unit-type *prior* to the last lexical constituent that could define a possible terminal boundary of a unit-type:

B2:   Know what 'cha mean (#) we went camping in Mojave last//
B1:   [Oh] didja go with Mark in August (?)[7]

or,

B: That sounds fantastic (#) not everybody can jus' spend a day in
       some//place
A: [Well] we've already established the fact that um he's not y'know
       just <u>anyone</u> (.)

The category of overlaps, as we have defined them, explicitly allows some margin of error in the transition between speaker turns. However, interruptions can be viewed as *violations* of the turn-taking system rules (which provide that the proper place for transition between speakers is at the terminal boundary of a unit-type or possible unit-type). How are these "errors" and "violations" distributed in our transcripts?[8]

Patterns of Overlap and Interruption

Because of the small number of observations involved, we have collapsed the results of our tabulations for same-sex conversations (male-male and female-female) into one table (see Table 1). There were 7 instances of simultaneous speech classified as interruptions and 22 classified as overlaps.[9] What is striking about Table 1 is that both overlaps and interruptions appear to be symmetrically distributed between speakers. That is, speaker transition errors (overlaps) and violations (interrupts) seem to be fairly equally divided between the first and second speakers in these conversations; or, put another way, the distribution approaches maximum variance.

Table 1
INTERRUPTIONS AND OVERLAPS IN 20 SAME-SEX
TWO-PARTY CONVERSATIONAL SEGMENTS

	FIRST SPEAKER*	SECOND SPEAKER	TOTAL
INTERRUPTIONS	43% (3)	57% (4)	100% (7)
OVERLAPS	55% (12)	45% (10)	100% (22)

*For a given segment, the person speaking first is designated first speaker; the person speaking second is thus a second speaker. There is no necessary implication that "first speaker" is the one who initiated the conversation, e.g., the first to utter a greeting, etc.

Turning to Table 2, in cross-sex conversations there were 48 instances of simultaneous speech classified as interruptions and 9 classified as overlaps. The pattern displayed by Table 2 is dramatic: virtually all the interruptions and overlaps are by the male speakers (98% and 100%, respectively). The cross-sex

Table 2
INTERRUPTIONS AND OVERLAPS IN 11 CROSS-SEX
TWO-PARTY CONVERSATIONAL SEGMENTS

	MALES	FEMALES	TOTAL
INTERRUPTIONS	96% (46)	4% (2)	100% (48)
OVERLAPS	100% (9)	——	100% (9)

conversational segments we examined are thus clearly asymmetrical with regard to the occurrence of violations and speaker errors.

Since our observations of simultaneous speech are based on a collection of conversational segments, it is possible that one or two conversational pairs could have contributed a disproportionate number of these instances to the overall pattern. If this were the case, it is conceivable that some unusual circumstances or some quirk of personality could have produced these remarkable distributions.

Reviewing the transcripts, we found that 5 out of the 11 male-female segments contained a total of 9 overlaps; 18 percent of the segments contained 66 percent of the overlaps. All were, of course, done by males. For the 20 same-sex pairs, half yielded a total of 22 overlaps, with 64 percent of the overlaps located in 15 percent of the segments. Thus if the distribution of overlaps across the segments is construed as evidence of clustering, we would have to conclude that the pattern is essentially identical for both cross-sex and same-sex pairs.

Ten of the 11 male-female segments exhibited interruptions, ranging from a low of 2 to a high of 13 and averaging 4.2 per transcript. The segment containing 13 interruptions (27 percent of the total) occurred between the female teaching assistant (see footnote 6) and a male undergraduate who repeatedly interrupted her attempts to explain a concept. The 7 interruptions that occurred in the same-sex conversations, in contrast, were concentrated in only 3 of the 20 or 15 percent of the segments. Thus it might be argued that the occurrence of interruptions is clustered in a few conversations for the same-sex pairs, while almost uniformly distributed across cross-sex pairs. This contrast in the distribution of interruptions vis a vis overlaps cannot be fully analyzed here, although it suggests, if anything, that interruptions are idiosyncratic in same-sex conversations and systematic in cross-sex conversations. For example, one possibility is that males conversing with females orient themselves to the role of listener differently than they do with one another. For, if interruptions are viewed as violations of a speaker's rights, continual or frequent interruption might be viewed as disregard for a speaker, or for what a speaker has to say.

Here, we are dealing with a class of speakers, females, whose rights to speak appear to be casually infringed upon by males.

Hence, on the basis of these observations, we note that at least for the transcripts we have inspected, there is a marked asymmetry between males and females with respect to interruption, and, perhaps to a lesser extent, with respect to overlap. The incidence of interruptions, which are violations of a speaker's right to complete a turn, and of overlaps, which we have viewed as errors indigenous to the speaker transition process, are much higher and more uniformly distributed across the male-female segments than proves to be the case for the same-sex transcripts.

USING THE MODEL: SILENCES

Silences in the conversational interchange are also possible outcomes provided by the model. The operation of the rule-set does not *command* participants to speak; even a next speaker selected by the current speaker (and thus obliged to take the turn thereby transferred) may pause before speaking. Moreover, since, at some points, potential next speakers may elect not to speak in the absence of selection by current speaker and current speaker may not elect to continue, a discontinuity in conversational flow—which Sacks *et al.* (1974) term a "lapse"—may occur. Many conversations proceed with few if any lapses; yet others are characterized by frequent and sometimes lengthy gaps between speaker turns. (Recall that our segments were selected partly on the basis of silence.)

There is nothing inherent in the turn-taking model which would suggest that, over a range of turns and of different conversations, one party to a conversation would fall silent more frequently than another. Indeed, all the model furnishes by way of a characterization of speakers are the categories "current speaker" and "next speaker." Accordingly, we would expect that on the average silences *between* speaker turns would tend to be symmetrically distributed (we cannot consider the silence within speaker turns here).

For two-party conversations, this assumption can be expressed as a ratio of silences (measured in seconds and tenths of seconds) with 1.0 indicating equality (either exactly equal silences or the absence of any gaps whatsoever). This is admittedly a crude measurement which does not distinguish between types of silences (e.g., those that represent a thoughtful pause before answering a question, or those following upon a brusque interruption), but it should inform us as to the existence of gross asymmetries.

The ratio of silence was computed as follows. The total silence in seconds (and tenths of seconds) for the least silent speaker was divided by the total for the most silent speaker for each of the same-sex pairs, thus avoiding any ratio greater than 1.0 (and hence, an arbitrary maximization of any differences that might exist).

A speaker's total silence was determined by counting the elapsed time prior to speaking after the previous speaker had concluded a turn. If a previous speaker spoke again after a period of time—without a next speaker beginning an utterance—the intervening silence was treated as *internal* to that speaker's turn and thus not counted.

Patterns of Silence

Figure 2 charts the silence ratios for the three sets of conversational segments. It is immediately evident that each female in the cross-sex segments exhibits the most silence, where for same-sex conversations, the distribution of silence is more nearly equal. It is also worth noting that the female-female and male-female distributions do not overlap, and that the other same-sex distribution does so only slightly. For our transcripts, there is an obvious asymmetry in the allocation of silences between men and women conversationalists relative to their same-sex counterparts.

What accounts for these differences? We can begin to address this question by observing that 62 percent of the females' aggregate silence in the cross-sex segments followed upon three types of events in the preceding turns: (1) a delayed "minimal response" by the male; (2) an overlap by the male; and (3) an interruption by the male. In the two instances where a female interrupted a male, there was no ensuing silence prior to the male speaking again. A few silences do follow delayed minimal responses, overlaps and interrupts in the same-sex conversations. However, there are fewer (45 percent vs 67 percent) of such ensuing silences spread across the three types of events and the average aggregate silence is 1.35 seconds (with a range from 1.0 to 2.2) as compared with 3.21 seconds (with a range from 1.0 to 12.0) for females in the cross-sex segments.

If we subtract all the silences following the delayed minimal responses, overlaps, and interruptions for the cross-sex segments, we may gain some information about the effect of these male-initiated events on their female co-conversationalists. (Since the delayed minimal response is, by our definition, preceded by at least one second of silence, these silences must also be excluded if the silence following them is to be disregarded.)

This operation yields a mean ratio of silence of .36 with the median falling at .28 and a range from 1 to 1.2. This adjusted mean is somewhat closer to those for the same-sex distributions (see Figure 3), but there is more variance (s^2 = .129 versus .033 for the original distribution). Although some slight

Figure 2

Distribution of silence ratios for female-female, male-male and male-female conversational segments

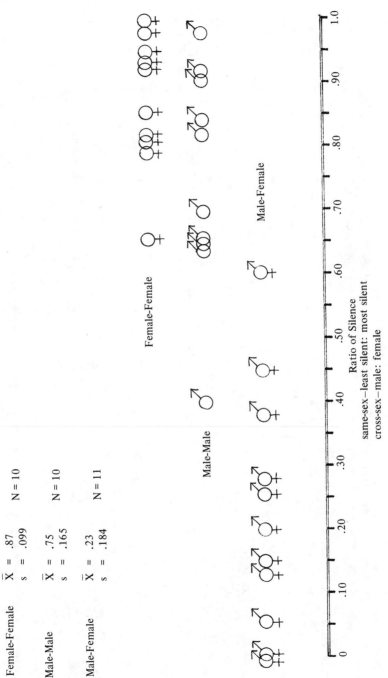

Figure 3

Distribution of silence ratios for female-female, male-male, and male-female conversational segments excluding silences in male-female segments due to overlaps, interruptions, and minimal responses

Female-Female $\overline{X}$ = .87   N = 10
                 s = .099

Male-Male $\overline{X}$ = .75   N = 10
                 s = .165

Male-Female $\overline{X}$ = .36   N = 11
                 s = .36

Female-Female

Male-Male

Male-Female

Ratio of Silence
same-sex — least silent: most silent
cross-sex — male: female

0   .10   .20   .30   .40   .50   .60   .70   .80   .90   1.0 1.20

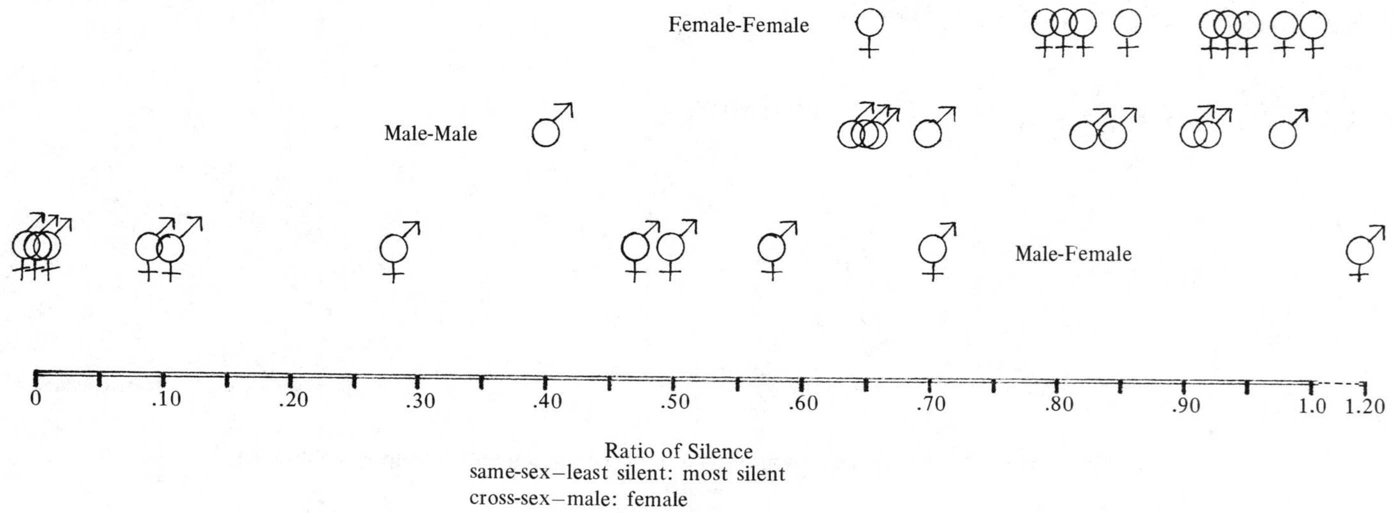

equalization in the silence ratio does occur by discounting silences following delayed minimal responses, overlaps and interruptions, it appears to us that the overall asymmetry between males and females still remains. One reason for this may be that the occurrence of one or more of these three silence-inducing events in the course of conversation may affect the subsequent conversational participation of the female, a possibility that we cannot elaborate here. It is quite evident, however, that there is a relationship between the occurrence of delayed minimal responses, overlaps, and interruptions, on the one hand, and noticeable silence prior to a next speaker's turn on the other. This relationship is most pronounced for females in cross-sex conversations. We now turn to a more detailed consideration of this relationship.

Delayed Minimal Responses

Consider the following excerpt from a male-female transcript:

(A is the male, and B the female)

| 1 | B: | This thing with uh Sandy 'n Karen |
| 2 | | 'n Paul is really bugging me |

(5.0)

| 3 | A: | Um |

(3.0)

4	B:	Well it's really <u>complicating</u> things
5		y'know between Sandy 'n Karen 'n I
6		because I know what's ( ) going on
7		'n I can see uh there's no contradiction
8		to me at all//

| 9 | A: | [Um] hmm |

(#)

10	B:	In between Sandy finding (#) I mean in
11		between Paul finding Sandy attractive (#)
12		'n Paul finding um uh <u>Karen</u>
13		attractive

(4.0)

| 14 | A: | Mm hmm |

(6.0)

```
15    B:    Y'know an' sleeping with either
16          of 'em of whatever (2.0) the
17          problem (x) problem is that when
18          he started finding Karen attractive
19          um (#) it was at the same
20          time uh as he was finding Sandy
21          unattractive
      (10.0)
```

It seems evident that B (the female) introduces a topic in lines 1 and 2 (her feelings about the relationship between the three persons mentioned) and attempts to elaborate it in her subsequent remarks. It is also obvious that A (the male), in response to B's attempts, employs several minimal responses ("Um," "Um hmm") which were discussed earlier as types of supportive responses one party gives to another in conversation (Fishman, 1973; Schegloff, 1972b). The difference here is that these minimal responses are (with the exception of the "um hmm" of line 9) preceded by pauses up to 10 seconds in length. Instead of finely timed placement within the structure of the current speaker's utterance, as suggested by Fishman (1973), these are retarded beyond the end of the utterance.

In our male-female segments, the mean silence for all females following a delayed minimal response was 3.85 seconds (versus 1.4 seconds for the three instances found in the same-sex conversations). Eleven of the 13 delayed minimal responses observed in our data were followed by perceptible silences, and ten of these were timed as longer than one second.

The difference between a monologue and a dialogue is not the number of persons present but the articulation of the roles of speaker and listener. We are inclined to the view that the "promptly" issued minimal response serves to display active listenership (in effect, "I understand what you are saying") with, moreover, the least intervention in the development of a topic by the other speaker (in effect, "Go on, say more."). That speakers currently holding the floor are oriented to the display of active listenership is sometimes indicated by the use of question-like forms ("you know") to elicit response from the putative listener.

Such displays of active listenership can, of course, be simulated. We have in mind here the "yes dear" response that husbands are said to utter while their wives talk and they read the newspaper, a kind of minimum hearership sustained by an artfully located standardized response. Poor timing (among other things) can quickly betray feigned involvement or at least call attention to some difficulty in the course of talk.

The delayed minimal response and the ensuing silence may thus *locate* a point in conversation found to be problematic by its participants. If we assume that the demonstration of active attention and the invitation to continue a turn support the speaker's developing a topic, then retarding the response may function to signal a lack of understanding or even disinterest in and inattention to the current talk. The silence that follows a delayed minimal response reflects, we believe, the other speaker's uncertainty as to her partner's orientation to the current state of the conversation, an uncertainty generated by these several possibilities. The implications of the foregoing in the context of the pattern of male-initiated retarded responses will be discussed in connection with the examination below of the silences following interruptions.

Interruptions and Ensuing Silences

We have already noted the tendency for speakers in our transcripts to fall silent for noticeable (if brief) periods of time subsequent to being interrupted. This observation relies almost entirely on the response of women in the cross-sex segments who, in the aggregate, paused for an average of 3.14 seconds after 32 or 70 percent of the interruptions recorded. Two women in the same-sex conversations each paused for 1 second in response to 2 of the seven or 29 percent of the interruptions recorded there. Silence also followed overlaps, but less frequently and for shorter average durations than it did interruptions.

Our position, which follows that of Sacks *et al.* (1974), is that interruptions are a violation of a current speaker's right to complete a turn, or more precisely, to reach a possible transition place in a unit-type's progression. In an earlier, unpublished manuscript, Sacks (n.d.) discusses the social control devices available to conversationalists in dealing with violations such as interruptions. One type of negative sanction is the complaint, i.e., a formulation of a speaker's previous utterance as a certain kind of act. Such a complaint could be: "You just interrupted me" or, in the case of a series of such acts, "You keep interrupting me."

We have observed a variant of this type of sanction which includes a counter-interruption reclaiming the turn just lost:

(A1 and A2 are both males)

1	A1:	Well (,) I moved again ya know (x)
2		<u>you</u> know Del Playa (?) Well I//
3	A2:	[Shee] :::et (!) You don't mean//
4	A1:	[Let] me finish::: no I didn't move
5		back in with Cathy (.)

The above example is the only instance in our data where an explicit negative sanction follows on an interruption and it occurs in a male-male segment. Indeed, even after repeated interruptions, women in our transcripts enter no such complaint, and, as the preceding remarks suggest, when the interrupting male completes his utterance, the female typically pauses before speaking again. A possible explanation for the relative absence of sanctioning in our data lies in the locally managed character of conversation. Elsewhere (Sacks: 1972 n.d.) it is suggested that complaints must be entered in the turns immediately subsequent to violations if they are to be effective. However, voicing a complaint also constitutes changing the topic of the talk at that point. A speaker interrupted in the course of topic development may choose to disregard the violation in order to continue her trend of thought. In this respect, the females' pauses before speaking again might indicate points at which the foci of topic development must be recollected after interruptions.

While we cannot demonstrate it here, we believe that both retarded minimal responses and interruptions function as topic control mechanisms. For example, if retarded minimal responses are indeed signals of non-support for the continued development of a topic by one speaker over a series of turns (or by continuation of the same turn) a series of retarded responses should serve, at a minimum, to bring the topic to a close. We have observed this pattern in 3 of the 10 male-female transcripts.

Similarly, repeated interruptions of the same speaker by her partner also seem to be followed by topic change. If the interrupter is the one who is developing a topic, the interruptions appear to restrict the rights of the person being interrupted to contribute to the developing topic. We view the production of both retarded minimal responses and interruptions by male speakers interacting with females as an assertion of the right to control the topic of conversation reminiscent of adult-child conversations where in most instances the child has restricted rights to speak and to be listened to (cf. Sacks, 1972b). Indeed, our preliminary work on a set of adult-child transcripts indicates that the patterns of interruption found there (adults interrupt children overwhelmingly) most closely resemble the male-female patterns and contrast with those of the same-sex adult conversants we have discussed in this paper.

CONCLUDING REMARKS

It will be useful at this point to recall that Sacks *et al.* (1974) view the turn-taking system as an economy in which the turn is distributed in much the same fashion as a commodity. Differences between males and females in the distribution of turns may, for example, be parallel to the differences between them in the society's economic system, i.e., a matter of advantage. It can be noted that, in effecting the distribution of turns, the operation of the turn-taking system determines the distribution of resources for accomplishing interactional events *through* conversation, e.g., introducing and developing topics. Just above, we suggested that males assert an asymmetrical right to control topics and do so without evident repercussions. We are led to the conclusion that, at least in our transcripts, men deny equal status to women as conversational partners with respect to rights to the full utilization of their turns and support for the development of topics. Thus we speculate that just as male dominance is exhibited through male control of macro-institutions in society, it is also exhibited through control of at least a part of one micro-institution.

Before closing, we wish to reiterate one point. We are not claiming that male-female conversations invariably exhibit the asymmetric patterns reported in this paper. A challenging task for further research is the specification of conditions under which they occur, i.e., the conditions under which sex roles become relevant to the conduct of conversationalists and sex-linked differences in conversational interaction emerge.

NOTES

[1]This paper does not concern itself specifically with the nonverbal component of conversational interaction. Gestures, posture, patterns of eye contact, and intonation are clearly involved in the total communicative exchange between speakers. Moreover, research by Duncan (1972) suggests that nonverbal cues (e.g., hand gesticulation) are relevant to turn-taking in the interview situation. However, since our data consist of transcripts of audiotapes, we obviously cannot address such matters. Thus, we ignore them in our discussion even though they are potentially important variables to consider.

[2]The transcribing conventions used for our data are presented in the Appendix to this paper. Here, the = sign following a speaker's last word indicates a transition to the first word of the next speaker's utterance which is free of any perceivable gap.

[3]The use of the term "decision" here does not necessarily imply any *conscious* choice or deliberation of the sort that could be retrieved by introspection or elicited by interview, but instead is used descriptively as a shorthand reference to the process of selection from sets of alternative acts that constitute different states of talk.

[4]The analogy to the notion of a generative grammar is obvious.

[5]The research plan called for ten segments each for the male-male, female-female and male-female conversations. In the course of recording these conversations, we were given a tape of a discussion section conducted by a female teaching assistant. One segment of this tape contained a two-party interaction with the teaching assistant and a male undergraduate. Inclusion of this segment increased the number of male-female segments to 11, but since it contained the only instances of a female interrupting a male we could not exclude it. It is worth noting that in this case of female-initiated interruption, the female is the status superior (teaching assistant vis-à-vis undergraduate). Nevertheless, the male undergraduate

interrupted this woman eleven times to her two. Our future research will, in part, deal with the relationship between sex role status differentials and other types of status inequalities, e.g., employer-employee.

[6]In coding instances of simultaneous speech in terms of our distribution between overlap and interruption, we relied on our intuitive knowledge of the English language to decide where possible completion points occurred. In cases where an utterance was ambiguous (e.g., could receive more than one syntactic analysis) we relied on the topical context for disambguation. We hope to employ more formal linguistic analysis in subsequent research.

[7]The careful reader will note that the excerpt to the left of the double slashes could be interpreted as a possibly complete sentence. However, the context of B2's utterance led the authors to decide that "last" was used as an adjective rather than an adverb; thus B1's intrusion constituted an interruption of B2's unit-type completion.

[8]In the analysis, we do not take certain steps that some would assume to be routine. We do not employ a chi-square test to our percentage tables because more than one of the units of analysis (interruptions and overlaps) can be contributed by each individual, thus violating the assumption of independent observations. Since our collection of segments is not a probability sample, we do not present tests of significance which depend for their interpretation on just such a sample. We feel that the regularities in our data are sufficiently strong to warrant reporting them here if caution is exercised in their interpretation.

[9]The segments from which these instances were drawn were not standardized, and the figures presented are thus not rates of interruption or overlap per some unit measure. Among the many possible units are number of words uttered, temporal duration of speech, number of turns, number of unit-types in a turn, number of unit-types, etc. There are a number of problems connected with each of these choices, not the least of which is determining the theoretical rationale for selecting among them. For present purposes, we have elected not to introduce any arbitrary standardization since whatever unit we selected would not alter the basic fact that in our transcripts an overwhelming proportion of interruptions are done by men to women. These considerations also pertain to the discussion of silences.

REFERENCES

Bernard, Jesse. (1968). *The sex game.* Englewood Cliffs, N.J.: Prentice-Hall.

Brend, Ruth M. (1972). Male-female intonation patterns in American English. *Proceedings of the Seventh International Congress of Phonetic Sciences, 1971.* The Hague: Mouton. Reprinted in Barrie Thorne and Nancy Henley (eds.) (1975), *Language and sex: difference and dominance.* Rowley, Mass.: Newbury House.

Duncan, Starkey, Jr. (1972). Some signals and rules for taking speaking turns in conversations. *Journal of Personality and Social Psychology,* 23, 283-92.

Fishman, Pamela. (1973). Interaction: the work women do. Unpublished master's paper, Univ. of California, Dept. of Sociology, Santa Barbara.

Henley, Nancy, & Thorne, Barrie. (1975). Sex differences in language, speech and nonverbal communication: an annotated bibliography. In Barrie Thorne and Nancy Henley (eds.), *Language and sex: difference and dominance.* Rowley, Mass.: Newbury House.

Key, Mary Ritchie. (1972). Linguistic behavior of male and female. *Linguistics,* 88 (August 15), 15-31.

Kramer, Cheris. (1973). Women's speech: separate but unequal? *Quarterly Journal of Speech,* 60, 14-24. Reprinted in Barrie Thorne and Nancy Henley (eds.) (1975), *Language and sex: difference and dominance.* Rowley, Mass.: Newbury House.

Lakoff, Robin. (1973). Language and woman's place. *Language and Society,* 2, 45-79.

Sacks, Harvey. (1972*a*). An initial investigation of the usability of conversational data for doing sociology. In David Sudnow (ed.), *Studies in social interaction.* Glencoe: The Free Press.

———. (1972*b*). On the analyzability of stories by children. In John Gumperz and Dell Hymes (eds.), *Directions in sociolinguistics.* New York: Holt, Rinehart & Winston.

———. (n.d.). Aspects of the sequential organization of conversation. Unpublished manuscript.

Sacks, Harvey, Schegloff, Emanuel A., & Jefferson, Gail. (1974). A simplest systematics for the organization of turn-taking for conversation. *Language,* 50, 696-735.

Schegloff, Emanuel. (1972*a*). Notes on a conversational practice: formulating place. In David Sudnow (ed.), *Studies in social interaction.* Glencoe: The Free Press.

———. (1972*b*). Sequencing in conversational openings. In John Gumperz and Dell Hymes (eds.), *Directions in sociolinguistics.* New York: Holt, Rinehart & Winston.

Schegloff, Emanuel A., & Sacks, Harvey. (1973). Opening up closings. *Semantica,* 8, 289-327.

Soskin, William F., & John, Vera P. (1963). The study of spontaneous talk. In Roger Barker (ed.), *The stream of behavior.* New York: Appleton, Century, Crofts.

Strodtbeck, Fred L., & Mann, Richard D. (1956). Sex role differentiation in jury deliberations. *Sociometry,* 19, 3-11.

Strodtbeck, Fred L., James, Rita M., & Hawkins, Charles. (1957). Social status in jury deliberations. *American Sociological Review,* 22, 713-19.

APPENDIX

TRANSCRIBING CONVENTIONS

The transcript techniques and symbols were devised by Gail Jefferson in the course of research undertaken with Harvey Sacks. Techniques are revised, symbols added or dropped as they seem useful to the work. There is no guarantee or suggestion that the symbols or transcripts alone would permit the doing of any unspecified research tasks; they are properly used as an adjunct to the tape recorded materials.

(x) I've (x) I've met him once	Parentheses encasing an "x" indicate a hitch or stutter on the part of the speaker.
// J: Well really//I C: I don't care	Double obliques indicate the point at which one speaker is overlapped or interrupted by another. When nothing appears to the right of this symbol, the speaker has been overlapped in the middle of the last syllable preceding the slashes.
[ ] J: If I//could D: [But] you can't	Brackets around the first part of a speaker's utterance mean that the portion bracketed overlapped or interrupted a previous speaker's utterance.
::: A: Well::: now	Colons indicate that the immediately prior syllable is prolonged.
= A: 'Swat I said= B: But you didn't	An equal sign is used to indicate that no time elapses between the objects "latched" by the marks. Often used as a transcribing convenience, it can also mean that a next speaker starts at precisely the end of a current speaker's utterance.
_____	Underscoring is utilized to represent heavier emphasis (in speaker's pitch) on words so marked.
(?), (!), (,), (.) Are you sure (?)	Punctuation marks are used for intonation, not grammar.
(word) If you (will) please	Single parentheses with words in them indicate that something was heard, but the transcriber is

not sure what it was. These can serve as a warning that the transcript may be unreliable.

( )
Why do you ( ) it

Single parentheses without words in them indicate that something was said but not caught by the transcriber.

((softly))
Ha ((chuckles))

Double parentheses enclose "descriptions," not transcribed utterances.

(#)
But (#) you said

Score sign indicates a pause of one second or less that wasn't possible to discriminate precisely.

(1.2)

Numbers encased in parentheses indicate the seconds and tenths of seconds ensuing between speaker's turns. They may also be used to indicate the duration of pauses internal to a speaker's turn.

SEX DIFFERENTIATION IN LANGUAGE*

Ann Bodine

INTRODUCTION

Sex differentiation in language has been variously discussed in anthropological and linguistic literature under the topic of gender and under the topic of women's language or speech (more rarely, men's and women's language or speech). Throughout the seventeenth and eighteenth centuries European scholars, explorers, and missionaries to Asia, Africa, the Americas, Australia, and the Pacific produced a steady stream of descriptions of languages with gender,[1] which they considered unremarkable, and languages in which women and men spoke differently, which they considered remarkable and treated as an entirely different phenomenon from gender.

In the nineteenth century there were new investigations of languages for which female-male speech differences had been repoited earlier by ethnographers who wanted to see how the female-male speech differences had survived colonization or other contact with Western society. There were also numerous second- and third-hand commentaries on the earlier primary sources, as well as descriptions of previously unreported languages with gender or with differences in the speech of women and men.

A groundbreaking early discussion of the general phenomenon of sex differentiation in language was Frazer (1900). Frazer stands out because he discussed together, as possibly related phenomena, both gender and speech differences between women and men. Frazer suggested the term "subjective gender" for differentiation based on sex of speaker, in order to relate it to the phenomenon of gender, for which he suggested the term "objective gender." The particular relationship which Frazer postulated between the two was that gender and differences between the speech of women and men may be connected through historical development, rather than that they may be related as different manifestations of similar social, psychological, or cognitive tendencies, which this writer considers more plausible. At any rate, Frazer's paper was groundbreaking in even treating the two phenomena together.

---

*An earlier version of parts of this paper was presented in a longer paper at the Conference on Women and Language, Rutgers University, April, 1973.

Remarkably, all of this interest in female-male speech differences inspired no serious investigations of such differences among Europeans. A possible explanation is that the forms which were described under the rubric "men's and women's languages (or speech)" were generally exclusively used by either one sex or the other. This type of differentiation, which may be called *sex-exclusive differentiation,* appears to be relatively uncommon in European languages. Differences in frequency of occurrence of any form between the speech of women and men, which may be called *sex-preferential differentiation,* are less accessible to conscious awareness and, since they require assessment of relative probability of occurrence, are more difficult to describe accurately. Some of those who discussed female-male speech differences among exotic peoples undoubtedly saw no connection with anything occurring in their own society.

Paradoxically, a diametrically opposite tendency also served to inhibit the empirical investigation of sex differences in the speech of Europeans; that is, the tendency of scholars of the period to serve forth as obvious fact, in need of no further investigation, what "everyone knows" about the "different" way women speak, while men's speech was automatically equated with *the* language. In general, everyone knew that "even our own (English/ French/ Spanish/ German. . .) women speak in their own (modest/ peculiar/ illogical. . .) way, using trivial vocabulary, avoiding harsh and unseemly words, speaking a conservative form of the language, talking too much. . . ." Such statements were sometimes made in the context of the description of female-male differences in exotic languages. This tendency inhibited the serious investigation of sex-preferential differentiation in European languages. Although most writers made only passing reference to their own or their culture's stereotypes of how women speak, the practice received its highest development in Jespersen (1922), who filled much of a chapter with what everyone knew about how "different" women's speech is. Jespersen's work also contains a critique of the widely accepted view that the sex-exclusive female-male speech differences among the Carib Indians should be considered separate languages. Instead Jespersen suggested that the Carib situation was merely an extreme development of a widespread sociolinguistic phenomenon.

Kraus (1924, cited in Reik, 1954) surveyed female-male speech differences in African, American Indian, and Australian Aboriginal languages and compared the avoidance of names of in-laws or words sounding like the names of in-laws (which in a society with unilineal descent produces some speech differences between men and women) to the inability of a psychoanalytic patient to pronounce the name of a person in a painful relationship. Kraus' work was summarized by Reik (1954), who compared female-male speech differences arising from other types of word taboos to the modification or distortion of emotionally charged words by psychoanalytic patients. Although in-law avoidance and other word taboos account for only a tiny fraction of female-male speech differences, Reik did make a serious attempt to compare sex differentiation in European languages with that of exotic languages and urged that the comparison be extended by others.

Two later reviews of sex differentiation in language were Haas (1944) and Furfey (1944). Haas presented new description of female-male speech differences in three Muskogean languages, in addition to reviews of other twentieth century reports. Furfey, like Frazer in an earlier period, considered both gender and female-male speech differences together. Unlike Frazer, Furfey postulated that the relation between the two is that of different manifestations of a similar social tendency. Furthermore, Furfey was unique among his contemporaries and predecessors in explicitly tying linguistic sex differentiation into wider considerations of social structure by comparing female-male language differences with language differences between social classes. However, the rich mine of possibilities for the investigation of relations between linguistic and nonlinguistic phenomena suggested by Furfey was neglected by a generation of social scientists in favor of the similar but socially less threatening problem of the relation between color terminology and nonlinguistic behavior. At the time of their publication the reviews by Haas and Furfey appear to have stimulated only a single new description, that of Flannery (1946), and, like earlier writing on the subject, inspired no investigation of sex differentiation in European languages.

With the belated awakening of interest in the general phenomenon of linguistic sex differentiation, its causes and consequences, which has been brought about by the resurgence of concern with sexually based social inequality, a new review seems justified. This paper attempts to consider and compare, in a comprehensive way, the various channels through which sex differentiation is manifested in a variety of widely differing languages. After this survey, attitudes toward linguistic sex differentiation are discussed—both the attitudes of the members of a speech community toward their own language's sex differentiation, as well as the attitudes of the ethnographers toward the linguistic sex differentiation they discovered.

CLASSIFICATION OF LINGUISTIC SEX DIFFERENTIATION

Aside from acoustic and prosodic differences, most types of sex-based language differences which have been reported can be displayed in a chart like that of Table 1, in which one axis of classification is the type of language difference (difference in pronunciation, difference in form) and the other axis of classification is the position in the conversational interaction of the person whose sex decides which form will be used (speaker, spoken to, speaker plus spoken to, spoken about). In Table 1 a variety of languages and language families are classified along these two axes, with each box numbered for row and column in the upper right corner. Thus category 1A contains those languages which have pronunciation differences based on sex of speaker. After some language names there is a parenthetic reference to another section. For example, in category 1A Gros Ventre is cross-referenced to 2A, indicating that in addition to having pronunciation differences based on sex of speaker, Gros Ventre also has differences in form based on sex of speaker, and is listed in category 2A as well. Table 2 lists the sources used in compiling Table 1.

The terms sex-exclusive and sex-preferential differentiation were introduced earlier in this paper in the context of language differences based on sex of speaker. Both terms apply equally to language differences based on sex of spoken to or spoken about. Thus, if a certain title (or pronoun, salutation, verb form, etc.) is used only in speaking to a woman, this is considered sex-exclusive differentiation. Similarly, if a certain adjective is usually applied to a man, this is considered sex-preferential differentiation. The term "sex-preferential" does not distinguish individual variation from total variation for the speech community (some of the women all of the time, all of the women some of the time, most of the women most of the time). No such ambiguity exists with sex-exclusive differentiation, which includes only those differences which are maintained by virtually all of the speakers virtually all of the time.

DIFFERENTIATION BASED ON SEX OF SPEAKER

This type of linguistic sex differentiation is tabulated in Column A of Table 1. Differentiation based on sex of speaker was widely reported in the seventeenth and eighteenth centuries, beginning with reports of the speech of Carib women and men, who were often said, incorrectly, to speak entirely different languages. Even today differentiation based on sex of speaker is the type which is most often mentioned in connection with linguistic sex differentiation.

This discussion will exclude single-sex secret languages, usually connected with secret societies, because use of such languages is restricted to ritual occasions. Linguistic differentiation based on sex of speaker is here understood to mean that women and men differ in their usual speech. This is not to discount the possibility that in some cases these differences may have arisen when a single-sex secret language was de-ritualized and gradually or suddenly came to be used in ordinary contexts.

Most of the pronunciation differences in the speech of women and men exhibited by languages in Table 1 category 1A may be summarized by the following three correspondences. First, one sex omits one or more speech sounds which the other sex uses. Examples are Chukchee (Bogoras, 1922) and Caraya (Ehrenreich and Krause, 1912, as reported by Chamberlain, 1912) with longer

TABLE 1: CROSS-CULTURAL SUMMARY OF SEX DIFFERENTIATION IN LANGUAGE

BASED ON SEX OF:

DIFFERENCE IN:	A. SPEAKER	B. SPOKEN TO	C. SPEAKER PLUS SPOKEN TO	D. SPOKEN ABOUT
1. PRONUNCIATION	1A Bengali, Caraya, Cham, Chukchee, Creek, Eskimo, Gros Ventre (2A), Hitchiti, Koasati, Zuñi (2A).	1B	1C Yana.	1D
2. FORM: INTERJECTIONS	2A Gros Ventre (1A), Zuñi (1A). Also, according to Flannery, Cree, Algonkin, Iroquois, Ojibwa, Sioux, Fox, Yokuts.	2B ONLY IN DIRECT ADDRESS	2C	2D
PARTICLES	Japanese (2B), Thai.			
PERSONAL PRONOUNS	Japanese (2B), Thai. Yuchi? (See discussion).	Tunica, Semitic languages, pre-modern Japanese (2A).	Chiquita—affixes and a few stems.	Widespread, but far from universal. Chiquita—only in M-M speech.
TITLES		Bengali.		Widespread, but far from universal.
KINSHIP TERMINOLOGY	Many languages of Amer. Indians, Asia, Africa, according to Dixon and Kroeber.	*See below.	Carib—stems, Chiquita—usually stems, probably Yana—affixes.	Generally used in all kinship terminologies for at least some relatives.

NOUNS	Many of these also differ on basis of sex of spoken about. Yuchi? (See discussion).	*See below.	Carib—stems, Chiquita—affixes, probably Yana—affixes.	Probably all languages have sex differentiation in some nouns. Different affix in some languages, as in gender, different stem in other languages. Chiquita—gender only in M-M version.
VERBS		Semitic languages—affixes.	Probably Yana—affixes, Biloxi—only in direct address.	Gender concord often manifested in verbs.
NOUN MODIFIERS	*Differentiation in any part of language (titles, kinship, nouns, verbs, etc.) based on sex of spoken about automatically implies differentiation when these forms are used in direct address.	*See below.	Yana—affixes.	Gender concord often manifested in noun modifiers.

TABLE 2: SOURCES FOR CROSS-CULTURAL SURVEY

LANGUAGE	INVESTIGATORS & DATES
Bengali	Chatterji (pronunciation) 1921 Das (terms of reference and address, titles) 1968
Biloxi (N. Amer. Ind.)	Dorsey and Swanton 1912
Caraya (S. Amer. Ind.)	Ehrenreich and Krause 1912, as reported by Chamberlain 1912
Carib	Jespersen 1922, Frazer 1900, and others
Cham (SE Asia)	Blood 1962
Chiquita (S. Amer. Ind.)	Adam and Henry 1880
Chukchee (NE Siberia)	Bogoras 1922
Creek (N. Amer. Ind.)	Haas 1944
Eskimo	Boas' editorial notes to Eskimo section of *Handbook of American Indian Languages* 1911-38, Egede 1818, as reported by Frazer 1900
Gros Ventre (N. Amer. Ind.)	Flannery 1946
Hebrew and Other Semitic	Brunswick 1973
Hitchiti (N. Amer. Ind.)	Haas 1944
Indo-European (reconstructed)	Meillet 1923
Japanese	Own knowledge and information supplied by several native speakers
Koasati (N. Amer. Ind.)	Haas 1944
Muskogean (Creek, Hitchiti, Koasati)	Haas 1944
Nootka (N. Amer. Ind.)	Sapir 1915
Thai	Haas 1944
Tunica (N. Amer. Ind.)	Haas 1944
Yana (N. Amer. Ind.)	Sapir 1929; Dixon and Kroeber 1903
Yuchi (N. Amer. Ind.)	Wagner 1933-38
Zuñi (N. Amer. Ind.)	Bunzel 1933-38

women's forms, and the three Muskogean languages (Haas, 1944) with longer men's forms. Second, both sexes use the same number of speech sounds with the same *position* of articulation for each, but for one or more sounds the *manner* of articulation is different for women and men. Examples are Koasati (Haas, 1944), where women's final *-l* or *-n* corresponds to men's final *-s;* Bengali (Chatterji, 1921), where women's initial *n-* corresponds to men's initial *l-;* and Eskimo (Egede, 1818, as reported in Frazer, 1900, for Greenlandic Eskimo; Boas, 1911-38) where men's oral stops correspond to women's nasals, with the same position of articulation. Third, both sexes use the same number of speech sounds with approximately the same manner of articulation, but for one or more sounds the position of articulation is different for women and men. Examples are Gros Ventre (Flannery, 1946) and Zuñi (Bunzel, 1933-38). In Zuñi, women's *ty* and *č* correspond to men's *ky,* and in Gros Ventre the reverse is true. What this means is that, in any language, pronunciation differences between women and men are remarkably small. On the other hand, in a few languages these small differences occur often enough to serve as constant markers of sex.

Differences in form in the sex-based versions of any language are similar to pronunciation differences in that both are remarkably superficial. Most sex-based differences in form exhibited by languages in Table 2 row 2, may be summarized by the following correspondences. First, one sex-based version omits an affix used in the other sex-based version. Examples are Yana and Chiquita with longer male-to-male forms, and Japanese with longer women's forms. Second, the sex-based versions have one or more different, analogously patterned affixes. Examples are gender differences in some European languages. Third, for from one to forty words the sex-based versions have entirely different stems, but these stems are handled the same syntactically. Examples are two Japanese personal pronouns and several dozen Carib nouns.

Conspicuous by its absence is any profound difference in syntactic patterning, such as difference in word order, between the sex-based versions of any language. In general, the only thing done by the sex-differentiated affix is to mark sex, while all other syntactic processes for the language are the same. However, as with pronunciation differences, superficial differences in form occur frequently enough in some languages (for example, the sex-exclusive differentiation in Yana, the sex-preferential differentiation in Japanese) to serve as constant markers of sex.

Differences in form based on sex of speaker, Table 1 category 2A, are common in interjections, particles, personal pronouns, and kinship terminology. In all languages, interjections are quite peripheral to language structure and in some cases are so firmly tied to gesture as to form a bridge between sex differentiation in language and in nonlinguistic behavior. The Gros Ventre interjection of joy is a good illustration of the continuum between sex differentiation in linguistic and nonlinguistic behavior. According to Flannery (1946: 133), for Gros Ventre women the interjection of joy is a sort of rattling of the tongue, whereas for men it is the gesture-plus-vocalization popularized by Hollywood as the "war whoop." Gros Ventre women and men also have differences in gestures that are not tied to vocalization.

Thai (Haas, 1944) and Japanese[2] are examples of languages in which women and men use some sex-exclusive particles and some sex-exclusive personal pronouns, in addition to particles and personal pronouns which are common to both sexes. In both languages the sex-exclusive particles differ only slightly, but the sex-exclusive personal pronouns are entirely different words. In Japanese the common word for *I* which may be used by any speaker is *watakushi*. But there is an abbreviated form of *watakushi,* namely *atashi,* which is exclusively used by females, and a completely different word for *I,* namely *boku,* which is exclusively used by males. Although the word *boku* is freely used by grown men as well as little boys with the meaning *I,* in the case of little boys the meaning is extended to *you* and occasionally even to *he,* so that adults of both sexes frequently say to or about little boys, for example: "Boku's going to be late for school." "Doesn't boku have to go to the potty now?"

Also, in present-day Japanese, second person pronouns are differentiated based on speaker's sex (although in most cases no second person pronoun is used, particularly in formal or honorific speech). In the minority of cases in which a second person pronoun is used, there is a common form, *anata,* which may be used by a woman or a man to a woman or a man. The second person pronoun *kimi* is used exclusively by men, in speaking to female or male equals or inferiors. An exception can occur in that a female adult, such as a teacher, might very rarely use *kimi* in addressing an unruly little boy, but a woman would never use *kimi* in addressing a girl (Obayashi, 1974). In this case, as well as in the case of *boku* being used to or about a little boy, there is a feeling of the adult assimilating to the child's speech.

Japanese also has sex-preferential differentiation which is much more widespread in speech than the sex-exclusive differentiation is, often affecting most words of an utterance. For nouns, sex-preferential differentiation in Japanese consists of the addition of an honorific prefix by women. For verbs, adjectives, and adverbs, Japanese sex-preferential differentiation consists of different suffixes for women and men, with the suffix more often used by women being longer than the suffix more often used by men.

The situation with Yuchi personal pronouns is more complicated than that for Thai and Japanese personal pronouns. In fact, it is so complicated as to be in great need of reanalysis.[3] The original description of Yuchi was given by Wagner (1933-38). Furfey (1944: 220) interprets Wagner's description and analysis to mean that Yuchi has "a complicated system of personal pronouns whose correct use depends on the sex of the speaker, the sex of the person spoken of, and the relationship between them."

Consulting Wagner's original data, sex is seen to be irrelevant in the first and second person pronouns. For third person pronouns Wagner gives long lists of terms with kinship-based meanings. For example,

> *se-, sio-, sedi-,* are used by both men and women and refer to a third person singular female Yuchi. If used by men they are restricted to a female relative of the same or a descending generation as the speaker (sister, daughter, niece, granddaughter) . . . . If used by women they refer to any female of the same or a descending generation whether related or not (Wagner, 1933-38: 326).

Wagner himself states, "The reflection of the social structure of the tribe in the pronominal forms is an interesting and rare example of an interrelation between culture and language" (1933-38: 327).

Although not mentioned by Furfey, Wagner states that there is a difference between male and female speech in the noun forms as well. However, closer examination shows that there is no difference in inanimate nouns based on sex of speaker, and similarly there is no difference in non-human animate nouns, and furthermore there is no difference in nouns referring to humans who are not Yuchi. Since the Yuchi constituted a very small community at the time of Wagner's work,[4] it seems to be the case that there is a difference in noun forms based on sex of speaker plus sex of spoken about only for kinship terminology, something which according to Dixon and Kroeber (1903: 15) is extremely common among the languages of the world. Similarly, there is a sex-based difference in what Wagner calls pronouns only for those referring to Yuchi tribe members, i.e., possibly only in the kinship terminology. It appears possible that Wagner and later Furfey have simply mistakenly analyzed as pronouns a type of kinship suffix, possibly noun classifiers.

In a large number of widely separated languages women and men use different kinship terminology, always a sex-exclusive differentiation. In many cases such differences constitute the bulk of the vocabulary lists heralded by early ethnographers as indicating separate language origins for women and men. This is even true of the Carib language, the language for which the strongest claims for truly separate women's and men's languages have been made. Rather than being taken as evidence for separate language origins, differences in kinship terms based on speaker's sex should more reasonably be compared, in magnitude of differentiation, with kinship terminology in which there is sex-exclusive differentiation based on sex of spoken about, such as in the English system. It is as if a girl calls all her parents' siblings *aunt,* while her brother calls the same individuals *uncle.* Many of these languages mark sex of spoken about as well, with mother's siblings called by a different term from father's siblings, and/or mother's female siblings called by a different term from mother's male siblings. But the unvarying fact in kinship differentiation based on speaker's sex is that a full sister and brother use different terms for what, in the English system (and in the minds of the early ethnographers who were so surprised by kinship differentiation based on speaker's sex), would be considered the "same" relationship. It is possible that an arbitrary linguistic development determines whether a language's kinship terminology marks speaker's sex or sex of spoken about. It is also possible that it may be related to inheritance rules or other social arrangements, but such a relationship has not been demonstrated so far.

DIFFERENTIATION BASED ON SEX OF SPOKEN TO

It appears to be a linguistic universal that, with the exception of direct address, there is no language which differentiates on the basis of sex of spoken to which does not also differentiate on the basis of sex of speaker. It should be noted in this connection that there are languages in which there is differentiation, not restricted to direct address, based on sex of spoken to *together with* sex of speaker. In this paper, differentiation determined by the sex of both members of a conversational interaction is considered separately from differentiation determined only by the sex of speaker or only by the sex of spoken to. Differentiation based on the sex of both members of the conversational interaction will be discussed in the next section.

Returning to the topic of this section, differentiation in direct address based only on sex of spoken to, it appears that there is no language which has pronunciation differences based only on sex of spoken to. That such differentiation is not incompatible with human sociolinguistic capabilities may be inferred from the widespread existence of baby talk by adults and from an unusual report by Sapir of the existence in the Nootka language of pronunciation differences based on

> physical characteristics of the person addressed or spoken of . . . . Consonantal play consists either in altering certain consonants of a word, in this case sibilants, to other consonants that are phonetically related to them, or in inserting meaningless consonants or consonant clusters in the body of the word. The physical classes indicated by these methods are children, unsually fat or heavy people, unusually short adults, those suffering from some defect of the eye, hunchbacks, those that are lame, left-handed persons, and circumcised males. (Sapir 1915, reprinted in Mandelbaum, ed., 1949: 180-81)

Thus, although a human language apparently *could* have pronunciation differences based only on sex of spoken to, there is no language known to this writer which does so.

Differences in forms used in direct address, based on sex of spoken to, include second person pronouns and verb inflections. Sex-differentiated second

TABLE 3: USE OF 2ND PERSON PRONOUN *kimi* IN 11TH-CENTURY JAPANESE AND IN PRESENT-DAY JAPANESE.

| | SPEAKER | | SPOKEN TO | |
	SEX	RANK	SEX	RANK
11TH CENTURY	both	lower	man	higher
PRESENT	man	higher or equal	both	lower or equal

person pronouns occur in Tunica (Haas, 1944), the Semitic languages (Brunsnick, 1973), and premodern Japanese. The Japanese case is interesting because a reversal of basis of differentiation has taken place. In eleventh-century Japanese the second person pronoun, *kimi,* was used by either a woman or a man exclusively in addressing a male superior (Obayashi, 1974). In present-day Japanese, as was discussed earlier in this paper, *kimi* is only used when a man talks to a male or female equal or inferior. Thus *kimi* has completely reversed itself, both with respect to sex and with respect to rank. This reversal is shown in Table 3. Tracing the evolution of the word from *Tale of the Genji* to the present day would be valuable.

The Semitic languages are unusual in that not only second person pronouns but also verbal suffixes used in direct address indicate the sex of the person spoken to (Brunsnick, 1973). A more common kind of sex differentiation in Semitic languages is the one which the Semitic languages have in common with any language which has gender. That is, when a noun is used as a term of address it is automatically marked for sex (i.e., "Amiga!" in Spanish), to the extent that the language's gender corresponds with sex. Similarly, a language which has differentiation based on sex of spoken about for some personal nouns, which is probably true of all languages, will automatically have sex differentiation when those nouns are used in address (i.e., "Boys!").

Also in Table 1 category 2B, Das (1968) states that in Bengali there are a variety of titles, terms of address, and terms of reference for men, while such words for women are virtually nonexistent.

DIFFERENTIATION BASED ON SEX OF SPEAKER
PLUS SEX OF SPOKEN TO

A language in which sex of speaker and sex of spoken to are both involved in the determination of what form will be employed could logically have four different versions. One version would be used by a woman speaking to a woman, a second version by a woman to a man, a third version by a man to a man, and a fourth version by a man to a woman. Apparently no language structurally differentiates all four of these dyads. The only language known to this writer to differentiate even three is Biloxi. Sex differentiation has been reported as occurring in Biloxi only in the imperative form of verbs (Dorsey and Swanton, 1912). Thus, Biloxi is like the languages discussed in the previous section in that its differentiation based on sex of speaker plus sex of spoken to occurs only in direct address, a relatively limited area of language use.

Three languages differentiate structurally on the basis of two of the above dyads, i.e., Carib (Du Tertre, 17th century, Labot, 17th and 18th centuries, both cited in Frazer, 1900), Chiquita (Adam and Henry, 1880), and Yana (Sapir, 1929). Many discussions of sex differentiation in Carib do not indicate, as do Du Tertre, Labot, and Frazer, that both sex of speaker and sex of spoken to determine which version of the language will be used, but instead give the impression that only speaker's sex is involved in the determination. Similarly, later commentators on the work of Adam and Henry have often neglected to mention that sex of spoken to is as important as speaker's sex in determining which version of Chiquita will be employed. Therefore, it is possible that some of the languages described earlier in this paper as differentiating on the basis of speaker's sex may actually differentiate on the basis of addressee's sex as well, but that this was not mentioned in the reports available to this writer.

For languages which differentiate on the basis of the sex of both members of the conversational interaction it is not strictly accurate, as Sapir pointed out (1929: 206), to speak of "women's speech" or "men's speech." Instead, these four languages will here be referred to as having sex-based versions of the following types: Carib, a F-F (female-to-female) version and another version for the other three dyads; Chiquita and Yana, a M-M (male-to-male) version and another version for the other three dyads; and Biloxi, a M-M version, a F-M version, and another version for the other two dyads. These relationships are displayed in Table 4.

When conversation is taking place within a group, the rule for both Carib and Chiquita appears to be that the presence of even one member of the opposite sex will cause the single-sex version, F-F for Carib and M-M for Chiquita, not to be used. Thus, if a Carib woman is speaking to another woman in the presence of a man, she uses the second version rather than F-F. Similarly, if a Chiquita man is speaking to another man in the presence of a woman, he uses the second version rather than M-M. For Yana and Biloxi the original ethnographers state the rule only for dyads, therefore, it is not known what happens in mixed groups. That the practice for Yana is probably not the same as that for Carib and Chiquita is suggested by the fact that a Yana woman uses the M-M version in quoting a man, indicating considerable exposure to the M-M version. With regard to Carib and Chiquita, the impression created by the ethnographers is that a Carib man does

TABLE 4: DIFFERENTIATION BASED ON SEX OF SPEAKER AND SEX OF SPOKEN ABOUT

SEX OF SPEAKER \ SEX OF SPOKEN TO	FEMALE	MALE
FEMALE	Carib form 1 Chiquita form 1 Yana form 1 Biloxi form 1	Carib form 2 Chiquita form 1 Yana form 1 Biloxi form 2
MALE	Carib form 2 Chiquita form 1 Yana form 1 Biloxi form 1	Carib form 2 Chiquita form 2 Yana form 2 Biloxi form 3

not know the F-F version and a Chiquita woman does not know the M-M version.

Pronunciation differences are found in Yana, between the M-M version and the version used by the other three dyads, in the pronunciation of final vowels. Differences in forms are more common than pronunciation differences in these four languages. There are some differences in third person pronouns in the two sex-based forms of Chiquita, as well as differences in kinship terms and in a few other nouns of personal relationship (friend, slave). The two sex-based versions of Carib also have different kin terms. Aside from kinship terminology, Carib has only a couple of dozen other nouns, all concrete objects, which are different in its two sex-related versions. (Various authors give slightly different lists, some of which are claimed to be exhaustive.) Although Sapir does not specifically mention kinship terminology in his discussion of differences between the two sex-based versions of Yana, the many correspondence rules he gives very likely encompass kinship terminology. Certainly kinship terms are not included in Sapir's short list of Yana forms which are the same in the two types of speech, and he clearly states that most other forms are different for the two versions of Yana, making it probably the most sex-differentiated language ever described.

Chiquita (Adam and Henry, 1880) exhibits a highly unusual type of sex differentiation. In this language women never use gender. However, men's speech to men has gender, with one category consisting of nouns referring to men and supernatural beings and the other category consisting of all other nouns. Given the semantic content of the gender categories in men's speech it is tempting to speculate that Chiquita men have tried to use language to symbolically elevate themselves, but that Chiquita women have refused to go along with it. This impression is reinforced by the fact that men drop their use of gender when speaking to women. Another difference is that there are some nouns which are declined by men but not by women and vice versa.

It should be noted that although the Caribs have often been cited, even recently (Kroeber, 1961: 28), as having separate languages for women and men, the two sex-based versions of Carib actually differ much less frequently than do the two sex-based versions of Yana and Chiquita. However, it is true that the difference between the two sex-based versions of Carib are due to the existence of a few dozen entirely different stems, whereas in Yana and Chiquita they are due to a small number of extremely productive rules which lead to a high rate of occurrence of affix differences.

DIFFERENTIATION BASED ON SEX OF SPOKEN ABOUT

There are no reports of pronunciation differences based on sex of spoken about. It seems probable that if such differentiation did occur it would have been reported, since it would have appeared exotic to European observers. Sapir's description, quoted earlier in this paper, of pronunciation differences in Nootka based on certain physical characteristics of the person spoken to or about suggests that it would be humanly possible for a language to include pronunciation differences based on sex of spoken about, but apparently this does not happen.

Differences in form based on sex of spoken about are common. In fact, differentiation in some nouns based on sex of spoken about (for example, *girl* and *boy*) is probably a universal linguistic feature, but precisely because of its feeling of "naturalness" it is not discussed in ethnographic literature. This leaves gender as a channel in which differentiation based on sex of spoken about is often manifested, but whose occurrence is not so "natural seeming" that it never occasioned discussion. Because gender occurs in some but not other European languages, and because it occurs as *grammatical* gender in some languages and *logical* gender[5] in others, the phenomenon was sufficiently visible to arouse interest and attention among European scholars before they became widely acquainted with the exotic languages. Consequently, the question "Why do languages have gender?" found an early place in the European scholarly tradition and, unlike the question "Why do women and men speak differently?", was not motivated by contact with the languages discussed in this paper. When a report on a newly contacted language appeared, it included the information that the language did or did not have gender, but either way the fact did not occasion much comment and was not related to "women's speech." Some of the vast literature discussing gender is mentioned by Jespersen (1922: 226-40).

ATTITUDES

The ethnographers give relatively little information about people's awareness of and attitudes toward the sex-based differences in their languages. Closely related and equally undiscussed is the question of the ethnographer's own attitude toward sex-based language differences, particularly as manifested in the ethnographer's decision as to which version, if any, should be considered basic and which derived.

According to Krause (1912, cited in Chamberlain 1912: 580), Caraya men are aware of the sex-based difference in their language. They told Krause that women's speech is "very bad," and they made jokes about a male non-native speaker who used a female form. No information is given about women's attitudes toward the differences, so it is not known whether this is a situation of mutual antagonism, where each sex has a low opinion of the other sex's speech, or whether there is a shared feeling of differential prestige between the two versions.

Among the Chukchee (Bogoras, 1922), women show their knowledge of the sex differences by using male forms when quoting a man in storytelling. We are not told whether the men also engage in this linguistic role playing. Bogoras gives his own reaction to Chukchee women's speech, stating that, "the speech of women, with its ever-recurring š, sounds quite peculiar, and is not easily understood by an inexperienced ear" (1922: 665). Obviously Bogoras associated principally with men and learned that variety of Chukchee first. Bogoras also states that "the pronunciation of men is considered as unbecoming a woman" (1922: 665), but he gives no indication how he ascertained that attitude—whether from men or from women or from both, or whether it is his own attempt to explain the situation.

Clearly, there is a need for caution in interpreting attitudes toward sex-based language differences, because the social world may look different to a woman than to a man, and both the sex of the informant and the sex of the ethnographer may influence the informant's expression of attitudes. This difficulty would in principle be surmountable by having both male and female ethnographers elicit information from both male and female informants, something which is often not possible and has apparently never been done with regard to sex differentiation in language. An even greater obstacle to uncovering people's attitudes toward sex differences in their language is that ambivalence may be present, so that distortion or denial may take place regardless of the sex of the ethnographer. This seems possibly to be the case with Gros Ventre.

According to Flannery (1946: 133), Gros Ventre speakers are aware of sex-based vocabulary differences, can state them explicitly, and use them correctly in quotation. They are also aware that men and women pronounce words differently, but a woman quoting a man uses female pronunciation, while a man quoting a woman uses male pronunciation, and according to Flannery (1946: 139), they are unable to state the difference between the two forms of speech. Since there is only one single pronunciation difference between men and woman in Gros Ventre, and since this difference is so simple, straightforward, consistent, and widespread in the language, it would be surprising if speakers had not figured it out.

Furthermore, consider the following anecdote related by Flannery (1946: 134). After Flannery had been given a Gros Ventre name, an old woman who had not been present at the naming ceremony asked her what her new name was. Flannery repeated her name as her male namer had pronounced it, iθenædjæ, and the old woman protested indignantly, "Your name is iθenækyæ. I knew that woman for whom you are named. Can't these men ever do anything right!" Again, it is suspicious that a person who could correct iθenædjæ to iθenækyæ could not pinpoint the difference. Perhaps the apparent antagonism associated with the different pronunciations blocked the speakers' conscious perception of the phenomenon or at least caused them to be unable or unwilling to state the difference to the ethnographer.

Flannery also collected attitudes among the Gros Ventre toward one sex using the other sex's forms in speech (1946: 135). According to one Gros Ventre woman, the expressions used by women are "more modest," and use of the other sex's forms would cause a woman to be labeled masculine or a man effeminate. An elderly Gros Ventre woman said that, in the past, frequent use of sex-inappropriate forms would cause a person to be labeled bisexual, and she told of a young man whose mother "bowed her head in shame when her son was heard talking like a woman." However, another young man who often used women's forms was excused on the basis of having been raised in a household with no men. Flannery felt that the stigma attached to using the wrong forms hastened the demise of the Gros Ventre language, because young people for whom English was the principal language and who consequently had imperfect control of Gros Ventre were so afraid of being labeled bisexual that they refused to speak Gros Ventre at all. A particularly puzzling statement made by a number of women informants was that prior to the introduction of English into the community, Gros Ventre children used the sex-appropriate version of Gros Ventre from the very beginning of speech and never had to be corrected.

This statement contrasts sharply with Haas' report from Koasati speakers (1944: 230), among whom an adult of either sex would correct the sex-inappropriate speech of a child of either sex, using the form appropriate to that child's sex. This fact, along with the use in storytelling of the form appropriate to the sex of the person being quoted, is used by Haas as proof that the Koasati have explicit knowledge of the sex-based differences in their language. As far as the Koasati's attitudes toward these differences are concerned, Haas reports only the judgment of a single male informant who told her that women's speech is better than men's speech. Women talk "easy, slow, and soft. It sounds pretty. Men's speech has too much *sss*" (1944: 229).

Most Japanese are aware of the sex-based differences in their language and can supply many examples of sex-specific forms, as well as smile at or correct the non-native speaker. Japanese children learn the sex-based differences at a very young age, with only occasional correcting by adults and older children of the 3-6-year-old child's errors. However, after having mastered the system, some adolescent Japanese girls rebel against it for several years and begin using male forms, more often preferentially male forms than exclusively male forms, to their girlfriends and occasionally even to adults. On the basis of attentive but not rigorous observation during two periods of study in Japan (academic year 1960-61 and spring 1972), it appears to this writer that Japanese women's and men's speech have become more similar in the last decade, but that in the fantasy world of television and film, women's and men's speech is becoming even more distinct.

Chatterji (1921) and Das (1968) are unique among the investigators discussed here in that they are reporting on their native language; that is, they are simultaneously linguist and informant. As linguist and informant, Chatterji makes an automatic, apparently undiscussed, undefended equation of the Bengali language with men's speech and reports that Bengali initial *l-* is often pronounced as *n-* by women, children, and the uneducated classes. Although he gives no numerical counts or estimates of either speakers or usage frequency, it would appear that women, children, and the uneducated must constitute the great bulk of the speakers of Bengali, and perhaps the description should read, "Bengali initial *n-* is sometimes pronounced as *l-* in pretentious speech, particularly that of status-conscious men." It is not clear that this is the better description, but it should be emphasized that even a simple phonetic statement may contain an implicit social evaluation.

Although the equation of the male version with *the* language is clearly a bias and should be considered a methodological error, it is true that these ethnographers needed to choose one version as analytically and descriptively basic. Had they been describing deep structure, this would not have been so important. Since most differences between men's and women's speech are superficial, the bulk of the description would be in common, with just two sets of terminal, phonetic realization rules. However, since these linguists were concentrating on surface structure, it would have been inefficient to give two separate descriptions of the language. Therefore, one version had to be chosen as descriptively basic and correspondence rules given for getting from the described to the undescribed.

In some cases the linguist might have to make an arbitrary choice as to which version to consider basic and which derived. In other cases, the choice might be largely determined by reasons of analytic efficiency—for example, if it would require 10 rules to get from women's forms to men's forms, or 25 rules to go the other way. Other factors might justifiably influence the choice, such as relative age of the two types of speech or the overall (not just male) view of the members of the speech community. Of course, in a society with great sex antagonism or with extremely separate male and female spheres of activity there may not be an overall view or consensus on the relative merits of the different-sex based versions of the language.

With the exception of Haas, Flannery, and Sapir, none of the investigators cited in this study even considered the basis of their choice of basic and derived. All automatically regarded the male version as basic. Of course, even after choice of basic version has been made, by whatever criteria, there is no justification for equating this version with *the* language, but almost all except Haas, Flannery, and Sapir did so. The widely employed article or chapter headings, "Women's Speech" or "Women's Language," themselves imply that male speech represents *the* language, with women's speech a deviation or special form.

CONCLUSIONS

Sex differentiation in language is universal, and various aspects of it have been discussed for centuries. Nevertheless, the picture given in this summary must be viewed as incomplete, since not all types of sex differentiation have been described as such in the literature surveyed. Although the phenomenon has received attention for several centuries, this attention has been colored and distorted by the French-German-English-Spanish linguistic backgrounds of the ethnographers. The presuppositions of the ethnographers, based on sex differentiation present in their own languages, have caused them to overstate and exaggerate types of linguistic sex differentiation which do not occur in their own languages and ignore or set apart types which do occur in their own languages. This resulted in, for example, the exaggerations showered on Carib, because it had sex-exclusive differentiation, and because this differentiation was based on speaker's sex. Similarly, differentiation in personal pronouns or kinship terminology based on speaker's sex was over-interpreted, while differentiation in the same semantic areas based on sex of spoken about was felt to be too natural to justify interpretation. Furthermore, because of the linguistic backgrounds of the ethnographers and later commentators, gender was usually set apart from all other types of linguistic sex differentiation.

Our knowledge of sex differentiation in language might be more complete, or at least different, if its investigation had been dominated by, for example, native speakers of Hungarian (which has neither grammatical nor logical gender, nor does it have differentiation based on sex of spoken about in personal pronouns), provided they did not suffer from secondary ethnocentrism induced by their knowledge of Western European languages. Use of a framework like that shown in Table 1, by bringing to mind the logically possible types of sex differentiation, circumvents the problem of the investigator's blindness to the types of sex differentiation with which they are familiar. If some such framework is not used, it cannot be known whether the absence of mention of a specific type of sex-based differentiation reflects its absence in the language or whether it was simply not commented on.

If descriptions of linguistic sex differentiation are uneven and incomplete for all languages, the social meaning of such differentiation has been even less explored. There is now a virtual explosion of investigations of sex differentiation, at least in English, as well as fruitful probing of the social implications of the sex differentiation which occurs in English. If this interest and effort continue we may soon have a good understanding of sex differentiation in English. However, it would be a mistake to generalize on the basis of a single language, or a small number of related languages, about sociolinguistic processes and regularities which can only be discovered from a broad cross-cultural base. Therefore, the work of the early ethnographers will remain valuable, because they were attentive to many kinds of linguistic sex differentiation in a variety of widely differing languages, many of which are now extinct. It is also important to be aware of the attitudes of the period which may have limited and biased some of their interpretations of sex differentiation in language.

NOTES

[1] For a language to have gender means that most or many nouns referring to females are treated differently grammatically from most or many nouns referring to males. For example, feminine nouns may be modified by a different adjective or take a different pronoun, article, or verb than masculine nouns.

[2] Based on the writer's own working knowledge of Japanese, as well as discussion with several native speakers.

[3] I am indebted to Hymes (1973) for referring me to Wolff's reanalysis of these forms (1948: 242-43). However, Wolff's reanalysis focused mainly on separating out the feature of "actor" and thus is not relevant to this discussion.

[4] Wagner gives no population count or estimate, but according to Terrell (1971) the Yuchi numbered about 2,500 in the year 1650 and must have been far fewer when Wagner did his work in 1928-29.

[5] If some nouns referring to females or to sexless objects are in the masculine category and some nouns referring to males or to sexless objects are in the feminine category, the system is called grammatical gender. If all and only nouns referring to females are in the feminine category and all and only nouns referring to males are in the masculine category, it is called logical or natural gender.

REFERENCES

Adam, Lucien & Henry, Victor. (1880). *Arte y vocabulario de la lingua chiquita.* Paris: Maisonneuve.

Blood, Doris (1962). Women's speech characteristics in Cham. *Asian Culture,* 3, 139-43.

Boas, Franz (ed.). (1911-38). *Handbook of American Indian languages.* Bureau of American Ethnology Bulletin 40. Washington: Government Printing Office.

Bogoras, Waldemar. (1922). Chukchee. In Franz Boas (ed.), *Handbook of American Indian languages.* Bureau of American Ethnology Bulletin 40. Washington: Government Printing Office.

Brunsnick, Norman. (1973). Personal communication.

Bunzel, Ruth. (1933-38). Zuñi. In Franz Boas (ed.), *Handbook of American Indian languages.* Bureau ˉof American Ethnology Bulletin 40, Part 3, 385-515. Washington: Government Printing Office.

Chamberlain, Alexander. (1912). Women's languages. *American Anthropologist,* 14, 579-81.

Chatterji, Suniti Kumar. (1921). Bengali phonetics. *Bulletin of the School of Oriental Studies,* 2 (1), 1-25.

Das, Sisir Kumar. (1968). Forms of address and terms of reference in Bengali. *Anthropological Linguistics,* 10 (4), 19-31.

Dixon, Roland & Kroeber, Alfred. (1903). The native languages of California. *American Anthropologist,* 5, 1-26.

Dorsey, James & Swanton, John. (1912). *A dictionary of the Biloxi and Ofo languages.* Bureau of American Ethnology Bulletin 47. Washington: Government Printing Office.

Flannery, Regina (1946). Men's and women's speech in Gros Ventre. *International Journal of American Linguistics,* 12, 133-35.

Frazer, James George. (1900). A suggestion as to the origin of gender in language. *Fortnightly Review,* 73, 79-90.

Furfey, Paul Hanly. (1944). Men's and women's language. *American Catholic Sociological Review,* 5, 218-23.

Haas, Mary. (1944). Men's and women's speech in Koasati. *Language,* 20, 142-49. Reprinted in Dell Hymes (ed.) (1964), *Language in culture and society.* New York: Harper & Row.

Hymes, Dell. (1964). *Language in culture and society.* New York: Harper & Row.

———. (1973). Personal communication.

Jespersen, Otto. (1922). *Language: its nature, development and origin.* New York: Macmillan.

Kroeber, Theodora. (1961). *Ishi in two worlds.* Berkeley: Univ. of Calif. Press.

Mandelbaum, David. (ed.). (1949). *Selected writings of Edward Sapir.* Berkeley: Univ. of Calif. Press.

Meillet, A. (1923). Le Genre féminin dans les langues indo-européenes. *Journal de psychologie: normale et pathologique,* 20, 943-44. Translated by Dell Hymes and reprinted in Dell Hymes (ed.) (1964), *Language in culture and society.* New York: Harper & Row.

Obayashi, Hiroshi. (1974). Personal communication.

Reik, Theodor. (1954). Men and women speak different languages. *Psychoanalysis,* 2 (4), 3-15.

Samarin, William. (1972). *Tongues of men and angels.* New York: Macmillan.

Sapir, Edward. (1915). *Abnormal types of speech in Nootka.* Canada Department of Mines, Geological Survey, Memoir 62, Anthropological Series, No. 5. Ottawa: Government Printing Bureau. Reprinted in David Mandelbaum (ed.) (1949), *Selected writings of Edward Sapir.* Berkeley: Univ. of Calif. Press.

———. (1929). Male and female forms of speech in Yana. In St. W. J. Teeuwen (ed.), *Donum Natalicium Schrijnen.* Nijmegen-Utrecht: Dekker and Van de Vegt. Reprinted in David Mandelbaum (ed.) (1949), *Selected writings of Edward Sapir.* Berkeley: Univ. of Calif. Press.

Terrell, John Upton. (1971). *American Indian almanac.* New York and Cleveland: World Publishing Co.

Wagner, Gunter. (1933-38). Yuchi. In Franz Boas (ed.), *Handbook of American Indian languages.* Bureau of American Ethnology Bulletin 40, Part 3, 385-515. Washington: Government Printing Office.

Wolff, Hans. (1948). Yuchi phonemes and morphemes with special reference to person markers. *International Journal of American Linguistics,* 14, 240-43.

CUES TO THE IDENTIFICATION OF
SEX IN CHILDREN'S SPEECH*

Jacqueline Sachs

A person's speech carries much information beyond the message. When we hear a person speak, even if we cannot see the person, we can often determine a number of speaker attributes. Each of us can identify many particular individuals from their voices. Even if the voice is that of a stranger, we might be able to identify the speaker's general age, mood, and socioeconomic status. If the speaker is an adult and is relatively neutral with respect to all other characteristics, we could almost invariably identify his or her sex. Differentiation between the adult male and female voice is undoubtedly the most salient of vocal characteristics. Some important aspects of the difference between male and female voices (such as the lower fundamental frequency of males) begin at puberty and are linked with the development of other secondary sex characteristics (Negus, 1949; Kirchner, 1970). Not all the cues to the identification of sex of speaker have their beginning at puberty, however. Although the differences are not as marked as they are in adults, it appears that cues to the sex of the speaker exist in prepubertal children's voices as well.

*This research was supported by a grant from the University of Connecticut Research Foundation. I would also like to acknowledge a number of people who have helped in carrying out this research: Dr. Ignatius Mattingly formulated the theory which was the starting point for these studies and has continued to offer insightful comments about the problem; Dr. Harry S. Cooker suggested using the backward sentences as stimuli; Dr. Gary B. Wilson provided valuable assistance with the semantic differential study; Ms. Louise Goldberg collected the semantic differential data and carried out the analysis; Dr. Arthur Abramson provided many helpful comments; and Dr. Philip Lieberman gave most generously of his enthusiasm and ideas. Some of these data were discussed at the Symposium on Women and Language which was held at Rutgers University in 1973.

Recent studies have shown that listeners are usually able to identify the sex of a child by listening to the voice (Weinberg and Bennett, 1971; Sachs, Lieberman, and Erickson, 1973). In the study by Sachs *et al.,* the listeners were quite surprised at their accuracy in the task. They often complained that they were only guessing on every voice, and yet their "guesses" were almost always correct. This raises an interesting question. If listeners can reliably and validly identify prepubertal boys and girls as to sex without having any intuitions about the basis for their judgment, what are the cues that they use? The purpose of this paper is to discuss some of the possible cues for differentiating male and female speakers and to present some experimental evidence that bears on the question.

Each speaker's particular voice quality and speech style is determined partially by physical makeup and partially by other factors, such as culture, socioeconomic status, personality, and communication setting. The most obvious difference between adult male and female voice quality is the pitch, or fundamental frequency of phonation. We assume that females have "high" voices and males have "low" voices. However, if a listener heard a male or female voice that crossed over into the pitch range that is expected of the opposite sex, the listener might still be able to identify the voice correctly. Pitch is not the only cue used in the classification. Studies which have eliminated fundamental frequency differences have shown that male and female voices remain differentiable. For example, Schwartz (1968) showed that speaker sex could be identified from isolated, voiceless fricatives, and Schwartz and Rine (1968) demonstrated that listeners could identify the sex of speaker from whispered vowels. These researchers and others have suggested that it is the pattern of formant frequencies, or resonances of the supralaryngeal vocal tract, that provides at least part of the cue to sex identification. Adult males, on the average, have larger supralaryngeal vocal tracts than females and produce lower formants as a result. Therefore, listeners may be responding partly to the formant frequency cues in identifying male and female speakers, even though they think that male voices are simply "low pitched" and female voices are "high pitched." A mismatching of the cues of fundamental frequency and formant frequencies might lead to confusion or to an assessment that the speaker was an unusually high-pitched male or low-pitched female.

The patterns of formant frequencies are determined by the size and shape of the vocal tract while producing speech. A person can use various means of articulation which cause the formants to be higher or lower than they would be in a "neutral" state. For example, spreading the lips while speaking would cause the formants to move upward, while protruding the lips would cause formant lowering. Mattingly (1966) suggested that the formant values observed in a group of men and women could not be due entirely to the unmodified vocal tract size. Using the Peterson and Barney (1952) data on vowel formants for 76 speakers of English, Mattingly correlated the distributions of the formants of each of 10 vowels. The correlations were lower than would be expected if vocal tract size were the only factor influencing those formant frequencies. Also, the separation between the distributions of formants for male and female speakers was very sharp, whereas one would expect overlap in the distributions based on the variability in male and female vocal tract size. Mattingly suggested that linguistic stylistic conventions must be involved. Adult men and women may modify their articulators, lowering or raising their formant frequencies, to produce voices that aim toward male-female archetypes. Presumably these archetypes are culturally determined. In other words, men may try to talk as if they are bigger than they actually are, and women may talk as if they are smaller than they actually are.

The possibility that there might be culturally determined differences in the speech styles of men and women is certainly not surprising. In many languages, the differences between the speech of males and females is quite marked. Since Bodine (1975) has provided an extensive review of sexual differentiation in speech, only a few examples will be mentioned here. The most extreme cases would be those in which a separate "men's language" or "women's language" exists, often for ritual purposes (see for example, Chamberlain, 1912). In most languages, however, there is a large amount of the language that is common to men and women, with only specific differences. In Thai, different sets of lexical items are considered appropriate for men and women (Haas, 1944). In English, the lexical stylistic differences are not as marked, but exist nevertheless, as has been shown in recent work by linguists such as Key (1972) and Lakoff (1973). While the most obvious example is the attitude that swear words are not appropriate for women, other differences may be much more pervasive. For example, Lakoff claims that the speech style expected of women is full of qualified statements, indirect ("polite") means of expression, and uncertainty.

As well as lexical and stylistic differences, phonological differences are quite common. Haas (1944) reported that phonological substitutions differentiated men's and women's speech in Koasati, an American Indian language. In a study in New England, Fischer (1968) found that boys said *fishin'* and *swimmin'*, while girls said *fishing* and *swimming*. A number of other linguists have found that women are more likely than men to use the more formal and prestigious phonological patterns in a language (Labov, Yaeger and Steiner, 1972; Shuy, Wolfram and Riley, 1967). Some intonation patterns in English also seem to signal feminine speech. Brend (1971) has described a number of patterns, such as the "surprise" pattern (Oh, that's awful!) and "cheerful" pattern (Are you coming? or Goodbye!), that are used mainly by women.

So, indeed, culturally based differentiation of language according to sex of speaker exists quite generally. The Mattingly hypothesis would imply that among these various aspects of linguistic style may be the way a person's voice sounds. Even if one did not have the signals of intonation, pronunciation, lexical selection, and so on, speakers could still be unfailingly identified as to sex from voice alone.

If Mattingly's hypothesis is correct—if males aim toward an ideal "male" speech and females toward "female" speech—then these culturally determined differences between male and female voice might also be found in children's voices, even though the vocal tract of the male had not yet started the growth which is connected with puberty. The first step in testing this hypothesis was to determine whether children can be identified as to sex from their voices before puberty.

THE EXPERIMENTAL EVIDENCE ON IDENTIFICATION OF SEX OF CHILD FROM VOICE

Weinberg and Bennett (1971) recorded 30-second samples of spontaneous speech from 66 normal 5- and 6-year old children. Judges were able to identify the sex of the children from these samples well above a chance level. 74% of all judgments were correct. Of the 29 boys, 20 were identified correctly and 2 were misperceived as girls. Of the 37 girls, 25 were correctly identified and 3 were misperceived as boys. Weinberg and Bennett analyzed the mean fundamental frequencies of the children's voices and found no significant differences between males and females. They suggested that differences in formant frequencies may have played a role in the judges' identifications. They noted that the boys in their study tended to be slightly bigger than the girls, and that this difference might imply that the boys had larger vocal tracts (and thus lower formants) than the girls.

Sachs, Lieberman and Erickson (1973) recorded a sentence-imitation from each of 26 boys and girls between the ages of 4 and 12. When judges heard these samples, they were able to identify the sex of the child correctly 81% of the time, an accuracy well above chance expectations. Of the 14 boys, 12 were correctly identified, and of the 12 girls, 9 were correctly identified and 2 were misperceived as boys. The average fundamental frequency (determined from a sample of isolated vowels from each child) was actually somewhat higher for the boys than for the girls, and therefore would likely not have been the cue for the accurate identification. These results, then, are quite comparable to Weinberg and Bennett's, but the explanation offered by Sachs et al. is different.

First, the size of the children in the Sachs et al. study was quite variable, since the age range was so great. It is unlikely, therefore, that judges were responding to absolute size of vocal tract alone, since then all small children should have been called girls and all large children, boys. It appears, instead, that the judges were able somehow to infer the general size of the child and make judgments relative to that size.

Secondly, Sachs *et al.* suggested that if Mattingly's hypothesis about cultural influences on the formant frequencies is correct, then the formant differences observed in adult male and female voices might be found in children's voices, even though the vocal tracts were the same size. If formants did differ, they could be a cue to sex identification. To test this possibility, 9 pairs of boys and girls, matched for height and weight, were formed from the original 26. (These children included some who were well identified, some who were misidentified, and some who were ambiguously perceived.) The rationale for matching on height and weight is that these measures would generally control for body size differences, including size of the vocal tract. Anatomical studies have shown that the larynx of a prepubertal boy and girl is likely to be the same size given the same height and weight (Kirchner, 1970). Also, there is no difference in mandible length between boys and girls before puberty (Walker and Kowalski, 1972; Hunter and Garn, 1972). Since mandible length accounts for half of the supralaryngeal tract length, it is likely that girls and boys of the same height and weight would have the same vocal tract size. Therefore, one would not have expected the boys and girls in the sample to exhibit different formant frequencies if vocal tract size were the sole determining factor. If, however, cultural influences play a role, the boys might have lower formants even with matched sizes.

Sachs *et al.* measured the first and second formants for three vowels, /a/, /i/ and /u/, for each of the 18 children. The formant values were significantly lower for the boys in the cases of /i/ and /u/. Since the matched pairs included both good and poor exemplars of boylike and girl-like voices, another analysis was done which selected on the basis of how accurately the sex of the child was identified. Three pairs of boys and three pairs of girls were formed, matched for height and weight, representing the best identified and least identified children in the sample for each sex. The most boylike voices had lower formants than the least boylike, and, conversely, the most girl-like voices had higher formants than the least girl-like. Sachs *et al.* discussed several possible interpretations of these results. Among these is the hypothesis that culturally acquired norms of male and female voice characteristics influenced the children's use of their articulators. For example, it was suggested that a speaker could change formant characteristics by pronouncing vowels with phonetic variations or by changing the configuration of the lips.

Though the formant differences could have been a cue for the sex identification, there were some children in the sample who were well identified even though their formant frequencies fell into the range typical of the opposite sex. Most of these were older girls with rather low formants who were not confused with boys. Therefore it appeared that other characteristics, as well as the formant patterns, must have played a role in the listeners' judgments. The judges, after all, listened to sentences, not isolated vowels, and it is certainly probable that some sentential cues might be more likely for males or females. The following experiments were run to eliminate sentential cues from the voice samples used by Sachs *et al.*, and to determine what role these may have played in the judges' accuracy.

Experiment I: Identification of Sex from Isolated Vowels

In Sachs *et al.*, the fundamental and formants had been measured from the 26 children's productions of the isolated vowels /a/, /i/ and /u/. The stimuli for the current judgments were made from these recordings. The samples had been collected from 14 boys (ages four years to 11 years, 10 months) and 12 girls (ages four years to 10 years, four months). The children had been recorded in their homes using a Sony TC800 recorder and a Sony microphone with flat frequency response to 8 kHz. The children were from middle-class homes. All of them had lived in the area for at least four years, with the exception of one who had recently moved from Kansas and two who had been in England for the previous academic year. One child was a bilingual speaker of Korean and English, but the rest were monolingual.

The stimulus tape was made of the three isolated vowels for each child said in succession, with a pause between sets for the judges to respond on their answer sheets. The order of children on the tape was randomized. Four voices were added at the beginning as a warm-up but were not identified as to sex. The judges were 75 University of Connecticut students (56 female and 19 male) enrolled in courses on language acquisition, and they listened as two groups. The judges were told that the tape would consist of children saying the vowels /a/, /i/ and /u/ and were instructed to listen to the voice of each child and then check on an answer sheet whether that voice was a girl's or a boy's. They were instructed to guess even when unsure. The judges received no feedback as to the correctness of their responses.

Analyses will be reported only for the 9 pairs of children that had been matched on height and weight in Sachs *et al.* to control for general size differences. Analysis of the judgments (see Table 1) revealed that the mean number of correct responses was significantly better than chance ($z = 3.20$, $p < .01$), with 66% of the responses correct. Using the proportion test, responses to each child's voice were analyzed. For both boys and girls, judges responded reliably. Sixteen of the 18 children were judged (correctly or not) at greater than chance level ($p < .01$) to be either a boy or a girl. Only two of the children were

TABLE 1

JUDGES' IDENTIFICATION OF SEX (p<.01) FOR 9 PAIRS OF MALE AND FEMALE CHILDREN, FROM SENTENCES, VOWELS, AND BACKWARD SENTENCES

Height of children in pair	MALE CHILDREN			FEMALE CHILDREN		
	Sentence stimuli	Isolated vowel stimuli	Backward sentence stimuli	Sentence stimuli	Isolated vowel stimuli	Backward sentence stimuli
42"-41"	Male	Female	Female	Female	Female	Female
45"-46"	–	Female	–	Female	Female	Female
49"	Male	Male	Female	Female	Female	Male
50"	Male	Male	Male	Female	Female	–
50"	Male	–	Male	Male	Male	Male
56"-54"	Male	Male	Male	Female	–	Female
57"	Male	Male	Male	Female	Male	–
59"-58"	Male	Male	Male	Male	Male	Male
61"-60"	Male	Male	Male	Female	Male	Male

ambiguously perceived from the isolated vowel stimuli. The validity of the judgments was not as great as the reliability. Of the 9 boys, 6 were correctly identified (p<.01), and 2 were judged to be girls (p<.01), with 72% of judgments being correct. Of the 9 girls, 4 were correctly identified (p<.01), and 4 were incorrectly thought to be boys (p<.01). Only 59% of the responses to girls' voices were correct. Two of the girls identified as boys in this study had also been overwhelmingly heard as boys in Sachs *et al.*

Looking at the 9 pairs in order of height and weight, we find that both children in the pair were judged to be girls for the 2 smallest pairs and both were judged to be boys for the 5 largest pairs. The two middle pairs were judged accurately. Thus it appears that the judges may have been influenced primarily by vocal tract size *per se* or by some other correlate of age of child in their decisions about the sex of the child. Larger (or older) children were called boys and smaller (or younger) children were called girls. However, the fact that a middle range of children was identified correctly even from isolated vowels may indicate that the sex cues can be discriminated when the age cue does not override them. The possibility that a narrower age range would lead to improved accuracy of judgments is currently being investigated.

These results suggest that the isolated vowels may carry some of the information that allows listeners to identify the sex of the child from the voice. However, responses to isolated vowels are less accurate than responses to sentences (z = 2.86, p<.01). Hearing sentences seemed to allow the listeners to judge sex independently of cues from age or size of the child. The sentences may simply provide more exemplars of phonetic material for making the judgment, or they may supply special sentential characteristics, such as rate, inflection, and so on. The next experiment was designed to look at these possibilities.

Experiment II: Identification of Sex from Backward Sentences

Since judgments were relatively poorer when the listeners heard only three isolated vowels from each child instead of sentences, we wished to expose them to more phonetic information, but not introduce sentential information. English sentences played backward sound like speech, but they seem to be sentences in a foreign language quite unlike English, especially in terms of intonation. Many listeners say it sounds to them like Russian or Swedish. These stimuli preserve some of the acoustic characteristics of the speech (for example, the formant frequencies of the vowels) but destroy the information gained from transitions in frequencies. Studies have shown that judges can identify certain voice characteristics from sentences played backward. For example, the degree of nasality in speech can be detected by listeners very reliably (Sherman, 1954; Spriestersbach, 1955; Colton and Cooker, 1968).

In this experiment, we asked judges to identify the sex of the same 26 children as in Experiment I, but by listening to the sentences from Sachs *et al.* played backward. The judges were the same 75 students who had participated in Experiment I. Precautions were taken to insure that hearing the isolated vowels did not influence their judgments on this task. The judges had not been given any feedback on Experiment I; one week had elapsed between testing; the order of children on the tape was different; and the judges were not informed that the samples came from the same children. They were informed that they would hear the English sentence "I thought I saw a big blue meanie," played backward, and they were told that the speakers were children. Four warm-up stimuli were played, and then the judges marked "boy" or "girl" on an answer sheet after hearing each of the 26 voices.

Again, only the responses to the 9 matched pairs will be reported to control for general body size of the children. Analysis of overall correctness of response for the 75 judges revealed that 59% of the judgments were correct. This falls short of being significantly different from chance performance ($z = 1.80$, $p = .07$). Looking at accuracy for each child's voice, we again find high reliability of judgments, with 15 of the 18 voices assigned to one category by most of the judges ($p < .01$). For boys, we find again that 6 of the 9 children were correctly identified ($p < .01$), and 2 were identified as girls ($p < .01$), with 69% of the responses being correct (see Table 1). (Although 69% of the responses were correct, we cannot conclude that the judges could identify the boys' voices above chance levels of performance, since overall performance is below chance. The correctness could reflect a bias to respond "boy" in the absence of knowledge, rather than reflecting actual ability to identify the sex of the speaker. If a bias were operating, as the percentage correct for boys' voices increased, the percentage correct for girls' voices would decrease.)

For the girls, the pattern is quite similar to that found in the experiment with isolated vowels, with very poor identification. Of the 9 girls, 3 were correctly identified (p<.01), and 4 were called boys (p<.01; see Table 1). Only 49% of the responses were correct. Again, the young girls tended to be heard as girls while the older ones were heard as boys. Two older girls, however, were not perceived as boys. One was correctly identified, and one was ambiguously perceived.

In comparing the overall accuracy of judgments in this experiment with that reported in Sachs *et al.*, we find that listeners respond less accurately when they hear sentences backward than they do when they hear normal sentences (z = 4.20, p<.01). The accuracy of response to backward sentences is not significantly different from the accuracy of response to isolated vowels (z = 1.25). These results suggest that there may be considerable information in normal sentences that provides a cue to the sex of the speaker, beyond the phonetic aspects of the voice. These results come as no surprise and suggest that we return to the sentences spoken by the children to see what further cues might be present.

In listening to the sentences spoken by the boys and girls, Sachs *et al.* had reported that "in general it seemed to us, subjectively, that boys had a more forceful, definite rhythm than the girls" (p. 81). Others who have heard the tapes have had various ideas about the qualitative differences between the boys and the girls. For example, some said that the girls sounded "smooth" or "gentle" and the boys sounded "rough." Someone thought that the boys' voices were "blocked" while the girls' voices were "clear like a bell." Unfortunately, no methods exist as yet for making objective, mechanical measurements of the sorts of characteristics that seemed, subjectively, to be present in the voices. We simply do not know what the underlying acoustic correlates are for most of these "qualitative" aspects of voice. Therefore, it seemed that some form of "subjective judgment" task was in order, and the following study represents an attempt to discover whether we could obtain reliable and meaningful assessments of other characteristics that correlate with the perceived sex of the speaker.

Experiment III: A Description of the Voices

The purpose of this study was to develop a measuring instrument for finding characteristics that are attributed to male and female voices or sentence productions. The semantic differential technique (Osgood, Suci, and Tannenbaum, 1957) has been used in many studies to measure qualitative characteristics of concepts and stimuli. Recently it has proved to be a useful technique in sociolinguistic research. When studying speech characteristics which are relatively hard to measure, such as degree of ethnicity or accentedness, researchers have found that groups of naive judges give reliable and useful ratings of these aspects of speech (Shuy, 1969). Some studies have used very brief samples of speech such as the ones used in Sachs *et al.*, so this method seemed appropriate for our purpose of studying the correlates of masculinity and femininity in children's speech.

In the semantic differential technique, judges rate the stimuli that are presented to them on a set of bipolar adjective scales. For example, a recording of a voice might be played, and then each judge would mark on a set of scales to indicate his or her evaluation of that voice. The judge would make about 20 decisions for each stimulus. Among these might be scales like:

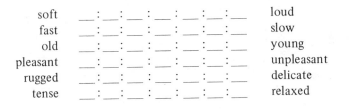

soft	__:__:__:__:__:__:__	loud
fast	__:__:__:__:__:__:__	slow
old	__:__:__:__:__:__:__	young
pleasant	__:__:__:__:__:__:__	unpleasant
rugged	__:__:__:__:__:__:__	delicate
tense	__:__:__:__:__:__:__	relaxed

In the analysis of the data obtained from the ratings, the mean ratings indicate the attitude that judges had toward the stimulus, on the average, and the variability in the ratings (measured by the variance) reveals whether the judges reacted to a particular stimulus consistently. Appropriate statistical analyses can also establish whether the judges reacted to different stimuli in the same way or in different ways. Furthermore, certain of the bipolar adjective scales will typically be correlated with one another. This "clustering" of certain scales reveals that each of the scales is not independent of every other one, but that various "factors" are involved in the judges' perceptions of the stimuli. For example, "soft" voices may tend to also be rated as "pleasant" and "relaxed," but whether the voice is heard as "young" or "old" may not be correlated with these other scales. We would then say that "soft-loud," "pleasant-unpleasant," and "tense-relaxed" form a cluster, and that "old-young" is independent of whatever underlying factor relates those three scales.

Obviously, it is crucial for the success of this method that the descriptive adjectives used to form the scales really reflect the characteristics that are in the stimuli. Therefore, the first step is to form scales empirically by eliciting descriptions of the stimuli under consideration from a population of judges. Six voices were chosen from the original 26, consisting of three boys and three girls who had been well identified as to sex when sentences were used as stimuli. A

TABLE 2
ADJECTIVES USED BY 15 JUDGES IN DESCRIBING 6 CHILDREN'S VOICES

USED FOR MALE VOICES	USED FOR FEMALE VOICES	USED FOR BOTH
afraid	angelic	breathy
bored	articulate	childlike
boy	authoritative	confident
broken	awed	cute
bully	bell-like	hesitant
confused	bright	high
content	clear	hoarse
crackly	cold	immature
deep	daring	low
denasal	dramatic	mature
fast	expressive	nasal
innocent	feminine	older
insecure	girl	raspy
halting	good	smart
hesitant	happy	soft
loud	intelligent	sweet
male	leader	young
meanie	little	
medium-pitch	loveable	
monotone	matter-of-fact	
precocious	melodic	
sad	normal	
self-conscious	playful	
shy	pleasant	
slow	poised	
tense	pouty	
thick	pure	
tired	self-assured	
unemotional	self-confident	
unintelligible	sexy	
uninterested	small	
unsure	smooth	
whining	steady	
	squeaky	
	tight	
	timid	
	unexpressive	
	whispery	

tape was constructed of the sentences with the children in random order. This tape was played to a group of judges to elicit descriptive adjectives.

The judges were 15 female students who were enrolled in an undergraduate speech course. Because we wanted to avoid responses that reflected sex-role stereotypes, the judges were completely naive as to the goals of the experiment. They were not informed that sex differences in voice were being studied, they were not asked whether the voice was that of a boy or girl, and sex of speaker had not been mentioned in the instructions. They were told that we were interested in how people evaluate children from their voices, and that they should write down as many adjectives as they wished to describe the voice, the speech, and the child. The instructions stressed the use of adjectives rather than descriptive phrases.

After they had generated adjectives describing each sample, these judges were asked to identify the sex of 12 children from a recorded sample of their speech. The 6 children they had described were among these, in random order. These judgments were used to determine whether these judges, like the 83 in Sachs *et al.,* heard the 6 children as the correct sex. These judgments were overwhelmingly correct, with only 3 errors out of 90 responses.

A total of 88 different descriptive adjectives were elicited from the judges (17 were used for both boys and girls, 33 only for boys, and 38 only for girls). Table 2 shows all the adjectives used by the judges in describing the 6 voices.

Among the adjectives used by the judges were many that appeared to be synonyms of each other or that reflected the same underlying concept, such as "confident," "self-assured," and "self-confident." From each of these groups, one term was chosen or a term was invented that seemed representative of the underlying concept involved. These words were combined with opposites (or very dissimilar concepts) to form 25 adjective scales. When no commonly known opposite term existed, "non-" or "not" was used as the other end of the scale, as in "nasal-nonnasal" and "whining-not whining." As is standard in semantic differential scales, the adjectives were arranged so that judges would not establish a bias for expecting certain types of characteristics on one side of the scale. For example, if all characteristics that people are likely to view as positive characteristics ("bright," "kind," "friendly," "graceful") appeared on the left side, the judges might begin to pay little attention to the actual adjectives which define each scale. The ratings were made along a 7-point scale, with the middle point representing a neutral judgment on that characteristic.

The judges for the semantic differential ratings were 50 students (40 female and 10 male) enrolled in an undergraduate speech course. They were not told that the research involved sex differences in voice. The instructions were as follows: "The purpose of this study is to find what characteristics are perceived in voices. You will hear a child saying a sentence. When the sentence is finished, you will rate the voice on a set of characteristics. There is a complete page of characteristics for each voice. You are to rate the voices on each of these scales in order." Then an example of a scale was given (that was not one used in the ratings) and judges were instructed in the use of the scales. They were told to work quickly and give the first impression that came to mind.

The stimuli consisted of 6 sentences from Sachs *et al.,* with 3 from females who had been well identified and 3 from males who had been well identified. The girls were ages 6 years, 8 months; 9 years, 10 months; 9 years, 11 months; and the boys were 7 years, 1 month; 7 years, 9 months; and 9 years, 9 months.

The ratings for each voice were separately factor analyzed by the principal components procedure, and the matrices were subjected to varimax rotation. Two-, 3-, and 4-factor solutions were performed on the data from the 25 scales. Five of these scales ("loud-soft," "kind-cruel," "breathy-nonbreathy," "mellow-harsh," and "whining-not whining") did not appear at all on the 4-factor solution and were dropped from further analyses. Subsequent analyses were performed with the 20 remaining scales.

Two-, 3-, 4-, and 5-factor solutions were performed on the judgment data. The 4-factor solution added only 10% to the explained variance, the 4th factor had an Eigenvalue of 1.03 (1.00 is the usual cut-off point), and the scales making up the fourth factor did not seem to form a coherent group. On the other hand, the scales making up the factors in the 3-factor solution appeared to have convincing face validity. Scales were accepted as being part of a factor if they had a high loading (.40 or higher) on one factor and did not load highly on any other factor. For the male voices combined, Factor I accounted for 47% of the variance, Factor II for 32%, and Factor III for 21%. For the 3 female voices combined, Factor I accounted for 56% of the variance, Factor II for 26%, and Factor III for 18%.

The scales that cluster together to form the factors seem to reflect the same underlying variables for each voice. Those forming Factor I seem to reflect judgments of the child's personality and mood as shown in the voice. "Active-Passive" is the highest loading scale for 3 of the voices, and we will refer to this factor by that scale name. The scales that form Factor II seem to be assessments primarily of the intelligibility or fluency of the child's speech. We will call this scale "Fluent-Disfluent." The scales that form Factor III ("masculine-feminine," "rugged-delicate," "rough-smooth," and "low-high" are the ones that do not appear in any other factor) seem to reflect the masculinity or femininity of the voice, and we will call this factor "Masculine-Feminine." Table 3 shows the factors and the scales that appeared in only one factor, across the 6 children's voices.

A description of each child's voice based on the mean ratings by the judges also supports the finding that a "masculinity-femininity" dimension exists in these voices. The ratings on the scales that make up the "Active-Passive" and "Fluent-Disfluent" factors appear to be independent of the perceived masculinity or femininity of the child's voice. The younger children in this sample were usually judged to be "slow, dull, and depressed" and "immature, disfluent, and tense." The older children were "happy, quick, and bright," and

TABLE 3
FACTORS IN JUDGMENTS OF 6 CHILDREN'S VOICES, AND THE
SCALES THAT APPEARED IN ONLY ONE FACTOR, IN ORDER OF
FREQUENCY OF OCCURRENCE ACROSS THE STIMULI

Active-Passive	Fluent-Disfluent	Masculine-Feminine
active-passive	relaxed-tense	rugged-delicate
happy-depressed	fluent-disfluent	low-high
eager-indifferent	intelligible-unintelligible	masculine-feminine
bright-dull	nonnasal-nasal	rough-smooth
quick-slow		

two of the three were judged to be "intelligible and fluent." Both the young children and the older ones were judged accurately as to sex. The boys in this sample were described as "rough, unsure, masculine, and high." The girls were perceived as "feminine, meek, delicate, high, and smooth." Table 4 shows the descriptions of the male and female children in terms of the scales that received mean ratings below 3.00 and above 4.00.

Thus it appears that the semantic differential technique may be useful for studying perceived sex differences in voice. Factor analyses of the ratings made in response to 6 children's voices produced 3 independent and meaningful dimensions. Although the Masculine-Feminine factor accounted for the smallest amount of the variance, there was great overlap in the scales making up this factor across the 6 voices. It might be possible in subsequent studies to find other scales that correlate highly with the perceived masculinity or femininity of the voice.

The factors revealed in this study can be compared with those found in other research on children's speech. Williams and his colleagues (Williams, 1970; Williams, Whitehead, and Miller, 1971a; Williams, Whitehead, and Miller, 1971b; Williams, 1973) have found two dimensions, ethnicity-nonstandardness and confidence-eagerness, in semantic differential scaling studies of the speech of children from various dialect and social status groups. The first of these, ethnicity-nonstandardness, would not have appeared in our study since dialect variations were minimal as compared with those in the studies reported by Williams, and no scales tapped such differences. Williams' studies used middle- and lower-class white, black, and Mexican-American children's voices as the stimuli. The second dimension, confidence-eagerness, was found to be very well correlated with the fluency and enthusiasm of the child. For example, counts of hestitation phenomena in the speech showed that as they increased, negative ratings on confidence-eagerness increased. In our study, Active-Passive (which included the scale "eager-indifferent") and Fluent-Disfluent (which included the scale "fluent-disfluent") appeared as two separate factors. Furthermore, there

TABLE 4
THE JUDGES' DESCRIPTIONS OF EACH CHILD'S VOICE, BASED ON MEAN RATINGS
ABOVE 4.00 AND BELOW 3.00, IN ORDER OF DEGREE OF DEVIATION FROM NEU-
TRAL POSITION ON SCALE (3.50)

	Active-Passive	Fluent-Disfluent	Masculine-Feminine	Others
Male, 7:1	dull depressed passive meek indifferent	disfluent immature tense unintelligible awkward	rough	unsure slow nasal masculine reserved careless
Male, 7:9	immature slow meek passive dull depressed indifferent	tense disfluent awkward	unsure masculine	reserved
Male, 9:9	quick eager active happy	immature tense nasal graceful	high	smooth masculine friendly
Female, 6:8	slow	immature nasal tense	feminine meek delicate high	unsure
Female, 9:10	calm happy friendly	intelligible fluent confident careful relaxed	smooth delicate meek	feminine graceful nonnasal high immature
Female, 9:11	graceful bright	intelligible fluent calm careful relaxed nonnasal	delicate	feminine confident smooth high mature

was evidence of the independence of these dimensions in the fact that one of the
children was generally high on the Active-Passive scales but low on the
Fluent-Disfluent. Our research would suggest that confidence-eagerness is not a
unitary dimension, but further research is necessary to resolve this point.

In Williams (1970), the judges rated whether 5th- and 6th-grade children sounded "male-like" or "female-like" and whether they were younger or older, as well as rating on other variables that were more related to dialect and class differences. The sex and age scales correlated to form a factor which accounted for only 6% of the variance in a 4-factor solution. Children who were judged to be male were rated as being older, and those who were judged to be female were thought to be younger. There were no other scales used in the study that would reasonably be expected to group together with sex differences. Since the purpose in obtaining the ratings was to study speech and social status, the factor which reflected sex and age was omitted from further consideration.

An important finding of Williams' work is that the judges' stereotypes may play a large role in the ratings. When brief descriptions of the children, or even simply ethnic labels, were supplied to judges for semantic differential rating, ratings and factors emerged that were very similar to the ratings obtained when judges had actually listened to the children's speech (Williams *et al.*, 1971a). This suggests that the judges may not really be rating such characteristics as fluency or confidence from the speech *per se,* but deciding rather quickly whether the voice is that of a white, black, or Mexican-American child and then making subsequent ratings relative to some internal expectations about these children. Another study showed the effect of such expectations on ratings (Williams *et al.,* 1971b). Judges were shown videotapes of white, black, and Mexican-American children with the children shown from side views so that their lips could not be read. Instead of playing the children's actual speech, however, recordings of standard English speech were played. Thus the speech to be rated had an "ethnic guise" when it was paired with a black or Mexican-American child's face. In these conditions, the ratings of the standard English speech moved toward the ethnic stereotype ratings, with the voice rated more ethnic-nonstandard and less confident-eager. The possible parallel with ratings of sex differences is clear. It is possible that judges may decide immediately that the child is a boy or a girl, and then assign other ratings to match their stereotypes of sex-appropriate characteristics. In this study, we attempted to avoid stereotyped reactions in both the initial descriptive part of the scale development and in the semantic differential ratings by not indicating that we were interested in sex differences. We hoped that the judges would pay attention to the actual characteristics of the voices, and that cues to sex would simply be among them. However, we have no way of knowing how much stereotypes were influencing the results in this study. Future studies which manipulate different aspects of the signal will allow a separation of the various factors involved in the ratings.

CONCLUSIONS

In this paper, we have reported three studies in which judgments were obtained about boys' and girls' voices. Boys and girls between the ages of 5 and

12 years typically sound different from one another, but the cues which allow identification of sex are subtle. The possibility exists that there may already be anatomical differentiation of the vocal tract at this age which would result in phonetic differences, even when children are matched on the basis of general body size.

We suggest that at least part of the reason that boys and girls sound different is that they have learned to use the voice and speech style that is viewed as appropriate for their sex in the culture. For example, sentences provide more cues for the identification of sex than do isolated vowels or backward sentences. The signals that differentiate voice by sex that exist in the child's voice before puberty may reflect the child's sex-role identification. In Sachs *et al.,* the two girls who were almost always perceived as boys were described by a neighbor as having characteristics that our culture associates with boys. One girl was "athletic, strong, and competitive," and the other was "a tomboy, very sports-minded, a real tough kid but well liked." In Experiments I and II reported in this paper, those two girls continued to be identified as boys from isolated vowels and backward sentences.

Many questions about sex differences in speech remain to be resolved:

1. What are the cues that allow listeners to identify sex from hearing a person speak? We have suggested that there are probably sentential cues, such as the smoothness of the sentence or the use of certain intonation patterns, and voice quality cues, such as the formant frequencies. Probably no one cue alone can account for the listeners' accuracy. Speech stimuli can be obtained and modified in various ways to determine the relative contribution of different cues.

2. To what extent are the voice cues (e.g., formant frequency patterns) physically determined, and to what extent are they culturally determined? Although we have argued for the possibility of cultural influences, following Mattingly's hypothesis concerning the differences observed in adult speakers, we cannot rule out the possibility that prepubertal boys have larger vocal tracts than prepubertal girls, given the same height and weight. More data are needed on the anatomical development of the vocal tract in males and females. There is currently no established external index of vocal tract dimensions, so that exact matching of boys and girls on vocal tract size would involve measurements from X-rays.

3. What is the course of development of the various cues to sex identification in speech? We have found that the youngest children in our sample, the four-year-olds, were not well identified. The boys tended to be called girls, even with sentences as stimuli. However, in these studies, the age range of the

children was very large and was likely a great source of confusion for the judges. It is possible that even younger children might be identified as to sex if the age range was limited. Since at least some of the cues (e.g., sentential cues) are certainly learned, we might expect to see them appearing in the speech of children along with other signs of the child's awareness of the appropriateness of certain speech styles. A related question would be whether children can identify the sex of speakers (especially of their peers) from their voices.

4. What is the function of sex differences in speech? Ordinarily, it is advantageous for a species if the sex of individuals is easily discernible to other members of that species. In humans, visual cues are usually available because males and females differ on a number of anatomical characteristics. Clothing and other decorations of the body often enhance these differences. Presumably, masculinity or femininity in voice and speech also functions to mark the sex of an individual clearly, even when visual cues are not available. Differences in speech that come about through acculturation would serve to make males and females more distinct. And, just as visual cues function to attract males and females to each other, sex differences in speech probably also function as an attractive stimulus to the opposite sex. There is also the possibility that the speech styles have taken on functions that are linked with the roles that the culture views as appropriate for each sex. For example, a man might use a more "feminine" voice in certain situations, and a woman, a more "masculine" voice. Sachs *et al.* suggested that both sexes might use exaggerated feminine characteristics in care-giving situations, such as when talking to babies or pets, because care-giving is considered most appropriate for women.

5. What are the effects of sex differences in speech? For males, presumably having a "masculine" speech style would have generally positive effects. Having an "effeminate" voice, on the other hand, would be detrimental in most social settings. For females, the situation may be somewhat more complex. A voice which is perceived as "feminine" would be beneficial to a woman in certain roles, but that speech style may carry connotations of the traditional female roles. For example, the woman with a sweet, gentle voice and very polite manner of speaking might be viewed as lacking in authority. Yet if she adopts a more "masculine" speech style, she might be thought of as "overly aggressive." As yet, we know very little about listeners' evaluations of speakers and the messages they are presenting as influenced by the speaker's voice and speech characteristics. Undoubtedly, one important topic for future research is the study of attitudes toward males and females (both children and adults) as a function of the degree of masculinity or femininity in their speech.

REFERENCES

Bodine, Ann. (1975). Sex differentiation in language. In Barrie Thorne and Nancy Henley (eds.), *Language and sex: difference and dominance.* Rowley, Mass.: Newbury House.

Brend, Ruth. (1972). Male-female intonation patterns in American English. *Proceedings of the Seventh International Congress of Phonetic Sciences, 1971.* The Hague: Mouton. Reprinted in Barrie Thorne and Nancy Henley (eds.) (1975), *Language and sex: difference and dominance.* Rowley, Mass.: Newbury House.

Chamberlain, Alexander F. (1912). Women's languages. *American Anthropologist,* 14, 579-81.

Colton, Raymond H. & Cooker, Harry S. (1968). Perceived nasality in the speech of the deaf. *Journal of Speech and Hearing Research,* 11, 553-59.

Fischer, J. (1958). Social influences in the choice of a linguistic variant. *Word,* 14, 47-56.

Haas, Mary. (1944). Men's and women's speech in Koasati. *Language,* 20, 142-49.

Hunter, W. S. & Garn, Stanley. (1972). Disproportionate sexual dimorphism in the human face. *American Journal of Physical Anthropology,* 36, 133-38.

Key, Mary Ritchie. (1972). Linguistic behavior of male and female. *Linguistics,* 88 (Aug. 15), 15-31.

Kirchner, J. A. (1970). *Physiology of the larynx,* rev. ed. Rochester, Minn.: American Academy of Opthalmology and Otolaryngology.

Labov, William, Yaeger, M., & Steiner, R. (1972). A quantitative study of sound change in progress. Final report on National Science Foundation contract NSF-GS-3287. Philadelphia, Pa.: U. S. Regional Survey.

Lakoff, Robin. (1973). Language and woman's place. *Language in Society,* 2, 45-79.

Mattingly, Ignatius M. (1966). Speaker variation and vocal-tract size. *Journal of the Acoustical Society of America* (abstract), 39, 1219.

Negus, V. E. (1949). *The comparative anatomy and physiology of the larynx.* New York: Hafner.

Osgood, Charles E., Suci, G. J., & Tannenbaum, P. H. (1957). *The measurement of meaning.* Urbana: Univ. of Illinois Press.

Peterson, G. & Barney, H. (1952). Control methods used in a study of the vowels. *Journal of the Acoustical Society of America,* 24, 175-84.

Sachs, Jacqueline, Lieberman, Philip, & Erickson, Donna. (1973). Anatomical and cultural determinants of male and female speech. In Roger W. Shuy & Ralph W. Fasold (eds.), *Language attitudes: current trends and prospects.* Washington, D. C.: Georgetown Univ. Press.

Schwartz, M. F. (1968). Identification of speaker sex from isolated, voiceless fricatives. *Journal of the Acoustical Society of America,* 43, 1178-79.

Schwartz, M. F. & Rine, Helen. (1968). Identification of speaker sex from isolated, whispered vowels. *Journal of the Acoustical Society of America,* 44, 1736-37.

Sherman, D. (1954). The merits of backward playing of connected speech in the scaling of voice quality disorders. *Journal of Speech and Hearing Disorders,* 19, 312-21.

Shuy, Roger W. (1969). Subjective judgments in sociolinguistics analysis. In Alatis, J. E. (ed.), *Linguistics and the teaching of standard English to speakers of other languages or dialects,* Washington, D. C.: Georgetown Univ. Press.

Shuy, Roger W., Wolfram, W., & Riley, W. K. (1967). A study of social dialects in Detroit. Final report, Project 6-1347. Washington, D. C.: U. S. Office of Education.

Spriestersbach, D. C. (1955). Assessing nasal quality in cleft palate speech of children. *Journal of Speech and Hearing Disorders,* 20, 266-70.

Walker, G. F. & Kowalski, C. J. (1972). On the growth of the mandible. *American Journal of Physical Anthropology,* 36, 111-18.

Weinberg, Bernd & Bennett, Suzanne (1971). Speaker sex recognition of 5- and 6-year-old children's speech. *Journal of the Acoustical Society of America,* 50, 1210-13.

Williams, Frederick. (1970). Psychological correlates of speech characteristics: On sounding "disadvantaged." *Journal of Speech and Hearing Research,* 13, 472-88.

Williams, Frederick. (1973). Some research notes on dialect attitudes and stereotypes. In Shuy, Roger W., and Fasold, Ralph W. (eds.), *Language attitudes: current trends and prospects.* Washington, D. C.: Georgetown Univ. Press.

Williams, Frederick, Whitehead, J. L., & Miller, L. M. (1971a). Attitudinal correlates of children's speech characteristics. Research Report, Project 0-0336. Washington, D. C.: U. S. Office of Education.

Williams, Frederick, Whitehead, J. L., & Miller, L. M. (1971b). Ethnic stereotyping and judgments of children's speech. *Speech Monographs,* 38, 166-70.

TEACHER-CHILD VERBAL INTERACTION:
AN APPROACH TO THE STUDY OF SEX DIFFERENCES*

Louise Cherry

Several psychologists who have reviewed studies reporting sex differences have concluded that the superior verbal fluency of females is one of the most consistent and stable psychological sex differences (Bardwick, 1971; Garai and Scheinfeld, 1968; Maccoby, 1966; Sherman, 1971; Terman and Tyler, 1954). This paper includes a critique of the methodology and assumptions of the naturalistic observational studies which have reported that preschool girls perform better than boys in this particular language usage, verbal fluency (Jersild and Ritzman, 1938; Smith and Connolly, 1972; Young, 1941). The paper also reports some findings from a study of the effect of the sex of child on teacher-child dyadic verbal interaction in classrooms, specifically focusing on verbal fluency, verbal initiation of verbal interaction, question-answer acknowledgment sequences, and control and attention-getting aspects of verbal interaction.

Some naturalistic observational studies have reported the superior verbal fluency or talkativeness of preschool girls compared with boys (Jersild and Ritzman, 1938; Smith and Connolly, 1972; Young, 1941). Young's study is a good example of the methods used to assess verbal fluency in these studies. The subjects of the study were 74 male and female preschool children, aged 30-65

*This paper is based on a doctoral dissertation presented to Harvard University, 1974. I thank Courtney B. Cazden, Carolyn Edwards, Nancy M. Henley, Aimee Dorr Leifer, Kathleen Sylva, Shelly E. Taylor, and Barrie Thorne for their helpful comments on earlier versions of this paper. This research was supported by a Dissertation Fellowship for Women's Studies, granted by the Ford Foundation.

months, from two socioeconomic groups, one whose parents were on relief, and one whose parents were from the middle and upper-middle classes. Data collection in this study consisted of the experimenter's observing each child in four settings: outside in play, inside in play, inside looking at books, and during dinner. There were 280 minutes of observation for each child.

> The experimenter made verbatim records of the meaningful and meaningless vocalizations of each subject. A system of abbreviations and symbols for names and common words was used to facilitate recording. (Young, 1941: 19)

In the data analysis verbal fluency or talkativeness was defined as the number of comprehensible words spoken per 10 minutes. Young justifies the use of only "comprehensible" words since "it seems inadvisable to put meaningless syllables on a par with words" (Young, 1941: 61). The results of this study showed that girls were significantly more verbally fluent (as measured by the number of comprehensible words per ten minutes) than boys.

In order to evaluate the sex difference finding, several issues must be raised about this research. First of all, the methods of data collection involved transformation of the "raw behavior" of speech into categories of "meaningful vocalizations" and "meaningless vocalizations" recorded by " . . . a system of abbreviations and symbols for names and common words" (Young, 1941: 19). Many language investigators have pointed out that it is impossible to write verbatim records of verbal interaction. The observer may, for example, edit some utterances, disregard others, overlook or neglect to record grammatical errors (Soskin and John, 1963). The categories of "meaningless" and "meaningful" vocalizations involve value judgments. Even if acceptable levels of reliability are obtained between observers who are "naive" to the hypotheses of the study, the observers probably share the same sex-role expectations, attitudes, and stereotypes of the culture, and this can influence their transformation of the "raw behavior" of speech. We have no way of assessing this source of error. For example, if the observers believe that girls are more fluent or that girls should be more fluent than boys, then these observers may be likely to hear and then record a girl's utterances as "meaningful" in comparison with a boy's utterances. The sex of the observer may also affect transformations of speech.

The second issue about Young's research is her assumption that verbal fluency is a characteristic of the individual speaker. Young measured verbal fluency as speech units per time units, a rate of speech production. This definition of verbal fluency is similar to vocalization rate, which has been used in some investigations of infant behavior.[1]

Is verbal fluency a characteristic of individual speech, as existing research has assumed? Or is verbal fluency better conceptualized as a part of verbal interaction between two or more speakers? Lewis and Lee-Painter (1974) have argued that models of dyadic interaction that define the behavior of only one participant deny the very nature of this interaction.

> Any study—regardless of direction—that fails to consider the dyadic relationship cannot accurately describe the elements. Once we consider the dyad we must at once conclude that *both* actors actively and significantly influence each other. (Lewis and Lee-Painter, 1974: 46)

How talkative you are depends on how talkative you are "allowed" to be in a particular conversation. Fluency can therefore refer to the length of verbal interaction, as measured in speech units; for example a verbal interaction between two people might consist of a total of 20 utterances; or it can be measured in minutes, for example a verbal interaction between two people might last five minutes. Fluency can also refer to qualitative aspects of verbal interaction, such as the reciprocity of verbal interaction. For example, in one verbal interaction, one participant might do most of the speaking, while the other listens. In another verbal interaction both participants might take an equal number of turns speaking and listening.

If fluency is regarded as a quality of verbal interaction rather than a characteristic of the individual speaker, then Young's distinction between "meaningless" and "meaningful" vocalizations eliminates part of the communicated meaning of the verbal interaction. For example, one person's turn at talking could consist of the nonlexical vocalization *mm,* which serves in some contexts as an affirmative answer to the other speaker's question.[2] Young's distinction between "meaningless" and "meaningful" vocalizations is one of articulation of speech rather than fluency.

A methodology appropriate to uncover sex differences in dyadic verbal interaction must include procedures of data collection and data analysis that avoid the problems inherent in previous research. The data collected should be actual speech, recorded by audio or video equipment for later analysis in the laboratory (see Cazden, 1975). "Good data" involve the gathering of large samples of well-recorded speech as it naturally occurs in conversations. The methodology for data collection should not alter the social reality under scrutiny; hence the researcher should, whenever possible, avoid intrusive methods of data collection. Wireless microphone (radio transmitter and receiver) and video recording equipment have made the task of collecting "good data" easier for the investigator now than at the time when Young was doing her research.

Data analysis must include units of analysis that measure the quality of verbal interaction itself, as well as characteristics of the speech of individual speakers, when appropriate to test the hypotheses. For example, the repeated finding that girls are more fluent than boys suggests that teacher-girl dyadic verbal interaction should be more fluent (i.e., longer and more reciprocal) than teacher-boy dyadic verbal interaction. A related question is who initiates the interactions. Levy (1972) has suggested that girls are socialized into patterns of nonindependence and noninitiation in preschool. It follows then, that a greater percentage of teacher-girl dyadic verbal interactions should be verbally initiated by the teacher rather than the child, as compared with teacher-boy dyadic verbal interactions.

Some characteristics of the speech of individual speakers in dyadic verbal interaction are also relevant to exploring sex-difference hypotheses. For example, one of the assumptions of dyadic relationships is that " . . . *both* actors actively and significantly influence each other" (Lewis and Lee-Painter, 1974: 46). Serbin *et al.* (1973) have reported that boys (compared to girls) are more disruptive and noncompliant in the preschool classroom. It is therefore expected that teachers' speech to boys (compared to girls) should contain more controlling speech, such as commands. Another example of when characteristics of an individual's speech can be used to test a sex difference hypothesis is derived from Brophy and Good's (1970) finding that boys receive more evaluative feedback from their teachers than girls. It is therefore expected that boys (compared to girls) should be more likely to receive verbal feedback from their teachers.

Dyadic relationships with teachers comprise one important interactional context for preschool children. The author of this paper conducted a study of dyadic verbal interaction between female preschool teachers and male and female children to find out how sex of child affected these verbal interactions. The specific details of this study are reported elsewhere (Cherry, 1974); this paper focuses on hypothesized differences in the quality of dyadic verbal interaction between female preschool teachers and the girls, and the boys, in their classes. Based on the findings of previous studies, the following qualitative differences in teacher-girl dyadic verbal interaction, and teacher-boy dyadic verbal interaction were expected:

1. Teacher-girl dyadic verbal interaction would be more fluent, i.e., longer and more reciprocal, than teacher-boy dyadic verbal interaction.

2. A greater percentage of teacher-girl dyadic verbal interaction would be verbally initiated by the teacher rather than the child, as compared with teacher-boy dyadic verbal interaction.

3. A greater percentage of teacher-boy question-answer sequences (a boy's answer to a teacher's question in sequence) would be verbally acknowledged by the teacher, as compared with teacher-girl question-answer sequences.

4. Teachers' speech to boys would be more controlling and attention-getting as compared with teachers' speech to girls.

METHOD

Subjects

The subjects of this study were four female preschool teachers, two (one head, one assistant) from each of two Boston area private schools, and the 38 children (16 girls and 22 boys) in their classes. The age of the students ranged from two years 9 months to four years 5 months. All the participants in the study were middle-class speakers of English. The parents of the children, the teachers, and the directors of the schools gave their informed consent for the study to take place, but none knew the specific hypotheses of the study. The schools chosen for the study were selected to be as similar as possible, both in the population served, as well as in the way the schools were run.

Data Collection

The data were collected by recording the spontaneously occurring conversations between teachers and children in the classrooms. The recordings were made by a small cassette tape recorder which each teacher carried over her shoulder. Each of the four teachers carried the recorder on five different days in two situations per day, so that 40 data samples of not more than 30 minutes each were collected, totalling more than 16 hours of recording. The situations were "juice," when the teacher was seated at a table drinking juice and eating crackers with the children; and "play," when the teacher was walking around the classroom engaged in various activities with the children. During recording the author stood or sat unobtrusively while making contextual notes.

The tape recordings were transcribed by two research assistants (one female, one male) who did not know the hypotheses of the study. They were instructed to record as accurately as possible everything that was said by the teacher and the child she was talking with, without altering the grammatical or verbal form of the speech. The research assistants recorded false starts, fragments of words and phrases, hesitations and filled pauses (including *um* and *ah*), nonlexical expressions, interruptions, and simultaneous or overlapping speech. Additional information relating to the text of the speech, such as "whispering" or unintelligible speech, was indicated. Reliabilities were calculated for this transcription process; the percentage agreement for words was 94 percent and for utterance boundaries, 93 percent. The transcripts were checked and then typed. The typist substituted letters of the alphabet for children's and teachers' names so that analysis of the data could be done "blind" with regard to the sex of the child.

Data Analysis

The unit of analysis of conversation was the *verbal interaction*. This was defined as all utterances between the teacher and one child in sequence. The analysis also included the *verbal initiator* of the verbal interaction—that is, the first speaker in the verbal interaction, and the *turn*—that is, all utterances of one speaker until the other speaker begins speaking. All these units of analysis refer to qualitative aspects of verbal interaction. In addition, the data analysis included the following measures of the speech of individual speakers: A *word* was defined as all words in the lexicon not including nonlexical items such as *shhh* or *ah.* An *utterance* was defined as a string of words communicating one idea and bounded by a pause of one second or more. An *attentional marker* was defined as a word in the first position of an utterance, followed by a pause of less than one second, which serves to catch or hold the listener's attention.[3] Attentional markers included the words *hey, see, look, watch, no, now, OK,* or the listener's name. A *repetition* was defined as the same utterance said by the same speaker within five utterances of the original utterance. A *directive* was defined as a request for action or object in the form of an imperative, a statement, or an interrogative. A *question-answer verbal acknowledgement sequence* was defined as when a teacher asks a child a question, the child answers it, and then the teacher responds to the answer with a verbal acknowledgement in sequence. The reliabilities of these codings were calculated as the percentage agreement of the research assistants' codings of a subset of the 40 transcripts. The reliabilities were all greater than 80 percent.

In order to test the hypotheses the following measurements were calculated for each teacher, as an average for all of that teacher's verbal interaction with boys, and an average of all of that teacher's verbal interactions with girls:

1. Fluency was measured by the number of utterances per verbal interaction (length) and the number of turns per verbal interaction (reciprocity).

2. Verbal initiation was measured as the percentage of all teacher-child verbal interactions that were verbally initiated by the teacher.

3. Verbal feedback or acknowledgement by the teacher was measured as the percentage of all teacher-child question-answer sequences that were verbally acknowledged by the teacher in sequence.

4. Control and attention-getting aspects of teachers' speech in verbal interaction with children was measured by the percentage of all teacher utterances that had attentional markers, the percentage of all teacher utterances that were directives, and the percentage of all teacher utterances that were repetitions.

RESULTS

The data were analyzed by two-way analyses of variance with repeated measures on the factors of Sex of Child, and Situation. It was hypothesized that teachers' verbal interactions with girls (compared with boys) would be more fluent, i.e., longer, as measured by utterances per verbal interaction, and more reciprocal, as measured by turns per verbal interaction. This hypothesis was not confirmed. The analyses of variance for both measures of fluency that were computed for Sex of Child yielded no significant results. There were no significant differences in either the length or the reciprocity of teacher-girl and teacher-boy dyadic verbal interactions.

It was hypothesized that teacher-girl verbal interactions would be more likely to have been verbally initiated by the teacher than by the child, in comparison with teacher-boy verbal interactions. This hypothesis was not confirmed. The analysis of variance for the number of verbal initiations per verbal interaction that was computed for Sex of Child yielded no significant results. There was no significant difference in the percentage of all teacher-boy verbal interactions and teacher-girl verbal interactions that were verbally initiated by the teacher.

It was hypothesized that in a question-answer sequence the teacher would be more likely to verbally acknowledge a boy's answer than a girl's. Not only was this hypothesis not confirmed, but the reverse was true. The analysis of variance for verbal acknowledgements that was computed for Sex of Child showed a highly significant result. Teachers verbally acknowledged a significantly greater percentage of teacher-girl question-answer sequences (87 percent) than teacher-boy question-answer sequences (75 percent; $F = 78.9$, df = 1,3, $p < .005$).

It was hypothesized that teachers' speech to boys compared to girls would be more controlling (greater use of directives and repetitions) and more attention-getting (greater use of attentional markers). This hypothesis was partially confirmed. The analysis of variance for attentional-marked utterances that was computed for Sex of Child yielded a highly significant result. Teachers used a significantly greater percentage of attentional-marked utterances in speech to boys (8 percent) compared with speech to girls (4 percent; $F = 27.0$, df = 1,3, $p < .01$). The analysis of variance for directive utterances that was computed for Sex of Child did not yield significant results, but the trend in the data was as predicted. Teachers used a greater percentage of directive utterances in speech to boys (15 percent) than to girls (12 percent), but this difference was not significant ($F = 3.0$, df = 1,3, $p < .20$). An analysis of repetitions was not done since the frequencies of exact repetitions were very low in these data.

DISCUSSION

The results of this study do not substantiate the frequently mentioned claim of girls' superior verbal fluency. No sex difference appeared in qualitative analysis of teacher-child dyadic verbal interaction, the reciprocity of interaction, nor in the length of verbal interaction. Some of the earlier studies which reported that girls were more fluent than boys, for example, Young (1941), were based on a research methodology that (1) relied on interpretive procedures which were made explicit (e.g., on-the-spot transformation of raw speech behavior); and (2) defined fluency as an individual characteristic of the speaker. This analysis assumed that fluency is a quality of verbal interaction and not a characteristic of an individual's speech. How talkative you are depends on how talkative you are "allowed" to be in a particular conversation.

The results of this study show that teachers, who to a great extent are the controllers of the course of interaction with children in the context of the preschool classroom, "allow" girls to take no more turns at talking than they "allow" boys, and the length of these verbal interactions is also about the same for the two sexes. Aspects of fluency as defined in this study that appear in the context of the preschool classroom are the same for boys, and girls, in their verbal interactions with teachers.

The findings reported in this study show that girls are more likely than boys to receive feedback in the form of verbal acknowledgement of their answers to teachers' questions. The following sequences (from the data) illustrate this pattern:

Teacher: Can you tell me what they're selling at that store over there?
Child: Ya.
Teacher: What are they selling?

Teacher: How many are there?
Child: Two.
Teacher: Two.

In interpreting this finding, however, there are two points to note. First, in most of the cases where boys' answers were not acknowledged, the next turn (where a teacher acknowledgement could have come but did not) was the beginning of a new verbal interaction with/by another child. In this naturalistic study, the probability of teacher verbal acknowledgement of a question-answer sequence with one child, and the probability of occurrence of a new verbal interaction with another child, was confounded. Secondly, the finding that girls were more likely to have their answers verbally acknowledged by the teacher suggests that girls were getting more feedback on their behavior at this "micro" level. However, this study examined only verbal feedback. It could be that girls are less likely, in general, to receive nonverbal acknowledgement from teachers.

The results give no evidence that girls are less verbally initiating than boys are, in this case in verbal interaction with their teachers in preschool classrooms. It is possible, however, that there are sex differences in other kinds of initiating behaviors.

The results of the study show that teachers' speech to boys in verbal interaction was more controlling and attention-getting as compared with teachers' speech to girls. One of the assumptions of an interactional model of the adult-child dyad is that the child's behavior affects the adult's behavior, and vice versa (Bell, 1971; Lewis and Lee-Painter, 1974). Many investigators have reported that preschool boys are more physically aggressive than girls (Feshbach, 1970; Maccoby, 1972) and more noncompliant and disruptive in the preschool classroom (Serbin *et al.,* 1973) than girls. Some have suggested that the preschool classroom is a situation of conflict for boys (Kagan, 1964; Lee and Wolinsky, 1973; Levy, 1972; Sherman, 1971). It is not surprising that teachers' speech to boys in the classroom contained more attention-getting features and was more controlling in the use of more directives. This teacher strategy to help boys control their asocial behavior may have included attempts by the teacher to channel boys into doing activities appropriate for the classroom context. The following conversation is an example of this. It occurred between one of the teachers and a three-year-old boy. The overall purpose of this conversation was directive—to get the boy to stop playing with "bombs" inside the classroom. The attentional markers and the directive utterances are italicized.

Teacher: *OK*, where you gonna put those bombs before you go to class?
Child: Outside.
Teacher: *Put them in your pocket before you go in the class.*
Child: My pocket got a hole in it.
Teacher: Both pockets.
Child: Yeah, both pockets.
Teacher: Maybe G can keep it in (her/his) pocket.

In conclusion, the results of this study raise other research questions, such as to what extent these findings can be generalized across different contexts. This study examined qualitative differences in teachers' dyadic verbal interactions with girls and boys in preschool classrooms. The results are generalizable to the middle-class English-speaking population of female preschool teachers and the children in their classes. The aspects of teacher-child verbal interaction considered in this study should be investigated in other contexts to understand the variation of sex difference in language performance. These contexts might include children's verbal interactions with male teachers and with other children in the classroom setting; or with parents and siblings in the home; or with peers outside the home and school settings.

Researchers investigating sex differences in behavior cannot rely on models which reduce human interaction to characteristics of individuals. It is hoped that studies of sex differences in other interactional contexts, such as the mother-infant dyad, will focus on the nature of the interaction as well as on the characteristics of the individual participants, and will examine how these combine to produce the complex network of behaviors we observe. Perhaps then we can better understand the dynamics of sex-differentiated behavior in interactional contexts.

NOTES

[1]Several investigators have found female infants superior in vocalization rate compared to male infants (Kagan, 1969; Goldberg and Lewis, 1969; Goldberg, Godfrey, and Lewis, 1967).

[2]Some investigators of conversational interaction have shown that nonlexical items and fragments of speech such as *uh* and *mmhm* are important in the organization of conversation (Jefferson, 1973; Schegloff, 1968; Schegloff and Sacks, 1973).

[3]This analysis was suggested by one of the analyses used in Shatz and Gelman (1973).

REFERENCES

Arrington, R. E. (1939). Time sampling studies of child behavior. *Psychological Monographs,* 51, 228.

Bardwick, J. M. (1971). *The psychology of women.* New York: Harper & Row.

Barker, R. (ed.). (1963). *The stream of behavior.* New York: Appleton, Century, Crofts.

Bell, P. (1972). Stimulus control of parent or caretaker behavior by offspring. *Developmental Psychology,* 4, 63-72.

Brophy, J. E. & Good, T. L. (1970). Teacher communication of differential expectations for children's classroom performance: some behavioral data. *Journal of Educational Psychology,* 61, 365-74.

Carmichael, L. (1954). *Handbook of child psychology.* New York: Wiley, Ch. 19.

Cazden, C. B. (1975). Methodologies for classroom interaction research: a reply to reviews of *Functions of language in the classroom.* In M. King and N. Flanders (eds.), *Research in the teaching of English.* Forthcoming.

Cherry, L. J. (1974). Sex differences in preschool teacher-child verbal interaction. Unpublished doctoral dissertation, Harvard Univ.

Feshbach, S. (1970). Aggression. In P. Mussen (ed.), *Carmichael's manual of child psychology.* New York: Wiley, 159-261.

Garai, J. E. & Scheinfeld, A. (1968). Sex differences in mental and behavioral traits. *Genetic Psychology Monographs,* 77, 169-299.

Goldberg, S., Godfrey, L., & Lewis, M. (1967). Play behavior in the year old infant: early sex differences. Paper presented at the Society for Research in Child Development.

Goldberg, S. & Lewis, M. (1969). Play behavior in the year old infant: some sex differences. *Child Development,* 40, 21-31.

Jefferson, G. (1973). A case of precision timing in ordinary conversation: overlapped tag-positioned address terms in closing sequences. *Semiotica, 9,* 47-96.

Jersild, A. & Ritzman, R. (1938). Aspects of language development: the growth of loquacity and vocabulary. *Child Development, 9,* 243-59.

Jones, N. B. (ed.). (1972). *Ethological studies of child behavior.* Cambridge, England: Cambridge Univ. Press.

Kagan, J. (1964). The child's sex role classification of school objects. *Child Development, 35,* 1051-56.

———. (1969). Continuity in cognitive development during the first year. *Merrill-Palmer Quarterly, 15* (1), 101-19.

King, M. & Flanders, N. (1975). *Research in the teaching of English.* Forthcoming.

Lee, P. & Wolinsky, A. (1973). Male teachers of young children: a preliminary empirical study. *Young Children, 28,* 342-52.

Levy, B. (1972). The school's role in the sex-role stereotyping of girls: a feminist review of the literature. *Feminist Studies, 1* (1), 5-73.

Lewis, M. & Lee-Painter, S. (1974). An interactional approach to the mother-infant dyad. In Lewis, M. & Rosenblum, L. (eds.), *The effect of the infant on its caregiver.* New York: Wiley.

Lewis, M. & Rosenblum, L. (eds.). (1974). *The effect of the infant on its caregiver.* New York: Wiley.

Maccoby, E. A. (ed.). (1966). *The development of sex differences.* Stanford, Calif.: Stanford Univ. Press.

———. (1972). Differential socialization of boys and girls. Paper given at the American Psychological Assoc.

———. (1966). Sex differences in intellectual factors. In E. Maccoby (ed.), *The development of sex differences.* Stanford, Calif.: Stanford Univ. Press.

Mussen, P. (1970). *Carmichael's manual of child psychology,* 3rd edition. New York: Wiley.

Schegloff, E. (1968). Sequencing in conversational openings. *American Anthropologist, 70,* 1075-95.

Schegloff, E. and Sacks, H. (1973). Opening up closings. *Semiotica, 7,* 289-327.

Serbin, L. *et al.* (1973). A comparison of teacher response to the preacademic and problem behavior of boys and girls. *Child Development, 44,* 796-804.

Shatz, M. & Gelman, R. (1973). The development of communication: modifications in the speech of young children as a function of listener. *Monographs of the Society for Child Development.* Serial No. 152.

Sherman, J. (1971). *On the psychology of women.* Springfield, Ill.: Charles C. Thomas.

Smith, P. & Connolly, K. (1972). Patterns of play and social interaction in preschool children. In N. B. Jones (ed.), *Ethological studies of child behavior.* Cambridge, England: Cambridge Univ. Press.

Soskin, W. F. & John, V. P. (1963). A study of spontaneous talk. In R. Barker (ed.), *The stream of behavior.* New York: Appleton, Century, Crofts.

Terman, L. & Tyler, L. (1954). Psychological sex differences. In L. Carmichael, *Handbook of child psychology.* New York: Wiley, Ch. 19.

Young, F. (1941). An analysis of certain variables in a developmental study of language. *Genetic Psychology Monographs,* 23, 2-141.

POWER, SEX, AND NONVERBAL COMMUNICATION*

Nancy M. Henley

In front of, and defending, the larger political-economic structure that determines our lives and defines the context of human relationships, there is a micropolitical structure that helps maintain it. The "trivia" of everyday life—using "sir" or first name, touching others, dropping the eyes, smiling, interrupting, and so on—that characterize these micropolitics are commonly understood as facilitators of social intercourse, but are not recognized as defenders of the status quo—of the state, of the wealthy, of authority, of all those whose power may be challenged. Nevertheless, these minutiae find their place on a continuum of social control which extends from internalized socialization (the colonization of the mind) at the one end to sheer physical force (guns, clubs, incarceration) at the other.

Micropolitical cues are, moreover, of particular importance in the study of woman's place in our society, for several reasons. First, like any other oppressed group, women should know all the chains binding them. Second, women are likely targets for this subtle form of social control for two reasons: they are particularly socialized to docility and passivity, and their physical integration

*Reprinted from the *Berkeley Journal of Sociology,* 1973-4, 18, 1-26. This paper was written with the partial support of Special Research Fellowship 1F03MH35977 from the National Institute of Mental Health. It has benefited from criticism and discussion with numerous friends and associates, including Roger Brown, Ann Calderwood, editors of the *Berkeley Journal of Sociology,* and many women, particularly women of the Center for Cognitive Studies, Harvard University.

around centers of power (as wives, secretaries, etc.) ensures their frequent interaction (verbal and nonverbal) with those in power.[1] Finally, women are more sensitive than men to social cues in general, as many studies have shown, and to nonverbal cues in particular (Argyle *et al.,* 1970).

This paper will seek to examine certain nonverbal behaviors, and some subtle verbal ones, in their social context as a step toward understanding the myriad faces of power.

SEXUAL DIMORPHISM OR UNIMORPHISM?

From the beginning we should guard against the mistake of assuming that the observed nonverbal (or even verbal) differences between the human sexes result from biology. In 1943 Galt pointed out humanity's long journey from an apparently little-acknowledged distinction between the sexes (and early bisexuality and natural "polymorphous perversity") to the present "Western" cultural assumption of extreme sexual distinction (and narrowly channeled sexuality). He writes,

> . . . it should be clear that the *either-or* type of sexual behavior demanded of man and woman by the mores of Western culture under threat of severe penalty is not in line with the trend of sexual adjustment as it has developed throughout biological evolution. (p. 9)

Birdwhistell (1970) writes that when different animal species are rated on a spectrum by the extent of their sexual dimorphism, on the basis of secondary sexual characteristics "man seems far closer to the unimorphic end of the spectrum than he might like to believe" (p. 41). He states that his work in kinesics leads him to postulate "that man and probably a number of other weakly dimorphic species necessarily organize much of gender display and recognition at the level of position, movement, and expression" (p. 42). Thus we must realize that much of our nonverbal behavior, far from being "natural," has been developed and modified to emphasize and display sex differences, much like our manner of dress. (Class differences are signaled and emphasized in these ways too.)

COMMUNICATION–VERBAL AND NONVERBAL

Our culture emphasizes verbal over nonverbal communication. English is taught in our schools through all grades, with the aims of both better understanding (diagramming sentences, learning Latin roots) and better expression (writing compositions). Nonverbal communication isn't taught: we never learn to analyze what certain postures, gestures, and looks mean, or how to express ourselves better nonverbally. (Of course, nonverbal communication is learned informally, just as language is learned before we enter schools to study it.) This doesn't mean everybody doesn't *know* that looks and postures mean something, perhaps everything, especially in emotion-charged interaction. But mentioning looks and postures is illegitimate in reporting communication; legal transcripts and newspaper accounts don't record them. And they are seldom allowed in personal argument ("What look? What tone of voice? Look, did I say OK, or didn't I?")

Yet, with all our ignorance about nonverbal communication, the evidence is that the nonverbal message greatly overpowers the verbal one; one estimate (Argyle *et al.,* 1970) is that it carries 4.3 times the weight. In the face of the facts that nonverbal communication is more important than verbal, that it helps maintain the power structure, that women are particularly influenced by it, and that it is glaringly ignored in our education and disallowed in argument, it becomes important for all those deprived of power, and particularly women, to learn all they can about how it affects their lives, and to apply that knowledge to their struggle for liberation.

Most of the literature on nonverbal communication emphasizes solidarity relations (friendship, liking, attraction) rather than power relations. The popular literature on "body language" (e.g., Fast, 1970; Montagu, 1971; Morris, 1971), where it's not charlatanry, concentrates primarily on intimacy and communication between supposed equals. The empirical literature (e.g., Duncan, 1969; Mehrabian, 1972; Scheflen, 1972) likewise tends to focus on the emotional and solidarity aspects of nonverbal communication.

For insights into the *status* aspects of nonverbal communication, a more fruitful source is the anecdotal descriptions of writers like Goffman and Haley. Haley in a well-known essay (1962) discusses "The Art of Psychoanalysis" from the point of view of gamesmanship. He notes the importance of the physical aspects of this status-laden interaction:

> By placing the patient on a couch, the analyst gives the patient the feeling of having his feet up in the air and the knowledge that the analyst has both feet on the ground. Not only is the patient disconcerted by having to lie down while talking, but he finds himself literally below the analyst and so his one-down position is geographically emphasized. In addition, the analyst seats himself behind the couch where he can watch the patient but the patient cannot watch him. This gives the patient the sort of disconcerted feeling a person has when sparring with an opponent while blindfolded. Unable to see what response his ploys provoke, he is unsure when he is one-up and one-down. . . . Another purpose is served by the position behind the couch. Inevitably what the analyst says becomes exaggerated in importance since the patient lacks any other means of determining his effect on the analyst. (pp. 209-210)

Goffman (1956), in his intriguing essay "The Nature of Deference and Demeanor," points to many characteristics associated with status. "Between superordinate and subordinate," he writes, "we may expect to find asymmetrical relations, the superordinate having the right to exercise certain familiarities which the subordinate is not allowed to reciprocate." Goffman cites such familiarities as using familiar address, asking for personal information, touching, teasing, and informal demeanor.

Some Conceptual Problems

As Mehrabian (1972) has pointed out, "nonverbal behavior," in its traditionally broad usage, has included subtle aspects of verbal behavior as well. This article will not dwell on problems of terminology in a rather confused field where distinctions are made or not made between such terms as paralinguistic, extralinguistic, linguistic, subtle, implicit, nonverbal, kinesic, and proxemic. I will discuss first some of those aspects of language which are not part of familiar linguistic analysis, and then a group of non-language behaviors. It should be kept in mind at all times, however, that the artificial divisions created by traditions of study and by this particular account are not real: communication is integral, carried on at many levels and in many channels simultaneously.

I will not investigate the relationships of these behaviors to *power* and *status* separately. Status and power are usually confounded; when writing of specific findings, I will be specific about which variable the researchers investigated. When writing of my own theories regarding nonverbal communication, however, I may refer either to power or to status or to both.

Since males are likely to have more status and power than females, it may be difficult to determine whether sex or status is the appropriate variable to be associated with a particular behavior. For example, are female secretaries touched because they are subordinates, or because they are females, or both? The answer is probably both. Many studies demonstrate separately the effects of status and sex, but for some questions we will have to await further research.

The relation of nonverbal cues to the exercise of power is complex. On a simple behavioral level, we may observe first that they are *associated* with power or the lack of it. Further they may *affect* the power relationship, for example, when in an established relationship a dominance gesture is not met with submission. On an analytical level, we may decide that the gestures act as cues *symbolic* of power, both to display for observers and to *express* for both sender and receiver the power relation. On a theoretical level, we may suggest that nonverbal behaviors are used overall to *maintain* the power relations of a society, but in individual situations may help *establish* such relations, as when people in a competitive situation begin to seek dominance over each other. For the most part this article will deal with the association between behavior and status in the maintenance of social structure.

The observations and descriptions cited in the following studies are based at times on somewhat unrefined methods of observation, but that only indicates the developing state of this field of investigation and ought not stop us from reviewing them and seeing the relations between them. The questions thus raised, and conclusions drawn, will point toward future directions for research, in the continual interplay that the relation between theory and research requires.

SUBTLE ASPECTS OF LANGUAGE

Although we are focusing on nonverbal communication, we know that language also carries messages of status in its structure and usage. Sociolinguists have for some years pursued political, class, and status aspects of language, but until recently only feminists looked into ("complained about") sexism in our language.

Male/Female Distinctions

Two comprehensive reviews of male/female distinctions in languages have now been made. Lakoff (1973) discusses both the concept of "woman's language" in English (which, when used, works against her) and the deprecation of women implicit in general usage. Examples of woman's language are given in the lexicon, syntax, intonation and other supra-segmental patterns. There is also provocative discussion of sex-differentiated language learning in children and of the interaction of sex and class with language. Lakoff illustrates the weakness introduced into woman's English by its use of tag-questions (e.g., "The Vietnam war is terrible, isn't it?") and tag-orders (e.g., "Won't you please close the door?"). Other examples can be added to this list: hesitating, apologizing, and disparaging one's own statement (e.g., "I don't know anything about it, but. . . .").

Key (1972) examines the linguistic behavior of males and females in phonological, grammatical, and semantic components, emphasizing analysis in situational context. She looks both at differences in women's and men's usages and at the implicit sexism in structure and usage in the phonological realm (pronunciation and intonation patterns, including pitch and stress), in the grammatical component (syntactic patterns and grammatical gender), and in the semantic component (grammatical categories, gender vs. sex, and pronominal and nominal referents). Recent papers by other authors have analyzed such topics as gender in English (Nichols, 1971), male-female differences in intonation (Brend, 1972) and anatomical and cultural determinants of male and female speech (Sachs *et al.,* 1973).

Austin (1965) has commented on sex and status differences in speech:

In our culture little boys tend to be nasal . . . and little girls, oral. Nasality is considered 'tough' and 'vulgar' and is somewhat discouraged by elders. 'Gentlemanly' little boys tend to be oral also. (p. 34)

... A 'little girl's voice' (innocence, helplessness, regression) is composed of high pitch and orality. (p. 37)

The dominant middle-class white culture in the United States has certain set views on lower-class Negro speech. It is 'loud,' 'unclear,' 'slurred,' 'lazy.' The myth of loudness should be exorcised at once. Any minority or 'out-group' is characterized as 'loud'—Americans in Europe, Englishmen in America, and so on. (p. 38)

When considering women as the out-group, at first it may seem that the characterization "loud" does not apply: their speech is renowned as soft, quiet (the "lady's" speech is golden). However, only the acceptable members of the out-group (i.e., those allowed into some legitimate relationship with the in-group) are identified as having the in-group characteristics and are not stereotyped as loud. Non-ladies are often characterized by their loudness, and female advocates of women's liberation are used to being described as "shrill." Of course, the word *shrill* simply adds the connotation of loudness to that of high pitch (commonly associated with the female voice, though not determined by biology—see Sachs *et al.*, 1973).

Terms of Address

The use of different terms of address is one very familiar distinction made with language. Inferiors must address superiors by title and last name (Mr., Dr., Professor Jones) or by other polite address, such as "sir," or polite second-person forms *(vous, Sie, usted)* in languages which have them. Superiors may address inferiors by first name or by the familiar form *(tu, du, tú)*. Brown and his colleagues (Brown, 1965; Brown & Ford, 1961; Brown & Gilman, 1960) have demonstrated how terms of address are used to indicate both status and solidarity relations: status is characterized by asymmetry of address as described above, and solidarity by symmetric use of familiar (close) or polite (distant) address. Historically the polite form has been used symmetrically within the upper classes, and the familiar form symmetrically within the lower classes.

In a detailed analysis of the status and solidarity dimensions of interpersonal relationships, Brown has gone beyond the terms of address to a generalization of the rules that govern their use; this generalization applies to other forms of communicative behavior we will examine later. He has pointed out a universal norm in terms of address that has the generalized formula: "If form X is used to inferiors it is used between intimates, and if form Y is used to superiors it is used between strangers" (Brown, 1965, p. 92). Furthermore, when there is a clear difference of status between two persons, the right to initiate a change to more intimate forms of relationship (e.g., mutual first name or familiar address) belongs to the superior.

Self-disclosure

Goffman (1956) writes:

> . . .in American business organizations the boss may thoughtfully ask the elevator man how his children are, but this entrance into another's life may be blocked to the elevator man, who can appreciate the concern but not return it. Perhaps the clearest form of this is found in the psychiatrist-patient relation, where the psychiatrist has the right to touch on aspects of the patient's life that the patient might not even allow himself to touch upon, while of course this privilege is not reciprocated. (p. 64)

A study of address and social relations in a business organization by Slobin, Miller, and Porter (1968) confirms both the basic analysis of address made by Brown and the observations about self-disclosure made by Goffman. Individuals in the company studied were "more self-disclosing to their immediate superior than to their immediate subordinates" (p. 292), that is, personal information flows opposite to the flow of authority. This finding may be juxtaposed with that of Jourard and Lasakow (1958) who found that females disclose themselves more to others than do males. Although this effect has been frequently replicated, a number of studies have failed to find sex differences in self-disclosure; however, no study has reported greater male disclosure (Cozby, 1973).

The whole question of the relation of self-disclosure to status, and its special importance for women, is further illuminated in comparing the controlled aura of the professional or VIP (doctor, corporation head, judge) with the more variable demeanor of ordinary people, particularly children, working-class people, women, and persons of "ethnic" background.[2]

"Cool" is nothing more than the withholding of information, that is, refusing to disclose one's thoughts and emotions, and the value it gives to street people, poker players, and psychiatrists is of the same sort. But while it is practically a class characteristic for the upper classes, for lower-class people it can only be an individual or situational variable. Disadvantaged people find it difficult to withhold personal information; poor people and national minorities are forced to reveal any information about themselves that is wanted by the authorities. They are the focus of endless questioning by social workers and government officials, and of endless investigation by anthropologists and sociologists. The cultures of most poor and "ethnic" peoples in our societies, and those of women and children, allow for a broader and deeper range of emotional display than that of adult white males, and members of those cultures are commonly depicted as "uncontrolled" emotionally. Male children are socialized away from this, but the socialization of female children to be more expressive emotionally sets them up for their vulnerability as "emotional" women, with little control over the visibility of their affect.[3] This involuntary self-disclosure, giving knowledge that gives power over oneself ("Whoever said 'Knowledge is power'/had power first"—Gitlin, 1971), is related to the self-disclosure that comes with visibility, which will be discussed in a subsequent section.

NONVERBAL COMMUNICATION

Demeanor

In the area of demeanor, Goffman (1956) observes that in hospital staff meetings, "medical doctors had the privilege of swearing, changing the topic of conversation, and sitting in undignified positions" (p. 78), while attendants were required to show greater circumspection. Furthermore, doctors' freedom to lounge on the nursing station counter and to joke with the nurses could be extended to other ranks only after it had been initiated by doctors.

The rules of demeanor recognized by Goffman may also be examined with special reference to women: women, too, are denied such privileges as swearing and sitting in undignified positions, which are allowed to men, and are explicitly required to be more circumspect than men by all standards, including the well-known double one.

Space

There are silent messages in the nonhuman environment as well as the human one, and the distribution of space is one carrier of such messages. The imposing height and space of courtrooms and governmental buildings intimidate, as they are meant to, the people whose lives are affected there. A storefront structure is designed to draw people in; a courthouse or library, with distant stone facade and discouraging high steps, is designed to turn people away.

Brown (1965, pp. 78-82) discusses spatial relations (as one of five types of interpersonal relationship) in terms of solidarity and status dimensions, noting that status differences are marked by being above or below, in front or behind. Sommer (1969) observes that dominant animals and human beings have a larger envelope of inviolability surrounding them than do subordinate ones (dominants may not be approached as closely).[4] Sex status in the unequal distribution of personal space is demonstrated in a study reported by Willis (1966). He found, in studying the initial speaking distance set by an approaching person, that women were approached more closely than were men, by both men and women.

Silveira (1972) reports that in public observations of who gets out of the other's way when passing on the sidewalk, the woman moved out of the man's way in 12 of 19 observed mixed-sex encounters (in four cases both moved, and in three cases the man did). When women approached women or men approached men, about 50% of the time both moved out of each other's way, the rest of the time only one moved.

Touch

Popular writers (e.g., Montagu, 1971; Morris, 1971) who have written on touching have generally advanced sexual explanations for it or see it only in a context of intimacy. Jourard and Rubin (1968) take the view that "touching is equated with sexual intent, either consciously, or at a less-conscious level" (p. 47). Lewis (1972) writes: "In general, for men in our culture, proximity (touching) is restricted to the opposite sex and its function is primarily sexual in nature" (p. 237).

But there are clearly status connotations in touching, and it will be valuable to consider the touching between the sexes in this light. Goffman (1956) writes of the "touch system" in a hospital: "The doctors touched other ranks as a means of conveying friendly support and comfort, but other ranks tended to feel that it would be presumptuous for them to reciprocate a doctor's touch, let alone initiate such a contact with a doctor" (p. 74).

Touching is also one of the closer invasions of one's personal space and may be related to the deference shown the space surrounding the body. It is even more a physical threat than space violation, pointing, or staring, perhaps a vestige of the days when dominance was determined by physical prowess. The status dimension of touching is illustrated in the following interactions between pairs of persons of differing status (which would be more likely to put an arm around the shoulder, a hand on the back, tap the chest, or hold the wrists?): teacher and student; master and servant; policeman and accused; doctor and patient; minister and parishioner; counselor and client; foreman and worker; businessman and secretary.

Even those who put forward a sexual explanation for males' touching of females have to admit that there is at least a status overlay: female factory workers, secretaries, students, servants, and waitresses are often unwillingly felt or pinched, but women of higher status (e.g., "boss ladies," "first ladies," and "ladies" in general) aren't.

In fact, women are expected to accept as normal behavior the daily violations of their persons. However, when they reciprocate or, especially, initiate touch with men they are likely to be interpreted as conveying specific sexual intent. The question of sexuality as explanation for touching will be taken up later.

What investigation of touching there has been by psychologists provides evidence in support of the thesis that females are touched by others more than males are (Jourard, 1966; Jourard & Rubin, 1968). Studies of child-mother interaction have reported greater touching of female than of male children, at least from age six months on (Clay, 1968; Goldberg & Lewis, 1969; Lewis, 1972).

It is interesting to examine some of the consequences of being handled more as a child. Lewis (1972) puts forward the thesis "that the major socialization process, in terms of attachment or social behavior, is to move the infant from a proximal mode of social interaction [e.g., touching, rocking, holding] to a distal mode [e.g., smiling and vocalizing]" (p. 234). His data suggest that boys are moved faster from the proximal to distal form of interaction than girls are, and indeed, that girls are never socialized as thoroughly as boys in this regard, i.e., to distal relations, associated with more independence. Thus, greater touching of females is part of the larger picture in which they are socialized to dependence, to be not the manipulators of their environment, but the objects in it.[5]

An observational study by this author (1970, 1973) investigated touching with regard to several status dimensions (socioeconomic status, sex, and age) and found that in all these cases those of higher status (higher SES, male, older) touched those of lower status significantly more. With regard to sex, observed frequencies were: for males (M) touching (T) females (F), 42; FTM, 25; MTM, 17; and FTF, 17. The pattern of touching between and within the sexes was particularly striking when other factors were held constant, i.e., when women did not have other status advantages in the absence of the sex one. A breakdown of observations into indoor and outdoor[6] settings showed a clear sex status touching pattern only outdoors. This finding was interpreted as suggesting either that subtler cues (e.g., eye contact, voice shifts) sufficed to maintain the status relation indoors, while grosser physical acts were necessary outdoors; or that more public outdoor settings necessitated stricter attention to the status structure than the more intimate indoor ones.

Sexual explanations of touching. The greater frequency of touching between the sexes, when compared to within sexes, may suggest components of both heterosexual attraction and homosexual inhibition. However, sexual attraction is not sufficient to explain men's greater touching of women, since it would predict that women would touch men as frequntly. It can hardly be claimed any longer that men have greater "sex drives,"[7] therefore a lesser expression of sex must be attributed to an inhibition on the part of women to display sexual interest in this manner. At this point we are back where we started: the question becomes one of why one sex feels free to express its motivation tactually and the other does not. The status difference, which is a common variable underlying the differential utilization of touch in other status dimensions, best explains the difference in touching between the sexes.[8]

Duality of touch symbolism. The hypothesis that touch communicates power is not necessarily in conflict with an alternative interpretation that it communicates intimacy. There is no question that persons who are close exchange touch more. Touch may be regarded as a nonverbal equivalent of calling another by first name; used reciprocally, it indicates solidarity; when nonreciprocal, it indicates status. Even when there is mutuality, however, we may note that there is some indication of status difference. Consider for example, who, over the course of dating by a couple, initiates touching: usually the male is the first to place his arm around the female, rather than vice versa.

Furthermore, as with Brown's (1965) status norm discussed previously, there is evidence that the behavioral form used toward subordinates or members of a lower class is found in reciprocal use among the members of that class: Clay (1968), Hore (1970), and Lewis and Wilson (1971) all report greater physical contact among mother-child pairs in lower classes than in higher ones.

Eye Contact

Perhaps the most extensively researched area in nonverbal communication is that of eye contact. And according to one researcher: "Perhaps the most powerful single variable [in eye contact] is sex" (Duncan, 1969, p. 129). There is, first of all, a common finding that in interactions, women look more at the other person than do men (Exline, 1963; Exline, Gray & Schuette, 1965; Rubin, 1970). Women also have a higher percentage of mutual looking; Exline, Gray, and Schuette (1965) suggest that this "willingness to engage in mutual visual interaction is more characteristic of those who are oriented towards inclusive and affectionate interpersonal relations" (p. 207).

It is important to put eye contact into its political context, taking into account the importance of social approval to women's survival. The hypothesis that "Ss maintain more eye contact with individuals toward whom they have developed higher expectancies for social approval" was supported in Efran and Broughton's (1966) study of visual interaction in males. And Exline (1963) writes: "Women . . . may look at other persons more than do men because they value more highly the kinds of information they can obtain through such activity" (p. 18).[9] More pointedly, Rubin (1970) suggests that "gazing may serve as a vehicle of emotional expression for women and, in addition, may allow women to obtain cues from their male partners concerning the appropriateness of their behavior" (p. 272).

There is another reason for women's greater eye contact: the listener in a conversation tends to look at the speaker rather than vice versa (Exline, 1963; Duncan, 1969), and men tend to talk more than women (Argyle, Lalljee & Cook, 1968).

Exline notes that Simmel (1921) specifically distinguishes the mutual, communion-signifying glance from the nonmutual one, and that Sartre implies that "when two glances meet, a wordless struggle ensues until one or the other succeeds in establishing dominance" (p. 3). Exline asks: "A dominance which is, perhaps, signaled by the lowered glance of the loser?" Here we have reverberations of the parlor game in which one person stares another down, but this "game" is enacted at subtler levels thousands of times daily when a subordinate averts or lowers the eyes from the gaze of a superior.

Dominance communicated through eye contact (with other nonverbal cues) is illustrated by O'Connor (1970) in this account:

> A husband and wife are at a party. The wife says something that the husband does not want her to say. . . . He quickly tightens the muscles around his jaw and gives her a rapid but intense direct stare. . . . The wife, who is actually sensitive to the gestures of the man on whom she is dependent, immediately stops the conversation, lowers or turns her head slightly, averts her eyes or gives off some other gesture of submission which communicates acquiescence to her husband and reduces his aggression. (p. 9)

Research reported by Ellsworth, Carlsmith, and Henson (1972) supports the notion that the stare can be perceived as an aggressive gesture. These authors write: "The studies reported here demonstrate that staring at humans can elicit the same sort of responses that are common in primates; that is, staring can act like a primate threat display" (p. 310). The suggestion that the averted glance may be a gesture of submission is supported by the research of Hutt and Ounsted (1966). These authors, in writing about the characteristic gaze aversion of autistic children, remark that

> . . .these children were never attacked despite the fact that to a naive observer they appeared to be easy targets; this indicated that their gaze aversion had some signalling function similar to 'facing away' in the kittiwake or 'head-flagging' in the herring gull—behavior patterns which Tinbergen (1959) has termed 'appeasement postures.' In other words, gaze aversion inhibited any aggressive or threat behavior on the part of other conspecifics. (p. 354)

There seems to be some discrepancy between the notions that dominance is established or maintained by the nonmutual glance, and that women do more looking. But there are several factors that resolve this conflict. First, of course, we must remember that a greater portion of women's looking consists of *mutual* eye contact. Also, women may look at the other more and still not use nonmutual looking to dominate, by looking when another is speaking (an act outside the realm of competition). They may furthermore be the first to look away (the submissive gesture) when mutual glance is maintained for some while. More detailed research on sex differences in the initiation and termination of eye contact, in coordination with speaking patterns, would further our understanding here.

Visibility

Visibility is related to both eye contact and self-disclosure: it is the availability of (visual) information about oneself to others, with all the power that information conveys. Further insight into the politics of visibility is given by Argyle *et al.* (1968), in whose experiments the visibility of one of the two communicators was varied. These authors hypothesize that "if A can see B better than B can see A, A becomes the 'perceiver' and comes to dominate the encounter" (p. 13). In their experiments, females found communication more difficult when they could not see the other person and wanted to see even when invisible themselves. While women when invisible *decreased* their speech by 40%, males when invisible *increased* their amount of speech by 40% in addition to talking more than females in general. A significant interaction between visibility and sex was found in which "males talk more when invisible *and* talking to females" (p. 12). These results suggest sex differences in the effects of invisibility; though invisibility conveys a certain advantage, perhaps women are not as able (because of past experience outside the laboratory) to take advantage of it as are men.

Argyle and Williams (1969) report that in interview situations an asymmetry is established, that subjects felt themselves to be subordinate, to be "observed" rather than "observer," when they were being interviewed (as opposed to interviewing), were female, were younger, or if female, were with a male. The authors' comments about females' reactions to visibility are interesting:

> It is expected that there would be sex differences. Women, in most societies, dress up more colorfully and decoratively than men, and can be regarded as taking the role of performer rather than audience. It is suggested that women are more concerned about their appearance, not because they are personally insecure, but because they are going to be performers and going to be 'observed.' We predict then that in a dyadic encounter between a male and a female the female will feel herself more observed than a male; and that this difference will not be due to differences of security or dominance. (pp. 398-99)

Later, however, they state:

> It is possible that people who feel observed have in the past been stared down by others, and adopted a low level of looking themselves—i.e., their feelings of being observed are based on real experiences of being looked at in the past. (p. 410)

In a society in which women's clothing is designed explicitly to reveal the body and its contours; in which women are ogled, whistled at, and pinched while simply going about their business; in which they see advertisements in magazines, on billboards, on TV in their own homes, showing revealingly clad women; in which tactual information about them is freely available, their bodies accessible to touch like community property; in which even their marital status is the first information by which a stranger identifies them—in such a society it is little wonder that women feel "observed." They are.

Gestures of Dominance and Submission

Dominant and submissive gestures have long been described by students of animal behavior, often with some reference to their similarity to the gestures of human beings. We noted earlier that the direct stare has been characterized as a threat, and the averted glance as a sign of submission, among humans. Anthony (1970) compares the "presenting" submissive gesture of chimpanzees to that of chorus girls, and O'Connor (1970) makes similar comparisons. O'Connor describes some subtle distinctions that make a gesture submissive rather than dominant:

> Women use [the direct stare] as well as men, but often in modified form. While looking directly at a man, a woman usually has her head slightly tilted, implying the beginning of a presenting gesture or enough submission to render the stare ambivalent if not actually submissive. (p. 9)

Staring, pointing, and touching may be considered as dominance gestures with the corresponding submissive gestures being respectively, lowering or averting the eyes, stopping action or speech, and cuddling to the touch. Veiled physical threats may be seen in the playful and casual lifting and tossing around that is often done by men with women—swinging them (hard) at square dances, picking them up and spanking them (in "play"), threatening to drop them or throw them in water (and doing it), or just lifting them to demonstrate their lightness and the male's strength. Smiling is another recognized submissive gesture, the badge of women and of the shuffling Tom.

Interruption may also be considered a dominance gesture, and allowing interruption, the corresponding submissive gesture. Argyle et al. (1968) allude to a finding that men dominate an interaction by interruption, though the supporting data are not directly presented. Our own conversational experiences will confirm that superiors can more readily interrupt others, and more readily resist interruption by others, than subordinates.

When Power Becomes Sex: Violation of Sex Status Norms

We noted earlier that women's touch was more likely to be interpreted as having sexual intent than men's. Similarly, women's stare, physical closeness, and loosening of demeanor may all be taken by men as sexual invitations. Other characteristics that are associated with men, such as a husky voice or the withholding of information (the "woman of mystery"), are considered sexy in women. We have seen that these behaviors and characteristics are not just "natural" or pointless properties in men, but carry status and power connotations, helping maintain their place in the social order. Why should these concomitants of status lose those connotations, and in addition, take on sexual connotations, when used by the wrong sex? It is because the implication of power is unacceptable when the actor is a woman, and therefore must be denied.

Sex is a convenient alternative interpretation because (a) many of these behaviors—touching, gazing, proximity, and relaxed demeanor—are also expressive of solidarity and intimacy, and appropriate to a sexual relationship; and (b) attribution of sexual aggressiveness to a woman both compliments the man and disarms the woman, and places her back in her familiar unthreatening role as sex object (as in "You're so cute when you're mad, baby."). There are other ways in which women are put down for exhibiting "male" characteristics: they are labeled deviant and abhorrent (castrating, domineering), or, when all else fails, lesbian.

CONCLUSION

We have noted the importance of nonverbal and subtle verbal cues in the maintenance of the social structure and of power relationships, and their particular importance in restricting women to "their" place. In grammar, vocabulary, voice quality, and intonation patterns, women's language keeps them at a disadvantage, while men's (the dominant) language tends to ignore women completely or deprecate them. Terms of address, conversational patterns, self-disclosure, demeanor, distribution of space, touch, eye contact, and visibility all contribute to the maintenance of the status quo. The accessibility of information about subordinate persons and groups, including women, is used to subordinate and subdue them.

When subordinate groups defy the norms governing micropolitical acts, authority's first attempt at control is the denial of the norm violation, and substitution of an interpretation (for women, sexual aggression) which re-establishes the former relationship. The dual nature of many of the signals, used differently as indicators of either status or solidarity, makes them particularly available for this ploy.

The findings presented here have certain implications for women and others in inferior positions who wish to counteract the power expressed over them. They may begin to become conscious of the nonverbal symbolism of power, in order to resist it when it is used by others to exert control, and to exercise it themselves to help reverse the power relationships in their environment (see Henley, 1971). Similarly, those reluctantly in positions of power, like men who wish to divest themselves of "foreskin privilege," can begin to monitor their own acts toward others and their reactions to others' acts, in an attempt to exorcise the subtle power indicators from their daily interactions.

Manipulating these status cues will not, of course, change the fundamental power relationships in our society. Knowledge of them will, however, raise consciousness and enable people to detect the subtle ways in which they are inhibited, coerced, and controlled.

NOTES

[1]Personal servants, of course, are also physically integrated around power. However, other oppressed groups in our society are often physically separated (e.g., in ghettos and reservations) from power centers.

[2]The unemotional demeanor associated with Anglo-Saxon culture is, of course, an asset in a society dominated by persons of Anglo-Saxon descent.

[3]Many factors in female socialization have this effect, such as the fostering of passivity, non-aggressiveness, physical weakness, unconcern with achievement, etc. One especially important, and usually overlooked, factor is the socialization of women to *care* more than men about personal relationships. Ross articulated in 1921 the "Law of Personal Exploitation" which states: "In any sentimental relation the one who cares less can exploit the one who cares more" (p. 136). It is put more broadly (without restriction to sentiment) by Waller and Hill (1951) as the "Principle of Least Interest": "That person is able to dictate the conditions of association whose interest in the continuation of the affair is least" (p. 191).

[4]Space, of course, is the prerogative of the rich and the powerful; only the poor must live in crowded rooms, without yards, in crowded cities.

[5]In fact, I relate this socialization to receive touch to the sexual abuse of girls and women. Rush (1971) argues that "sexual abuse of [female] children is permitted because it is an unspoken but prominent factor in socializing and preparing the female to accept a subordinate role; to feel guilty, ashamed, and to tolerate, through fear, the power exercised over her by men. . . . In short, the sexual abuse of female children is a process of education which prepares them to become the sweethearts and wives of America" (p. 10).

[6]Indoors: bank, stores, restaurant, doctor's office, college buildings. Outdoors: shopping plaza, beach, college campus, concert, party.

[7]Sherfey (1966), in fact, has written of (primitive) woman's sexual drive as "too strong" for society's good: "the *forceful* suppression of women's inordinate sexual demands was a prerequisite to the dawn of every modern civilization and almost every living culture" (1970, p. 224; emphasis hers. See also Sherfey, 1973).

[8]Of course, Millett's (1970) analysis has shown us that the realm of sexuality certainly does not exclude the political.

[9]Exline relates women's "visual dependence" in the social field, however, to a supposed personality variable, that women are more field-dependent in studies in the physical field (i.e., in making judgments of horizonticality and verticality they tend to rely on reference points in the environment rather than on their own internal body cues). This explanation overlooks the social context in which the visual information is both more important to women and generally less available to them (because of their exclusion from informative interaction, and men's greater concealment of affect). Both the physical and social examples, nevertheless, do illustrate women's reliance on visual perception rather than gut feelings (both literally and figuratively), perhaps because of learned distrust for their own judgments.

REFERENCES

Anthony, N. (1970). Open letter to psychiatrists. *Radical Therapist,* 1, 3, 8.

Argyle, M., M. Lalljee, & M. Cook. (1968). The effects of visibility on interaction in a dyad. *Human Relations,* 21, 3-17.

Argyle, M., V. Salter, H. Nicholson, M. Williams, and P. Burgess. (1970). The communication of inferior and superior attitudes by verbal and nonverbal signals. *British Journal of Social and Clinical Psychology,* 9, 222-31.

Argyle, M., and M. Williams. (1969). Observer or observed? A reversible perspective in person perception. *Sociometry,* 32, 396-412.

Austin, W. M. (1965). Some social aspects of Paralanguage. *Canadian Journal of Linguistics,* 11, 31-39.

Birdwhistell, R. L. (1970). *Kinesics and context: essays on body motion communication.* Philadelphia: Univ. of Pennsylvania Press.

Brend, R. M. (1972). Male-female differences in American English intonation. *Proceedings of the Seventh International Congress of Phonetic Sciences, 1971.* The Hague: Mouton. Reprinted in Barrie Thorne and Nancy Henley (eds.) (1975), *Language and sex: difference and dominance.* Rowley, Mass.: Newbury House.

Brown, R. (1965). *Social psychology.* Glencoe, Ill.: Free Press.

Brown, R. & M. Ford. (1961). Address in American English. *Journal of Abnormal and Social Psychology,* 62, 375-85.

Brown, R. & A. Gilman. (1960). The pronouns of power and solidarity. In T. A. Sebeok (ed.), *Style in language.* Cambridge, Mass.: M. I. T. Press.

Clay, V. S. (1968). The effect of culture on mother-child tactile communication. *Family Coordinator,* 17, 204-10.

Cozby, P. C. (1973). Self-disclosure: a literature review. *Psychological Bulletin,* 79, 73-91.

Duncan, S. (1969). Nonverbal communication. *Psychological Bulletin,* 72, 118-37.

Efran, J. S. & A. Broughton. (1966). Effect of expectancies for social approval on visual behavior. *Journal of Personality and Social Psychology*, 4, 103-107.

Ellsworth, P. C., J. M. Carlsmith, & A. Henson. (1972). The stare as a stimulus to flight in human subjects: A series of field experiments. *Journal of Personality and Social Psychology*, 21, 302-11.

Exline, R. (1963). Explorations in the process of person perception: visual interaction in relation to competition, sex, and need for affiliation. *Journal of Personality*, 31, 1-20.

Exline, R., D. Gray, & D. Schuette. (1965). Visual behavior in a dyad as affected by interview content and sex of respondent. *Journal of Personality and Social Psychology*, 1, 201-209.

Fast, J. (1970). *Body language.* New York: Evans.

Galt, W. E. (1943). The male-female dichotomy in human behavior. *Psychiatry*, 6, 1-14.

Gitlin, T. (1971). On power structure research. *100 Flowers*, 1, 35.

Goffman, E. (1956). The nature of deference and demeanor. *American Anthropologist*, 58, 473-502. In E. Goffman (1967), *Interaction ritual.* New York: Anchor, 47-95.

Goldberg, S. & M. Lewis. (1969). Play behavior in the year-old infant: early sex differences. *Child Development*, 40, 21-31.

Haley, J. (1962). The art of psychoanalysis. In S. I. Hayakawa (ed.), *The use and misuse of language.* Greenwich, Conn.: Fawcett, 207-18.

Henley, N. (1970). The politics of touch. Paper read at American Psychological Association. In P. Brown (ed.) (1973), *Radical psychology.* New York: Harper & Row, 421-33.

———. Facing down the man. *Radical Therapist* 2, 2, 22. In Rough Times Staff (eds.) (1973), *Rough Times*, New York: Ballantine.

———. (1973). Status and sex: some touching considerations. *Bulletin of the Psychonomic Society*, 2, 91-93.

Hore, T. (1970). Social class differences in some aspects of the nonverbal communication between mother and preschool child. *Australian Journal of Psychology*, 22, 21-27.

Hutt, C. & C. Ounsted. (1966). The biological significance of gaze aversion with particular reference to the syndrome of infantile autism. *Behavioral Science*, 11, 346-56.

Jourard, S. M. (1966). An exploratory study of body accessibility. *British Journal of Social and Clinical Psychology*, 5, 221-31.

Jourard, S. M. & P. Lasakow. (1958). Some factors in self-disclosure. *Journal of Abnormal and Social Psychology*, 56, 91-98.

Jourard, S. M. & J. E. Rubin (1968). Self-disclosure and touching: a study of two modes of interpersonal encounter and their inter-relation. *Journal of Humanistic Psychology*, 8, 39-48.

Key, M. R. (1972). Linguistic behavior of male and female. *Linguistics,* 88 (August 15), 15-31.

Lakoff, R. (1973). Language and woman's place. *Language in Society,* 2, 45-79.

Lewis, M. (1972). Parents and children: sex-role development. *School Review,* 80, 229-40.

Lewis, M. & C. D. Wilson. (1971). Infant development in lower-class American families. Paper read at Society for Research in Child Development.

Mehrabian, A. (1972). *Nonverbal communication.* Chicago: Aldine-Atherton.

Millett, K. (1970). *Sexual politics.* Garden City, N. Y.: Doubleday.

Montagu, A. (1971). *Touching: the human significance of the skin.* New York: Columbia Univ. Press.

Morris, D. (1971). *Intimate behavior.* New York: Random House.

Nichols, P. C. (1971). Gender in English: syntactic and semantic functions. Paper read at Modern Language Association.

O'Connor, L. (1970). Male dominance: the nitty gritty of oppression. *It Ain't Me Babe,* 1, 9-11.

Ross, E. A. (1921). *Principles of sociology.* New York: Century.

Rubin, Z. (1970). Measurement of romantic love. *Journal of Personality and Social Psychology,* 16, 265-73.

Rush, F. (1971). The sexual abuse of children. *Radical Therapist,* 2, 4, 9-11.

Sachs, J., P. Lieberman & D. Erickson. (1973). Anatomical and cultural determinants of male and female speech. In Shuy, R. & Fasold, R. (eds.), *Language attitudes: current trends and prospects.* Washington, D. C.: Georgetown Univ. Press.

Scheflen, A. E. (1972). *Body language and the social order.* Englewood Cliffs, N. J.: Prentice-Hall.

Sherfey, M. J. (1966). The evolution and nature of female sexuality in relation to psychoanalytic theory. *Journal of the American Psychoanalytic Association,* 14, 28-128. In R. Morgan (ed.) (1970), *Sisterhood is powerful.* New York: Random House, 220-30.

———. (1973). *The nature and evolution of female sexuality.* New York: Random House.

Silveira, J. (1972). Thoughts on the politics of touch. *Women's Press* (Eugene, Oregon), 1, 13, 13.

Simmel, G. (1921). Sociology of the senses: visual interaction. In R. E. Park & E. W. Burgess (eds.), *Introduction to the science of sociology.* Chicago: Univ. of Chicago Press.

Slobin, D. I., S. H. Miller & L. W. Porter (1968). Forms of address and social relations in a business organization. *Journal of Personality and Social Psychology,* 8, 289-93.

Sommer, R. (1969). *Personal space.* Englewood Cliffs, N. J.: Prentice-Hall.

Tinbergen, N. (1969). Comparative study of the behavior of gulls: a progress report. *Behavior*, 15, 1-70.

Waller, W. W. & R. Hill. (1951). *The family, a dynamic interpretation.* New York: Dryden.

Willis, F. N., Jr. (1966). Initial speaking distance as a function of the speakers' relationship. *Psychonomic Science*, 5, 221-22.

NOTES ON THE AUTHORS

ANN BODINE is in the Department of Sociology at Rutgers University.

RUTH BREND is in the Department of Linguistics at Michigan State University.

LOUISE CHERRY is at the Institute of Human Development of the Educational Testing Service.

ALMA GRAHAM is Executive Editor, Dictionary Division, with the American Heritage Publishing Company.

NANCY HENLEY is in the Department of Social Sciences, University of Lowell, Massachusetts.

CHERIS KRAMER is in the Department of Speech Communication at the University of Illinois, Urbana.

JACQUELINE SACHS is in the Department of Speech at the University of Connecticut.

MURIEL SCHULZ is in the Department of English at the California State University, Fullerton.

MARJORIE SWACKER is in the Department of English, Texas A & M University.

BARRIE THORNE is in the Department of Sociology, Michigan State University.

PETER TRUDGILL is in the Department of Linguistic Science of the University of Reading (England).

CANDACE WEST is in the Department of Sociology, University of California, Santa Barbara.

DON H. ZIMMERMAN is in the Department of Sociology, University of California, Santa Barbara.

Sex Differences in Language, Speech, and Nonverbal Communication:

An Annotated Bibliography

Compiled by
Nancy Henley and Barrie Thorne

CONTENTS

INTRODUCTION

This bibliography, which began as a modest effort to pull together what we thought were very few published sources on language and sex, grew very rapidly to reach its present size. Part of the growth was due to the uncovering of sources buried in a wide range of places, and often not directly billed as dealing with this topic. For example, experimental psychologists have often used sex as a variable (mainly because it's an obvious, discrete way to categorize subjects), and among their findings are some bearing on this subject. Much of the growth of the bibliography, however, is due to the increased attention which this general topic is receiving; the reader might note that by far the bulk of references are dated since the late 1960's, that is, since the inception of the women's liberation movement.

Our goal has been to compile this information in the most useful form possible. Each item is annotated and arranged by topic. The topics include various dimensions of language and nonverbal communication; this is only one of several alternative ways of organizing this information. One important distinction is between language *about* the sexes (included under II-A, "Sexist Bias of English Language"), and differences in the way women and men *use* language (differences in word choice, syntactic usage, and language style; phonology; conversational patterns; speech in multilingual situations; language acquisition; verbal ability). A final section, on sex differences in nonverbal communication, does not claim to be comprehensive; it is included to raise the issue of the interrelationship between verbal and nonverbal behavior, and to break down the artificial isolation of speech from other modes of communication.

Some of the items are annotated or referred to under more than one topic. This cross referencing is indicated in brackets at the end of the annotation. An index to the bibliography, arranged by author, is also included. Where papers are unpublished, we have tried, where possible, to provide the address of the author(s). Italics and brackets indicate that the editors are commenting, sometimes providing cross references, and at other points providing asides, criticisms, reminders, and explanatory discussions.

I. COMPREHENSIVE SOURCES: LANGUAGE AND SPEECH

BODINE, ANN.
"Sex Differentiation in Language." In Barrie Thorne and Nancy Henley, eds., *Language and Sex: Difference and Dominance.* Rowley, Mass.: Newbury House, 1975.

Bodine reviews the history of the study of sex differentiation in language, offers a comprehensive analysis of the various forms sex differentiation takes in a wide variety of languages, and reviews the attitudes of the speakers and the linguists toward linguistic sex differentiation. Sex differentiation may be *sex-exclusive* (forms used exclusively by one sex) or *sex-preferential* (forms differing in frequency of occurrence in speech of women and men), and has been generally discussed under separate topics of gender and "women's language." Earlier linguists (1) generally failed to see any connection between gender in language (assignment of sex to certain forms) and sex differentiation of other types; (2) took the notion of gender for granted, but marveled at descriptions of (presumably) sex-exclusive differentiation in far-off cultures; (3) ignored the evidence of sex-preferential speech in their own European languages, though (4) they thought that in their own languages women spoke differently; and (5) generally equated "men's language" (including their own) with *the* language. Chatterji, for example, equated Bengali language with men's speech, stating that the initial *l-* is often pronounced as *n-* by women, children, and the uneducated—who must constitute the great bulk of Bengali speakers. Obviously the difference might be represented otherwise, perhaps better, by the statement that "initial *n-* is sometimes pronounced as *l-* in pretentious speech, particularly that of status-conscious men." Bodine develops a classificatory scheme of axes: (1) type of language differences (pronunciation, form—acoustic and prosodic differences are omitted), and (2) the basis of language difference (sex of speaker, spoken to, speaker plus spoken to, or spoken about), and reviews the literature describing sex differences for each category of the classification. Differences based on sex of *speaker*, in both pronunciation and form, are remarkably superficial, nor is there profound difference in syntactic patterning. With regard to sex of *spoken to*, it seems to be a linguistic universal that no language differentiates on this basis which doesn't also differentiate on the basis of sex of speaker (excepting in direct address). Differentiation based on both *speaker and spoken to* could produce four versions, but no language with all four is known. There are no reports of pronunciation differences based on sex of *spoken about*, but differences in form on this basis are common (e.g., gender). The discussion of attitudes toward sex differentiation involves speakers' awareness of the differences; reports are often spotty with regard to whether both sexes are aware of the differences and/or can reproduce them. Ethnographers, generally male, tended to associate with male informants and may have given biased reports on attitudes toward sex differentiation in language. Descriptions of linguistic sex differentiation are uneven and incomplete for all languages, and the social implications are even less explored, though the present explosion of investigations (at least in English), concurrent with interest in social questions, suggests we may soon have a good understanding of sex differentiation in English. For a full understanding of sociolinguistic processes and regularities, however, a broad cross-cultural base is necessary. [*See V.*]

CONKLIN, NANCY FAIRES.
   "Toward a Feminist Analysis of Linguistic Behavior." *The University of Michigan Papers in Women's Studies*, 1, No. 1 (1974), 51-73.

   Conklin examines "various ways in which languages set women apart as a distinct group and how women set themselves apart." She surveys sex-marking in various languages in the form of specific words, endings, distinctions embedded in kinship systems, politeness-marking systems, taboos circumscribing women's use of speech, and in the speech genres and vocabularies specific to each sex. When the speech forms of men and women merge, change is usually in the direction of women adopting male language. Conklin discusses the pronoun structure, the subtleties of sexist use of language, and the question of how each sex learns appropriate speech forms. Dialect studies reveal patterns of female speech: "hypercorrectness, respect for and acquiescence to 'standard' speech, judgments of persons' value and status on the basis of their accents, standardness, and style of speaking." Overall, Conklin argues, women have "acute sociolinguistic sensitivity," which entails being attuned to the behavior of others and relying on external norms. As a result, women may allow themselves to be defined by standards not necessarily their own; they may become alienated from their own culture and from other women. "But women's sensitivity to the behavior of others could be turned into a powerful tool for their liberation." There are strengths in female skill in manipulating language, in having a "large range of stylistic repertoires," in "attentiveness to what others are saying." "Both in dealing with the power structure, and in dealing with other women, an awareness of the ebb and flow below the surface of the interaction is a useful tool and also a valuable weapon." [*See II-A-2, II-B, IV-C, V, VI.*]

JESPERSEN, OTTO.
   "The Woman," Chapter XIII of *Language: Its Nature, Development and Origin*. London: Allen & Unwin, 1922, pp. 237-254.

   Among traditional books on language, Jespersen's discussion is the only extensive treatment of sex differences. He draws on a variety of sources: old ethnographies, novels, statements by Cicero and Lord Chesterfield, and makes many generalizations without even that sort of supporting evidence. Jespersen covers the following topics: (1) Ethnographic studies indicating that there are tribes in which men and women "speak totally different languages, or at any rate distinct dialects." These include differences in vocabulary, word taboos, and some grammatical forms unique to each sex. Jespersen suggests that these differences may be traced to the separate activities and roles of the sexes and to differences in rank. (2) The attitude of each sex toward language change. Jespersen presents a mixed picture: some believe women are more conservative than men with regard to language change, and that innovations are due to the initiative of men (he cites a source claiming that in France and England, women avoid coining new words; later, Jespersen himself asserts that "woman as a rule follows the main road of language, where man is often inclined to turn aside into a narrow footpath or even to strike out a new path for himself." On the other hand, he mentions a South American tribe where women "busied themselves in inventing new words," and a report that in Japan women are less conservative than men in pronunciation and in the selection of words and expressions. (3) Sex differences in phonetics. Although there are assorted examples of differences in pronunciation (e.g. women took the lead in weakening the old fully trilled tongue-point *r*), Jespersen claims that phonetically "there is scarcely any difference between the speech of men and that of women." (4) Choice of vocabulary and adverbs. Jespersen claims that women are more euphemistic than men, "instinctively" avoiding the coarseness of male speech. Men not only swear, but invent and use slang, and are more given to punning. The vocabulary of women, Jespersen claims, is less extensive than that of men, and women are more given to hyperbole, to adverbs of intensity. He claims that men use more complicated sentence constructions, building sentences "like a set of Chinese boxes," with clauses containing one within another. Women build sentences "like a string of pearls, joined together on a string of ands and similar words." Jespersen concludes with a barrage of generalizations, about "the greater rapidity of female thought" and the "superior readiness of the speech of women"–not "proof of intellectual power," but of talk without much prior thought ("a woman's thought is no sooner formed than uttered"). He attributes this to the domestic occupations of women which "demanded no deep thought, which were performed in company and could well be accompanied with a lively chatter." [*See II-B, V, VI.*]

KEY, MARY RITCHIE.
   "Linguistic Behavior of Male and Female." *Linguistics,* 88 (Aug. 15, 1972), 15-31.

   While linguists have dealt with dimensions of language variety such as age, socio-economic differences, and literary differences, they rarely discuss linguistic distinctions between the sexes. Sex differences in language may vary with group, situation, and role. Key summarizes findings by others and makes observations of her own about phonological differences in women's and men's speech, intonation patterns, male-female differences in syntax, the semantic component, and pronominal and nominal referents. [*See II-A-1, II-B, III-B-3.*]

KEY, MARY RITCHIE.
    Male/Female Language. Metuchen, N.J.: Scarecrow Press, 1975.

KRAMER, CHERIS.
    "Women's Speech: Separate But Unequal?" *Quarterly Journal of Speech,* 60 (Feb., 1974), 14-24. Reprinted in Barrie Thorne and Nancy Henley, eds., *Language and Sex: Difference and Dominance.* Rowley, Mass.: Newbury House, 1975.

    Kramer considers "evidence for there being systems of co-occurring, sex-linked linguistic signals in the United States" ("genderlects" or "sexlects"). She emphasizes the need to consider not only sex differences in grammar, phonology, and semantics, but also "possible differences in verbal skills, instrumental use of language, and the relationship of non-verbal uses to verbal behavior." Kramer reviews literature on male vs. female languages in primitive societies, and on phonetic differences between male and female speakers. She suggests the value of examining popular stereotypes about women's speech (how people think women speak or should speak), and from such stereotypes she draws out an imaginative list of research questions, e.g. on the relative verbosity of female vs. male speakers; patterns of question-asking; volume and pitch as they vary by situation; differences in the written work of men and women. Kramer hypothesizes that "women's speech reflects the stereotyped roles of male and female in our society, i.e., women in a subservient, nurturing position in a male-dominated world," although researchers should also be aware of differences among female speakers (related, for example, to differences of class, race, origin, age). Research into sex differences in speech should take account of the varied components of speech events [*see Dell Hymes, "Models of Interaction of Language and Social Setting," Journal of Social Issues, XXXIII (1967), 8-28*]: channel (oral, written, or other medium); key (tone, manner, or spirit of the act); setting or scene; participants (addressor, addressee, audience); topic; ends or purposes; norms of interaction; genres (categories or types of speech events, e.g. conversation, curse, lecture). [*See II-B, III-A, III-B-2, IV-A, IV-C, VIII-C.*]

LAKOFF, ROBIN.
    "Language and Woman's Place." *Language in Society,* 2 (1973), 45-79. Briefer version, "You Are What You Say," *Ms.,* 3 (July, 1974), 63-67. Also in the author's *Language and Woman's Place.* New York: Harper & Row, 1975.

    A lengthy paper which discusses two aspects of linguistic discrimination and prejudice against women: (1) The existence of a "woman's language," a style which avoids strong or forceful statements and encourages expressions that suggest triviality of subject matter, and uncertainty. Women are taught to use this special style of speech, which is later used against them in claims that women are unable to speak precisely, forcefully, or to take part in serious discussion. (2) General linguistic use which treats women as objects and defines them as secondary beings, having existence only when defined by a man. Lakoff uses data from her own speech and that of her acquaintances, and from the media. She concludes that language provides clues that some external situation needs changing, although social change creates lexical change, not the reverse. [*See II-A-1, II-B, III-B-3, V, VII.*]

THORNE, BARRIE AND NANCY HENLEY.
   "Difference and Dominance: An Overview of Language, Gender, and Society." In
   Barrie Thorne and Nancy Henley, eds., *Language and Sex: Difference and Dominance.*
   Rowley, Mass.: Newbury House, 1975.

This overview of literature on the sexual differentiation of language begins with a brief history of this field of research (with emphasis on the contributions of the women's movement), and a review of the diverse disciplines, frameworks, and methods of research which have converged on this topic. Sociolinguistic distinctions—verbal repertoire, speech style, and the social context of communicative events—are used to interpret and organize various findings about sex differences in speech, and to suggest leads for further research. The bulk of the article is devoted to the issue of social context, to trying to account for the sexual differentiation of language by drawing on theories and research on the sociology, anthropology, and psychology of the sexes. There are three central themes: (1) The social elaboration of gender differences through learned, including linguistic, behavior; (2) Language and male dominance, expressed in sexist language (language about women) and, in actual speech use, in verbal gestures of dominance and submission between men and women (e.g., patterns of interruption, hesitation, amount of talk; the less obtrusive speech of women; speech genres such as asymmetric joking). The finding that female speech is more polite and "correct" is related to the greater circumspection required of subordinates and to the connection Trudgill suggests between masculinity and less standard speech forms. There is a discussion of whether men's speech is superior, drawing attention to the dangers in assuming the male as the norm, and suggesting that there is a need to reevaluate, but perhaps not discard female speech patterns. And there is analysis of under what conditions and with what consequences women and men use the speech style associated with the opposite sex; (3) The division of labor by sex—language is part of the ideological association of women with family, and men with occupational roles. There may be a sexual division of labor in conversational topics and lexicons, and male and female speech can be compared for range, extent, and locales of use. The traditional responsibility of women for child-rearing gives them a central role in transmitting language; the roles of the family and of peer groups in language acquisition, and the tie of language to single-sex bonding are discussed. Finally, the paper turns to the issue of change, and summarizes some of the many questions and topics awaiting systematic inquiry.

II. VOCABULARY AND SYNTAX

A. Sexist Bias of English Language

1. Analysis of Sexism in Language

BODINE, ANN.
   "Androcentrism in Prescriptive Grammar." *Language in Society,* in press.

Although prescriptive grammarians have, at least since the 18th century, claimed that there is no sex-indefinite pronoun for the third person singular and stated that *he* is to be used, English "has always had other linguistic devices for referring to sex-indefinite referents, notably, the use of *they* (their, them)," as in the sentence: "Who dropped their ticket?" Prior to the 18th century, the singular *they* was widely used in written and presumably also spoken English. It is significant, Bodine suggests, that grammarians sought to correct it by focusing on agreement with the antecedent in number, but not in gender. "A non-sexist 'correction' would have been to advocate *he or she,* but rather than encourage this usage the grammarians actually tried to eradicate it also, claiming *he or she* is 'clumsy,' 'pedantic,' or 'unnecessary.' Significantly, they never attacked terms such as *one or more* or *person or persons,* although the plural logically includes the singular more than the masculine includes the feminine. These two situations are analogous. In both cases the language user is confronted with an obligatory category, either number or sex, which is irrelevant to the message being transmitted." Current junior high and high school grammars condemn *he or she* as clumsy, and the singular *they* as inaccurate; "and then the pupils are taught to achieve both elegance of expression and accuracy by referring to women as *he!*" Bodine cites examples she has collected from ordinary conversations of people using *they* for singular antecedents. The continuing attack of textbook writers and teachers on *he or she* and the singular *they,* she notes, also indicates "both forms are still much a part of American English." Earlier changes in second person pronouns (e.g. the elimination of *thou-thee* under egalitarian pressures) demonstrate that pronominal systems are susceptible to alteration in response to social change. Bodine predicts that the feminist counter-attack on the sex-indefinite *he* will affect English pronominal usage; "during the next few years students of language development may have the opportunity to follow the progress of a particularly visible type of language change." Such change will bear on general linguistic issues: post-childhood linguistic acculturation; conscious vs. unconscious change; and compensatory adjustment within the linguistic system (e.g. the possible weakening of number concord).

BOSMAJIAN, HAIG A.
  "The Language of Sexism." *ETC.,* 29 (1972), 305-313.

This is a general article about sexism in language, which takes off from the point that language has often been used to "define and dehumanize individuals or groups of individuals into submission" (e.g. the Nazi use of language to redefine and dehumanize the Jews; the language of white racism). Examples of "male supremist language" are given: the use of male as generic; the "firstness of *men*" when listed with *women* (an ordering that appears even in the N.O.W. 1966 Statement of Purpose, which begins "We, men and women who hereby constitute ourselves as the National Organization for Women"); the language of religions and of organizations (*spokesmen*); the ritual of women adopting the name of their husbands upon marriage, and of giving the newborn child the male parent's surname. In short, men have a power of defining through naming, and, the author argues (citing examples of such efforts), the liberation of women "will have to be accompanied with a conscious effort on the part of women to allow themselves to be defined by men no longer."

BURR, ELIZABETH, SUSAN DUNN, AND NORMA FARQUHAR.´
  "Women and the Language of Inequality." *Social Education,* 36 (1972), 841-845.

A brief article which points to sexist writing customs, especially in textbooks. Examples: Subsuming masculine terms in fact operate to exclude females (a phrase like "men of goodwill" does not bring to mind a group of amicable females). In textbooks, hypothetical persons are usually male ("a discontented man could move west"). Girls and women are usually referred to mainly in terms of those who "own" them, as nameless wives, daughters, and mothers of named males. Because women have traditionally been expected to assume the full burden of childcare, textbooks describe children who still need care as the mother's ("Sacajewea carried her infant son"); male offspring seen as heirs and female offspring of marriageable age are described as the father's. Women are often described as if they were luggage ("the pioneer took his family west in a covered wagon"), which is inappropriate unless the woman moved involuntarily. Textbooks should also acknowledge the fact that single women and female heads of family participated in the westward movement. Terms which are applicable to either or both sexes are often defined as applying exclusively to males (*monarchy* = 'a nation ruled by a king').

CONNERS, KATHLEEN.
   "Studies in Feminine Agentives in Selected European Languages." *Romance Philology,* 24 (1971), 573-598.

A lengthy analysis of the history of the formation of feminine agentives, especially for occupational terms (e.g. *aviatrix*), in the major Romance languages, English, and German. Feminine agentives behave as the marked category vis-à-vis the masculine terms (which serve as the generic, and to designate mixed groups). Yet feminine agentives are no more uniform in derivation than masculine ones, a fact Conners attributes to four non-linguistic factors: (1) In most occupations the need for an explicitly feminine label arises infrequently because the masculine can represent both sexes in its unmarked generic function, and most occupations have been confined to men; (2) The feminine counterparts of masculine terms often designate the wife of the man practicing the occupation (*duchess* is the spouse of *duke*); (3) The form potentially fit to serve as a feminine agentive has often been preempted by the corresponding name of an instrument, container, or product (e.g. in French *faucheuse* means 'mowing machine'); (4) Individual feminine agentives and suffixes have repeatedly taken on derogatory or facetious connotations "regardless of whether the society involved regarded women with respect and nourished their ambitions." While many new feminine agentives are coined, sometimes experimentally, there does not seem to be spreading acceptance and use of such forms proportionate to the movement of women into the labor force, at least in Western European societies. In these societies, "as the socially marked category, women in public life, becomes gradually less marked (i.e., as women become more and more common in traditionally 'masculine' occupations), it gradually becomes less rather than more appropriate to distinguish sex morphologically." On the other hand, "in modern Russia and Israel, where for political and historical reasons women have shared greatly in the work of a society in the making, feminizers seem to enjoy great productivity, unblocked by any threat of confusion with words for machines, where skilled labor is at issue, or by any strong tendency toward facetious connotations . . . Could the high frequency of female occupational terms actually tend to lessen the possibility of their degradation to facetious use?"

DENSMORE, DANA.
   "Speech Is the Form of Thought." Reprint (10 pp.) available from KNOW, Inc., P.O. Box 86031, Pittsburgh, Pa. 15221.

Sexism is so pervasive that language reflects it, for example, in pronouns (*he* as the generic for *he* or *she,* even in a group which is 99% women). Densmore proposes a new glossary of personal pronouns: nominative case, *she* (includes in one word both the old *he* and the old *she*); objective case, *herm* (includes *her* and *him*); possessive case, *heris* (used for *her* or *his*, including both words in spelling and sound). In place of *man* as the generic, there should be more use of *human, person, people*. The author concludes: "Androcentric language is first a symptom of sexism, but it also reinforces it and permits abuses such as subtly shutting women out. To the extent that it is a symptom, enforcing these changes will not abolish sexism. But it would raise consciousness and permit women to begin to feel that they are not a different species, not, in fact, a useful afterthought lodged between man and nature."

FARB, PETER.
   Word Play: What Happens When People Talk. New York: Alfred A. Knopf, 1973.

   Written in a lively style for a general audience, this book includes several sections which summarize studies of sex differences in language. On pp. 141-144, Farb writes of "the unequal treatment many languages give to the two sexes": the use of male generics, the notion that the average person is always masculine (as in "the man in the street" and hypothetical person in riddles), the connotations of various sets of words (males *roar, bellow,* and *growl;* females *squeal, shriek,* and *purr*). While *woman* began as an "Adam's-rib word" (derived from Old English *wife* plus *man*), *female* came from the Middle English word, *femelle,* meaning 'small woman,' but due to its apparent resemblance to the word *male,* it got changed to *female.* Masculine words like *master* and *father* are usually used to refer to leadership and power; feminine words more often imply unpredictability or treachery (e.g. feminine names for hurricanes). Farb also discusses sexism in French (feminine nouns are formed by adding *-e* to the masculine; words for high-prestige roles are usually masculine). [*See II-B, III-A, III-B-2, V.*]

FARWELL, MARILYN.
   "Women and Language." In Jean R. Leppaluoto, ed., *Women on the Move.* Pittsburgh: KNOW, Inc., 1973, pp. 165-171.

   The English language, Farwell writes, "reflects and rigidifies the social status of women"; its structure "solidifies the either/or pattern of masculine and feminine and discourages an equalization pattern, one that would emphasize the person instead of the role." Structures like the generic male pronoun and nouns like *poet, actor,* and *Jew* define woman as "secondary or other, even as deviant." The connotations of various words imply that women are weak, immature, and even childish; terms like *effete* and *effeminate,* and the use of the term *masculine* to describe accented and therefore strong endings in poetry, imply that to be female is to be weak. The feminine sometimes connotes seductive and dangerous. To overcome sexist language, Farwell suggests spreading awareness of these patterns, introducing non-male generic terms and pronouns (our goal should be to make terms like *chairperson* familiar), and drawing upon the creative language of writers like Sylvia Plath and Adrienne Rich.

FAUST, JEAN.
   "Words That Oppress." *Women Speaking,* April, 1970. Reprint (2 pp.) available from KNOW, Inc., P.O. Box 86031, Pittsburgh, Pa. 15221.

   Language "oppresses and diminishes the female of the species, reducing her to an appendage or an extension of the male." Titles, professions, occupations are masculine, and are diminished when made feminine by adding *-ess* or *-ette* (*sculptress, jockette*). Male athletic teams have forceful names (*Lions, Tigers, Rams*); female teams are called names like *Rockettes, Mercurettes, Cindergals.* Language emphasizes differences between the sexes; language controls behavior and thought. Women are often defined by their sexuality (rarely are men "defined so wholly and irrevocably in a single word"), e.g. *whore, slut, tart.* Since World War II, Faust claims, sexual insults have increased. She concludes that men's fear of women, and of sexual inadequacy, is behind this derogatory language.

FEMINIST WRITERS WORKSHOP.
>   (Proposed by Ruth Todasco; commentaries by Ruth Todasco, Ellen Morgan, Jessie Sheridan, and Kathryn Starr). *An Intelligent Woman's Guide to Dirty Words: English Words and Phrases Reflecting Sexist Attitudes Toward Women in Patriarchal Society, Arranged According to Usage and Idea.* Vol. One of *The Feminist English Dictionary.* Chicago: Loop Center Y.W.C.A. (37 South Wabash Ave.), 1973.

This is the first in a series designed to review language as a prime force in the deprecation of women, to jar lexicographers to "perceive the prejudice inherent in their scholarship," and to provide a new set of definitions to substitute for those, like Webster, whose authority derives from male-dominated culture. Vol. One draws material from established dictionaries of the English language, arranging words and definitions under the categories: "Woman as Whore"; "Woman as Whorish"; "Woman as Body"; "Woman as Animal"; "Woman as -Ess"; "Woman as -Ette"; "Patriarchal Stereotypes." The commentators note that language functions to keep women in their place, that it embodies "the self-deluding myths of patriarchal man," that it deprecates, diminishes, and expresses contempt toward women, and defines them as a subspecies "different from the human standard." Ellen Morgan comments that "neo-feminists" are building consciousness of the conditioning force of language, and instituting reforms to negate the force of linguistic sexism. Neo-feminists also "try to create in their writing an affirmation of femaleness, to develop a linguistic mode which conditions positively," for example by describing female sexuality and femaleness in complimentary terms reflecting the value of "gentleness and other qualities which they believe have been concomitants of women's powerlessness and oppression." While many men use an authoritative and declarative linguistic mode, neo-feminists "tend to reject elitism and authoritarianism, and base their politics on personal experience, their style is more descriptive and, if not more tentative, more relative, more inclined to the many-faceted, less structured by the desire to assert one idea to the exclusion of others than to convey the multiple and personal character of experience."

GRAHAM, ALMA.
>   "The Making of a Nonsexist Dictionary." *Ms.,* 2 (Dec., 1973), 12-16. Reprinted in Barrie Thorne and Nancy Henley, eds., *Language and Sex: Difference and Dominance.* Rowley, Mass.: Newbury House, 1975.

An account of the construction of the *American Heritage School Dictionary* (American Heritage Publishing Co., 1972), the first ever published in which lexicographers made a conscious effort to correct the sex biases of English. The dictionary, a wordbook for children, contains 35,000 entries selected after a computer analysis of 5 million words encountered by American children in their schoolbooks. 700,000 citation slips were prepared, each showing a word in 3 lines of context. These slips gave the analysis a reflection of the culture talking to its children, and enabled them to compile statistics on sex-linked word usage in context. Some of the statistics: the ratio in schoolbooks of *he* to *she, him* to *her,* and *his* to *hers* was almost 4 to 1; there were over 7 times as many men as women in the books, and over twice as many boys as girls. *Mother* occurred more frequently than *father, wife* 3 times as often as *husband;* women are referred to in terms that identify their relation to men and children. Additionally, the citation slips showed that boys and girls were being taught separate sets of values, expectations, and goals, along expected lines: "masculine" activity, strength, etc., were contrasted with "feminine" inactivity and beauty. The lexicographers consciously combatted these images, developing new illustrative usages running counter to stereotypes. Graham also identifies some ways that sexism works in the language: (1) the "my-virtue-is-your-vice" tactic: a man's tears are *womanish*, a woman's uniform, *mannish;* (2) labelling the "exception to the rule," as in *woman doctor* and *male nurse;* (3) the "trivializing tactic," producing female forms like *poetess* and *libber;* (4) the "praise him/blame her" tendency, as in the contrast between *queen, madam, dame,* and *prince, lord, father;* (5) the "exclusionary tactic" that assumes all the world is male. Graham discusses the use of male forms to refer to human beings in general, and cites a finding from a survey of pronoun citations: out of 940 citations for *he*, 744 were applied to male humans, 128 to male animals, and 36 to persons in male-linked occupations; only 32 referred to the unspecified singular subject. Thus the reason most pronouns in schoolbooks were male was because most of the subjects being written about were males, not because the references were to unidentified human beings.

GREER, GERMAINE.
The Female Eunuch. New York: McGraw-Hill, 1971.

In a chapter on "Abuse," Greer discusses "the language of women hatred." She notes that some terms which originally applied to both sexes have become pejorative when applied to women (e.g. *witches* may be either sex, but as a term of abuse, the word is directed at women). Class antagonism enters into the vocabulary of female status with the ironic use of terms like *madam, lady,* and *dame.* "The most offensive group of words applied to the female population are those which bear the weight of neurotic male disgust for illicit or casual sex" (e.g., *tramp, piece of ass, pig, pussy*). Many of these terms are "dead, fleshy and inhuman." There is also food imagery (*honey, sweety-pie*), pretty toy words *(doll)*, cute animal terms *(chick)*.

HAUGEN, EINAR.
"Sexism and the Norwegian Language." Paper presented at Society for the Advancement of Scandinavian Study meeting, 1974. (Haugen is in the Program in Scandinavian Germanic Languages and Literatures, Harvard Univ.)

Haugen traces controversy in Scandinavia over sexism in language. The women's rights movement in Norway has called attention to language as a factor in male dominance, and the writings of Rolf M. Blakar (a social psychologist at the Univ. of Oslo) on sexism in language have "caused a bit of a stir." Blakar offers evidence from use of titles of address, descriptions of occupations, the synonyms for *man* and *woman,* word association tests, and the listing of husbands and wives in official registers. As counter-measures, Blakar proposes what amount to "consciousness-raising" techniques, e.g., reversal, such as speaking of a "male judge" or "career man" or "chatterbox men." In his conclusion, Haugen notes that "language expresses faithfully, if a little conservatively, the realities as the vast number of men and women have seen it down to our day." When the reality changes, the language will respond. [One of Blakar's writings: Rolf M. Blakar, "How Sex Roles are Represented, Reflected and Conserved in the Norwegian Language," *Olso Univ. Working Papers in Linguistics,* 5 (1974). [*See III-A.*]

KEY, MARY RITCHIE.
  "Linguistic Behavior of Male and Female." *Linguistics,* 88 (Aug. 15, 1972), 15-31.

There are different male and female images in language: men *bellow,* women *purr;* men *yell,* women *scream* or *squeal; vivacious* women, but not *vivacious* men; women *fret,* men *get angry;* men *have careers,* women *have jobs;* married women engage in *homemaking,* single women *keep house.* Key gives examples, drawn from written and spoken language, of groupings in which "women" occur, e.g., "the blind, the lame, and the women" (Nathan Pusey); signs on Mohammedan mosques: "Women and dogs and other impure animals are not permitted to enter"; it is difficult to tame "oceans, fools, and women" (Spiro Agnew); women are often classified with slaves and children. Key discusses pronominal referents; although grammar books may say the stated pronoun *he* is used in reference to an unspecified, unknown person, in actual usages certain occupational roles may be referred to as *she* (nurses; elementary school teachers; secretaries), in contrast with the invariable *he* with doctor; sailor; plumber; president. Pronominal and nominal referents are often inconsistent. [*See I, II-B, III-B-3.*]

LAKOFF, ROBIN.
  "Language and Woman's Place." *Language in Society,* 2 (1973), 45-79.

  Lakoff explores ways in which language refers to women, as distinct from men: (1) There are more euphemisms for "woman" than for "man" (e.g., *lady; girl*). Euphemisms indicate the subject is a source of strain or discomfort; there are often derogatory epithets for which the euphemism substitutes. To banish *lady* in its euphemistic sense, we would need first to get rid of *broad* and other derogatory terms for women (and the idea that women *are* broads). The euphemisms may themselves be degrading, e.g. *lady* tends to trivialize the subject matter *(lady doctor); girl* in stressing the idea of immaturity, removes the sexual connotations lurking in *woman,* but also suggests irresponsibility. (2) Language forms which define women as secondary beings who achieve status only through men, e.g., supposedly parallel words, which in fact are imbalanced (and indicate social inequities): *master* and *mistress* have diverged in time; *master* now refers to a man who has acquired consummate ability in some field, while *mistress* is restricted to its sexual sense of 'paramour' (and, unlike *master,* is preceded by a possessive masculine noun: not "she is a mistress," but "she is John's mistress"). Analogously, we say "Mary is John's widow," but not "John is Mary's widower" (though he is dead, she is still defined by her relationship to him, but the bereaved husband is no longer defined in terms of his wife). There is a lack of parallel in terms of address for each sex: *Mr.* (ambiguous re marital status) vs. *Mrs./Miss.* There is a tendency to use first names sooner and to be more apt to use them (rather than last-name-alone, or title-plus-last-name) in referring to and addressing women. In terms of changes, Lakoff argues that language is a clue to social inequities, which must be changed before language will change. She maintains that there is currently too much emphasis on neutralizing pronouns (removing the generic *he*), an area which is less in need of changing than other areas of linguistic sexism, and which is more difficult to change than many other disparities. [*See I, II-B, III-B-3, V, VII.*]

LAWRENCE, BARBARA.
  "Dirty Words *Can* Harm you." *Redbook,* 143 (May, 1974), 33.

An essay which points to the systematic derogation of women implicit in many obscenities. Various tabooed sexual verbs (e.g. *fuck; screw*) involve origins and imagery with "undeniably painful, if not sadistic, implications, the object of which is almost always female." When not openly deprecating to women, tabooed male descriptions may serve to "divorce a male organ or function from any significant interaction with the female" (e.g., *testes,* suggesting "witnesses" to the sexual and procreative strengths of the male organ). Female descriptives, on the other hand, are usually contemptuous of women (e.g. *piece*). Lawrence notes that many people who are shocked at racial or ethnic obscenities do not question obscenities which derogate women.

LEGMAN, G.
  Rationale of the Dirty Joke: An Analysis of Sexual Humor. Castle Books, 1968.

This study analyzes over 2000 erotic jokes and folklore collected in America and abroad. It is arranged by subjects (such as "the male approach," "the sadistic concept," and "women"), with extensive tangents, e.g. into the significance of jokes about mothers-in-law and about pubic hair. Legman claims that most "dirty jokes" are originated by men and there is no place in such folklore for women, except as the butt of humor. "It is not just that so preponderant an amount of the material is grossly anti-woman in tendency and intent, but also that the situations presented almost completely lack any protagonist position in which a woman can identify herself—*as a woman*—with any human gratification or pride." Legman argues that speech is a form of sexual display for males, akin to bodily ornamentation for females. [*See III-B-4; IV-C.*]

MAINARDI, PATRICIA.
  "Quilts: The Great American Art." *Radical America,* 7, No. 1 (1973), 36-68.

In this article on quilting as women's unrecognized art, Mainardi shows the sexism implicit in much writing on quilts. For example, in his catalogue essays for recent exhibitions of quilts by the Whitney and Smithsonian museums, "Jonathan Holstein praises pieced quilts [which bear superficial resemblance to the work of contemporary formalist artists such as Stella, Noland, and Newman] with the words 'strong,' 'bold,' 'vigorous,' 'bravado,' and 'toughness,' while he dismisses the appliqué quilts [which current male artists have not chosen to imitate] as 'pretty,' 'elegant,' 'beautiful but decorative.' This is the kind of phallic criticism women artists are sick of hearing, and is made all the more ridiculous by the fact that women actually made *both* types of quilts" (p. 64). In a footnote, Mainardi adds, "... from my experience in researching this article [I found that] sentence structure can be sexist—as in the constant use of the passive voice in reference to quilts ('quilts were made,' 'quilting was done,' 'names changed,' never 'women made quilts,' 'women changed the names'), and the subtle sexism in the constant use of the word 'pattern' instead of 'design' " (p. 68).

MILLER, CASEY AND KATE SWIFT.
   "De-sexing the English Language." *Ms.,* 1 (Spring, 1972), 7.

The generic personal pronoun (*he*) has an effect on personality development, implying that women are a human subspecies, whereas it bolsters male egos. In response to women's liberation, people are "trying to kick the habit of using *he* when they mean anyone, male or female"; politicians are more careful, and *his/her* is appearing in print. Adding the feminine to the masculine pronoun is often awkward, as are other devices, such as *they* used as a singular pronoun. There is need for a new singular personal pronoun that is truly generic. The authors suggest: nominative case, *tey* (to replace *he and she*); objective case, *tem* (for *him and her*); possessive case, *ter(s)* (in place of *his and her[s]*). Once *tey* or a similar word is adopted, *he* can become exclusively masculine, just as *she* is now exclusively feminine.

MILLER, CASEY AND KATE SWIFT.
   "One Small Step for Genkind." *New York Times Magazine,* April 16, 1972, pp. 36+.
   Reprinted as "Is Language Sexist?" *Cosmopolitan,* Sept., 1972, pp. 89-92+.

Sexist language is "any language that expresses stereotyped attitudes and expectations or assumes the inherent superiority of one sex over the other." *Masculine* and *feminine* are more sexist than *male* and *female,* because the words invoke strong cultural stereotypes. Words associated with males (*manly, virile, masculine*) often imply positive traits like courage, strength, independence; corresponding words associated with females are defined with fewer attributes (weakness is often one of them), and are often used in a negative way (*feminine wiles; womanish tears*). *Sissy,* derived from *sister,* is pejorative; *buddy,* from *brother,* is positive. The media use language in a sexist way: when a woman or girl makes the news, her sex is identified at the beginning of a story, if possible in the headline (which reveals an assumption that woman's achieving is rare). Because people are assumed to be male unless otherwise identified, the media have developed an extensive vocabulary to avoid repetition of *woman.* The results ("Grandmother Wins Nobel Prize"; "Blonde Hijacks Airliner") convey information that would be ludicrous if the subjects were male. The addition of feminine endings to non-sexual words (*poetess; aviatrix*) declined before the start of the new feminist movement, but there is now a kind of counter-movement, e.g. for *chairwoman; congresswoman.*

MURRAY, JESSICA.
   "Male Perspective in Language." *Women: A Journal of Liberation,* 3, No. 2 (1973), 46-50.

Language reflects "the archetypical assumption" that "all people are male until proven female." For example, the supposedly generic and neutral meaning of *man* is often confused with the male meaning; a lecture beginning with a general philosophical question, "How does Man see himself?", continued "As a salesman? A doctor? A dentist?" Hence the scope was shifted from man, the species, to man, to male. Was Eve the vehicle of man (the male)'s Fall or of man (the species)'s Fall? This involves a paradox: women being part of humanity, but conceptually excluded from it. Murray offers other examples from art, literature, and textbooks showing that people are assumed to be male unless specified female. A conspicuous example of woman-as-special-case is the sexualization of women, the assumption in language, writing, and the media, that a woman's gender is the most significant thing about her (while men are considered full people, whose sexuality is only a small part of their whole make-up). Murray concludes, "the role of language in perpetuating the archetype of women-as-extra-human could be changed by adopting new language conventions" (e.g. *Ms.,* and changes in the pronoun system), but "let us not do away with male-initiated terminology until we fully understand from whence it came."

NICHOLS, PATRICIA C.
"The Uses of Gender in English." Unpublished (graduate student) paper (12 pp.), Committee on Linguistics, Stanford Univ.

Nichols argues (as does Lakoff) that since pronouns are so integral to language, it would be difficult to introduce a new, non-sexist set of gender pronouns into English. But "there exist now within the language other means by which to change the uses of gender which relegate women to an invisible or inferior status." Increasingly, people are experimenting with gender usage: *he or she* is increasingly used generically; in informal usage, many speakers select a plural pronoun to refer to an indefinite pronoun or noun of unknown sex ("If a person were in trouble, they could have someplace to go"). There are deviations, especially in informal language, from the convention that masculine is the unmarked or norm, and feminine, the marked or deviation from the norm, e.g. the chairman of a grocery store in a television interview: "The consumer is entitled to all of the information she wants" (reflecting a view that women are the consumers). Nichols suggests more systematic study of uses of gender in everyday language, and research on children's acquisition of the generic *he* (is it part of casual language or more a feature of school language?)

NILSEN, ALLEEN PACE.
"The Correlation Between Gender and Other Semantic Features in American English." Paper presented at Linguistic Society of America meetings, Dec., 1973.

Nilsen found 500 dictionary items which included either a visible marker of +Masculine (e.g., *fellow, son, man*) or of +Feminine (e.g., *daughter, girl, frau*), the gender markers achieved through derivation rather than coincidence. These terms were analyzed for the existence of certain semantic features, and the results compared with the masculine/feminine markers, with the following results noted: There were 385 masculine terms and only 132 feminine ones, a ratio of roughly 3:1. This ratio was approximated in the category of archaic or rare words, but with all other areas the ratio differed considerably. Among words marked for +Person in the generic sense, all 90 were +Masculine. Among words marked +Occupation, the ratio of masculine to feminine words is almost 5:1 (and a larger proportion of the masculine than of feminine ones are also archaic/rare). For words marked +Prestige, there were 108 masculine and 18 feminine words (about 6:1, double the overall ratio). In words marked for +Negative connotation, feminine words outnumbered masculine ones 25 to 20 (and many are occupation-related). Among words marked −Human (no longer referring to a person although the lexical base originally did, such as *lady slipper, king pin*) 82 were masculine and 35 feminine. Words marked +Abstract are similar to the −Human, but they are also −Concrete; the ratio of masculine to feminine words was about 2:1 (43 to 21). The feminine words for these two categories (−Human, +Abstract) "tended to deal with aesthetically pleasing little things," e.g., *lady bird, maidenhair fern;* the masculine words were more serious, e.g., *mastermind, fraternalism.* For words marked +Unusual age, there were 34 feminine and 27 masculine terms, supporting the idea that age is more relevant to women than to men in our culture. Nearly all the age terms have positive connotations, incorporating the concept of youth, but there were five negative-connotation terms denoting old females, and none for old males. Among words marked for +Family relationship feminine terms most outnumbered masculine ones, 46:32. There was a correlation between the generic and prestige terms (both highly masculine). For some of the generic terms, specifically feminine terms have been created, but this doesn't guarantee linguistic equality; for example, the masculine term travels into other lexical items, as in *king-queen-kingdom* (but not *queendom*). There is another group of words in which the basic word is not gender-marked, but a feminine word has been derived, e.g., *author-authoress* and *major-majorette* (the latter having a different meaning). Apparently the *-er/-or* suffix, meaning "doer," has acquired a male connotation. It also seems that "the higher the prestige . . . of the word, the more important it becomes to make a separation between males and females." Nilsen raises several questions relating to feminists' desires to attack linguistic sexism, and concludes that feminists might best concentrate efforts on "educating children and the general public to the way language is rather than by trying to change the language," particularly seeing that, for instance, when generic male terms are used, illustrations of both males and females are given.

NILSEN, ALLEEN PACE.
    "Sexism in English: A Feminist View." In Nancy Hoffman, Cynthia Secor, and Adrian Tinsley, eds., *Female Studies VI.* Old Westbury, N.Y.: The Feminist Press, 1972, pp. 102-109.

    Culling through a standard desk dictionary, Nilsen found a variety of examples of sexism in English, which fit into three patterns: (1) "In our culture it is a woman's body which is considered important while it is a man's mind or his activities which are valued. A woman is sexy. A man is successful." Far more words have been derived from male names (e.g. *pasteurization, sousaphone, shick test*) than from female names (the only two in common use, *bloomers* and *Mae West jacket,* are both related to woman's physical anatomy). In geographical names, there is a preoccupation with women's breasts *(The Tetons, Little Nipple Top, Maiden's Peak),* but not with male anatomy *(Jackson Hole, Pike's Peak).* In words with a male and female counterpart, the female word often has sexual connotations, while the male word retains "a serious business-like aura," e.g. *sir* vs. *madam; master* vs. *mistress.* In other pairs of words, the masculine is usually the base with a feminine suffix added (e.g. *hero* and *heroine*); the masculine word "travels into compounds while the feminine word is a dead end" (e.g. *kingdom* but not *queendom*). Sex and marriage is the only semantic area "in which the masculine word is not the base or more powerful word," e.g. *prostitute* is the base word, and *male prostitute,* the derivative; *bridegroom* is derived from *bride,* and *widower* from *widow.* (2) Language indicates that women are expected to play a passive role, and men an active one, e.g. the frequent identification of women with something to eat (*a peach*), with plants (*wall flower*), the passivity of many female names

(Ivy, Pearl). Females are also identified with pets (*pony tails;* dressed in *halters*). Another aspect of women's passivity: their definition in relationship to husbands, brothers, and fathers. (3) In language, the concept of masculine usually has positive connotations, while the feminine has either trivial or negative connotations (compare *chef* with *cook; tailor* with *seamstress; major* with *majorette*). Telling a child to *be a lady* often means to sit with her knees together; *to be a man* means to be noble, strong, virtuous. "The chicken metaphor tells the whole story of a girl's life. In her youth she is a *chick,* then she marries and begins feeling *cooped up,* so she goes to *hen parties* where she *cackles* with her friends. Then she has her *brood* and begins to *hen-peck* her husband. Finally she turns into an *old biddy.*"

SCHNEIDER, JOSEPH W. AND SALLY L. HACKER.
"Sex Role Imagery and the Use of the Generic 'Man' in Introductory Texts." *American Sociologist,* 8, No. 8 (1973), 12-18.

Students in introductory sociology classes were asked to submit pictures to represent the major sections of an introductory text. When the terms used the generic *man (social man, political man, economic man, urban man),* 64% of the pictures showed male only. When the generic label *man* was removed (so the terms were *social behavior, political behavior,* etc.), 50% of the students illustrated the concepts with pictures of males only. Women were seldom elicited as the image under the generic term *man.*

SCHULZ, MURIEL R.
"The Semantic Derogation of Woman." In Barrie Thorne and Nancy Henley, eds., *Language and Sex: Difference and Dominance.* Rowley, Mass.: Newbury House, 1975.

This is a study of the tendency for terms designating women in English to acquire debased or obscene reference (pejoration), and an analysis of the reasons for it, since language reflects the thoughts, attitudes, and culture of its creators and users, who in the case of English are, according to Schulz, "largely men." Schulz examines a collection of terms which have been thus abased, comparing them often with their male equivalents; terms for males have almost totally escaped such pejoration. A common tendency of the terms applied to women has been for them to become sexually abusive, i.e., to finally acquire the meaning of morally loose, whore. Women have not coined the terms; it is men who refer to women in sexual terms, and the wealth of terms reveals their hostility. Endearments for women (but not for men) have similarly undergone pejoration; a number of the terms began as references to either sex, but specialized to refer to women at the time they began pejorating. Ullman has suggested three origins for pejoration, which might bear on the causes for the degeneration of terms designating women: association with a contaminating concept, euphemism, and prejudice. Contamination may be a factor, but Schulz rejects the notion "that there is a quality inherent in the concept of *woman* which taints any word associated with it." Women are acknowledged as the *less* promiscuous, more proper, of the sexes, yet have the largest category of words designating humans in sexual terms (Schulz knows about 1000, and cites other sources). Euphemism seems out; though many terms for prostitutes are euphemistic, most are dysphemistic. Prejudice seems the most likely explanation—"woman" is a "label of primary potency"(Allport) by which a stereotype is maintained, and evidence is brought forward for fear of women as the source of the prejudice. Schulz concludes that though we generally cannot know the extent to which language influences its users, words "highly charged with emotion, taboo, or distaste do not only reflect the culture which uses them. They teach and perpetuate the attitudes which created them . . . to brand a class of person as obscene is to taint them to the users of the language."

STANLEY, JULIA P.
"Paradigmatic Woman: The Prostitute." Paper presented, in briefer versions, at South Atlantic Modern Language Assoc., 1972; American Dialect Society, 1972; and Linguistic Society of America, 1973.

Stanley has compiled and analyzed 220 terms for sexually promiscuous women (she stopped at that number because she'd "reached the point of diminishing returns"; she notes "the very size of the set and the impossibility of collecting ALL the terms for prostitute is a comment on our culture. As linguists we assume that the existence of a new lexical item indicates a cultural need for a term that expresses a new concept. Isn't it strange that the set of terms that refer to prostitutes is one that's constantly expanding?") In contrast, there are relatively few terms for promiscuous men; Stanley lists 22, and notes "there's no linguistic reason why the set is so small." Stanley sets out the semantic features that define the categories represented by the terms for prostitutes: A. Denotative: 1. cost (cheap; expensive); 2. method of payment (direct, indirect); 3. type of activity (little; much); and Connotative: 1. negative; 2. neutral; 3. positive. B. Dysphemistic or euphemistic (whether the term exposes male disdain for the sexuality of women or conceals his disdain). C. Metonymic (whether the term refers to women through reference to a specific portion of their bodies). D. Metaphoric (whether the term refers to women through comparison to another object or animal). This semantic set provides "a paradigm of the definition of women in our culture." "The names that men have given to women who make themselves sexually available to them reveal the underlying metaphors by which men conceive of their relationships with women, and through which women learn to perceive and define themselves. The metaphors that underlie the terms for sexually promiscuous women define and perpetuate the ambivalent sex-role stereotypes that a male-dominated culture sets forth for women."

STRAINCHAMPS, ETHEL.
"Our Sexist Language." In Vivian Gornick and Barbara K. Moran, eds., *Woman in Sexist Society*. New York: Basic Books, 1971, pp. 240-250.

An article with a philological bent, tracing the historical origins, use, and censorship of *fuck, cunt, twot, condom, diaphragm* (the author claims that women, compared with men, have a "sane and rational attitude toward taboo words"). Strainchamps cites evidence of male dominance in English: *man* and *he* as generics; words which were nonemotive when they referred to either gender have become contemptuous after being applied to women alone, and some that were pejorative lost that sense when they acquired an exclusively male reference (*shrewd-shrewish* illustrate both trends). Strainchamps claims that English "retains more vestiges of the archaic sexual attitudes than any other civilized tongue."

TOTH, EMILY.
"The Politics of Linguistic Sexism." Paper presented at Modern Language Assoc., 1971. (Toth is at the Humanities Center, Johns Hopkins.)

Language shows that men have power and superiority, whereas women are defined as Other, often as passive, inferior, or invisible. Male terms are used as the unmarked forms (*man, mankind, one-man show*), with women subsumed in the male generic. Occupations, professions, careers are male (including *bachelor's* and *Master's* degrees, and *fellowships*). When a woman enters the "man's world," this is marked by a peculiar vocabulary (*female judge, madam chairman*). Abstractions, to be revealed or controlled by men, are often personified as female (science, liberty, victory, fortune). Machines or other items run or manned by men are often called *she* (ships, cars, ejaculations like "fill 'er up!" and "Thar she blows!"). Expressions for which there is no opposite-sex equivalent indicate power relationships: *brotherly love* (whereas *sisterly love* implies lesbianism); a man can be *cocksure,* but the most a woman can do is make a man feel *hen-pecked;* a man cannot be a *shrew, fishwife, virago,* or *bitch.* There are no female equivalents for *effeminate* or *emasculated.* Women's terms are often associated with littleness, confinement, cuteness (e.g. *women's liberation* abbreviated to *lib* and *libbers,* in contrast with Black Liberation and the National Liberation Front); also the *little woman,* and the *little black dress.*

VARDA ONE.
"Manglish." Reprint (4 pp.) available from KNOW, Inc., P.O. Box 86031, Pittsburgh, Pa. 15221. (Copyright by Everywoman Pub. Co., Venice, Calif., 1971.)

This paper compiles some of the material from Varda One's "Manglish" columns in the feminist newspaper, *Everywoman.* "Manglish" is the "process of the degradation of women in language," and operates by various mechanisms: (1) "The myth of lexicographic objectivity" (dictionaries, like the Bible, are treated as absolutes, yet are full of prejudice: more space is given for male items, sex-stereotyped examples are used in illustrative sentences, the masculine is presented first in a sequence where the feminine is also present, more insulting terms are included for women than men, prejudiced comments are included, and there are more drawings of men and male animals). (2) "The appendage complex" (it is assumed that men are humans and women an afterthought, e.g. in the use of the male form for both sexes, and the use of the male form as neuter, with feminine qualifiers added). (3) "Relating function to gender, usually reserving low prestige jobs for women" (the incorporation of a gender suffix in words like *policeman* and *policewoman,* and the assumption of one sex even without an explicit indicator, e.g. *tycoon* and *secretary*). (4) "Devolutionary process of words involving women" (the degeneration of previously neutral terms like *harlot* and *wench*). (5) "The subsuming of identity" (in patronymics, married names, first names, and historical omissions [words based on names of people tend to immortalize men, but not women]). (6) "The woman as 'the other' " (men postulate women as "a goal outside themselves to be mastered and conquered," e.g. anything overwhelming in nature is feminine, such as *Mother Earth, Hurricane Ida,* and the *sea,* as is anything difficult or big, such as *ships, mines, dams*). (7) "The double standard of titles" *(Miss/Mrs.* vs. *Mr.).* (8) "The use of compliments and insults." (9) "Slang expressions for sexual organs." (10) "Sexist maxims" (e.g., "women hate to work for other women"). (11) "The use of double-think" (a woman who is aggressive is called *pushy;* a man, a *go-getter*). (12) "Sexist expressions" ("we call the deadliest insect a *black widow spider,* the cruelest torture instrument an *iron maiden,* a carnivorous plant is a *Venus flytrap,* and the device for hauling prisoners is a *black Maria*").

2. Protest Against Sexist Language

Political protest is implicit in many of the writings on sexism in language, and proposals for change (e.g., for changing pronoun structures and introducing new terms like Ms., chairperson, chairone, herstory, humankind). *This movement for language change—and the conflict and controversies which have developed in its wake—is a phenomenon in itself worthy of study, as suggested in the following references.*

CONKLIN, NANCY FAIRES.
"Perspectives on the Dialects of Women." Paper presented at American Dialect Society, 1973. (Conklin is in the Linguistics Dept., Univ. of Mich.)

Popular and feminist literature show growing interest in women's dialects, and a questioning of linguistic convention (e.g., the introduction of *Ms.* as a term of address; criticisms of the pronoun system). Ratification of the Equal Rights Amendment may have linguistic ramifications; federal forms, such as employment forms, which currently read, "Do not mention the race, religion, or national origin of the applicant," may have to add "sex of applicant." "It will be extremely difficult to avoid some sex-marking item such as title or third person pronoun. Perhaps some language planning is in order." Younger women, and feminist women of all ages, have begun to punctuate their speech with what have been male epithets and, in general, to avoid extremely polite styles. This change in speech may be an important predictive variable for research on the political and social attitudes of the young, middle-class, particularly college women. [*See IV-B, V.*]

CONKLIN, NANCY FAIRES.
"Toward a Feminist Analysis of Linguistic Behavior." *The University of Michigan Papers in Women's Studies,* 1, No. 1 (1974), 51-73.

The women's movement has made some attempts to deal with sexism in language, but has "unfortunately focused primarily on rather marginal problems," e.g. false etymologies like *herstory* (to replace *history*) and *himacane* (to replace *hurricane*). The third-person singular pronoun is significant as the only obligatorily sex-marked category in English, but the outlook for new, artificial forms (such as *te* or *co* for *he and she*) coming into general use is very poor, since historically pronoun systems are resistant to outside influence. *They* has strong colloquial usage as the third-person singular pronoun, and feminists should encourage the acceptability of *they.* The new title *Ms.* still embodies a sex marker (although eliminating mention of marital status); a "thorough-going program of de-sexing the language" would require replacing the *Ms.* and *Mr.* address forms by a neutral form, such as *M.* The most serious problems appear in the sexist use of language (e.g. the special connotations of the language for talking about women). One of the marks of the feminist in American society is the everyday use of the four letter epithets (*shit, fuck,* etc.) which have traditionally been taboo for women. "Obscene language is used to add emphasis to one's speech, to call attention to one's statements, and stress one's commitment to them. Feminists should be aware that they are using obscenities not just for their shock value, but because they are 'strong language' in the most literal sense of the word." [*See I, II-B, IV-C, V, VI.*]

DALY, MARY.
   Beyond God the Father: Toward a Philosophy of Women's Liberation. Boston:
   Beacon, 1973.

   One of the premises of this insightful argument for feminism is that "the symbolic and
linguistic instruments for communication—which include essentially the whole theological
tradition in world religions—have been formulated by males under the conditions of
patriarchy." Women have had the power of naming stolen from them. "We have not been
free to use our own power to name ourselves, the world, or God." Part of liberation is
discovering the inadequacy of existing language, and establishing a new reality by creating
new words and meanings; for example, "the word *sisterhood* no longer means a subordinate
mini-brotherhood, but an authentic bonding of women on a wide scale for our own
liberation." Daly refers to the "gift of tongues" as an example of "the failure of religious
charisma to uproot alienative structures," since speaking in tongues "has functioned as only
a temporary release for individuals in elite groups," and these same individuals and groups
"have been most stubbornly conservative and sexist in their adherence to 'real' language,
outside the special moments of charismatic occurrences." "Women's new hearing and
naming is cosmic upheaval, in contrast to this charism which is a controllable and cooptable
ripple of protest. Feminist naming is a deliberate confrontation with language structures of
our heritage. It transcends the split between nonrational sounds of 'tongues' and the merely
rational semantic games of linguistic analysis, for it is a break out of the deafening noise of
sexist language that has kept us from hearing our own word."

EBLE, CONNIE.
   "How to Name a Revolution." Paper presented at Southeastern Conference on
   Linguistics, 1973. (Eble is in the English Dept., Univ. of North Carolina.)

   With the development of the women's liberation movement, "the problem that has no
name" (as Betty Friedan referred to the female plight in 1966) has acquired many names.
Eble divides the "working vocabulary" of the movement into four subject areas: (1) "The
vocabulary of male supremacy" (e.g. *patriarchy, sexism, male chauvinist, male heavies*);
(2) "The vocabulary of female unity" (e.g. *sisters, sisterhood, uppity women*); (3) "The
vocabulary of action-reform-revolution" (e.g. *politics of experience, psychology of
oppression, consciousness-raising*); (4) "The vocabulary of shock" (deliberate use of hostile
and obscene terms to overcome stereotypes of feminine language). The media have also
coined terms, many of them designed to trivialize the movement (e.g. *women's lib, lib lady,
libber, libbie, bra-burners*).

HOLE, JUDITH AND ELLEN LEVINE.
   Rebirth of Feminism. New York: Quadrangle Books, 1971.

   The first overall history of the new wave of feminism includes a section on "The Politics
of Language," which describes language as one of the institutions feminists are questioning
and seeking to change. The authors also note that the feminist movement has developed its
own special language and set of symbols, e.g. *sexism, male chauvinist, sexist.*

McDOWELL, MARGARET B.
  "The New Rhetoric of Woman Power." *The Midwest Quarterly*, 12 (1971), 187-198.

McDowell raises general questions, e.g., what types of rhetoric (of speakers, writers, aims, methods, and tone) can be found in the women's liberation movement? What kinds of writing and speeches oppose the movement? "What rhetorical stance on the woman question do contemporary advertising, television, and educaters assume?" How do various magazines react to the movement? How does the rhetoric of the women's movement compare with that of other protest movements, such as the New Left, black power, and 19th century feminism? The author categorizes branches of the women's movement, from radicals to members of government commissions on the status of women, and comments upon their varied rhetorics. The radical women's movement uses terms common to New Left protest of the 1960's, e.g., nouns or verbs become adjectives (*life* styles; *movement* women); extreme words replace moderate ones (*impoverished, dehumanized* vs. *discontent, frustration*); in spite of their anti-war stance, movement women have a militarist vocabulary (*struggle, power, solidarity, organize, attack, liberate*); guerilla theater groups use obscenity. Males in audiences often laugh at feminist speakers, as they did at abolitionists and suffragists in earlier times. [*This article is sometimes misinformed; its rhetorical stance, especially towards the radical movement, is mildly negative.*]

PEI, MARIO.
  "The Paeon of the Liberated Woman," Chapter 6 of *Double-Speak in America*. New York: Hawthorn Books, 1973.

Writing in a chatty and critical vein about newly-minted phrases in the American public language scene, Pei catalogues various terms brought into parlance by the women's liberation movement, e.g. *sexism, sexist, male chauvinist pig, sex object, chairperson*. He notes feminist protest against media phrases like *Women's Lib Gals* and against the masculine generic pronoun structure. He also mentions satiric responses to feminist proposals for language change, such as Russell Baker's column in the *New York Times*, proposing male terms parallel to *Mrs.* and *Miss*, namely *Murm* abbreviated to *Mrm.* for a married man, and *Smur* or *Smr.* for a bachelor.

SAFILIOS-ROTHSCHILD, CONSTANTINA.
  Women and Social Policy. Englewood Cliffs, N.J.: Prentice-Hall, 1974.

This book sets out to "delineate the entire map of strategies, social action, policies, and laws necessary to effectively eradicate sexism from all aspects of our lives and from the entire society" (p. viii). Under the section on "Social Policy to 'Liberate' Language" (pp. 122-126), the author mentions the effect of sexist language on the socialization of children into gender stereotypes, and on the expression and formulation of ideas. She proposes that writers should start writing high quality short stories and novels which are free of sex stereotypes; that historians and scientists should assess "established truths" to look for sexist biases; that "all the different types of explicit and implicit forms of sexism in the language must be detected, uncovered, and widely publicized and ridiculed." Passage of a legislative act could make it legal to sue mass media or leading figures or experts for using sexist rhetoric or expressions or carrying sexist features. "The gradual disappearance of sexist references, expressions, and connotations from our everyday language would have a very important effect upon women's self-concepts and degree of self-esteem, as well as upon the degree of esteem for and the type of image men have of women" (p. 126).

B. Sex Differences in Word Choice, Syntactic Usage, and Language Style

BARRON, NANCY.
> "Sex-Typed Language: The Production of Grammatical Cases." *Acta Sociologica*, 14, No. 1-2 (1971), 24-72.

An analysis of the use of grammatical case as it varies by sex. Assuming that non-linguistic, sex-typed behavior would show up in language use, Barron drew on studies by Maccoby and others which suggest that in cognitive style, men are more analytic and women more synthetic; and that in interaction style, men are more self-oriented and women more other-oriented. From this, Barron hypothesized that "the speech of men is characterized by action and the projection of themselves as actors upon their environment; women are concerned with internal states and behaviors which would integrate other persons with themselves into the social situation." Recorded samples of teachers and pupils engaged in regular classroom activities were reconstructed (by adding implicit information deleted by grammatical or situational reduction rules), and each nominal phrase was coded for case, and by gender of speaker. It was found that the choice of case (which gives the meanings and uses of nouns in sentences) was sex-typed. Women, compared with men, produced a greater proportion of explicit participative cases (nouns with psychological state verbs, e.g. *hear, think, love*) and purposive cases (specifying the function or rationale of a person's actions). This, Barron claims, is because women are more concerned with internal psychological states and with the functions of objects for interpersonal use. Men made more use of instrumental and source cases (showing more involvement with implementation of action by means of objects), and objective cases (verbally emphasizing things, and particularly things acted upon). No sex differences were found in the use of agentive and locative cases.

BERNARDEZ-BONESATTI, TERESA.
> "Feminist and Non-Feminist Out-Patients Compared." Paper presented at American Psychiatric Association, 1974. (Bernardez-Bonesatti is in the Dept. of Psychiatry, College of Human Medicine, Michigan State Univ.)

The author writes from her experience as a psychiatrist whose clinical practice in the last four years has included 32 non-feminist women and 28 feminists, ranging in ages from 18 to 45, of varied racial, educational, and marital backgrounds. These observations are based on the first two or three interviews with these patients. Non-feminists—who presented their problems as signs of personal inadequacy, and were compliant, submissive, and unassertive in the therapeutic context—tended to speak using passive self-references, defining the self via others, and rarely using the personal pronoun *I*. The feminists, all of whom had had experience in consciousness-raising groups, were less submissive and compliant, and more active, inquisitive, and critical towards the therapist. They were more autonomous in self-definition than the non-feminists, and used more active self-references. The author concludes that "feminists are healthier persons although they are outside the [biased] 'norm' for female behavior."

BODINE, ANN.

"Sex Differentiation in Language." Paper presented at Conference on Women and Language, Rutgers Univ., 1973 [*this part of paper not included in revised version cited in I*].

In an informal study, Bodine found that along the East Coast men say *half dollar* for the coin that American women call *fifty cent piece* (although the introduction of the *Kennedy half dollar* has broken down that pattern). There is sex differentiation in first names and in most common titles in English. One sixth of personal nouns are sex differentiated; of those, 20% refer to religious and court hierarchy (abbess, countess), and hence are low in usage; another 20% are high usage kinship terms. Bodine discusses the origin of *man* as a generic term, and the historical and current controversy over the use of *they* with a sex-indefinite singular antecedent.

CONKLIN, NANCY FAIRES.

"Toward a Feminist Analysis of Linguistic Behavior." *The University of Michigan Papers in Women's Studies,* 1, No. 1 (1974), 51-73.

The sexes have different word domains: women are more likely to control the terminology of sewing and fabric terms, cooking methods and utensils, and child care; men, the jargon of sports and of auto mechanics. This specialization reflects the roles and functions of each sex in society. "Since men may be professionals in any field, it is quite conceivable that men who command the vocabulary of what are generally women's subjects may be taken for professional (rather than 'amateur,' like the housewives) practitioners of that subject matter area (i.e., chefs, child psychologists, designers). Because women are more rarely professionals of any sort and almost never achieve professional status in areas which are viewed as 'male,' they are less likely to be given the benefit of the doubt (i.e., assumed to be trained mechanics, sportscasters, or even chemists, lawyers, or film directors, the 'neutral' areas)." [*See I, II-A-2, IV-C, V, VI.*]

EBLE, CONNIE C.

"How the Speech of Some Is More Equal Than Others." Paper presented at Southeastern Conference on Linguistics, 1972. (Eble is in the English Dept., Univ. of North Carolina.)

There are sex differences in the frequency and context of use of certain words, e.g. endearment terms *(sweetie, honey, dear)* have more limited use by men; while both sexes can say, "Hi *love*," to members of the opposite sex, in America only women can say it to the same sex (in England men can say it to men). Females can use both *my boyfriend* and *my girlfriend* in relation to themselves, but men can use only *my girlfriend* in this way. In contrast, terms of hostility are more associated with men. There are sex differences in choice of adjectives, and possibly in the connotation of words. Some phrases have different meanings if spoken by a male vs. a female, e.g., "You caught me with my pants down" is a "metaphorical admission of embarrassment on the part of a man but is almost always interpreted literally and physically if a woman says it." The phrase, "he's got great legs" suggests active athletic stamina; "she's got great legs" implies a passive sexual quality. [*See III-B-3.*]

FARB, PETER.
  Word Play: What Happens When People Talk. New York: Alfred A. Knopf, 1973.

  This summary of sociolinguistic literature, designed for a general audience, includes a discussion of sex differences in speech use. On p. 49, Farb writes that words like *goodness, gracious,* and *dear me* are usually considered female speech. Women's speech is also associated with the expressive use of intensifiers like *so, such,* and *vastly* (a female usage which has also been observed in German, Danish, French, and Russian). [*See II-A, III-A, III-B-2, V.*]

GARCIA-ZAMOR, MARIE A.
  "Child Awareness of Sex Role Distinctions in Language Use." Paper presented at Linguistic Society of America, Dec., 1973. (Garcia-Zamor is with the International Bank for Reconstruction and Development, 1818 H St., N.W., Washington, D.C. 20433.)

  Garcia-Zamor tested eight nursery school children for their tendency to *attribute* certain expressions to males or females. Boys were more in agreement over their attributions, particularly in attributing statements to males. Aggressive expressions, bright colors, cars, *shit,* and *daddy* were seen as male. *Dum dum* (associated with breaking something), light colors, tag questions, and *drat* were associated with females. [*See VII.*]

GILLEY, HOYT MELVYN AND COLLIER STEPHEN SUMMERS.
  "Sex Differences in the Use of Hostile Verbs." *Journal of Psychology,* 76 (1970), 33-37.

  In this experimental study 50 males and 50 females were asked to make up sentences from a given pronoun and a given verb. There were 20 "neutral" and 20 "hostile" verbs; subjects were in either a personal-reference condition for the pronouns (*I* or *we*) or an other-reference condition (*he* [sic] or *they*). There were five blocks of 20 trials, run by a male experimenter who gave neither positive nor negative reinforcement. Male subjects used hostile verbs at a greater average frequency (40.38 over 100 trials) than did female subjects (35.86). The authors review previous research on use of hostile and neutral verbs in an operant conditioning technique.

GLESER, GOLDINE C., LOUIS A. GOTTSCHALK, AND JOHN WATKINS.
"The Relationship of Sex and Intelligence to Choice of Words: A Normative Study of Verbal Behavior." *Journal of Clinical Psychology,* 15 (1959), 182-191.

Samples of speech were elicited from 90 white, "occupationally adjusted, medically healthy" subjects (most employees of Kroger Manufacturing Co.). The sample was divided into three IQ levels (which correlated closely with education), with each group evenly divided by sex. Each subject was asked (by a male examiner) to tell about "any interesting or dramatic life experiences you have had." The taped responses were coded by grammatical composition and by "psychological functions." Most IQ differences were found in grammatical categories, while all differences in verbal behavior related to sex were found in the psychological categories. Females used significantly more words implying feeling, emotion, or motivation (whether positive, negative, or neutral); they also made more references to self and used more auxiliary words and negations. Men used significantly more words implying time, space, quantity, and destructive action. There was a tendency (not statistically significant) for sex differences to disappear in the "highest IQ" group, with the exception of the relative frequency of words expressing emotion. The more intelligent (better educated) women were like men in less frequent use of self-references and negation. But the more intelligent (better educated) men were like women in using fewer references to place or spatial relations and fewer words implying destructive action.

HALL, EDWARD T.
The Silent Language. Doubleday, 1959.

Hall writes that the *can* and *may* distinction in English "originally developed informally and was linked to sex; men and boys said 'can,' women and girls 'may' " (Fawcett Premier Third Edition, p. 120). Since *may* sounded more refined to women, they tried to push it on men, along with the grammatical "gobbledygook" about possible and not possible, and teachers are still trying to instill the distinction in children. As sex role distinctions diminish, however, he says, the *may-can* distinction "now is so mixed up it's almost impossible to develop any rules," and either is applicable in many situations. He cites no references for his claims.

HIRSCHMAN, LYNETTE.
"Analysis of Supportive and Assertive Behavior in Conversations." Paper presented at meeting of Linguistic Society of America, July, 1974.

Probing sex differences in conversational assertiveness and supportiveness, Hirschman had pairs of subjects discuss a question for ten minutes (there was a total of four single-sex and eight mixed-sex conversations). In terms of word choice, the data were analyzed for presence of qualifiers (like *maybe, sort of, I think, I guess*), taken to accompany less conversational assertiveness; for frequency of fillers (*uhm, well, like, you know*) indicative of less fluent speech; frequency of affirmative words (*yeah, right, mm hmm*) indicating supportiveness (a positive response to the other's statements). The only striking female-male difference in word choice was in use of *mm hmm*: females outnumbered males 53 to 8, and every woman produced more *mm hmm*'s than any of the males, in fact, more than all the males put together. In the case of *yeah* (also interpreted as an affirmative word), one male accounted for almost 70% of the male total; otherwise the sexes were about the same in using this word, as they were in the use of *right,* and in the frequency of affirmative words in general. Although *mm hmm, yeah,* and *right* all are used to indicate the listener's attention, understanding, or agreement, *yeah* and *right* have more freedom of distribution than *mm hmm* (they can appear alone, at the beginning, middle, or end of an utterance; in strings of affirmatives [*right right yeah*] ; and after an interjection; while *mm hmm* is more restricted). For the speaker, hearing an *mm hmm* is a good indication that the other person isn't going to say anything more, while *yeah* or *right* are more likely to lead directly into an utterance. *Mm hmm* is conversationally less obtrusive. It was also found that females use more *mm hmm*'s in female-female conversations than in mixed-sex conversations. There was also a sex difference in the use of *I think;* males used it almost twice as much as females (118 to 66). *I think* correlated with word output (it was used more by the more assertive speakers); in these conversations, *I think* seemed to function not so much as a qualifier as a polite way of stating an opinion. [*See IV-A, IV-D, VIII-B.*]

HIRSCHMAN, LYNETTE.
  "Female-Male Differences in Conversational Interaction." Paper presented at meeting of Linguistic Society of America, Dec., 1973.

  In Hirschman's sample of six dyadic conversations, females used a much higher percentage of fillers (e.g. *uhm, you know*) than males. No differences were found in the proportion of qualifiers (e.g. *maybe, probably, I think, I guess*) used, though different speakers did use different kinds of qualifiers: a female used many of the *I think, I'd say* type, while a male used many of the *most, many* type. Females more often used pronouns involving the other speaker than they used third-person references; the reverse pattern was true for males. Females used the *mm hmm* response much more often than males, particularly with each other. [*See IV-A, IV-B, IV-D, IV-E.*]

JESPERSEN, OTTO.
  "The Woman," Chapter XIII of *Language: Its Nature, Development and Origin.* London: Allen & Unwin, 1922, pp. 237-254.

  (1) Word choice: according to Jespersen, women are euphemistic, exercising "a great and universal influence on linguistic development through their instinctive shrinking from coarse and gross expressions and their preference for refined and (in certain spheres) veiled and indirect expressions" (p. 246). While men swear, women use euphemistic substitutes (e.g. men say *hell;* women say *the other place*). Through the invention and use of slang (which Jespersen calls a "secondary sexual characteristic"), men are the "chief renovators of language." "This is not invalidated by the fact that quite recently, with the rise of the feminist movement, many young ladies have begun to imitate their brothers in that as well as in other respects" (p. 248). (2) Vocabulary: Jespersen claims that women's vocabulary is less extensive, and more in the central field of language (avoiding the bizarre) than is that of men, and that "men take greater interest in words as such and in their acoustic properties" (pp. 248-249). (3) Adverbs: women are "fond" of hyperbole, using more adverbs of intensity *(awfully, pretty, terribly nice, quite, so).* (4) Sentence construction: "Women

much more often than men break off without finishing their sentences, because they start talking without having thought out what they are going to say" (p. 250). The sexes, Jespersen claims, have different ways of building sentences: men use more intricate structures, with clause within clause (like a set of Chinese boxes); women add on clauses (building sentences like stringing pearls), the gradation between ideas marked not grammatically, but "emotionally," by stress and intonation. [*See I, V, VI.*]

KEY, MARY RITCHIE.
   "Linguistic Behavior of Male and Female." *Linguistics,* 88 (Aug. 15, 1972), 15-31.

Females may more often use the intensifiers, *so, such, quite, vastly* ("It was *so* interesting"; "I had *such* fun"). Key refers to Shuy's claim that females are more sensitive than males to indicators of lower status, and are less likely to use syntactic features with such connotations. [*See I, II-A-1, III-B-3.*]

KRAMER, CHERIS.
   "Folklinguistics." *Psychology Today,* 8 (June, 1974), 82-85.

Kramer discusses and compares stereotypes of female and male speech (as depicted in *New Yorker* cartoons) with differences found in actual speech in an experimental study. Kramer analyzed 156 cartoons containing adult human speech, from 13 consecutive issues (in 1973) of *The New Yorker.* In addition, she had 25 male and 25 female students indicate, for each caption, whether they thought the speaker was male or female (there was clear consensus in their choices). In the cartoons, male characters swear more freely than female characters (the student raters commented that, in general, profanity and harsh language distinguish male from female speech, and that men use a simpler, more direct, more assertive type of language, while women tend to "flower up" their remarks). Adjectives (such as *nice* and *pretty*), which are popularly associated with female speech, sometimes serve in the cartoons to identify a woman as having traditional ideas about the female role; at other times such adjectives are the basis for a joke (especially when a woman uses them while talking about a "masculine" topic); occasionally, male cartoon figures use these adjectives to indicate role reversal. Kramer emphasizes that folk-linguistics, as shown in the cartoons and the student responses, may not fit empirical data about the way people talk. She designed an experiment to explore generalizations often made: that men use a greater variety of words; that women use more adverbs ending in *-ly;* that women are more interested in people, and men in objects. The participants (17 men and 17 women) were shown two photographs, one of people and the other of a building, and asked to write paragraphs describing them. Analysis of these written descriptions indicated *no significant sex differences.* Men did not use a greater variety of prenominal adjectives; women did not use a significantly larger number of *-ly* adverbs, nor did women use more words in describing either the people or the building. Kramer then had 11 female students examine a random sample of the typed paragraphs (5 by women, 5 by men) and try to identify the sex of the writer; in all there were 59 correct guesses, and 51 incorrect ones. Kramer notes that this study was limited to written language, to essays written for a general audience, and to college freshmen—all of which may have bearing on the findings. She concludes that in communication research, "beliefs about sex-related language differences may be as important as the actual differences. As long as women play a subordinate role, their speech will be stereotyped as separate and unequal" (p. 85). [*See IV-B, IV-D, IV-F.*]

KRAMER, CHERIS.
"Stereotypes of Women's Speech: The Word From Cartoons." *Journal of Popular Culture,* in press.

Expanding the study of cartoons to include samples from *Ladies Home Journal, Playboy,* and *Cosmopolitan,* as well as *The New Yorker,* Kramer gave university students lists of cartoon captions and asked them to assign each caption to a male or female speaker and to give reasons for their decisions. Sex of the speaker of the captions was clearly stereotyped in more than three-fourths of the cartoons. Students of both sexes characterized stereotyped women's speech as being "stupid, vague, emotional, confused, and wordy"; men's speech was stereotyped as logical, concise, businesslike, in control. In the world of cartoons, women's speech is weaker than men's speech in emphasis, with fewer uses of exclamations and curse words. Often male speakers are putting down another person, while often when the woman talks, it is her speech itself that is the joke. Women are restricted both in how they talk and in where they talk. Women, who are found in fewer places than male speakers in the cartoons, were "seldom shown otherwise than as housewife, mother, sex object. Statements that indicated the speaker held an authoritarian position were attributed to men. Women's statements were defined primarily by personality traits rather than by professional occupation." [*See IV-D*].

KRAMER, CHERIS.
"Women's Speech: Separate But Unequal?" *Quarterly Journal of Speech,* 60 (Feb., 1974), 14-24. Reprinted in Barrie Thorne and Nancy Henley, eds., *Language and Sex: Difference and Dominance.* Rowley, Mass.: Newbury House, 1975.

Complete word taboos for one sex or the other are probably rare in English; most differences appear to be a matter of context and frequency, e.g., women knowing but not using swear words in the same context or with the same frequency as men, or women using words like *pretty, cute,* and *oh dear* in contexts and frequencies which differ from men. Men may have a claim not only on swear words, but on slang words in general. In his preface to the *Dictionary of American Slang* (New York: Thomas Y. Crowell, 1960), Flexner claims that "most American slang is created and used by males. Many types of slang words—including the taboo and strongly derogatory ones, those referring to sex, women, work, money, whiskey, politics, transportation, sports, and the like—refer primarily to male endeavor and interest. The majority of entries in this dictionary could be labeled "primary masculine use'" (p. xii). [*What if a woman compiled a dictionary of slang, and paid attention to women's speech, including that of all-female groups? Are these studies biased?*] Several sources, including Jespersen, claim women use more hyperbole than men, especially the intensive *so* (which Lakoff suggests can be used like a tag-question to avoid full commitment to a statement; Kramer notes that "since being emphatic is not seemingly a characteristic of women's speech, it would be useful to determine in what situations and with what topics women do use the intensive *so*"). Jokes and novels allude to a "syntactic looseness in women's speech"; Jespersen claims women are prone to jump from one idea to another, and not to complete sentences; Mary Ellman (*Thinking About Women,* New York: Harcourt, Brace & World, 1968) writes of the stereotyped formlessness of women's speech as represented in the writing of men like Joyce, Sartre, Mailer, and Hemingway. These stereotypes suggest areas for empirical research. One could also examine the written work of men and women to see if the dialogue is different for the sexes in novels, and if women writers treat dialogue differently. [*See I, III-A, III-B-2, IV-A, IV-C, VIII-C.*]

LAKOFF, ROBIN.
  "Language and Woman's Place." *Language in Society,* 2 (1973), 45-79.

Women have a distinctive style of speech which avoids strong statements and has
connotations of uncertainty and triviality. A woman who wants to be taken seriously learns
to adopt male ("neutral") vocabulary and style of speech. Specifics: (1) There are, Lakoff
claims, differences between the sexes in choice and frequency of lexical items, e.g. women
make far more precise discriminations in naming colors, and the domains where women have
elaborate vocabularies are of little concern to men, and have a connotation of triviality.
(2) Use of non-referent particles: the sexes use different expletives; women are more likely
to say *oh dear, goodness,* or *fudge,* while the men use stronger expletives *(shit, damn).*
Hence, men are allowed stronger means of expression than are open to women, which
further reinforces men's position of strength in the real world (men are listened to with
more deference). (3) Adjective choice: females are more likely to use adjectives like
adorable, charming, lovely, divine; male or "neutral" adjectives include *great, terrific,
neat.* The women's words suggest that the referent is frivolous, trivial, unimportant to the
world at large. (4) Syntax: women more often use tag questions ("John is here, isn't he?" as
opposed to the direct question form, "Is John here?") The tag form is midway between
an outright statement and a yes-no question; it is used when the speaker is stating a claim
but lacks full confidence in the truth of that claim; it gives the addressee leeway, not forcing
him or her to go along with the views of the speaker. This is another way in which women's
speech patterns avoid making strong statements. Women are also more likely to couch
wishes in the form of requests (while men more often use commands)—another way in
which women's language sounds more "polite" than men's, avoiding imposing views or
claims on the addressee. [*See I, II-A-1, III-B-3, V, VII.*]

PEI, MARIO.
  Words in Sheep's Clothing. New York: Hawthorn Books, 1969.

Pei sets out to catalogue "weasel words"—words whose "semantics are deliberately
changed or obscured, to achieve a specific purpose," or which are used "for the sole purpose
of impressing and bamboozling the reader or hearer." He jumps from Madison Avenue to
the world of moving pictures, arts, journalism, science, politics, and touches on the language
of women in Chapter 5, "Debs, Mods, and Hippies" [*note the grouping in which women are
placed.*] He describes female terms of address *(honey, sweetie, you're a doll, darling)* and
complains, "What women use among themselves is their own business, but must they inflict
it on us?" [*He apparently assumes an all-male readership.*] Pei claims that there is a "special
feminine vocabulary" in English, that men "may not, dare not, and will not use." The
vocabulary is characterized by abbreviation, and a "feminine diminutive suffix": *hanky,
panties, nightie, meanie, cutie.* It includes French borrowings, e.g. for color names like
beige, mauve, taupe (words which "normally mean nothing to men"). Women use more
extravagant adjectives *(wonderful, heavenly, divine, dreamy).* Pei traces to "feminine
influence" the use of *fun* as an adjective ("a fun dress"); the suffix *-ette (majorette),* and the
prefix *mini-* ("miniskirt"). Pei concludes that feminine (and teen-age) language are meant to
"proclaim that their user is a member of a certain class, and to flaunt the word-slogan like a
battle-flag in the faces of mere men or of the older generation." He concludes, "a
thoroughly male and adult vocabulary" [*note again the grouping*] "could form the subject
of a chapter, too; but then our book might be banned in Boston."

SHUSTER, JANET.
"Grammatical Forms Marked for Male and Female in English." Unpublished (graduate student) paper (9 pp.), Dept. of Anthropology, Univ. of Chicago, 1973.

Shuster points to a usage of active vs. passive voice, and transitive vs. intransitive verbs, which is differentially marked for men's and women's speech. (1) In the following verb usages, passive forms are more common if females are speaking or being referred to: *to be laid, to be fucked, to be taken* (sexually), *to be had* (sexually), *to come across* (perform sexually), *to* (be) *put out* (sexually), *to be walked.* Active forms are more common if males are speaking or being referred to: *to lay, to fuck, to take* (sexually), *to have* (sexually), *to put* (her) *out, to walk* (her). (2) Intransitive verb forms are more often used in reference to females, or by female speakers: *fuck with him, walk home with him, go with him* on a date, *make love with him, marry with him.* Transitive forms are more common in male speech or in reference to male speakers: *fuck her, walk her home, take her out* on a date, *make love to her, marry to her.* These nonreciprocal grammatical forms express the asymmetrical power relationship of men over women. Shuster examines the active/transitive, passive/intransitive verb complexes in the speech and discourse about three characters in Mailer's novel, *Deer Park.* Dorothea, an independent woman respected by men, uses and is referred to by male forms of speech ("guys I've had for a one-night stand"). Elena and Lulu fit female stereotypes (weak; dependent on men), and male speakers refer to them as objects to be acted upon (man referring to Lulu: "I was able to take her again").

SWACKER, MARJORIE.
"The Sex of the Speaker as a Sociolinguistic Variable." In Barrie Thorne and Nancy Henley, eds., *Language and Sex: Difference and Dominance.* Rowley, Mass.: Newbury House, 1975.

Swacker had 34 informants (17 men and 17 women, all Caucasians, in their early 20's, and students) look at 3 pictures by Albrecht Dürer, and describe what he or she saw, taking as much time as needed for the description, and trying to leave nothing out. The responses were tape recorded, and results analyzed for sex differences in speaking patterns. There were distinctions in *verbosity,* with men on the average speaking for longer intervals than women. Men used considerably more *numerals* in their descriptive passages (e.g., counting as part of their description; no women counted). Women preceded half of their numerals with indicators of approximation (". . . about six books"); only one man used a term of estimation. The sexes differed in *topic shift* markers. Both used pause patterns to mark shifts; women used significantly more conjunctions than did men, while men (but no women) used interjections to mark topic shifts (". . . a small shelf with some books piled up on it—*OK*—the man seems to be wearing a great big robe . . ."). [*See IV-D, IV-G.*]

TUCKER, SUSIE I.
Protean Shape: A Study in Eighteenth-Century Vocabulary and Usage. London: Athlone Press, 1967.

Chapter II ("Censure and Protest") describes 18th century language practices greeted with disapproval by critics like Dr. Johnson—e.g., foreign words, affectations, cant, sailors' language, and "women's usage" (pp. 78-80). Tucker notes that the critics would have put women speakers low down in the scale of good, or desirable speech, not because they were uneducated, but because women had "particular vogue words." One commentator referred to the ladies "whose main ornaments to their correspondence were an ah! and an oh!" Mrs. Piozzi, a woman writer, was criticized for overuse of *such, so,* and *somehow,* and the indefinite *one* ("*one,*" Tucker notes, "pinpoints a deficiency of English, a singular common gender pronoun corresponding to *they*" p. 79). Another female writer was criticized for the indiscriminate use of *fine* ("a fine sense of honor"), and another, for her affected use of *mentally* ("she mentally preferred").

WARSHAY, DIANA W.
   "Sex Differences in Language Style." In Constantina Safilios-Rothschild, ed., *Toward a Sociology of Women.* Lexington, Mass.: Xerox College Pub., 1972, pp. 3-9.

Warshay had 263 white, middle-class students in a midwestern university respond to the Important Events Test (writing down events in the past important to them). These language samples were analyzed for differences in grammar (ratio of verb to noun forms of reference to events), content analysis, and word counts. Warshay found that, compared with females, males tended to write with less fluency, to refer to events in a verb (rather than noun) phrase, to make more time references (of a vague sort; females gave more specific dates). Males also tended to involve themselves more in their references to events (while females referred more to others), to locate the event in their personal sphere of activity (while females located events in their interacting community), and to refer less to others. "Thus the male is shown to be more active, more ego-involved in what he does, and less concerned about others. His achievements are personal, underscoring and rewarding his individuality." The female adult "exhibits concern with 'being.' Blocked or largely excluded from public achievement, she seeks satisfaction in primary relations in the local community" (p. 8).

WOOD, MARION M.
   "The Influence of Sex and Knowledge of Communication Effectiveness on Spontaneous Speech." *Word,* 22, No. 1-2-3 (1966), 112-137.

This is an experimental study varying sex of speaker (18 subjects of each sex were individually tested), stimuli evoking spontaneous speech (speakers were asked to describe photographs of the same person with different facial expressions), sex of person spoken to, and knowledge of communication effectiveness (subjects were given different sets of "pseudofeedback" about success and failure). Interaction between speaker and hearer was limited to speech by the speaker (i.e., it was one-way, with no nonverbal communication). There were quantitative findings (men had greater verbal output) and findings about sex differences in speech style and word choice. "The analysis of the 90,000-word corpus of spontaneous speech . . . revealed distinctive styles of approach for men and women. A chi-square test showed (1) a correlation between the male utterances studied and an empirical style of speech, characterized by descriptions of observable features with objectively oriented concepts, and (2) a correlation between the female utterances studied and a creative style of speech, characterized by interpretive descriptions of associate images with predominantly connotative concepts." The author suggests an "intuitive" link between these two styles and the role differentiation Robert F. Bales *(Interaction Process Analysis,* Cambridge, Mass.: Addison-Wesley, 1950), and others posit in small experimental groups (task-oriented, instrumental roles, linked to males; and socio-emotional roles tied to females). Wood also looked at specific lexical sets associated with each sex, drawing on the speech of 3 of the male and 3 of the female subjects. This analysis suggested that some words seemed more associated with males: nouns such as *background, centimeter, dots, fraction,* and *V-shape;* and verbs such as *intersect, joins, parallels, protruded,* and *right-triangular.* Only one-third of the female-exclusive lexical selections were words of this type. The female list was instead characterized by nouns such as *bird, cheese, death, family,* and *spinach;* verbs like *enjoying, gotten up, might be posing, might have just put,* and *has been surprised;* and modifiers such as *confused, distasteful, peek-a-boo, questioning,* and *skeptical.* Females varied verb tenses and used more active than passive voice, compared with men. [*See IV-D.*]

III. PHONOLOGY

A. Phonetic Variants

ANSHEN, FRANK.
   "Speech Variation Among Negroes in a Small Southern Community." Unpublished Ph.D. dissertation, New York Univ., 1969.

Anshen studied phonological variables (e.g., postvocalic *r*; pronunciation of *th* as in *this;* the suffix *-in* vs. *-ing*) in the black population of Hillsboro, North Carolina. Among his findings: women use fewer stigmatized forms than men, and, compared with men, women are more sensitive to the prestige pattern.

FARB, PETER.
   Word Play: What Happens When People Talk. New York: Alfred A. Knopf, 1973.

In a general discussion of sociolinguistic literature concerning sex differences, Farb refers to the studies [*cited in this section*] of Labov, Trudgill, and Fischer, which indicate that, at least phonologically, "women (compared with men of the same age, social class, and level of education) speak in ways which more closely resemble the prestige way of talking" (p. 51). Farb reiterates Trudgill's explanation for this phenomenon. [*See II-A-1, II-B, III-B-2, V.*]

FASOLD, RALPH W.
   "A Sociolinguistic Study of the Pronunciation of Three Vowels in Detroit Speech." Washington, D.C.: Center for Applied Linguistics, mimeo, 1968.

Using data from the Detroit Dialect Study, Fasold found that the fronting of three vowels, /æ/, /a/, and /ɔ/, was more characteristic of lower-middle-class speakers than of upper-middle-class or working-class speakers. He also found that, especially in the lower-middle-class, women outscored men in the fronting of all three vowels. Younger informants predominated in fronting these vowels.

FISCHER, JOHN L.
"Social Influences on the Choice of a Linguistic Variant." *Word,* 14 (1958), 47-56. Reprinted in Dell Hymes, ed., *Language in Culture and Society.* New York: Harper & Row, 1964, pp. 483-488.

Analyzing recorded interviews with 24 children (half of each sex, ages 3-10) in a semi-rural New England village, Fischer found variations in the use of *-in* and *-ing* as verb endings. While all of the children used both forms to some extent, "a markedly greater number of girls used *-ing* more frequently, while more boys used more *-in.*" Hence, in this community "*-ing* is regarded as symbolizing female speakers and *-in* as symbolizing males." There was a slight tendency for *-ing* to be associated with higher socio-economic status. Personality was also a factor; a boy regarded as "model" used the *-ing* ending almost exclusively; a boy seen as "typical" used *-in* more than half the time. There were situational differences; *-ing* was used in more formal, and *-in* in more informal interviews. Finally, more "formal" verbs *(criticizing, correcting, reading)* were associated with the *-ing* pronunciation, and more informal verbs with the *-in* variant *(punchin, flubbin, swimmin).*

HAUGEN, EINAR.
" 'Sexism' and the Norwegian Language." Paper presented at Society for the Advancement of Scandinavian Study meeting, 1974.

Referring to Scandinavian materials, Haugen summarizes various studies of language variation by sex. Magnes Oftedal analyzed local dialects in Norway and observed greater "carefulness" in speech of women, a trait he attributes to the greater vulnerability of women to severe judgments about their behavior, especially their "moral" behavior. Females tend to adopt urban expressions in preference to rural ones, and, Oftedal says, women are usually about one generation ahead of men in linguistic development. Anders Steinsholt made similar observations: in urbanizing areas women use a more urban dialect than their sons, and "it is almost a rule that the members of a family divide into three groups linguistically: the father in one, the sons in one, and the mother and daughters in a third." While women go on adapting their language, men stop changing their language by age 30. Steinsholt attributes this to the greater demands made on proper female behavior. In a study of linguistic innovations in an urbanizing rural community in Denmark, Anker Jensen reported a similar finding in 1892: the women were ahead of the men in adopting urban speech patterns. In a study in French Switzerland, Gauchat made the same finding in 1905. [*See III-A-1.*]

KRAMER, CHERIS.
"Women's Speech: Separate But Unequal?" *Quarterly Journal of Speech,* 60 (Feb., 1974), 14-24. Reprinted in Barrie Thorne and Nancy Henley, eds., *Language and Sex: Difference and Dominance.* Rowley, Mass.: Newbury House, 1975.

Kramer reviews research indicating that women are more likely than men to use phonetic forms considered correct (research by Shuy; Shuy, Wolfram, and Riley; Fischer; Labov; Levine and Crockett). [*See I, II-B, III-B-2, IV-A, IV-C, VIII-C.*]

LABOV, WILLIAM.
 Sociolinguistic Patterns. Philadelphia: Univ. of Pennsylvania Press, 1972, pp. 243;
 301-304.

In careful speech women use fewer stigmatized forms than men and are more sensitive
than men to prestige patterns; lower-middle-class women show the most extreme form of
this behavior. There are implications for the role of women in furthering linguistic change.
Writing in 1905, L. Gauchat reported that in Paris, women used more of the newer linguistic
forms than men did. Recent studies in New York (see William Labov, *The Social
Stratification of English in New York City,* Washington, D.C.: Center for Applied
Linguistics, 1966), Detroit (research of Shuy, Wolfram, and Riley), and Chicago (Labov's
research) also show that women use the most advanced forms in their casual speech, and
correct more sharply to the other extremes in their formal speech. Women do not, however,
always lead in the course of linguistic change; Labov's study of Martha's Vineyard found
male speakers carried some new forms; Trudgill suggests that in Norwich, men lead in the
use of new vernacular forms in casual speech. "The correct generalization then is not that
women lead in linguistic change, but rather that the sexual differentiation of speech often
plays a major role in the mechanism of linguistic evolution." [*See VII.*]

LEVINE, LEWIS AND HARRY J. CROCKETT, JR.
 "Speech Variation in a Piedmont Community: Postvocalic *r.*" In Stanley Lieberson,
 ed., *Explorations in Sociolinguistics.* The Hague: Mouton, 1966, 76-98.

The authors studied speech variation and social structure in a North Carolina Piedmont
community, interviewing 275 white residents to elicit word pronunciations. Pronunciation
of the postvocalic *r* (as in *bare*) varied by age, length of residence in the community,
occupation and education, and sex. Females were more likely than males to pronounce the
postvocalic *r* (i.e., to use the more "correct" form), as were those of higher education, those
in prestigeful occupations, newer community residents, and younger people. These groups
may "spearhead" linguistic change, as the community shifts to the national norm. On the
other hand, there may be a difference in points of reference, with these groups taking the
national norm as their speech model, while "the linguistic behavior of males, older people,
long-term residents, and blue-collar respondents is referred to a Southern prestige norm—the
r-less pronunciation of the coastal plain."

SHUY, ROGER W., WALTER A. WOLFRAM, AND WILLIAM K. RILEY.
 Linguistic Correlates of Social Stratification in Detroit Speech. Final Report, Project
 6-1347. Washington, D.C.: U.S. Office of Education, 1967.

This extensive study of the speech of 700 randomly selected Detroit residents correlated
linguistic and social variables, including sex. With some variation by class, women showed
greater sensitivity than men to multiple negation and pronominal apposition (as in "my
brother *he* went to the park"). Males had a greater tendency to use nasalized vowels, e.g.
/mǽ/ for *man,* and to use *-in* rather than *-ing* (supporting Fischer's findings).

TRUDGILL, PETER.
    "Sex, Covert Prestige, and Linguistic Change in the Urban British English of Norwich." *Language in Society,* 1 (1972), 179-195. Reprinted in Barrie Thorne and Nancy Henley, eds., *Language and Sex: Difference and Dominance.* Rowley, Mass.: Newbury House, 1975.

    Trudgill reviews studies and presents his own data for speakers of urban British English in Norwich, showing that "women, allowing for other variables such as age, education and social class, consistently produce linguistic forms which more closely approach those of the standard language or have higher prestige than those produced by men, or, alternatively, that they produce forms of this type more frequently." He offers several "speculative" explanations for this finding: (1) Women are more status-conscious than men; their insecure and subordinate social position makes it "more necessary for women to secure and signal their social status linguistically and in other ways." Men can be rated socially by their occupation, by what they *do,* while women are rated on how they *appear*—hence reliance on non-occupational signals of status, such as speech. (2) Working-class speech and culture have connotations of masculinity, being associated with roughness and toughness, while refinement and sophistication are considered feminine characteristics. In a sometimes covert way, men value non-standard speech as a signal of masculinity and of group solidarity. Trudgill found an age difference: males of all ages, and females under 30, valued non-standard speech forms more than females over 30. In terms of linguistic change, standard forms are introduced by middle-class women, and non-standard forms by working-class men.

WOLFRAM, WALTER A.
    A Sociolinguistic Description of Detroit Negro Speech. Washington, D.C.: Center for Applied Linguistics, 1969.

    Wolfram drew on data from the Detroit Dialect Study (reported in Shuy, Wolfram, and Riley, 1967) to include more linguistic variables, and with a focus on the black population. He found that within each social class, black females approximated the standard English norm more than males. Females of all classes had fewer *f, t,* or $\emptyset$ realizations of *th* (as in *tooth*); females more often pronounced final consonant clusters (as in *friend*) and the postvocalic *r* (as in *car*).

B. Suprasegmentals

1. General

ADDINGTON, D. W.
    "The Relationship of Selected Vocal Characteristics to Personality Perception." *Speech Monographs,* 35 (1968), 492-503.

    Addington used an experiment to explore whether male and female speakers using the same vocal characteristics elicit different personality perception. Two male and two female trained speakers alternately made their voices more breathy, tense, thin, flat, throaty, nasal, and orotund; they also varied rate and pitch. Students listened to tapes of these voice variations and described the speaker's personality. Factor analysis of the results indicated that "changes in male voice affect personality perception differently than do similar changes in female voices" (497); female vocal manipulations altered personality ascriptions more than those of males. For example, increased thinness of voice quality had no effect on perception of males, but for female voices elicited perceptions of increased social, physical, emotional, and mental immaturity; also more sensitivity and sense of humor. Males using increased vocal tension were perceived as being older, more unyielding, and cantankerous, while females were seen as younger, more emotional, feminine, high-strung, and less intelligent. Increased throatiness in male speakers led to their being stereotyped as older, more realistic, mature, sophisticated, and well adjusted. Females with more throaty voices were seen as "cloddish or oafish" (less intelligent, lazier, more boorish, ugly, sickly, careless, etc.).

AUSTIN, WILLIAM M.
"Some Social Aspects of Paralanguage." *Canadian Journal of Linguistics,* 11 (1965), 31-39.

Paralanguage is defined as significant noises, in a code situation between sender and receiver, made by the non-articulated vocal tract (any articulations tend to be stylistic variants). Vocal modifiers, one paralinguistic category, indicate changes in the vocal tract only; one vocal modifier is in the oral/nasal distinction. "In our culture little boys tend to be nasal . . . and little girls, oral. Nasality is considered 'tough' and 'vulgar' and somewhat discouraged by elders. 'Gentlemanly' little boys tend to be oral also." Certain signals are highly suggestive of "paramorphology": "A 'little girl's voice' (innocence, helplessness, regression) is composed of high pitch and orality." In the paralanguage of courtship, the male is low and nasal, the female high, oral and giggling; in the final stages of courtship speech, it is low and nasal in both, but with "wide pitch and intensity variation on the part of the female." Derogatory imitation, "one of the most infuriating acts of aggression one person can commit on another," is illustrated for both male and female, with mention of the "even stronger" case in which "male or female imitates a male with derogatory female imitation." For upper-class paralanguage, Austin writes, it must be clear, low, and oral in men; and clear and oral, with a choice of high or low for women. "Low pitch has lately become fashionable for women, but fifty years ago all 'ladies' spoke with a high pitch." Japanese speech has both marked linguistic differences between male and female, and striking paralinguistic differences: males loud and low, "in Samurai movies almost a bark"; females soft and high, almost a squeak.

CRYSTAL, D.
"Prosodic and Paralinguistic Correlates of Social Categories." In Edwin Ardener, ed., *Social Anthropology and Language.* London: Tavistock, 1971, pp. 185-206.

Crystal calls attention, in a general way, to the non-segmental phonetic and phonological characteristics of speech: pitch, loudness, speed of utterance, and use of qualities of voice such as nasalization or breathiness in order to communicate specific meanings. He claims that non-segmental phonology is "one of the main ways of establishing the identity of social groups in speech," and notes that non-segmental features have been found to correlate with sex, age, status, occupation, and speech genres. "Intuitive impressions of effeminacy in English, for example, partly correlate with segmental effects such as lisping, but are mainly non-segmental; a 'simpering' voice, for instance, largely reduces to the use of a wider pitch-range than normal (for men), with *glissando* effects between stressed syllables, a more frequent use of complex tones (e.g., the fall-rise and the rise-fall), the use of breathiness and huskiness in the voice, and switching to a higher (falsetto) register from time to time." Crystal cites data from other languages about non-segmental correlates of sex. He also suggests that *responses* to non-segmental vocal effects can be a valuable part of a description; for example, in Mohave the breaking of the male voice in adolescence is not considered an important or relevant indication of puberty, whereas in English it is.

LAVER, JOHN D. M.
"Voice Quality and Indexical Information." *British Journal of Disorders of Communication,* 33 (1968), 43-54.

Laver outlines a descriptive model of voice quality (which is determined by anatomy and voluntary muscular "setting," and includes variations in phonation type, pitch range, and loudness range of laryngeal setting, and supralaryngeal modifications, such as nasalization). Voice quality is an index to biological, psychological, and social characteristics of the speaker. Laver includes "sex and age" under "biological information about the speaker": "One usually forms fairly accurate impressions, from voice quality alone, of a speaker's sex and age . . . Deviations from 'normal' expectations about the correlation between a speaker's voice and his sex and age seem to have a powerful effect on impressions of personality" (p. 49). Several references are included to support these statements.

2. Pitch

FARB, PETER.
Word Play: What Happens When People Talk. New York: Alfred A. Knopf, 1973.

Drawing on Crystal's comments about sex differences in voice types [*see annotation in III-B-1*], Farb notes that in English-speaking communities, some women are said to have "sexy voices," and some men are said to sound "effeminate" (the common explanation is that this involves a lisp). The effeminate voice has a wider pitch range than the male norm; it uses sliding effects between stressed syllables, has more breathiness in voice quality, and uses complex tonal patterns. [*See II-A-1, II-B, III-A, V.*]

HENNESSEE, JUDITH.
"Some News Is Good News." *Ms.,* 3 (July, 1974), 25-29.

Reporting on the experiences of female TV news reporters, Hennessee comments on the presumed relationship between a low-pitched voice and credibility. In American culture the norm for an authoritative voice is male; "higher-pitched voices are still associated with unpleasantness, evoking nagging mothers or wives, waspish schoolteachers, acerbic librarians." (In France, women's voices are preferred for news broadcasting.) Yet a survey of attitudes toward television newswomen, done by researchers at the Univ. of Wisconsin, showed that "only about one-fifth of those polled (a sample which included small-town conservative families) said they would be more likely to believe a news report by a man.

Newswomen, it appears, have more support from their viewers than from their employers." Women newscasters with the deepest voices are sometimes called the most authoritative of women in TV news.

KRAMER, CHERIS.
"Women's Speech: Separate But Unequal?" *Quarterly Journal of Speech,* 60 (Feb., 1974), 14-24. Reprinted in Barrie Thorne and Nancy Henley, eds., *Language and Sex: Difference and Dominance.* Rowley, Mass.: Newbury House, 1975.

Kramer comments upon cultural stereotypes about the pitch level of women's speech. In cartoons and novels the talk of all-female gatherings is loud and high-pitched (Kramer suggests a research question: "Do women change volume and pitch, depending on the situation and the ratio of men and women present?"). High pitch is a stereotyped attribute of females; on Sesame Street boy monsters are "brave and gruff" and girl monsters are "high-pitched and timid" (cited from Letty Cottin Pogrebin, "Down with Sexist Upbringing," *Ms.,* 1 [Spring, 1972], p. 28). People do not associate the higher-pitched voice with serious topics—a reason broadcasters give for not employing female news announcers. Kramer suggests researching the response of each sex to women's voices, and studying whether women with broadcasting jobs change their pitch and volume for performance on the air more than male broadcasters. "At what age does this preference for the male voice begin? And in what situations other than broadcasting?" [*See I, II-B, III-A, IV-A, IV-C, VIII-C.*]

LIEBERMAN, PHILIP.
Intonation, Perception, and Language. Cambridge: M.I.T. Press, 1967.

Lieberman cites a study of the vocalizations of a 10-month-old boy and a girl of 13 months which found that the average fundamental frequency of the babies' vocalizations was 50-100 cps lower when they were "talking" with their fathers than when they were "talking" with their mothers. This suggests that intonation patterns may vary with the sex spoken to (pp. 45-46).

MATTINGLY, IGNATIUS G.
"Speaker Variation and Vocal-Tract Size." Paper presented at Acoustical Society of America, 1966. Abstract in *Journal of the Acoustical Society of America,* 39 (1966), 1219.

This study tested the hypothesis that differences in the formant-frequency value sets (among speakers of the same dialect) are due chiefly to variations in individual vocal-tract size. For three speaker classes—men, women, children—the distribution of values for each of three formants of each of ten vowels was correlated with every other such distribution. If the differences were due to size of the vocal tract, the correlations should have been high, but most scores were low. Furthermore, the separation between male and female distributions for some vowel formants was much sharper than variation in individual vocal-tract size could reasonably explain. The author concludes: "The variation within class must be stylistic, not physical; and the difference between male and female formant values, though doubtless related to typical male and female vocal-tract size, is probably a linguistic convention."

SACHS, JACQUELINE.
"Cues to the Identification of Sex in Children's Speech." In Barrie Thorne and Nancy Henley, eds., *Language and Sex: Difference and Dominance.* Rowley, Mass.: Newbury House, 1975.

Prepubertal boys and girls can typically be identified as to sex from their voices. This paper presents three studies on the cues used in this identification. (1) Judges were able to guess the sex of the child from hearing isolated vowels, though not as well as from sentences. (2) Judges could not accurately determine sex from sentences played backwards, suggesting that, beyond the phonetic aspects of the voices, there is considerable information in normal sentences that carries information about the sex of the speaker. (3) When judges rated spoken sentences on semantic differential scales, a factor emerged that was correlated with the perceived masculinity or femininity of the voice, along with two other factors, Active-Passive and Fluent-Disfluent. This result suggests that there is an independent cue to the sex of the speaker that does not involve how active the voice sounds or how fluent it is. [*Author's annotation.*] [*See VII.*]

SACHS, JACQUELINE, PHILIP LIEBERMAN, AND DONNA ERICKSON.
"Anatomical and Cultural Determinants of Male and Female Speech." In Roger W. Shuy and Ralph W. Fasold, eds., *Language Attitudes: Current Trends and Prospects.* Washington, D.C.: Georgetown Univ. Press, 1973, pp. 74-84.

In the phonetic differentiation between adult male and female voices, the most obvious factor is pitch, or fundamental frequency of phonation. The lower fundamental frequencies of the male are a consequence of secondary sexual dimorphism occurring at puberty (the larynx of the male is enlarged and vocal cords become longer and thicker). There is, however, evidence that "the acoustic differences are greater than one would expect if the sole determining factor were simply the average anatomical difference that exists between adult men and women." Adult men and women "may modify their articulation of the same phonetic elements to produce acoustic signals that correspond to the male-female archetypes. In other words, men tend to talk as though they were bigger, and women as though they were smaller, than they actually may be." To explore this possibility, Sachs *et al.* studied preadolescent children (with larynxes of the same size relative to weight and height, and hence with no obvious anatomical basis for a sex difference in formant frequencies). They recorded samples of speech for 14 boys and 12 girls ranging in age from 4 to 14 years and had 83 adult judges listen to the tape and try to identify each voice as male or female. The results: "Judges could reliably and validly identify the sex of children from their voices. Boys on the average had higher fundamentals but lower formants than girls." The authors examined possible explanations: while they found no average difference in articulatory mechanism size, there may be differential use of anatomy, or there could be hormonal control over certain aspects of the motor output. Or "the children could be learning culturally determined patterns that are viewed as appropriate for each sex." A speaker could change the formant pattern, e.g., by spreading the lips to shorten the vocal tract and raise the formants ("the characteristic way some women have of talking and smiling at the same time would have just this effect"). The judges may have drawn on cues other than formant pattern to identify the sex of the child speaker, e.g., it seems that "boys had a more forceful, definite rhythm of speaking than the girls"; there may have been differences in vocabulary items and in intonation patterns. The paper suggests that pitch may not be determined totally by anatomical structure, but also by sex roles and cultural expectations. [*See VII.*]

3. Intonation

BREND, RUTH M.

"Male-Female Intonation Patterns in American English." *Proceedings of the Seventh International Congress of Phonetic Sciences, 1971.* The Hague: Mouton, 1972, pp. 866-870. Reprinted in Barrie Thorne and Nancy Henley, eds., *Language and Sex: Difference and Dominance.* Rowley, Mass.: Newbury House, 1975.

While speakers of American English have some intonation patterns in common, certain patterns seem to be completely lacking from men's speech, while others are differently preferred by men and women. For example, men tend to use the incomplete "deliberative" pattern, i.e., the small upstep from the low ('Yes, 'yes, I/'know.), while women prefer the "more polite" incomplete longer upstep ('Yes, 'yes I 'know.). Certain patterns are used predominantly if not solely by women, e.g. the "surprise" patterns of high-low down-glides ('Oh 'that's 'awful!), the "request confirmation" pattern (You do!); the hesitation pattern (Well, I/'studied . . .); and the "polite, cheerful" pattern (Are you 'coming?). Furthermore, men rarely, if ever, use the highest level of pitch that women use; most men have only three contrastive levels of intonation, while many women have four.

EBLE, CONNIE C.

"How the Speech of Some Is More Equal Than Others." Paper presented at Southeastern Conference on Linguistics, 1972.

"It is generally thought that women have more extremes of high and low intonation than do men and that there are some intonation patterns, impressionistically the 'whining, questioning, helpless' patterns, which are used predominantly by women." [*See II-B.*]

KEY, MARY RITCHIE.

"Linguistic Behavior of Male and Female." *Linguistics,* 88 (Aug. 15, 1972), 15-31.

"It is quite likely that women use patterns of uncertainty and indefiniteness more often than men—patterns of PLIGHT" (p. 18). One of Key's students, in a brief exploratory experiment, listened to children in the 3rd, 4th, and 5th grades retell a story. "The girls spoke with very expressive intonation, and the boys toned down the intonational features, even to the point of monotony, 'playing it cool' " (p. 18). Radio and TV broadcasters are concerned with pronunciation features; one handbook for announcers concludes that women's delivery "is lacking in the authority needed for a convincing newscast." However, in Germany and in the South, women's voices are heard frequently on the air. [*See I, II-A-1, II-B.*]

LAKOFF, ROBIN.

"Language and Woman's Place." *Language in Society,* 2 (1973), 45-79.

There is a peculiar sentence intonation pattern found in English only among women: a declarative answer to a question, but with a rising inflection typical of a yes-no question, and conveying hesitance, as though one were seeking confirmation. Example: (Q) "When

will dinner be ready?" (A) [using this intonation style] "Oh . . . around six o'clock . . . ?"
As though the second speaker is saying, "Six o'clock, if that's OK with you, if you agree."
Speaker (A) comes out sounding insecure and unsure of her opinion. This pattern indicates
the unwillingness of women to state an opinion directly. [*See I, II-A-1, II-B, V, VII.*]

SAMARIN, WILLIAM.
    Tongues of Men and Angels. New York: Macmillan, 1972.

Samarin notes sex differences in the production of glossolalia. One of his respondents
commented that "men speak more forcefully as a rule, and some women have a crying or
weeping tone (something I have observed as well); even voice quality may be different" (p.
96).

4. Speech Intensity

LEGMAN, G.
    Rationale of the Dirty Joke: An Analysis of Sexual Humor. Castle Books, 1968.

This extensive analysis of erotic folklore includes a section on "the voice as phallus" (pp.
336-337), which begins with a psychoanalytic argument that there is an unconscious
identification of the voice as "the virile prerogative of the dominant sex." When a female
"usurps" this prerogative through a powerful speaking voice or forthright self-expression,
she becomes "attractively dominant to some men, and repellent (the man-eating,
song-singing Siren, Harpy or Rhine-maiden) to others." She may be seen as immoral.
Legman also asserts that where men are in "dominated situations, as in armies or on college
faculties, very hedged and repressed ways of speech become habitual," and he notes that
"the Milquetoast or Dagwood has, traditionally, a weakly faint or absurdly screeching
voice." [*See II-A-1, IV-C.*]

MARKEL, NORMAN N., LAYNE D. PREBOR, AND JOHN F. BRANDT.
    "Bio-social Factors in Dyadic Communication: Sex and Speaking Intensity." *Journal
    of Personality and Social Psychology,* 23 (1972), 11-13.

An experimental study in which male and female subjects spoke to male and female
experimenters, at near and far distances. Average speaking intensity was determined by
means of a graphic level recorder. Male subjects spoke with greater intensity than females,
and there was a significant interaction between sex of subjects and sex of experimenter such
that all subjects decreased intensity to the same-sex experimenter and increased intensity to
the opposite-sex experimenter. These results are interpreted as reflecting a greater affiliation
to an experimenter of the same sex.

IV. CONVERSATIONAL PATTERNS

A. General References

HIRSCHMAN, LYNETTE.
> "Analysis of Supportive and Assertive Behavior in Conversations." Paper presented at meeting of Linguistic Society of America, July, 1974.

Hirschman ran two experiments, each with two female and two male subjects (all white college students, previously unacquainted). The four subjects were separated into two pairs and given a question to discuss for ten minutes (the question dealt with love, sexuality, and marriage). Pairs were rotated, producing four single-sex and eight mixed-sex conversations, which were recorded, transcribed, and analyzed. It was hypothesized that in conversational behavior females would be more supportive, and males more assertive (although supportiveness and assertiveness were not understood to be opposites; "ideally it would be possible to be simultaneously assertive and supportive"). Assertiveness was measured by patterns of obtaining and holding the floor (interrupting, talking a lot, not losing the floor to an interrupter); relative absence of qualifiers *(maybe, sort of, I think, I guess);* fluency in speech (related to frequency of fillers and ratio of clauses finished to clauses started). Supportiveness was measured by frequency of affirmative words *(yeah, right, mm hmm)* indicating positive response to the other's statements; picking up on the other's statement (e.g. using interutterance connectives like *and*); asking questions to draw out the other speaker. Data was sparse or inconclusive on some variables (interruptions, questions, utterance classification). Overall, the amount of speech, and the average percentage of word output were equal for the sexes. Differences in mean length of utterance, frequency of affirmative words, frequency of fillers, and ratio of completed to attempted clauses were not statistically significant. The only striking overall female-male difference was in the use of *mm hmm,* where females outnumbered males 53 to 8. There was also a difference in the use of *I think;* contrary to expectation, males used almost twice as many *I think*'s as females (118 to 66). Comparing same-sex with mixed-sex conversations, no significant differences were found. "There seemed to be a tendency for the subjects to use a higher frequency of affirmative words in the same-sex conversations than in the mixed-sex conversations. Also the males use fewer *I think*'s in the male-male conversations, and the females use more *mm hmm*'s." Hirschman concludes that the lack of correlation between most of the variables and sex can be interpreted in several ways: (1) the variables chosen do not represent assertiveness and supportiveness (there is some evidence to this effect, e.g. the finding that *I think* may be a more polite way of stating an opinion than a qualifier, and the fact that the more fluent people did not particularly dominate the bulk of the conversations—in several cases the less coherent speakers took many more words to communicate one idea, so their word output was high, but not their contribution in terms of content); (2) the situation did not lend itself to differences in female-male display of supportive or assertive behavior (the situation was awkward socially for the participants; the conversations were strained and generally very polite; the questions dealt with human relations, an area usually considered of more interest to females than to males); (3) the hypothesis may be incorrect; males and females may be equally supportive and equally assertive in conversational behavior. [*See II-B, VI-D, VIII-B.*]

HIRSCHMAN, LYNETTE.
"Female-Male Differences in Conversational Interaction." Paper presented at Linguistic Society of America, Dec., 1973. (Research conducted by Hirschman, Jill Gross, Jane Savitt, and Kathy Sanders.)

Two male and two female white college students (all unacquainted) were taped in dyadic conversation, in all possible pairs of the four, with topic controlled, for ten minutes per pair, giving a total of 60 minutes of tape. The conversations were analyzed for, first, certain speech characteristics: length of time each person held the floor; number of words produced by each; percent of time used for talking (by either) in each conversation; and proportion of fillers and qualifiers used. Second, some features of conversational interaction were examined: use of personal pronouns which include the other, as opposed to third person pronouns and generic collectives; affirmative and other responses to other speaker; and interruptions (successful and unsuccessful). Finally, the investigators looked at aspects of the "flow of conversation," such as initiation, elaboration, and change of topic; and asking and answering of questions. No conclusions are drawn about differences in female and male speech patterns, though the following results are reported: word-count data and that from speaking time were parallel, and the informants were neatly ordered in both. More time was used in talking, in conversations with a female present. Females had a much higher percentage of fillers than did males. No differences were found in proportion of qualifiers, though there were individual differences in types of qualifiers used, as there were other individual differences in speech styles. Females had a much greater frequency of pronouns involving the other speaker than third-person references, and males had the reverse. Females used the *mm hmm* response much more often than males, particularly with each other. The two females interrupted (or overlapped) each other more than any other pair. In "flow of conversation," the females when talking to each other tended to elaborate on each other's utterances, the males to argue; a female-question/male-answer pattern emerged in several conversations. These results aren't subject to generalization, but the study both suggests and tests some promising measures, and permits the formulation of interesting hypotheses. Hirschman suggests the above measures be used with larger samples, though with further refinement of the interruption variable. Females may talk more easily to each other than to men. Differences in style may be related to differences in assertiveness. Perhaps "voluminous female speakers compensate for their possible aggressiveness by increased indications of hesitancy and increased responsiveness." The female-question/male-answer pattern suggests a possible role of the female as facilitator of the conversation. It's also possible in examining flow of conversation that "males tend to dispute the other person's utterance or ignore it, while the females acknowledge it, or often build on it." [*See II-B, IV-B, IV-D, IV-E.*]

KRAMER, CHERIS.
"Women's Speech: Separate But Unequal?" *Quarterly Journal of Speech,* 60 (Feb., 1974), 14-24. Reprinted in Barrie Thorne and Nancy Henley, eds., *Language and Sex: Difference and Dominance.* Rowley, Mass.: Newbury House, 1975.

Kramer examines stereotypes about women's speech—about how people think women speak or should speak—as shown in etiquette manuals, speech books, cartoons, and novels, and she uses these stereotypes to suggest empirical questions to research. Kramer relates these questions to "the larger hypothesis that women's speech reflects the stereotyped role of male and female in our society, i.e., women in a subservient, nurturing position in a male-dominated world." Areas for research: (1) "great verbosity is not the prescribed behavior for females" (e.g., etiquette books advise females not to talk as much as males, to draw out males in a conversation and let them talk about themselves). Since women are not supposed to talk as much as men, perhaps a "talkative" woman is one that does talk as much as a man. Kramer suggests experiments, e.g. that measure the total amount of talking time for men and women in a variety of situations; that see if the ratio of men to women in the situation makes a difference in the relative verbosity of each sex; that measure how much talking a woman can do before she is labelled "talkative" (including types of sentence construction used, volume of voice, speech topics). (2) Do women use more questions and fewer declarative sentences than men? Do women (as Lakoff claims) actually use tag-questions more than men? Do their declarative sentences contain more qualifiers? In what situations, and on what topics? Do women, as Lakoff believes, use more polite request forms? How do such patterns relate to patterns of subordination and submission to men? (3) A stereotype of women's gatherings is that the talk is loud and high-pitched (the "hen session" stereotype, with speech called a "cackle"). Do women change volume and pitch, depending on the situation and the ratio of men and women present? The pitch of the female voice (usually higher because of physical reasons) is a stereotyped attribute of females, associated with other undesirable, but "feminine" traits, e.g., timidity, and trivial topics (a broadcaster explaining why so few U.S. television networks employ women reporters said, "As a whole, people don't like to hear women's voices telling them serious things"). One could compare women to men in attitudes to hearing women's voices over radio and television. (4) What are the speech patterns of women in positions of some power? Do "submissive" speech patterns continue? [*See I, II-B, III-A, III-B-2, IV-C, VIII-C.*]

B. Conversational Styles

ABRAHAMS, ROGER.
"Negotiating Respect: Patterns of Presentation Among Black Women." *Journal of American Folklore,* forthcoming.

Theoretically grounded in the dramaturgical approach of Goffman, this paper presents a conceptualization of the relationship between language styles of black women and the use of such styles for the assertion of status as *women.* Abrahams argues that "the essence of . . . negotiation lies in a woman being both sweet and tough depending upon her capacity to define and reasonably manipulate the situation." Ideally she has the ability to *talk sweet* with her infants and peers, but *talk smart* with anyone who might threaten her self-image. Considerable material illustrative of black women's presentational styles and forms and their role in the maintenance of Afro-American social and cultural structures is presented. [*Annotation by Laurel Walum.*]

BERNARD, JESSIE.
    "Talk, Conversation, Listening, Silence," Chapter 6 of *The Sex Game*. New York:
    Atheneum, 1972, pp. 135-164.

Using a wide assortment of studies, anecdotes, and observations, Bernard generalizes
about how the sexes talk and converse. Experimental studies of face-to-face groups
distinguish "instrumental" talk (having to do with orientation, facts, and information) from
"expressive" talk (dealing with feelings). "Traditionally the cultural norms for femininity
and womanliness have prescribed appreciatively expressive talk or stroking for women . . .
They were to raise the status of the other, relieve tension, agree, concur, comply,
understand, accept" (p. 137). Women may ask for suggestions, directions, opinions, or
expressions of feeling, "drawing men out," and conceding dominance in talking
relationships. Instrumental talk (more associated with males than females) orients, and
conveys information or facts. It may involve lecturing; it may become argumentative in style
(demanding evidence and proof, and insisting that everything be based on reason or logic); it
may involve a debating style which regards all talk as a competitive sport. This conflictful
and competitive style may be particularly inhibiting to women, since women tend to be less
competitive than men. Women furthermore "tend to be handicapped in fact-anchored talk.
In circles where conversation is most likely to occur, they are usually less well educated than
the men, less likely to have a hard, factual background, less in contact with the world of
knowledge. Personality is more important; personal opinion, attitudes, and observations give
them a wider berth to move in and are therefore more important for them than facts" (p.
153). [*See IV-D, IV-G.*]

CHESLER, PHYLLIS.
    Women and Madness. New York: Doubleday, 1972.

Many dialogues between women seem "senseless" or "mindless" to men; the women
seem to be reciting monologues at each other, neither really listening to or judging what the
other is saying. But the women are approaching a kind of emotional resolution and comfort,
telling separate confessions, feelings, in parallel. Each "comments upon the other's feelings
by reflecting them in a very sensitive matching process." Their theme, method, and goal are
nonverbal; facial expressions, pauses, sighs, and seemingly unrelated responses are crucial to
such a dialogue. On its most ordinary level, this conversational sharing gives women
emotional reality and comfort they cannot find with men; on its highest level, "it
constitutes the basic tools of art and psychic awareness" (p. 268).

CONKLIN, NANCY FAIRES.
    "Perspectives on the Dialects of Women." Paper presented at American Dialect
    Society, 1973.

"No major study of language use in natural social groups has attempted to study
women's speech." Labov justifies choosing to study only male adolescent peer groups on the
grounds that males are the "chief exemplars of the vernacular culture." But there is no
conclusive evidence that women do not participate fully in the vernacular culture.
"Sociolinguistic data do *not* show that women are less 'nonstandard' in casual, relaxed,

natural speech, only that they are less likely to exhibit their most relaxed speech styles in front of a linguistic investigator, especially a male investigator, due to their extreme social sensitivity. Women's speech in natural interaction groups, especially the female-only group, which has not been investigated at all, may be quite different from the so-called 'vernacular' styles so far reported." The weekly "consciousness-raising" discussion group of the women's movement developed out of the traditional female *Kaffeeklatsch;* this may be "an interaction type specific to women," and it may be "in these natural kinds of environments, in all-female groups, contrasted with data from more public, male/female interactions, that the essence of the dialect of women may be found, and women's whole, wide range of dialectal variation be recognized." [*See II-A-2, V.*]

COSER, ROSE LAUB.
   "Laughter Among Colleagues." *Psychiatry,* 23 (1960), 81-95.

   Coser recorded all conversations in which humor and laughter occurred at staff meetings of a mental hospital for a period of three months (total of 20 meetings). The meetings were formally structured and attended by individuals of different status positions (psychiatrists, residents, paramedical staff). Coser found "the use of humor took place in such a way as to relax the rigidity of the social structure without, however, upsetting it. Those who were of higher status positions more frequently took the initiative to use humor; more significant, still, the target of a witticism, if he was present, was never in a higher authority position than the initiator" (p. 95). There was a hierarchy of joking: senior staff made witticisms more often than junior members (whereas the humor of the latter was more often directed against patients and their relatives, and against themselves). Sex differences also figured into the hierarchy of humor: "at the meetings, men made by far the more frequent witticisms—99 out of 103—but women often laughed harder" (p. 85). This was not due to fewer numbers; there were more women at the meetings than there were junior staff. This pattern, Coser suggests, is in line with a cultural expectation that women should not challenge male authority, that women should be passive and receptive rather than active and initiating. "A woman who has a good sense of humor is one who laughs (but not too loudly!) when a man makes a witticism or tells a good joke. A man who has a good sense of humor is one who is witty in his remarks and tells good jokes. The man provides; the woman receives" (p. 85). [*See IV-C.*]

FASTEAU, MARC.
   "Why Aren't We Talking?" *Ms.,* 1 (July, 1972), 16.

   Emphasizing the need for men's liberation, Fasteau criticizes the competition, the impersonality, the obstacles to communication among men. "We've been taught that 'real men' are never passive or dependent, always dominant in relationships with women or other men, and don't talk about or directly express feelings, especially feelings that don't contribute to dominance ... There is nothing among men that resembles the personal communication that women have developed among themselves. We don't know very much about ourselves, and we know even less about each other." In his closest friendships with males, Fasteau writes, competition was a continual theme. "We always needed an excuse to talk. Getting together for its own sake would have been frightening. Talking personally and spontaneously involves revealing doubts, plans which may fail, ideas which haven't been thought through, happiness over things the other person may think trivial—in short, making ourselves vulnerable. That was too risky."

GRIER, WILLIAM H., AND PRICE M. COBBS.
  Black Rage. New York: Basic Books, 1968. (New York: Bantam, 1969).

Psychiatrists Grier and Cobbs offer a lengthy discourse on the black patois and its origins, with particular attention to its use by black men as a tool of seduction (section V of Chapter VI, pp. 96-108, Bantam edition). In their analysis, the patois from early slave times, though a product of the white masters' control of the slaves' language, has served as a bond of unity and "secret language" for blacks. They state that "the patois which was imposed as a brand of humiliation, defeat and suffering . . . has been turned to express defiance against the oppressor and, in a subtle but significant way, vanquishment of the white oppressor" (p. 107). This vanquishment is a symbolic one, acted out in their "vanquishment" of women. The authors report that a group of black men revealed, without exception, that as a technique of seduction they "reverted to the patois" at a crucial point. "Black women [according to these men] said that they experienced an intensification of excitement when their lovers reverted to the 'old language' " (p. 107). Grier and Cobbs describe several case histories of competent black men who use the patois, particularly in this way. "It is as if in his sexual conquests," they write, "the black man welcomes the opportunity to show his skill, his desirability, and his superiority over his white oppressor in the ultimate competition men engage in" (p. 107). [*As many feminists have pointed out, this book is pretty sexist.*]

HARDING, SUSAN.
  "Women and Words in a Spanish Village." In Rayna Reiter, ed., *Towards an Anthropology of Women.* New York: Monthly Review Press, 1975.

An ethnographic account of the verbal role of women in the village of Oroel in northeastern Spain, this paper indicates a division of verbal skills, topics, and genres of speech that follows the division of labor between men and women. Women's verbal specialties center around home and family: the talk that accompanies childrearing; "intuition"—a special kind of empathy, an engagement with the needs and concerns of others; worry about the well-being of others; verbal finesse at penetrating the secrecy of men (secrecy that goes with the greater power and resources of males); chatting; story-telling; and gossip. "The skills and genres are essential to, integrated with, or extensions of the tasks and obligations of women as wives and mothers. However, women also use their verbal acts to reach beyond the official limits of their role in response to their subordinate economic and political position in the society. Whatever power and influence women have in the daily affairs of Oroel depends on how well they can wield words in certain ways. Yet each of the verbal skills has a double edge. At the same time it reflects a woman's effort to reach beyond her subordinate position in the village society, it returns and keeps her in that position." [*See IV-C, IV-F.*]

HEILBRUN, CAROLYN G.
  Toward a Recognition of Androgyny. New York: Alfred A. Knopf, 1973.

In discussing the advantages of androgyny—"a condition under which the characteristics of the sexes, and the human impulses expressed by men and women, are not rigidly assigned"—Heilbrun quotes from a commentary by J. B. Priestley ("Journey Down the Rainbow," *Saturday Review,* Aug. 18, 1956, p. 35) on life between the sexes in Dallas, Texas: "I am convinced that good talk cannot flourish where there is a wide gulf between the sexes, where the men are altogether too masculine, too hearty and bluff and booming, where the women are too feminine, at once both too arch and too anxious. Where men are leavened by a feminine element, where women are not without some tempering by the masculine spirit, there is a chance of good talk. And if there cannot be a balance of the two eternal principles, then let the feminine principle have the domination. But here was a society entirely dominated by the masculine principle."

HIRSCHMAN, LYNETTE.
    "Female-Male Differences in Conversational Interaction." Paper presented at Linguistic Society of America, Dec., 1973.

The females in Hirschman's analysis, in conversation together, interrupted or overlapped each other more than the male or mixed-sex pairs. Though they used a much higher percentage of fillers than did males overall, females showed their lowest percentage in conversation together, suggesting that they may be more at ease (more fluent, less hesitant) with a female than with a male. A "flow of conversation" analysis gave the impression that females talking to each other would elaborate on the other's utterance, while the males would dispute or ignore it. In mixed-sex dyads, a female-question/male-answer pattern emerged in several conversations. Hirschman found individual styles which *might* be gender-associated, e.g., one female used qualifiers of the type *I think, I'd say, I guess,* while a male used qualifiers of the type *most people, many females,* etc. Another style difference: one female made many false starts, repeated words as a hesitation device, left many sentences unfinished, and didn't leave many long pauses unfilled; both males generally finished the sentences they started, but often had long internal pauses in their utterances. Hirschman regards these as suggestive findings to be further investigated. [*See II-B, IV-A, IV-D, IV-E.*]

KEENAN, ELINOR.
    "Norm-Makers, Norm-Breakers: Uses of Speech by Men and Women in a Malagasy Community." In J. F. Sherzer and R. Baumann, eds., *Explorations in the Ethnography of Speaking.* New York: Cambridge Univ. Press, in press.

In the Merina tribe in Madagascar, strong value is placed on speaking indirectly and avoiding open confrontation. Men are regarded as skillful at this type of speech; they use an illusive and formal style. Women are seen as norm-breakers; they are associated with a direct, straightforward, impolite manner of speech, blurting out what they mean and communicating anger and negative information. Women are associated with bargaining, haggling, reprimanding children, and gossiping about shameful behavior. Men dominate situations where indirectness is desirable, such as ceremonial speech situations and inter-village relations.

KRAMER, CHERIS.
    "Folklinguistics." *Psychology Today,* 8 (June, 1974), 82-85.

According to popular belief (but not carefully controlled research), the speech of women is "emotional, vague, euphemistic, sweetly proper, mindless, endless"; in general it is supposed to be weaker, less effective, and more restricted than the speech of men. Kramer found such stereotypes reflected in *New Yorker* cartoons: women characters speak less, and in fewer places; when not shown in the home (where women are most often pictured), women often seem incapable of handling the language of the location, and their speech is the focus of humor. In general, women in the cartoons speak less forcefully than men, uttering fewer exclamations. Males use exclamations when they are angry or exasperated; women, more to convey enthusiasm. Male characters swear more freely than female characters. Kramer emphasizes that the stereotypes may not be true of actual speech, and reports an experiment which turned up no sex differences in choice of words. She also notes, "words, phrases, and sentence patterns are not inherently strong or weak. They acquire these attributes only in a particular cultural context. If our society views female speech as inferior, it is because of the subordinate role assigned to women. Our culture is biased to interpret sex differences in favor of men." [*See II-B, IV-D, IV-F.*]

ROSENFELD, HOWARD M.
"Approval-Seeking and Approval-Inducing Functions of Verbal and Nonverbal Responses in the Dyad." *Journal of Personality and Social Psychology*, 4 (1966), 597-605.

Rosenfeld experimentally constructed an approval-seeking condition for 13 male and 13 female dyads, and an approval-avoiding condition for 11 pairs of males and 9 pairs of females, by secretly instructing one member of each dyad either to gain or to avoid the approval of the other member. He examined verbal and nonverbal responses (gestures, speeches, utterances, and words) as they varied in each condition. In general, women used shorter utterances than men, especially in the approval-avoiding condition, and a greater proportion of their utterances consisted in answers to questions than did the utterances of men.

SOSKIN, WILLIAM F. AND VERA P. JOHN.
"The Study of Spontaneous Talk." In Roger Barker, ed., *The Stream of Behavior*. New York: Appleton-Century-Crofts, 1963.

To study spontaneous talking behavior in natural settings, the authors used miniature radio transmitters worn by a husband and wife at a large summer resort. The talk of the couple (Roz and Jock) during a 16-hour day was analyzed into episodes and phases; quantity of talk; frequency of different message types and functions (e.g. informational functions—factual statements about oneself and one's world, vs. relational functions—the range of verbal acts by which a speaker manages his interpersonal relations). In terms of message types, Roz (the wife) produced more affect-discharging messages; Jock (the husband), more directive and informational statements. When the two were in private, Roz produced more expressive messages than when they were in the presence of others. While Jock's conversation followed a single theme for some time, Roz on a number of occasions seemed to be trying to shift the conversation to other topics. In one episode, Roz and Jock were rowing and nearly capsized; Jock's dominant position was reflected in the low percentage of questions he asked (he mainly gave regulative statements—demands, suggestions, prohibitions—which "functioned to enhance his ego, control his environment, and allay anxiety"). Roz gave more descriptions of her present physical or psychological state; at the peak of the crisis, she made many requests for information; when the crisis passed, she expressed more delayed affect. In interacting with larger groups, Roz was more sensitive than Jock to her own impact on the group and to the possible interests and needs of other group members; she frequently acted as a "governor" for Jock, attenuating his impact on the group. Jock used a disproportionate amount of available talking time, and produced longer units of speech. The greatest similarity between husband and wife appeared in social settings calling for heavy reliance on informational language, and the greatest difference in social contexts of more intimacy where much of their talk consisted of relational language. [See IV-D, IV-G.]

STRODTBECK, FRED L. AND RICHARD D. MANN.
   "Sex Role Differentiation in Jury Deliberations." *Sociometry,* 19 (1956), 3-11.

Mock jury deliberations were recorded in a laboratory situation, with participants drawn from regular jury pools of Chicago and St. Louis courts. Analyzing the interaction of the jurors, the authors claim to have found a sex-role differentiation similar to that Bales and others have suggested for adults in the family: males played an instrumental, and females, an expressive (social-emotional) role. "Men *pro-act,* that is, they initiate relatively long bursts of acts directed at the solution of the task problem, and women tend more to *react* to the contributions of others." Almost twice as much of the women's talk consisted of agreeing, concurring, complying, understanding, and passively accepting; and less than half as much of the women's talk showed antagonism or deflated the status of others. [See IV-D.]

C. Speech Genres

In a given social group, there may be specific types of speech events, genres, rituals, or games particular to either sex. For example, in Turkey there is a form of *verbal dueling* unique to groups of teenage boys, involving homosexual content and a specific sequence and rhyme form (Alan Dundes, Jerry W. Leach, and Bora Ozkok, "The Strategy of Turkish Boys' Verbal Dueling Rhymes," in John J. Gumperz and Dell Hymes, eds., *Directions in Sociolinguistics* [New York: Holt, Rinehart & Winston, 1972], 130-160). Verbal dueling among black speakers in urban areas ("the dozens"; "sounding"; "signifying") may involve distinctions according to the sex of speakers and audience. Most studies of these speech forms have been based primarily on male informants (e.g., Roger Abrahams, *Deep Down in the Jungle,* revised edition [Chicago: Aldine, 1970]; Thomas Kochman, " 'Rapping' in the Black Ghetto," *Trans-Action,* 6, 4 [1969], 26-34; William Labov, "Rules for Ritual Insults," in David Sudnow, ed., *Studies in Social Interaction* [New York: Free Press, 1972], 120-169). An exception, which draws largely on female informants, is Claudia Mitchell-Kernan, "Signifying," in Alan Dundes, ed., *Mother Wit From the Laughing Barrel* (Englewood Cliffs., N.J.: Prentice-Hall, 1973), 310-328; and "Signifying and Marking: Two Afro-American Speech Acts," in Gumperz and Hymes *(op. cit.),* 161-179. Mitchell-Kernan notes that the sex of informants is important since males are more likely to engage in verbal dueling. "This is not to say that no woman ever engages in such speech acts as *sounding* or *playing the dozens,* but when she does, they are typically not in the context of the speech event 'verbal dueling.' Because verbal dueling permits a great deal of license (not absolute in any sense), women cannot be suitably competitive because other social norms require more circumspection in their verbal behavior" (Mitchell-Kernan, 1973, p. 328).

Riddling is another speech event in which sex differences have been found. Among the Dusun, in Southeast Asia, women prefer riddles using archaic words or syllables, while men use the more simply metaphoric type (John W. Roberts, and Michael L. Forman, "Riddles: Expressive Models of Interrogation," in Gumperz and Hymes, *op. cit.,* 180-209). Other speech genres in which the sex of speakers, audience, and target may make a difference include *joking* (Rose Coser, "Laughter Among Colleagues," *see IV-B;* G. Legman, *Rationale of the Dirty Joke, see II-A-1*); *swearing* (Cheris Kramer, "Women's Speech; Separate But Unequal?" *see II-B;* J. Klein, "The Family in 'Traditional' Working-Class England," *see IV-F*); and *story-telling* (Barrie Thorne, "Women in the Draft Resistance Movement: A Case Study of Sex Roles and Social Movements," *see IV-F*). Susan Harding ("Women and Words in a Spanish Village," *see IV—B*) discusses story-telling, *chatting,* and *gossip* as speech genres associated with women.

Referring to the U.S., Nancy Faires Conklin ("Toward a Feminist Analysis of Linguistic Behavior," *see I*) notes that women's talk is often characterized as *gossiping,* an activity with low value; if women elevate themselves above gossip, they are said to carry out *conversation,* which is still regarded as a form of entertainment. In contrast, professional men are said to engage in *discussions, conferences, meetings;* their talk is described as "business-like" and "talking straight from the shoulder." Women who enter the public domain may take on this type of speech; otherwise they may not be taken seriously. Conklin urges women to "develop strategies for dealing with the new interactional situations presented by board room and locker room talk, either acquiring the style of speaking which is considered appropriate for these occasions or establishing their credentials as group members with women's own forms. They must recognize, legitimize, and creatively develop their own speech genres. Clearly the back-slapping joke will never be a female vehicle."

Vocal music genres may vary by sex. H. J. Ottenheimer ("Culture and Contact and Musical Style: Ethnomusicology in the Comoro Islands," *Ethnomusicology,* XIV [1970], 458-462) reports that on the Comoro Islands between Madagascar and Mozambique, there is a sexual division in musical styles. In call and response vocal music genres, the men emphasize the solo part and women, the chorus; choral singing among men is restricted to religious chant; women provide ululation for men's music in their role as spectators.

D. Amount of Speech

ARGYLE, MICHAEL, MANSUR LALLJEE, and MARK COOK.
"The Effects of Visibility on Interaction in a Dyad." *Human Relations,* 21 (1968), 3-17.

An experimental study in which visibility was varied in a dyad, and measures of several factors, including speech production, were made. The authors found that in male-female pairs, males spoke more than females, and that when males were invisible, their amount of speech increased by an average of 40%, while females reduced their speech by a similar amount. [*See IV-E; IX-F.*]

BERNARD, JESSIE.
The Sex Game. New York: Atheneum, 1972.

"Women in task-oriented groups of mixed-sex composition often have a hard time getting the floor. An informal survey of television panel discussion programs showed that men out-talked the women by a considerable margin, as indeed they do also in laboratory studies," (e.g. Strodtbeck, "Husband-Wife Interaction Over Revealed Differences," [*in this section*]). "Perhaps because their voices are less powerful, women have a harder time getting the attention of the group; and they are more likely to lose it by successful interruption from men. Unless someone in the group makes a special effort to give time to the women, they may sit for long periods contributing nothing" (pp. 145-146). [*See IV-B, IV-G.*]

BROWNELL, WINIFRED and DENNIS R. SMITH.
"Communication Patterns, Sex, and Length of Verbalization in Speech of Four-Year-Old Children." *Speech Monographs*, 40 (1973), 310-316.

An experimental study of 79 four-year-old children (half of each sex) doing a verbal task. The independent variables were communication pattern (dyad; triad; role-playing triad; small group) and sex. The dependent variables were mean length of verbalization and mean length of verbalization minus repetitions. (The authors note that the variable, "amount of speech produced," has been measured in various ways: average total number of words produced, amount of speech in a sentence, time periods of speech, length of response, and mean number of words per pause. Individual rates of speaking, size of group, and aggressiveness affect these measures.) The findings: a greater amount of speech was elicited in the small group situation than in the dyad. "Females produced significantly more speech across all conditions than did males. This evidence confirms earlier reports of female linguistic superiority in samples of white, middle-class children." [*See VIII-B.*]

CHESLER, PHYLLIS.
"Marriage and Psychotherapy." In the Radical Therapist Collective, eds., produced by Jerome Agel, *The Radical Therapist*. New York: Ballantine, 1971, pp. 175-180.

"Even control of a simple—but serious—conversation is usually impossible for most wives when several men, including their husbands, are present. The 'wife'—women talk to each other, or they listen silently while the men talk. Very rarely, if ever, do men listen silently to a group of women talking. Even if there are a number of women talking, and only one man present, he will question the women, perhaps patiently, perhaps not, but always in order to ultimately control the conversation, and always from a 'superior' position." [*See IV-G.*]

HILPERT, FRED, CHERIS KRAMER, and RUTH ANN CLARK.
"Participants' Perceptions of Self and Partner in Mixed-Sex Dyads." *Central States Speech Journal,* Spring, 1975.

Fifty-seven pairs of mixed-sex dyads discussed a specified problem for ten minutes. After the discussion each participant completed a questionnaire indicating whether self or partner contributed more to feelings of trust and friendship, contributed to the decision, and talked more. Both women and men selected their partners slightly more frequently than themselves as the person who contributed more to feelings of trust and friendship. In perceptions of who contributed more to the decision, men selected their female partners as often as themselves; women chose their male partners far more frequently than they chose themselves. In response to questions about perceived amount of speech, "women selected the man as the one who talked more 72 percent of the time, whereas the men selected themselves 58 percent of the time. Analysis of the actual amount of time talked revealed that the man spoke more in 59 percent of the dyads." (Overall women had accurate perceptions of who spoke more in 78% of the dyads and men in 70%, but where women were incorrect, their errors tended to be systematic, designating the man as dominant speaker when in reality it was the woman.) Women apparently were not unhappy with this situation; they expressed as much satisfaction with the decision and with their influence on it as did the men.

HIRSCHMAN, LYNETTE.
"Analysis of Supportive and Assertive Behavior in Conversations." Paper presented at meeting of Linguistic Society of America, July, 1974.

Probing sex differences in conversational assertiveness and supportiveness, Hirschman had pairs of subjects discuss a question for ten minutes (there was a total of four single-sex and eight mixed-sex conversations). Amount of speech (or obtaining and holding the floor, measured by quantity of speech, number of interruptions, and mean utterance length) was taken as one indication of assertiveness. It was hypothesized that men would be more assertive, and women more supportive in conversational behavior. No sex differences were found in amount of speech; "the number of conversations in which women talked more equalled the number of conversations in which men talked more. The average percentage of the word output was also equal for females and males." The differences in mean length of utterance were not statistically significant. In several cases the less coherent speakers had a high word output (taking more words to communicate one idea), but did not make a higher contribution to conversational content. [See II-B, IV-A, VIII-B.]

HIRSCHMAN, LYNETTE.
"Female-Male Differences in Conversational Interaction." Paper presented at Linguistic Society of America, Dec., 1973.

Hirschman found no clear gender differences in amount of speech, as measured by the length of time a person held the floor or the number of words produced, though informants were in the same order on the two measures. However, when the percent of time used for talking in a conversation (by either participant) was examined, it was found that more time was spent talking in conversations which had at least one female participant, suggesting that females may play a role in facilitating the flow of conversation. Referring to the style of her informant with the most floor time and word production, Hirschman suggests a possible female style, that "voluminous female speakers compensate for their possible aggressiveness by increased indications of hesitancy and increased responsiveness." [See II-B, IV-A, IV-B, IV-E.]

KENKEL, WILLIAM F.
"Observational Studies of Husband-Wife Interaction in Family Decision-Making." In Marvin Sussman, ed., *Sourcebook in Marriage and the Family*. Boston: Houghton Mifflin, 1963, pp. 144-156.

This is a laboratory study of two groups of 25 married couples at Iowa State Univ. The couples were young, well-educated, had at least one child, and the wife was a homemaker. Each couple was observed in a decision-making situation (deciding how to spend a sum of money); their behavior was analyzed using Bales' interaction process categories and other classifications. Among these couples, 52% of all husbands did most or more of the talking; the remaining 48% were divided between equal-talking couples and those where wives talked more (Kenkel doesn't give exact figures). Kenkel examined the relationship of amount of talk to influence ("influence" defined as "the degree to which a person is able to have his own wishes reflected in the decision of the group"). Among males, there was a tendency for high influence to be related to amount of talking. "For wives, the picture is less definite, partly because only four wives had a high degree of influence. There were, however, as many wives with medium influence as there were husbands. Among such wives only one did more of the talking; in most of the remaining cases, moreover, the husbands did the greater share of the talking. Apparently then, wives can actually achieve a medium degree of influence when their husbands do more of the talking or when the talking is distributed evenly. The reverse was untrue for husbands. Husbands had a two-to-one chance of achieving medium influence if they did the greater share of the talking; their chances were reduced to about one in three of influencing to this extent if the talking was distributed evenly; and in only one case did a husband achieve medium influence when his wife did more of the talking." Kenkel asked his subjects to rate who did the most talking; only "17 of the 50 individuals were able to judge accurately the distribution of the total amount of talking in their decision-making session."

KOMAROVSKY, MIRRA.
Blue-Collar Marriage. 1962; rpt. New York: Vintage, 1967.

In an intensive case study of 58 blue-collar couples, which included examining patterns of marital communication and power, Komarovsky found that, contrary to experimental findings with small groups, e.g., Strodtbeck, "Husband-Wife Interaction Over Revealed Differences," [*in this section*], amount of talk and dominance do not always go together. In several of the couples studied, the dominant partner was the less talkative of the two. "One can readily see that in a group of strangers a silent person can hardly make his influence count. In marriage, however, we deal not only with a smaller group but an enduring one. Over the years of marriage a person can exert his influence in other ways than through sheer volume of words. 'He doesn't say much but he means what he says and the children mind him,' a mother says about the father. The same may apply to the couple's marital relationship" (p. 353). [*See IV-F.*]

KRAMER, CHERIS.
"Folklinguistics." *Psychology Today,* 8 (June, 1974), 82-85.

Analysis of *New Yorker* cartoons revealed a "striking finding": women cartoon figures "did not speak in as many of the cartoons as did men" (a finding that goes against the popular stereotype that women talk too much). In the 156 cartoons in Kramer's sample, men speak 110 times, and women only 44. "In fact, the number of men goes up to 112 if we assume that a commanding voice from the clouds is that of a masculine God, and that a voice on the phone telling an elephant trainer to 'Give him two bottles of aspirin and call me in the morning' belongs to a male veterinarian." Kramer suggests several possible explanations for the relative silence of women: most cartoonists are men, and they may depict the people and activities they know best (male ones); men may try harder to be funny and make more comic statements; "or perhaps the cartoons reflect real life, where men like to have the last, topping word." [See II-B, IV-B, IV-F.]

KRAMER, CHERIS.
   "Stereotypes of Women's Speech: The Word From Cartoons." *Journal of Popular Culture*, in press.

This study of the speech of the sexes in cartoons in *The New Yorker, Ladies Home Journal, Playboy,* and *Cosmopolitan* does not confirm the claim that women's speech is "everlasting" (i.e., that women talk more than men). In the sample of *Playboy* cartoons, men talk 57 times, and women 32 times; in *New Yorker* cartoons men talk as much as two-and-a-half times more frequently than women; in *Ladies Home Journal* the caption is given to men as many times as to women (17 and 17); only in *Cosmopolitan* do women control more of the captions (11 men, 17 women). Females in the *Cosmopolitan* cartoons were more wordy than males (they had a higher average word count). Some of the length, Kramer suggests, "comes from an attempt on the part of women to soften the effect of their words." [See II-B.]

PARKER, ANGELE M.
   "Sex Differences in Classroom Intellectual Argumentation." Unpublished M.S. thesis, Pennsylvania State Univ., 1973.

Observations were made of 200 college students in discussion sections of introductory courses in history and sociology. Verbalizations were categorized by skill at intellectual argumentation. A questionnaire was administered, and subjects rated discussion behavior from "highly masculine" to "highly feminine" on a 4-point scale. Findings: males participated significantly more often than females, yet a greater number of females made at least one statement. Students rated intellectual participation behaviors as "masculine." The instructors participated significantly more frequently than the 200 students added together.

SOSKIN, WILLIAM F. AND VERA P. JOHN.
   "The Study of Spontaneous Talk." In Roger Barker, ed., *The Stream of Behavior.* New York: Appleton-Century-Crofts, 1963.

Studying the talk of a husband and wife at a summer resort (recorded by radio transmitters), the authors looked, among other things, at how much time each individual spent in talk (including variations in this amount by situation, activities, altered role relations). They found that the husband's claim on available talking time varied from 29% where he was having golf lessons, to 79% when talking with his wife. His total share of talking time across all situations was 50.6%. Not only did the husband talk more than the wife, but when the two were together, he produced longer units of speech. [See IV-B.]

STRODTBECK, FRED L.
"Husband-Wife Interaction Over Revealed Differences." *American Sociological Review,* 16 (1951), 468-473.

Strodtbeck had married couples fill out identical questionnaires as individuals and then, together, arrive at common answers for questions on which their initial responses disagreed. These discussions were taped and analyzed; two of the dimensions used were participation rates (amount of talk) and who "won" more of the contested decisions. Husbands talked more in 19 of the cases and wives in 15. For both husbands and wives, greater rate of talking was related to greater influence (winning more contested decisions).

STRODTBECK, FRED L., RITA M. JAMES and CHARLES HAWKINS.
"Social Status in Jury Deliberations." *American Sociological Review,* 22 (1957), 713-719.

Exploring the relation of status differences in the larger community to power and participation in face-to-face situations, the authors conducted mock jury deliberations with participants drawn by lot from the regular jury pools of Chicago and St. Louis courts (the jurors listened to a recorded trial, deliberated, and returned their verdict; 49 deliberations were recorded and analyzed, with 588 different jurors involved). Analysis of interaction showed that "men, in contrast with women, and persons of higher in contrast with lower status occupations have higher participation, influence, satisfaction and perceived competence for the jury task" (p. 718). Speaking time was distributed accordingly: in all occupational levels, males talked more than females.

STRODTBECK, FRED L. and RICHARD D. MANN.
"Sex Role Differentiation in Jury Deliberations." *Sociometry,* 19 (1956), 3-11.

In a study of the interaction of jurors involved in mock jury deliberations, the authors found that although men constituted about two-thirds of the juries studied, they contributed almost four-fifths of the talk. [*See IV-B.*]

SWACKER, MARJORIE.
"The Sex of the Speaker as a Sociolinguistic Variable." In Barrie Thorne and Nancy Henley, eds., *Language and Sex: Difference and Dominance.* Rowley, Mass.: Newbury House, 1975.

Thirty-four informants (17 men and 17 women) were separately shown three pictures by Albrecht Dürer and asked to describe what they saw, taking as much time as needed for their descriptions. Men were more verbose than women. The female mean time for all three descriptions was 3.17 minutes, and for males was 13.0 minutes; there were no significant sex differences in the speed of the discourse (words per minute). "These statistics are not entirely accurate because there were three male informants who simply talked until the tape ran out." Their times were arbitrarily set at 30 minutes for statistical purposes; even without "these exceptionally verbose males, the mean for men was significantly longer than that for females." [*See II-B, IV-G.*]

WOOD, MARION M.
    "The Influence of Sex and Knowledge of Communication Effectiveness on Spontaneous Speech." *Word,* 22, No. 1-2-3 (1966), 112-137.

An experimental study varying sex of speaker (18 subjects of each sex were individually tested); stimuli evoking spontaneous speech (speakers were asked to describe photographs of the same person with different facial expressions); sex of person spoken to; and knowledge of communication effectiveness (subjects were given different sets of "pseudofeedback" about success and failure). Interaction between speaker and hearer was limited to speech by the speaker (i.e., it was one-way with no nonverbal communication). It was found that: (1) "men tend to use more words per utterance in a given verbal task than do women"; and (2) "the length of the verbal output of males, but not of females, tends to increase under conditions of ineffective communication and to level off under conditions of successful communication." Wood suggests that "males are more sensitive to success or failure of communication than are females," and that "males may have a greater tendency to repeat" (related to their greater verbal output). [*See II-B.*]

E. Interruption

ARGYLE, MICHAEL, MANSUR LALLJEE, and MARK COOK.
    "The Effects of Visibility on Interaction in a Dyad." *Human Relations,* 21 (1968), 3-17.

An experimental study in which visibility was varied in a dyad, and speech patterns, among other things, were analyzed. The authors report that in an attempt to dominate, males interrupted more than did females (no figures are provided about this finding). [*See IV-D; IX-F.*]

HENNESSEE, JUDITH and JOAN NICHOLSON.
    "NOW Says: TV Commercials Insult Women." *New York Times Magazine,* May 28, 1972, 12+.

The New York branch of the National Organization for Women studied 1,241 television commercials. Almost all showed women inside the home doing household tasks or as domestic adjuncts to men. The commercials assume male authority; women never tell men what to do, but men continually give women advice and orders. The study found that 89.3% of the voice-overs are male (i.e., a woman may be the main figure in the ad, but her voice is followed by a male voice-over, the voice of authority, conferring the stamp of approval on the product). [*Voice-overs can be analyzed as a kind of interruption pattern.*]

HIRSCHMAN, LYNETTE.
> "Female-Male Differences in Conversational Interaction." Paper presented at Linguistic Society of America, Dec., 1973.

Analyzing a small sample of dyadic conversations, Hirschman found that the female pair interrupted each other with a much higher frequency than the four mixed-sex pairs or the male pair. She suggests that her interruption measure may need to be refined, however, to exclude overlapping that occurs when one speaker anticipates the end of the other speaker's utterance, rather than is attempting to gain the floor. Such a measure would require "a much more sophisticated understanding of the set of cues used to signal the end of an utterance." [See II-B, IV-A, IV-B, IV-D.]

ZIMMERMAN, DON H. and CANDACE WEST.
> "Sex Roles, Interruptions and Silences in Conversation." In Barrie Thorne and Nancy Henley, eds., *Language and Sex: Difference and Dominance*. Rowley, Mass.: Newbury House, 1975.

This paper is based on Harvey Sacks' work on rules governing the organization of conversation, e.g., rules that only one party speaks at a time, and that speaker change recurs. Related to this is the notion of a speaker's turn (bounded rights to speak, which may be violated by interruptions and speaking out of turn), and mechanisms for transition between speaker turns. Zimmerman and West examined transcripts of brief, two-party conversations, covertly recorded in public places. There were 11 male-female, 10 female-female, and 10 male-male pairs, all white, middle-class, from 20-35 years old, with relationships ranging from close friendship to casual acquaintanceship. The authors examined transcripts for instances of simultaneous speech—overlaps (where the current speaker has reached a point in her utterance that can be treated as a complete sentence and a non-speaker begins to talk while the current speaker continues; the speaker might protest, "I wasn't quite finished"); and interruptions (a non-speaker begins to talk at a point in the current speaker's utterance which cannot be viewed as a possible sentence completion point; the protest here would be, "You interrupted me"). In the single-sex conversations, which were combined for analysis, there were 7 interruptions and 22 overlaps, both symmetrically distributed between speakers. In male-female conversations there were 48 interruptions and 9 overlaps, which showed a dramatic asymmetric pattern: "virtually all the interruptions and overlaps are by the male speakers (98% and 100% respectively)." In no case did the woman who was interrupted protest. While in same-sex conversations the distribution of silence was nearly equal, in cross-sex conversations females showed more silence than males; women tended to fall silent for noticeable periods of time after being interrupted. Retarded minimal responses (e.g., "mm" or "um hmm") and interruptions—both more prevalent in the speech of males in cross-sex conversations—function as mechanisms to control the topic. This is reminiscent of adult-child conversations where the child, like women in these cross-sex conversations, has restricted rights to speak and to be listened to. The authors conclude that male dominance encompasses "routine chit-chat," since the woman's right to complete a speaking turn was routinely infringed upon without apparent consequence. [See IV-G.]

F. Conversational Topics

BARRON, N.M. and M.J. MARLIN.
"Sex of the Speaker and the Grammatical Case and Gender of Referenced Persons."
Technical Report No. CI 53, Center for Research in Social Behavior. Columbia: Univ.
of Missouri.

Videotapes of teachers and pupils in 6th and 11th grade classrooms were recorded,
reconstructed, and coded for a number of interpersonal and linguistic characteristics.
Analysis of the language of the teachers indicated, among other things, that both male and
female teachers talked about men more than about women. "It is presently a man's world in
the classroom despite its predominantly female population. The effects of this bias toward
the dominant masculine subcultures are yet to be documented, and then perhaps changed."

HARDING, SUSAN.
"Women and Words in a Spanish Village." In Rayna Reiter, ed., *Towards an
Anthropology of Women.* New York: Monthly Review Press, 1975.

In the village of Oroel in northeastern Spain, differences in conversational topics parallel
the division of labor between the sexes: men (whose domain is work in agriculture,
livestock, and in some shops and trades) talk of the land, crops, weather, prices, wages,
inheritance, work animals, and machinery. "On the side they may discuss hunting, play
cards, quote facts and figures of all sorts and argue about sports." The primary work of
women is at home; their talk is "wrapped around people and their personal lives," and the
needs and concerns of household members. [*See IV-B, IV-C.*]

KLEIN, J.
"The Family in 'Traditional' Working-Class England." In Michael Anderson, ed.,
Sociology of the Family. Baltimore, Md.: Penguin, 1971, pp. 70-77. Excerpted from
J. Klein, *Samples from English Culture,* Vol. 1. London: Routledge & Kegan Paul,
1965, pp. 103-113.

Within the culture of miners, there is strong segregation between the sexes. The woman's
place is in the home; the man's place is outside it, in his world of work, and with male
friends at the club, the pub, the corner, the sports-ground. "It is with other men that they
are at their most relaxed, at ease and emotionally expansive"; the bond between men is so
deep that in some ways they form a secret society, deliberately excluding women, children,
and strangers, partly through "pit-talk" or swear-words used familiarly within the group,
and offensively to those outside. "Women are not supposed to hear these words from men,
though they may use them in their own women's circle. Thus for instance the bookie's
office is part of the men's world, where women have no place. A woman going into the
office is subjected to jokes and language which in a more neutral locality would lead to a
fight." "Just as men in the clubs talk mainly about their work and secondly about sport and
never about their homes and families, so do their wives talk first of all about *their* work, i.e.

their homes and families, and secondly within the range of things with which they are all immediately familiar. The men discourage any transgressions over the line of this division of interests. When a woman does express any interest in politics or other general topics, she speaks rather apologetically, and can be prepared for her husband to tell her not to interrupt intelligent conversation: 'What the hell do you know about it?' " (p. 73). [See IV-C.]

KOMAROVSKY, MIRRA.
   Blue-Collar Marriage. 1962; rpt. New York: Vintage, 1967.

   This is an intensive case study of 58 blue-collar couples, based on interviews and covering topics like conjugal roles, the division of labor, patterns of interpersonal communication, marriage and power, kinship relations, social life, and leisure. Looking at communication patterns, Komarovsky found a strong pattern of sex segregation of activities, interests, and talk. Each sex felt it had little to say to the other, and even in social situations involving couples, the sexes split up to talk. The men felt their wives talked about gossip and "silly" matters ("dirty diapers stuff," one said); the men talked to their male friends about cars, sports, work, motorcycles, carpentry, local politics. The women (who were aware that men deprecated their conversations) talked to women friends about family and interpersonal matters. Women were more dissatisfied than men with their mates' patterns of marital communication; the women complained that their husbands didn't listen, didn't reveal their worries, and didn't talk enough in general. [See IV-D]

KRAMER, CHERIS.
   "Folklinguistics." Psychology Today, 8 (June, 1974), 82-85.

   Kramer analyzed 156 New Yorker cartoons. Among her findings: women and men discuss different topics. "Men hold forth with authority on business, politics, legal matters, taxes, age, household expenses, electronic bugging, church collections, kissing, baseball, human relations, health, and—women's speech. Women discuss social life, books, food and drink, pornography, life's troubles, caring for a husband, social work, age, and life-style." Students read the cartoon captions and tried (quite successfully) to indicate the sex of the speaker; several of the students said they considered all statements about economics, business, or jobs to be male. Men, wherever they happen to be, are pictured in control of language, while women, especially if they step over the topical boundary, often seem incapable of handling the language appropriate to the new location, and their speech is a source of humor. [See II-B, IV-B, IV-D.]

LANDIS, CARNEY.
   "National Differences in Conversations." Journal of Abnormal and Social Psychology, 21 (1927), 354-375.

   Landis collected 200 fragments of conversation overheard in London on Oxford and Regent Streets during the late afternoon and early evening, noting the sex of the speaker and the person spoken to. As in the Columbus sample (M.H. Landis and H.E. Burtt [annotated below]), the man-to-man conversations were about business and money (35%), amusements or sports (16%), and other men (15%). Englishwomen talked to each other of other women (26%), of themselves (20%), and showed a tendency to converse on a greater variety of topics than the women in the American sample. There were contrasts with the American sample in conversation between the sexes: Englishmen talked to Englishwomen about women (20%), clothes (16%), and themselves (16%). Englishwomen talked to Englishmen about other women (24%), and about themselves (12%). This study, Landis concludes, shows "the Englishman when talking to a feminine companion adapts his conversation to her interests while American women adapt their conversation to the interests of their masculine companions."

LANDIS, M.H. and H.E. BURTT.
    "A Study of Conversations." *Journal of Comparative Psychology,* 4 (1924), 81-89.

Following a method similar to Moore's [*annotated below*], the authors "wore rubber heels and cultivated an unobtrusive manner," overhearing and recording 481 conversations in Columbus, Ohio, in a variety of settings (street cars, railroad and subway stations, on campus, at athletic events, parties, churches, restaurants, etc.). They noted the conversational topic, time, place, sex of partners involved, and estimated social status. In male-male conversations, the most frequent topics were business and money (49%), sports or amusements (15%), and other men (13%). Women talked to women about men (22%), clothing or decoration (19%), and other women (15%). Women talked of persons in 37% of the cases. In sexually mixed groups, men talked to women of amusement or sports (25%), money and business (19%), and themselves (23%). Women talked to men of amusement or sports (24%), clothing or decoration (17%), and themselves (17%).

LANGER, ELINOR.
    "The Women of the Telephone Company." *New York Review of Books,* 14 (March 12, 1970 and March 26, 1970). Reprinted by New England Free Press, 60 Union Sq., Somerville, Mass. 02143.

After three months working (and observing) as a Customer's Service Representative in the New York Telephone Co., Langer concluded that in her department, staffed mainly by women, religion and politics were avoided in conversation. "This is not characteristic of the men's departments of the company where political discussion is commonplace, and I believe the women think that such heavy topics are properly the domain of men: they are not about to let foolish 'politics' interfere with the commonsensical and harmonious adjustments they have made to their working lives."

MARSHALL, LORNA.
    "Sharing, Talking, and Giving: Relief of Social Tensions Among !Kung Bushmen." *Africa,* 31 (1961), 231-246. Excerpted in Joshua A. Fishman, ed., *Readings in the Sociology of Language.* The Hague: Mouton, 1970, pp. 179-184.

Marshall reports ethnographic observations of talk among a hunting-gathering group in the Nyae Nyae region of South West Africa. Talking keeps up open communication among the members of the band; it is an outlet for emotions and means of social control. People cluster in little groups during the day to talk, and at night, talk late by their fires. Food is the subject talked about most often. The men's talk is often about hunting: about people's past hunts, wondering where the game is at present, and planning next hunts with practicality. "Women (who, incidentally, do not talk as much as men) gave me the impression of talking more about who gave or did not give them food and their anxieties about not having food. They spoke to me about women who were remembered for being especially quick and able gatherers, but did not have pleasurable satisfaction in remembering their hot, monotonous, arduous days of digging and picking and trudging home with their heavy loads" (p. 181 in Fishman).

MOORE, H.T.
"Further Data Concerning Sex Differences." *Journal of Abnormal and Social Psychology,* 4 (1922), 81-89.

Moore walked down Broadway in New York City, overhearing and recording 174 fragments of conversation, and classifying them according to the sex of the interlocuters. He found that men in talking to men discussed money and business (48% of the fragments), amusements or sports (14%), and other men (13%). Women talking to women discussed men (44%), clothing or decoration (23%), and other women (16%). Men talked to women about amusements or sports (25%), and money and business (22%). Women talked to men about other men (22%), and other women (13%).

THORNE, BARRIE.
"Women in the Draft Resistance Movement: A Case Study of Sex Roles and Social Movements." *Sex Roles: A Journal of Research,* 1, No. 2 (1975).

In a participant-observation study of the draft resistance movement from 1968-1969, Thorne found that women participants were continually placed in a secondary and subordinate role. Risk-taking (breaking ties with the Selective Service System through turning in a draft card, refusing induction, etc.) was a central Resistance tactic, and a criterion for full acceptance within the movement. Women (who were not eligible for the draft) were largely barred from risk-taking and from the central dramatic arenas of the movement: confrontations with draft boards at hearings, with army officials at pre-induction physicals and induction refusals, with judges at arraignments and trials. These confrontations lived on in a rich repertoire of anecdotes, which belonged to men and not to women. In story-telling sessions (a central conversational activity within the movement), women tended to listen while the men performed. This is an example of a more general phenomenon: the prevalence of all-male activities involving risk, violence, and danger, which become a basis for later story-telling (with women pushed into a listening role)—e.g. sports, army experiences, sailing, mountain climbing, hunting, and cockfighting. Childbirth may be one sphere of risky experience (which makes for good stories) available to women, but not to men, although prepared childbirth opens this sphere to males, at least in an observer role. [*See IV-C.*]

G. Control of Topics

The study of how topics are raised, dropped, developed, changed, and diverted in conversations may indicate sex differences; this is part of the general issue of control of conversations (see Phyllis Chesler, "Marriage and Psychotherapy," *under IV-D*). Don H. Zimmerman and Candace West ("Sex Roles, Interruptions and Silences in Conversation," *see IV-E*) found that when a female tried to develop a topic in her turns at talk, the male made minimal response ("um, um hmm"), which, along with more frequent interruptions by males, functioned as a mechanism by which men controlled the topic in mixed-sex conversations. Jessie Bernard (*The Sex Game, see IV-A*) uses a tennis metaphor for this pattern of minimal response: one partner (often the female) supplies all the balls, with none being returned. In a study of the talk of a couple in naturalistic settings, William F. Soskin and Vera P. John ("The Study of Spontaneous Talk," *see IV-B*) found that the husband's conversation followed a single theme, while the wife tried to shift the conversation to other topics. Bernard cites research by Harold Feldman (*Development of the Husband-Wife Relationship* [Ithaca, N.Y.: Cornell Univ. Press, 1965]) indicating that, at least in his sample of married couples, the woman's initiative in starting conversations was not rewarded. Initiation of discussion by the wife was found to be negatively related to the amount of time spent talking with one another daily. "The less he talked, the more she tried to get him to talk; or, equally probable, the more she tried to get him to talk, the less likely he was to want to talk." In an experimental study in which subjects separately described pictures, Marjorie Swacker ("The Sex of Speaker as a Sociolinguistic Variable," *see II-B*) found sex differences in markers used for shifting topics: women used significantly more conjunctions, and men more interjections. (e.g., "OK").

V. WOMEN'S AND MEN'S LANGUAGES, DIALECTS, VARIETIES

There is a fairly old literature about male-female language distinctions in non-Western societies. Key (see I) notes that "around the turn of the century and for a while thereafter interest in 'women's languages' ran high—perhaps triggered by the exotic accounts brought back by travelers who reported this phenomenon in far off places" (p. 15). This topic overlaps with others in the bibliography, especially "Sex Differences in Word Choice, Syntactic Usage, and Language Style" (II-B) and "Conversational Topics" (IV-F). In a more general way it points to a taxonomical issue: do these variations constitute separate languages, dialects, or language varieties or styles? (For a discussion of these terms see Joshua A. Fishman, The Sociology of Language, Rowley, Mass.: Newbury House, 1972, pp. 15-18; and Susan Ervin-Tripp, "On Sociolinguistic Rules: Alternation and Co-occurrence," in John J. Gumperz and Dell Hymes, eds., The Ethnography of Communication, New York: Holt, Rinehart & Winston, 1972, pp. 213-250.) See also the discussion at the end of this section.

BODINE, ANN.
"Sex Differentiation in Language." In Barrie Thorne and Nancy Henley, eds., *Language and Sex: Difference and Dominance.* Rowley, Mass.: Newbury House, 1975.

Bodine's comprehensive review of the cross-cultural literature on sex-based differentiation in language draws heavily from ethnographic studies of non-European societies, particularly Amerindian, but also including Bengali, Carib, Cham, Chukchee, Hebrew/Semitic, Indo-European, Japanese and Thai. A table based on her classification scheme (sex differentiation in (1) pronunciation, or any of several forms, (2) based on sex of speaker, spoken to, speaker plus spoken to, or spoken about) lists which languages contain which types of differentiation. She traces the history of the literature and notes tendencies, often influenced by the linguists' European backgrounds, influencing their reports. In particular, they failed to classify gender with other forms of sex-based differentiation, overstated and exaggerated types of differentiation not occurring in their own languages, and made presumptions that the language used by males was the basic language, and that used by females a deviation (hence the prevalence of the term "women's language" over "men's language"). [*See I, II-B.*]

CAPELL, A.
Studies in Socio-Linguistics. The Hague: Mouton, 1966.

In Chapter 7, "Language and Social Groupings," Capell discusses "group or social dialects," which may be distinguished along the lines of sex, rank, profession and occupation. He reviews cross-cultural literature (from North and South America, and Asia) showing sex differences in morphology, lexicon, and phonetic use.

CHAMBERLAIN, ALEXANDER F.
"Women's Languages." *American Anthropologist,* 14 (1912), 579-581.

This article reviews theories offered to explain the existence of separate "women's languages" among primitive peoples. Older theories accounted for women's language among the Carib by speculating that women belonging to foreign tribes were saved and incorporated by the Caribs when the male members were exterminated. This theory has been refuted. Others have looked to social-economic factors, such as differentiation of occupation and labor; also "religious and animistic concepts in woman's sphere of thought," and "the play-instinct, which often makes itself felt longer in woman."

CONKLIN, NANCY FAIRES.
"Perspectives on the Dialects of Women." Paper presented at American Dialect Society meeting, 1973.

Conklin reviews some of the early literature (Chamberlain, Flannery, Sapir) on systematic differences between men's and women's speech, with emphasis on the issue of language change. "Numerous cases have been recorded in which languages have lost male/female distinctions. When a language is dying due to influence from some other language (as with native American languages and English), male/female differences are apparently among the earliest linguistic fine points to be omitted by nonperfect learners. In many reports the existence of male/female differences is known only from tales or other archaic forms. Sex distinctions such as those discussed here seem, even in languages in full use, to be quite vulnerable to loss or merger. In the cases of natural linguistic change and of language decay which have been reported, it is the male forms which become generalized to all speakers, not the female ones." [*See II-A-2, IV-B.*]

CONKLIN, NANCY FAIRES.
    "Toward a Feminist Analysis of Linguistic Behavior." *The University of Michigan Papers in Women's Studies,* 1 No. 1 (1974), 51-73.

    Under the general rubric of "sex-marking in languages," Conklin discusses the literature on "so-called women's speech" (noting that the only cases which have been studied extensively are those where women's and men's speech differ radically, so distinctions are hard to overlook, e.g., Yana, Carib, Koasati). In these studies, "the men's language is always taken as the norm, and the women's language as deviating from that norm." Where the sexes use diverse language forms, there must be "some strong social motivation for stratification along sex lines to counteract the natural integration processes which normally go along with language contacts." In Carib society, the sexes were socially separate in types of labor; the women lived together with small children, and the men in their own quarters. Hence, social stratification was reflected in linguistic stratification. There is evidence from several dying native American languages that as native culture is westernized, "the men's form of speech becomes generalized and is used by both sexes." [*See I, II-A-2, II-B, IV-C, IV-D, VI.*]

FARB, PETER.
    Word Play: What Happens When People Talk. New York: Alfred A. Knopf, 1973.

    Written in a lively style for a general audience, and reporting the sociolinguistic research of others, this book includes discussion of sex differences. On pp. 47-50, Farb reviews some of the literature on male/female differences in pronunciation, vocabulary, grammar, and use of speech, among the Chukchi, the Yana, the Vakinankaratra of Madagascar, the Chiquito Indians of Bolivia, the Japanese, and the Gros Ventre Indians of Montana. Farb suggests that sex differences in English were probably more marked in the past, when the social lives of the sexes were more separate (and women, in particular, were more insulated than they are now). Farb concludes that "sexual distinctions in speech arose as assertions of male superiority" (p. 49), and that "differences disappear as the social status of women becomes more nearly equal to that of men" (p. 50). [*See II-A-1; II-B, III-A, III-B-2.*]

FARLEY, ALISON.
    "Sexism and Racism: A Linguistic Comparison." Unpublished paper, 1972 (Berkeley, Calif.).

    Farley draws social and linguistic parallels between blacks and women: both are minorities, experiencing discrimination in employment and status; both have indulged in group hatred and rejection; both minorities are now beginning to realize and accept their group identities with enthusiasm and pride. These two minorities "have in turn created separate linguistic systems" (the dialect of blacks is more unique than that of women, since women have not been physically isolated from the dominant white male culture, in the way blacks have [the special situation of black women is not discussed]). The lack of real power of both minorities is mirrored in language use: female speech has a connotation of lack of seriousness and importance; blacks may be extra verbal as a compensation for lack of power and prestige. Both blacks and women have used games of verbal subterfuge (for women, flirting, playing dumb, buttering up, being cute) to gain control over their lives. The verbal style of blacks and of women are more linguistically complex than that of the standard white male (e.g., women have been constrained to be indirect; blacks have developed a fluent and lively "rapping" style). Linguistically, women have a distinctive lexicon in some domains ("the conversation of the beauty parlor, the bridge shop or the kitchen would leave most men at a loss"). There is a long lexicon of distinctively black terms. In grammar, there are a few characteristically female forms (e.g., tag questions; the polite subjunctive); black dialect has systematic grammatical and phonological variants. "The final question is whether minority groups such as blacks or women will be integrated into the dominant culture to such an extent that the linguistic differences will disappear or dwindle to inconsequence, or whether the groups will achieve and maintain social, economic and linguistic independence."

FLANNERY, REGINA.
   "Men's and Women's Speech in Gros Ventre." *International Journal of American Linguistics,* 12 (1946), 133-135.

   Studying the Gros Ventre of the Fort Belknap Reservation in Montana, Flannery noted differences in vocabulary and pronunciation in the speech of men and women. In addition, there are gestures in the sign language used only by women, and women and men have distinctive calls. The Gros Ventre are aware that the sexes "talk differently," though no one could formulate the difference. When telling a story, the old people could give the interjections proper to the sex of the character quoted, but did not make the appropriate variation in pronunciation. But apart from such contexts, it was said that if a woman used men's words she would be considered mannish, and a man using women's words would be considered effeminate.

FURFEY, PAUL HANLY.
   "Men's and Women's Language." *The American Catholic Sociological Review,* 5 (1944), 218-223.

   Like Jespersen, Furfey believes that the terms "men's language" and "women's language" imply more than the facts warrant, since "there is no instance known to the writer in which the men and women of the same tribe speak entirely distinct tongues. The sex distinctions which have been discovered involve, not the language as a whole, but certain specific features of the languages, such as phonetics, grammar, or vocabulary." Phonetic differences between men and women have been reported from the Chukchi (a Mongoloid tribe in Siberia), in the Bengali language in eastern India, and from the Eskimo of Baffin Land. Among the Chiquito of Bolivia there are two genders in the men's language, which are not found among women. Less extensive grammatical differences have been reported from various American Indian tribes (the Yuchi, Koasati, Cree, Hitchiti) and the Thai. Differences between the sexes in vocabulary have been reported from the Carib, and the Yana (in northern California). Furfey concludes "sex may affect linguistic forms in three ways; for such forms may be modified by (1) the sex of the speaker, (2) the sex of the person spoken to, and (3) the sex, real or conventional, of the person or thing spoken of" (p. 221). On the social significance of linguistic sex distinctions, there is evidence that "the distinctions in question are bound up with a masculine assertion of superiority" (e.g., among the Chiquito, men and supernatural beings were classed in one category; women, the lower animals, and inanimate objects in another).

HAAS, MARY R.
"Men's and Women's Speech in Koasati." *Language,* 20 (1944), 142-149. Reprinted in Dell Hymes, ed., *Language in Culture and Society.* New York: Harper & Row, 1964, pp. 228-232.

In Koasati, a Muskogean language spoken in southwestern Louisiana, there are well-defined differences in the speech of men and women (involving indicative and imperative forms of verbal paradigms). Haas lays out rules governing these differences by setting up the forms used by women as basic and the male forms as derived from these (e.g., "if the women's form ends in a nasalized vowel, the men's form substitutes an *s* for the nasalization"). While this procedure is largely arbitrary, in a few instances "the speech of women is seen to be somewhat more archaic than that of men and to this extent it is possible to justify the procedure on historical grounds." Members of each sex are familiar with both types of speech, and can use either as the occasion demands (e.g., a man can use women's forms when telling a story about a woman character). At the present only middle-aged and elderly women use the women's forms; younger women have adopted men's speech. Other Muskogean languages at one time had similar differences, but they have largely disappeared. Haas summarizes other evidence of sex differences in speech: from the Yana, the Eskimo, the Carib, the Chukchee, the Thai.

HERTZLER, JOYCE O.
A Sociology of Language. New York: Random House, 1965.

Under "The Biosocial Categories and Groups" (pp. 318-321) Hertzler briefly summarizes some of the studies of segregation of language by sex groups "among primitive people" (the Caribs; in Madagascar; among the Guaycurus of Brazil; in Surinam; in Micronesia; among American Indian tribes; in Japan). He concludes that "major differentiations of language between the sexes of a society are rare. Contact between the sexes is so continuous and so extensive that sharp differences cannot long be maintained" (p. 319).

JESPERSEN, OTTO.
"The Woman," Chapter XIII of *Language: Its Nature, Development and Origin.* London: Allen & Unwin, 1922, pp. 237-254.

"There are tribes in which men and women are said to speak totally different languages, or at any rate, distinct dialects." For example, there are reports dating back to 1664 that among the Caribs of the Small Antilles, each sex has expressions which the other sex understands but never uses. However, these special words account for only about one tenth of the vocabulary, and the sexes share the same grammar; hence there are *not* really "two distinct languages in the proper sense of the word." Verbal taboos distinguish the sexes in various societies; e.g., among the Caribs, men on the war-path use words forbidden to women, and among the Zulu in Africa, a woman is not allowed to mention the name of her father-in-law and his brothers. There are grammatical differences between the sexes among the Chiquitos in Bolivia. Jespersen variously attributes these sex differences in language to the social separation of the sexes, to different activities and interests, and to differences of rank and male domination. [*See I, II-B, VI.*]

KRAUS, FLORA.
> *"Die Frauensprache bei den primitiven Vokern."* Imago (Leipzig), 10, 215 (1924), 296-313. Kraus, psychoanalyst in Vienna between the wars, read this paper on May 14, 1924 before the Wiener Psychanalytischen Vereinigung; its written form unfortunately remains untranslated from the German.

Kraus's paper, concerned with women's language in primitive societies, is important for the data contained and the insights presented but is of particular interest to those concerned with the history of ideas within the area of sex specific speech. The paper is divided into three parts: a survey of data showing sex specific items in a number of languages, a review of numerous attempts put forth to explain how language varieties developed along sex lines, and Kraus's own psychoanalytical explanation for the phenomena. The data, lexical and phonological and morphological, are drawn from a number of sources; nearly all of it may also be found in Jespersen, Reik, and/or Furfey. The second part concisely presents almost all of the theories, past and present, on the reasons for origins of sex specific language patterns; Kraus provides historically, sociologically, psychologically and religiously based notions with copious examples and thorough documentation. The last and most innovative section, Kraus's psychoanalytic theory on the origin of women's language, attributes its origin to *turned tongue,* a term designating a set of verbal ploys which allows the speaker to secretly discuss the socially unacceptable without actually naming the item or concept under discussion. [*Annotation by Marjorie Swacker.*]

LAKOFF, ROBIN.
> "Language and Woman's Place." *Language in Society,* 2, No. 1 (1973), 45-79.

Lakoff asserts that women have a special style of speaking (which avoids strong or forceful statements; uses indirect, "polite" means of expression; and is often associated with triviality). This contrasts with the more male or neutral style (associated with power, forcefulness, important matters). Women are socialized to the special style (and considered "unfeminine" if they don't use it), but are also punished for it (accused of being unable to speak precisely, to express themselves forcefully, or to take part in a serious discussion). Hence, a woman is caught in a bind: to be less than a woman (if she doesn't use the accepted style) or less than a person (which the style implies). A male is faced with no such dilemma; if he learns the language of his male peers, he is accepted both as a man and as a person. Adult males use woman's language less than vice versa; women may learn to switch to the neutral (male) form under appropriate situations (in class, talking to professors, at job interviews, etc.). This, in effect, makes women bilinguals; perhaps they never really master either language; it may take extra energy to shift languages appropriately. Lakoff asks if linguistic indecisiveness (trying to decide whether to use neutral or woman's language) is one reason why women may participate less than men in class discussions. [*See I, II-A-1, II-B, III-B-3, VII.*]

REIK, THEODOR.
"Men and Women Speak Different Languages." *Psychoanalysis*, 2, No. 4 (1954),
3-15.

This is a rambling, psychoanalytic article which notes that in a number of "primitive"
societies each sex has unique words and expressions never used by the other sex, and which
are surrounded by taboos. Interprets "primitive word avoidances" psychoanalytically: e.g.,
avoidances of names (as in societies where women are not to pronounce the names of their
fathers or brothers-in-law) as protection against the danger of having contact with forbidden
objects. Word taboos are also present in our "civilization," e.g., in cases where husband and
wife avoid addressing each other by name. In modern societies "women form a speech
community of their own," their talk, especially about sexual and bodily matters, being
"elusive and allusive," "indirect," and "delicate" (perhaps, Reik claims, because "speaking
means doing in words"). "Men may use certain feminine expressions when they imitate
women's talking or when they are making fun of women's way of expressing themselves."
Reik does not emphasize the reverse phenomenon: men's talk; women making fun of men,
though he does say that men may show consideration for "well-bred members of the other
sex" by avoiding coarse or vulgar expressions, e.g., a sailor who told his "lady physician"
about having "intimate union with a girl"; since the patient couldn't talk freely, Reik urged
the female psychiatrist to transfer him to a male physician. Reik notes sex differences in
topic and in adjectives (male: "a regular guy," "a good Joe," "paying through the nose,"
"hell," "damned," "it stinks" . . . female: "darling," "divine," "sweet," "adorable," and
emotional expressions like "I could just scream"; "I nearly fainted"; "I died laughing").

TRUDGILL, PETER.
"Language and Sex." Chapter 4 of *Sociolinguistics: An Introduction*. Harmonds-
worth, Middlesex, Eng.: Penguin, 1974.

This chapter surveys sex differences in Amerindian languages, Jespersen's explanations,
the Koasati examples, data from studies of phonology in Detroit, and data from South
African English, Norwich British English, and Norwegian. [*Annotation by the author.*]

ADDITIONAL REFERENCES

Blood, Doris. "Women's Speech Characteristics in Cham." *Asian Culture*, 3 (1962),
139-143.
Bogoras, Waldemar. "Chukchee." In Franz Boas, ed., *Handbook of American Indian
Languages*, BAE-B 40, Part 2 (1922). Washington: Smithsonian Institution, 631-903.
Bunzel, Ruth. "Zuni." In Franz Boas, ed., *Handbook of American Indian Languages*, BAE-B
40, Part 3 (1933-1938). Washington: Smithsonian Institution, 385-515.
Chatterji, Suniti Kumar. "Bengali Phonetics." *Bulletin of the School of Oriental Studies*, 2,
No. 1 (1962), 1-25.
Das, Sisir Kumar. "Forms of Address and Terms of Reference in Bengali." *Anthropological
Linguistics*, 10, No. 4 (1968), 19-31.

Dixon, Roland and Alfred Kroeber. "The Native Languages of California." *American Anthropologist*, 5 (1903), 1-26.

Dorsey, James, and John Swanton. *A Dictionary of the Biloxi and Ofo Languages*, BAE-B47 (1912). Washington: Smithsonian Institution.

Frazer, James George. "A Suggestion as to the Origin of Gender in Language." *Fortnightly Review*, 73 (1900), 79-90.

Kroeber, Theodora. *Ishi in Two Worlds*. Berkeley: Univ. of California Press, 1961.

Sapir, Edward. "Male and Female Forms of Speech in Yana." In St. W. J. Teeuwen, ed., *Donum Natalicium Schrijnen* (1929). Reprinted in David C. Mandelbaum, ed., *Selected Writings of Edward Sapir: In Language, Culture and Personality*. Berkeley: Univ. of California Press, 1949, pp. 206-212.

Wagner, Gunter. "Yuchi." In Franz Boas, ed., *Handbook of American Indian Languages*, BAE-B 40, Part 3 (1933-1938). Washington: Smithsonian Institution, pp. 293-384.

Women's Language as Deviant or a Special Case?

Many of these writings suggest not that women and men have separate, parallel languages, but that there is a woman's language as distinct from "regular," "normal," or "neutral" language (which is presumably a basically male turf, into which women may venture, but sometimes at the risk of being considered "unfeminine"). This may partly reflect a sexist bias in description (taking male behavior as the normal, the basepoint, and female behavior as deviant or abnormal), a practice Bodine (above) so well illuminates. It may also reflect real differences of power: since men dominate positions of public power (economic, political, religious institutions), their language forms have more recognized authority and legitimacy than those of women. As Lakoff (above) notes, men's language is being pre-empted by women, but women's language is not being adopted by men—just as women are moving into men's jobs more than vice-versa, and women are adopting male clothing styles more than the reverse. In short, "the language of the favored group, the group that holds the power, along with its non-linguistic behavior, is generally adopted by the other group, not vice-versa" (Lakoff, p. 50). This trend, which is of long standing, illustrates a broader social phenomenon known as "imitating the oppressor." On the general issue of whether or not women have—and/or should develop—a culture independent from that of men, see Ann Battle-Sister, "Conjectures on the Female Culture Question," Journal of Marriage and the Family, 33 (1971), 411-420.

VI. MULTILINGUAL SITUATIONS

CONKLIN, NANCY FAIRES.
  "Toward a Feminist Analysis of Linguistic Behavior." *University of Michigan Papers in Women's Studies*, 1, No. 1 (1974), 51-73.

Bilingual situations often present barriers to women, especially where women follow men to the latter's places of work or to live with the husband's family. In immigrant situations, men working outside the home come into contact with the dominant language;

women, located in the home, are isolated from the community at large. Youth may learn the dominant language, isolating older women still further. Conklin refers to Ervin-Tripp's study of Japanese "war brides" on the West Coast, whose bilingualism involved conflicting sets of values (Susan Ervin-Tripp, "An Analysis of the Interaction of Language, Topic and Listener," *American Anthropologist*, 66, No. 6, Part 2 [1964], 86-102). [*See I, II-A-2, II-B, V.*]

DIEBOLD, A. RICHARD.
    "Incipient Bilingualism." *Language*, 37 (1961), 97-112. Reprinted in Dell Hymes, ed., *Language in Culture and Society*. New York: Harper and Row, 1964, pp. 495-506.

In a peasant Indian village in Oaxaca, Mexico, the inhabitants speak Huave as a first language; Spanish is learned relatively late in life, if it is spoken at all (learning Spanish goes along with greater social contact with and participation in the national life). Diebold conducted a census of the village to ascertain who was monolingual, and who bilingual, and to what degree. 81% of the total were monolingual. With regard to sex, "bilingualism is predominantly a male skill, 80% of bilinguals of both the subordinate and coordinate groups being males." Sex is related to occupation; monolingual Huave speakers (proportionately more female than male) had less contact with the outside than subordinate and coordinate bilinguals (the latter made frequent marketing trips or actually lived outside the community for periods of time).

HANNERZ, ULF.
    "Language Variation and Social Relationships." *Studia Linguistica*, 24 (1970), 128-151.

Hannerz discusses a bi-dialect situation: that of ghetto blacks who have their own dialect, in addition to using standard English. In this case women are often more skillful at speaking standard English than are men, partly, Hannerz suggests, because "ghetto mothers often seem to attach greater weight to the schooling of daughters than sons." The working patterns of ghetto women expose them more to standard English than do the jobs of men; women are often found in "service roles" (domestic helper, waitress, sales person) which give them an opportunity to listen to and to practice standard English. In contrast, many ghetto men are in manual labor occupations where there is less extensive communication in standard English.

HUGHES, EVERETT C.
    "The Linguistic Division of Labor in Industrial and Urban Societies." *Georgetown University Monograph Series on Languages and Linguistics*, 23 (1970), 103-119. Reprinted in Joshua A. Fishman, ed., *Advances in the Sociology of Language II*. The Hague: Mouton, 1972, pp. 296-309.

Starting from the general assumption that "language encounters, hence bilingualism, are a function of social organization," Hughes describes the linguistic division of labor in Montreal, where French is spoken by the majority of the population, and English is spoken by a numerical, but economically dominant, minority. In the delivery of professional services (e.g., medicine, religion, education) there are two sets of institutions: one French-speaking, the other English. In industrial and commercial organizations, the top levels usually use English to communicate with themselves and with their peers in other organizations. In communicating information and instructions downward through the organization, at some point translation into French must occur, for at the middle and bottom ranks, personnel are nearly all French-speaking. White collar occupations in Montreal include the female bilingual private secretary, who provides liaison communication. "Usually of upper middle-class French family, she has taken the bilingual secretarial course offered by a certain convent. She has developed to a fine point the art of answering a phone call in the right language, French or English." The male bilingual executive assistant "has some of the liaison functions of the bilingual secretary, but he also deals with people lower in the ranks inside the organization" (p. 110).

JESPERSEN, OTTO.
"The Woman," Chapter XIII of *Language: Its Nature, Development and Origin.* London: Allen & Unwin, 1922, pp. 237-254.

"Among German and Scandinavian immigrants to America the men mix much more with the English-speaking population, and therefore have better opportunities, and also more occasion, to learn English than their wives, who remain more within doors. It is exactly the same among the Basques, where the school, the military service and daily business relations contribute to the extinction of Basque in favor of French, and where these factors operate much more strongly on the male than on the female population: there are families in which the wife talks Basque, while the husband does not even understand Basque and does not allow his children to learn it ... Vilhelm Thomsen informs me that the old Livonian language, which is now nearly extinct, is kept up with the greatest fidelity by the women, while the men are abandoning it for Lettish. Albanian women, too, generally know only Albanian, while the men are more often bilingual." [*See I, II-B, V.*]

LEOPOLD, WERNER F.
"The Decline of German Dialects." *Word,* 15 (1959), 130-153. Reprinted in Joshua A. Fishman, ed., *Readings in the Sociology of Language.* The Hague: Mouton, 1970, pp. 340-364.

In postwar Germany many population movements contributed to the demise of local dialects and the strengthening of colloquial standard German. Leopold reports a study by Otto Steiner comparing south and north German dialects; Steiner found that "boys use the local dialect far more commonly than girls, who prefer High German (standard German). In both regions, for both sexes, the share of High German is much larger in the cities than in the adjoining rural districts" (p. 359).

LIEBERSON, STANLEY.
 "Bilingualism in Montreal: A Demographic Analysis." *American Journal of Sociology,* 71 (1965), 10-25. Reprinted in Joshua A. Fishman, ed., *Advances in the Sociology of Language II.* The Hague: Mouton, 1971, pp. 231-254.

Based on Canadian census data, this article analyzes trends in language usage in Montreal from the 1920's to the 1960's. Over this time, although the French are far more bilingual than the English, the two populations have been in contact without the decline of either language. Children are generally raised as monolinguals who do not become bilingual until they leave the home context for school and/or work; hence the bilingualism of parents does not lead to loss of the mother tongue among the next generation. Sex differences in bilingualism enter into this process. Men in Montreal are more bilingual than women; hence "many of the bilingual members of each ethnic group are married to monolingual mates who share only the same mother tongue." This helps maintain the common mother tongue in the next generation, since this is the one language both parents could use with the children. Lieberson compares male age cohorts with female age cohorts. The degree of bilingualism among girls under 15 is similar to that found for boys of the same ages (well under 1%). "Beginning with the late teens, at the age when formal education ends for many and participation in the labor force begins, we find increasing differences between the sexes in their bilingualism. By the early twenties, the sex differences in bilingualism are considerable." Women have a consistently lower increase in bilingualism, and they also show a net decline in bilingualism at an earlier age than men. Lieberson attributes these gender differences to "the influence of male participation in the labor force and female withdrawal into the home and child-rearing," contending that "the main supports of bilingualism are school and occupational systems."

RUBIN, JOAN.
 "Bilingual Usage in Paraguay." In Joshua A. Fishman, ed., *Readings in the Sociology of Language.* The Hague: Mouton, 1970, pp. 512-530.

Paraguay has a high degree of bilingualism; more than half of the population speaks both Guarani (an Indian language) and Spanish (which has generally higher social status than Guarani). Rubin used a questionnaire to probe social factors influencing choice of language among bilinguals. Among other things, she found sex to be a variable. Men whose first language was either Spanish, or both Guarani and Spanish, tended "to use more Guarani with other men, but to use Spanish with women who are their intimates. Women, on the other hand, whose first language was either Spanish or both, tend to use Spanish to both male and female intimates" (p. 528).

TABOURET-KELLER, ANDREE.
 "A Contribution to the Sociological Study of Language Maintenance and Language Shift." In Joshua A. Fishman, ed., *Advances in the Sociology of Language II.* The Hague: Mouton, 1971, pp. 365-376.

A study of the shift to Standard French from the regional *patois* in Pays D'Oc and from a German dialect in Alsace, based on data about the linguistic usage of children ages 7 to 15. The analysis stresses economic and migration patterns, but also mentions sex differences in use of the *patois*. In Pays D'Oc 28% of girls and 23% of boys in the sample speak the *patois* (the difference is not statistically significant). Children tend to speak *patois* more with their fathers (58.5%) than with their mothers (45.7%), a statistically significant difference; use of *patois* with the father increases from the age of 12 onwards.

Note on Black English and U.S. Minorities

This Bibliography, relying largely on middle-class white academic sources, reflects its middle-class white academic bias: there is little material available on sex differences in the language of blacks and other U.S. racial and ethnic minorities. The following papers, cited in this section and elsewhere in the Bibliography, will be helpful to those seeking information relevant to the intersection of race and sex with language:

III-A	Anshen, Wolfram
IV-B	Abrahams, Grier and Cobbs
IV-C	Abrahams, Kochman, Labov, Mitchell-Kernan (two references)
V	Farley
VI	Conklin (on Ervin-Tripp), Hannerz
VII	Stewart
IX-A, D, F	Johnson

VII. LANGUAGE ACQUISITION

[Note: For further reference on language acquisition, see also VIII, VERBAL ABILITY, since many of the papers cited there report studies of children.]

BERNSTEIN, BASIL, ed.
  Class, Codes and Control, II: Applied Studies Towards a Sociology of Language. Boston: Routledge & Kegan Paul, 1973.

This book, reporting sociolinguistic research of Basil Bernstein and his colleagues at the Sociological Research Unit of the University of London Institute of Education, reflects their concern with class differences in "maternal language" (the language spoken by mothers to children). Among the topics explored: maternal orientations to communication; different strategies mothers use in controlling their children; interrelations among sex, class, and hesitation phenomena.

CHERRY, LOUISE.
  "Teacher-Child Verbal Interaction: An Approach to the Study of Sex Differences." In Barrie Thorne and Nancy Henley, eds., *Language and Sex: Difference and Dominance.* Rowley, Mass.: Newbury House, 1975.

Cherry recorded spontaneously occurring conversations among four female preschool teachers and their 38 children (16F, 22M) in the Boston area; there were ten data samples from each teacher, and over 16 hours of recording. *All* vocalizations were transcribed by two assistants (1F, 1M), with high agreement, and children's names were coded on transcripts so that sex could not be known. Cherry analyzed verbal interactions with attention to *initiator* (of the interaction), speaker *turns, words, utterances, attentional markers, repetitions, directives,* and *question-answer verbal acknowledgement* sequences. Totals were analyzed and tested for significance by two-way analysis of variance. A hypothesis that teachers' verbal interactions with girls would be more fluent (more utterances and more turns per interaction) than with boys was not confirmed, nor was one that teacher-girl verbal interactions would be more likely than teacher-boy interactions to have been initiated by the teacher. Teachers verbally acknowledged a significantly greater percentage of teacher-girl question-answer sequences than teacher-boy ones, contrary to expectation. Teachers used more "controlling" speech—more attentional-marked and more directive utterances—to boys, though the latter finding was not statistically significant. [*See VIII-B.*]

GARCIA-ZAMOR, MARIE A.
   "Child Awareness of Sex Role Distinctions in Language Use," paper presented at Linguistic Society of America, Dec., 1973. (Garcia-Zamor is at International Bank for Reconstruction and Development, Washington, D.C.)

   Eight nursery school children, four boys and four girls 5½-6 years old (middle and upper middle class), were interviewed twice: first, with a questionnaire designed to elicit overt attitudes toward sex roles: second, in a situation designed to determine how aware they are of "male" vs. "female" language. In the latter, the children gave judgments about whether a girl- or boy-doll prop uttered sentences containing terms of endearment, hostility, aggression, color terminology, elevating and derogatory terms, automotive terms, expressions of thoughtfulness, and tag questions. In the first interviews, traditional notions about sex roles were exhibited, with girls voicing far more of these views than boys, despite the fact that the nursery school is one that consciously attempts to combat sexism. Specifically, the girls had already begun to define themselves and females in general as inferior to males, and to circumscribe a limited range of life choices for themselves based on sex. In the language study, there was more agreement among the male subjects than among the females about whether an item was uttered by a male or female; and most of their instances of agreement were around terms ascribed to the male doll. The results are somewhat complex, and the following serves as only a suggestive summary of the findings: "Aggressive" (and competitive) expressions were consistently associated with the male doll; *"Dum-dum"* (devaluative) combined with accidental breaking was female-associated. Bright colors describing clothing were male-associated, light ones female-associated. Cars were more associated with males than females, across the automotive-term and color sentences. Tag questions tended to be female-associated. Judgments for terms of endearment and for epithets were mixed, though *shit* was seen by both boys and girls as male, and *drat* was seen by both as female; *daddy* was seen by both as male. Garcia-Zamor sees these results as "pointing to the durability of sex-based attitudes" and suggesting that "at this age boys make more consistent judgments about the appropriateness of language use on the basis of sex than girls do," though the girls had stronger sex-biased notions than the boys. She suggests that "it is the boys who are currently learning a new language—male language . . .

With his heightened level of linguistic sophistication the child can now differentiate between woman's language, his pre-school language, and the language of the male with whom he prefers to identify . . . The girls . . . merely continue in the language of the nursery. The only aspects of male language they need learn are those proscribed to them (for example, strong epithets), which this study shows they do learn." [See II-B.]

GLEASON, JEAN BERKO.
"Code Switching in Children's Language." In Timothy E. Moore, ed., *Cognitive Development and the Acquisition of Language,* pp. 159-167. New York: Academic Press, 1973.

This paper reports an observational study of the child's emerging control of different language styles, made on natural conversations in families with several children, ranging in age from infancy to eight years. In adult-to-child communication, distinctions were found between the manners of address to boy and girl children. Boy babies might be addressed in a "Hail-Baby-Well-Met style," especially by fathers, while being played with heartily. "Girl babies were dealt with more gently, both physically and verbally." A sex difference is mentioned in children's own language, in the sound effects accompanying play: though the actual differences aren't described, "the boys played more violent games and accompanied them with appropriate sound, but the girls made a lot of noises as well."

LABOV, WILLIAM.
Sociolinguistic Patterns. Philadelphia: Univ. of Pennsylvania Press, 1972, pp. 243, 301-304.

In terms of phonology, women are more sensitive to prestige patterns, and often use the most advanced forms in their own casual speech. Hence women play an important part in the mechanism of linguistic change. "To the extent that parents influence children's early language, women do so even more; certainly women talk to young children more than men do, and have a more direct influence during the years when children are forming linguistic rules with the greatest speed and efficiency. It seems likely that the rate of advance and direction of a linguistic change owes a great deal to the special sensitivity of women to the whole process" (p. 303). [See III-A.]

LAKOFF, ROBIN.
"Language and Woman's Place." *Language in Society,* 2, No. 1 (1973), 45-79.

Children are ostracized, scolded, or made fun of by adults and peers for not speaking the correct language for their sex. But if the little girl learns her lesson well, her "women's language" will later be an excuse others use to keep her in a demeaning position and to refuse to take her seriously. In a long footnote Lakoff amplifies on children's learning of sex-differentiated language. Probably both boys and girls first learn "women's language" (in Japanese, both sexes start out with particles proper for women, but boys are ridiculed if they speak them after about 5 years). As they mature, boys go through a stage of rough talk, which is discouraged in girls; at around 10, when they split up into same-sex peer groups, the two languages seem to be present. Boys have unlearned their original language and adopted new forms, while girls retain their old speech. Most of the phonological, syntactic, and semantic structure of language is in active use by 4 or 5, but social-contextual factors are not put into use until much later. Note that children have not learned the rules of polite conversation and blurt out inappropriate remarks. Lakoff suggests research in the acquisition of rules of contextual appropriateness, perhaps more accessible to research than syntactic and semantic acquisition. In suggesting that women who want to be taken seriously, who enter the public domain (professions, classrooms, etc.), learn the more male or "neutral" forms, Lakoff points to another language learning (and unlearning) process. [*See I, II-A-1, II-B, III-B-3, V.*]

LEWIS, MICHAEL.
   "Parents and Children: Sex-Role Development." *School Review,* 80 (1972), 229-240.

Lewis reviews his own research and that of others regarding sex-role socialization, and points out that from before the child is born, its sex is the characteristic most attended and responded to. With regard to vocal interaction, he reports that "It has been found repeatedly that from the earliest age mothers look at and talk to their girl infants more than they do their boy infants. In fact, looking-at and talking-to behaviors are greater for girls over the entire first two years of life."

SACHS, JACQUELINE.
   "Cues to the Identification of Sex in Children's Speech." In Barrie Thorne and Nancy Henley, eds., *Language and Sex: Difference and Dominance.* Rowley, Mass.: Newbury House, 1975.

Prepubertal boys and girls can typically be identified as to sex from their voices. This paper presents three studies on the cues used in this identification. (1) Judges were able to guess the sex of the child from hearing isolated vowels, though not as well as from sentences. (2) Judges could not accurately determine sex from sentences played backwards, suggesting that, beyond the phonetic aspects of the voices, there is considerable information in normal sentences that carries information about the sex of the speaker. (3) When judges rated spoken sentences on semantic differential scales, a factor emerged that was correlated with the perceived masculinity or femininity of the voice, along with two other factors, Active-Passive and Fluent-Disfluent. This result suggests that there is an independent cue to the sex of the speaker that does not involve how active the voice sounds or how fluent it is. [*Author's annotation.*] [*See III-B-2.*]

SACHS, JACQUELINE, PHILIP LIEBERMAN, and DONNA ERICKSON.
   "Anatomical and Cultural Determinants of Male and Female Speech." In Roger W. Shuy and Ralph W. Fasold, eds., *Language Attitudes: Current Trends and Prospects.* Washington: Georgetown Univ. Press, 1973, pp. 74-84.

In our culture there are variations in speech style when adults speak to babies; some aspects of this speech style "may be an exaggeration of features that distinguish feminine from masculine speech, such as higher perceived pitch and variability in intonation. The situations in which people use this speech style have a feature in common—they are what

J. P. Scott [*Animal Behavior,* Chicago: Univ. of Chicago Press, 1958] has called care-giving, or 'epimeletic,' situations. Courting couples sometimes speak a type of 'baby-talk' and some people use it when talking to pets. The care-giving role in our culture is considered most appropriate for females, but both women and men typically are embarrassed about using baby-talk, or claim they don't use it." In Arabic, however, both men and women use a conventionalized baby-talk to babies, although it is considered more appropriate for women. [*See III-B-2.*]

STEWART, WILLIAM A.
    "Urban Negro Speech: Sociolinguistic Factors Affecting English Teaching." In Roger
    W. Shuy, ed., *Social Dialects and Language Learning.* Champaign, Ill.: National
    Council of Teachers of English, 1964, pp. 10-18.

This paper on teaching standard English to speakers of "radically nonstandard dialects" contains brief comments on the range of dialects spoken by blacks in Washington, D.C. The least standard dialect (which Stewart calls the *basilect*) is largely restricted to young children. At about the age of seven or eight, there is (at least for boys) a noticeable dialect shift (e.g., the acquisition of new grammatical morphemes) which "appears to take place quite automatically, and in fact seems fairly independent of formal education, although the change may be accelerated and linguistically affected by it" (p. 17). The change coincides with the shift males make at that age from the status of "small-boy" to "big-boy" in the informal social structure of the local peer group. "Since 'big-boys' seem to regard basilect as 'small-boy talk' (just as adults do), the continued use of pure basilect probably becomes undesirable for a boy who aspires to status in the older age group." (p. 17). Stewart adds in a footnote (which leads one to wonder if all of his previous comments were about males only) that this kind of rapid dialect shift is less frequent among lower class girls, because age-grading is much less rigid among them than among boys. In the case of girls, dialect change seems to be more a direct result of formal education.

VIII. VERBAL ABILITY

A. General

GARAI, JOSEF E., and AMRAM SCHEINFELD.
    "Sex Differences in Mental and Behavioral Traits." *Genetic Psychology Monographs,*
    77 (1968), 169-299.

Females have better fluency and facility with language than males, giving them superiority in literature, essay writing, spelling, grammar, and foreign language learning. Earlier maturation of the speech organs leads to earlier age of speech onset of girls. Girls have better articulation than boys, and all speech disturbances are more frequent among males of all ages. Girls' earlier speech development, greater fluency, and greater language consciousness are related to earlier maturation of their speech organs, "their innate tendency toward more sedentary pursuits," closer contact with mothers, greater interest in people, socialization to social responsiveness and compliance, and perhaps to genetic factors which produce more speech defects in boys. These findings and others more related to intelligence testing (e.g., "verbal reasoning") are discussed in relation to reasoning and intelligence, and their implications for vocational and social roles. [*See VIII-B, VIII-C.*]

McCARTHY, DOROTHEA.
   "Some Possible Explanations of Sex Differences in Language Development and Disorders." *Journal of Psychology,* 35 (1953), 155-160.

   McCarthy claims small but important differences favoring girls over boys, in "practically all aspects of language development which show developmental trends with age" among white American children, from the age of onset of true language. [*See VIII-C.*]

THOMPSON, WAYNE N.
   Quantitative Research in Public Address and Communication. New York: Random House, 1967.

   This volume summarizes and evaluates quantitative research on public speaking, drawing mainly on research published in speech journals, such as *Quarterly Journal of Speech* and *Journal of Communication.* For each topic the author lists studies, with brief annotations, and then draws conclusions (which often claim more than the studies support). There are sections reporting differences between the sexes as public speakers and as listeners (audience members). In the area of public speaking, the following sex differences have the most research support: Women speakers are superior in such uses of language as vocabulary, sentence structure, and grammar; they are also less fidgety and better integrated than male speakers. Men speakers are "less withdrawn, have greater confidence, are more animated, and have more useful physical activity" (p. 88). Thompson continues, "The one study indicating that verbal comprehension and reasoning were negligibly correlated with speaking effectiveness for women raises the interesting question: If female persuasiveness is not dependent on reasoning, what are its constituents?" (p. 88). Later, Thompson reports on sex differences in stage fright. Three studies found that male public speakers report more self-confidence and less fear than female public speakers. These were self-reports; judges, however, observed stage fright more in men than in women (e.g., the findings that men are more fidgety as public speakers). One study reported that men were more fidgety, unintegrated, and had poorer sentences and poorer articulation as public speakers. In another section, Thompson generalizes about the sexes as listeners: (1) As listeners, "women may be more persuasible than men"; "the range of topics and situations producing greater persuasibility for females is impressive, and in no study published in the speech literature were the men more impressionable" (pp. 45-46). (2) As listeners, women are "more responsive, perceptive, flexible, impressionable, and teachable than men" (p. 47). The studies cited include one that found that in learning a new language, boys were less able to make articulatory coordinations; another concluded that women were more accurate than men in identifying emotion portrayed nonverbally by two different instructors; a third found that women were more sensitive to nonverbal communication through tones. (3) "College men may retain more from an oral presentation than college women" (p. 48), based, for example, on a study comparing scores of men and women on a multiple choice retention test. Thompson acknowledges that the data are not clear-cut: there are 5 studies, with women scoring higher than men in one of them, and nonsignificant differences in 2. (4) "Men and women do not differ significantly in their responses to communication when the emotional involvement is minimal" (p. 49), based on 6 diverse studies (e.g., one finding that sex was not a factor in ratings of voice quality, personality, and teaching effectiveness;

another finding that the sexes did not differ in ability to choose the best reason in support of a conclusion). The author further concludes (without really clarifying the terms used); "The boundary between areas of significant and nonsignificant sex differences seems clear. In those matters in which perceptiveness, flexibility, and emotional responsiveness are of primary importance, a difference exists; in those requiring deliberate judgment, there is no difference" (p. 50). [*There is a literature, not included in this bibliography, on sex differences in persuasability of listeners, and on the credibility which audiences grant male vs. female speakers; this reference is a lead into some of that literature.*]

WINITZ, HARRIS.
    "Language Skills of Male and Female Kindergarten Children." *Journal of Speech and Hearing Research,* 2 (1959), 377-386.

Although previous investigations have generally shown girls to be superior to boys on several language skills (Winitz cites 7 studies), the differences have been small and rarely significant, and other studies have contradicted the findings. A table summarizes the findings on 6 common measures, from 9 studies with a total of 124 tests: the differences favor girls almost two to one, though they are seldom significant (6 out of 7 significant differences favor girls, however). In many studies IQ and socioeconomic status have been uncontrolled and there are suggestions of boy-girl differences in them. Winitz's aim is to conduct language measures on equivalent and fairly large populations of boys and girls, to determine whether previous findings of female superiority are real or due to chance. The subjects were 75 girls and 75 boys—white, urban, nonstutterers of normal IQ and hearing—about to enter kindergarten in the Iowa City area, proportionately sampled from all kindergartens in the system. Measures of intelligence, socioeconomic status, and family constellation (older or younger siblings, both, or none) shows the two sex groups to be essentially equivalent on nonlanguage measures. On 6 measures of verbalization, elicited by stimulus pictures, girls were significantly superior in two (mean of longest responses, mean standard deviation); all differences in the other measures (response length, one-word responses, number of different words, structural complexity) also showed (nonsignificant) superior performance by girls. Girls were also significantly superior in one test of fluency, giving child names. On the other fluency measures (giving rhymes, adult names, and thing names) and on measures of articulation and vocabulary there were no significant differences, boys and girls showing superiority about equally. Winitz concludes that "the hypothesis of no language difference between the sexes is tenable in the population of five-year-old children with regard to major verbalization measures, articulatory skills, vocabulary skills, and three of four word-fluency measures." The differences in verbalization were not significant in the measures "generally regarded as of major importance," i.e., response length, structural complexity, and number of different words. "Female superiority in naming children may be the result of the tendency for girls to be more sociable than boys." He takes up but dismisses the possibility that a reason for not obtaining significant differences was that the examiner was male. [*Interestingly enough, the authors of all (8) studies cited as finding female superiority are female (one study had four female authors!). Of the two cited finding male superiority, one was co-authored by a male and female; the*

other was specifically mentioned as having used three male investigators out of ten.] Child
development has been primarily a women's field, and was especially so in the days of these
studies.

B. Fluency

BROWNELL, WINIFRED, and DENNIS R. SMITH.
    "Communication Patterns, Sex, and Length of Verbalization in Speech of
    Four-Year-Old Children." *Speech Monographs,* 40 (1973), 310-316.

This is an experimental study of 79 four-year-old children (half of each sex) in six Head
Start centers. The children were shown objects and asked to name them, to indicate which
of the objects go together, and to tell why. The independent variables were communication
pattern (dyad; triad; role-playing triad; small group) and sex. The dependent variables were
mean length of verbalization and mean length of verbalization minus repetitions. The
findings: a greater amount of speech was elicited in the small group situation than in the
dyad. "Females produced significantly more speech across all conditions than did males.
This evidence confirms earlier reports of female linguistic superiority in samples of white,
middle-class children." [*See IV-D.*]

CHERRY, LOUISE.
    "Teacher-Child Verbal Interaction: An Approach to the Study of Sex Differences."
    In Barrie Thorne and Nancy Henley, eds., *Language and Sex: Difference and*
    Dominance. Rowley, Mass.: Newbury House, 1975.

A finding of superior verbal fluency in females has been reported as one of the most
consistent and stable psychological sex differences to be found. Cherry examines the bases
for this claim (with reference to preschool children), with a critique of the methodology and
assumptions of the naturalistic observational studies cited, and reports her own research on
teacher-child dyadic verbal interaction. Previous studies often transformed the raw data
(e.g., omitting "meaningless vocalizations"), and depended on hand transcription, leaving
the possibility that the observers' preconceptions biased their transcriptions. There has
further been an assumption that verbal fluency is a characteristic of an individual speaker,
whereas it is better conceptualized as a part of verbal interaction between two or more
speakers. Cherry recorded spontaneously occurring conversations among four female
preschool teachers and their 38 children (16 F, 22 M) in the Boston area and looked at,
among other factors, fluency as an interactive variable. She failed to find greater fluency
(measured either by utterances or by turns per interaction) in teacher-girl interactions than
in teacher-boy ones. [*See VII.*]

GALL, MEREDITH D., AMOS K. HOBBY, and KENNETH H. CRAIK.
    "Non-Linguistic Factors in Oral Language Productivity." *Perceptual and Motor Skills,*
    29 (1969), 871-874.

This study provides evidence that women are more verbally fluent than men: "women
attained a higher mean word count than men in eight of nine descriptions of verbal displays.
On three of the comparisons, the sex differences are statistically significant." Correlating

word count scores with personality variables as assessed by the California Psychological Inventory, the authors found that, for women, verbal fluency had a negative correlation with "good impression"; but for men, the correlation was consistently positive.

GARAI, JOSEF E., and AMRAM SCHEINFELD.
  "Sex Differences in Mental and Behavioral Traits." *Genetic Psychology Monographs,*
  77 (1968), 169-299.

Females have been reported to possess greater verbal fluency than males from infancy on. Earlier maturation of the speech organs leads to the widely observed earlier age of speech onset of girls. Girls have been observed to show greater verbal fluency from 12 months on with the beginning of articulate speech, throughout the preschool period, throughout elementary school, and in high school and college. From 18 months on, girls made fewer grammatical errors than boys; in sentence complexity, girls surpass boys at all ages from 18 months on, and were also ahead of boys in sentence length from 18 months. Girls have been reported to have better articulation than boys, and speech defects of all kinds are more prevalent in boys. [*See VIII-A, VIII-C.*]

HIRSCHMAN, LYNETTE.
  "Analysis of Supportive and Assertive Behavior in Conversations." Paper presented at
  meeting of Linguistic Society of America, July, 1974.

Probing sex differences in conversational assertiveness and supportiveness, Hirschman had pairs of subjects discuss a question for ten minutes (the resulting conversations included four single-sex, and eight mixed-sex). It was assumed that fluency would be related to assertiveness. Fluency was measured by absence of fillers *(uhm, well, like, you know)* and ratio of clauses finished to clauses started. There were no statistically significant sex differences in these dimensions. [*See II-A, IV-A, IV-D.*]

C. Speech Disturbances

GARAI, JOSEF E., and AMRAM SCHEINFELD.
  "Sex Differences in Mental and Behavioral Traits." *Genetic Psychology Monographs,*
  77 (1968), 169-299.

Many studies report females to have superior language abilities of various sorts. Girls have better articulation than boys, and all speech disturbances, such as stuttering or poor articulation, aphasia and dyslexia, are much more frequent among males of all ages. Various reasons explaining female superiority are suggested; it may be that genetic factors produce more speech defects in boys. [*See VIII-A, VIII-B.*]

KRAMER, CHERIS.
  "Women's Speech: Separate But Unequal?" *Quarterly Journal of Speech,* 60 (Feb., 1974), 14-24. Reprinted in Barrie Thorne and Nancy Henley, *Language and Sex: Difference and Dominance.* Rowley, Mass.: Newbury House, 1975.

  In the literature on the ratio of male to female stutterers, there is general agreement that there are more male stutterers than female. But there is disagreement about biological vs. social causes. Some scholars claim stuttering is a hereditary trait, but "recent studies indicate that a male is more likely to stutter than a female because our culture places more importance on speech fluency in males than speech fluency in females. There is more pressure to speak well, and consequently the male feels more insecurity about his speech" (p. 6). (She cites Ronald Goldman, "Cultural Influences on the Sex Ratio in the Incidence of Stuttering," *American Anthropologist,* 69 [1967], 78-81.) [*See I, II-B, III-A, III-B-2, IV-A, IV-C.*]

McCARTHY, DOROTHEA.
  "Some Possible Explanations of Sex Differences in Language Development and Disorders." *Journal of Psychology,* 35 (1953), 155-160.

  There are small but important differences favoring girls, in "practically all aspects of language development which show developmental trends with age" among white American children, from the age of onset of true language. Boys more frequently suffer language disorders, particularly stuttering and reading disabilities; perhaps 65-100% of such disorders occur among boys. The differences appear at such an early age that their roots must be in early infancy, and there are enough environmental differences that genetic ones need not be postulated. (1) The early home environment is more satisfying to the girl infant, who can identify with and imitate the mother's speech, than to the boy, who needs to identify with and imitate the father's speech. Echo-reaction in girls will be closer to mother's speech, in any case, than boys' will be to father's speech, since the father's voice is much deeper. This stage, then, will be less satisfying for boys, even confusing, perhaps fear-producing. (2) If girls are as much preferred as natural children as they are as adoptive ones, they are more welcomed in the family and treated with more warmth. Boys suffering from insecurity and rejection in the home may be prone to later language disorders. (3) Sex role prescriptions separate boys from adult linguistic skills—they are sent outside to play, are not in as close range to the mother as girls. They hear less adult speech, and get less practice, both for this reason and because of the dissatisfaction (above) associated with echo-reaction. Girls not only have these advantages, but their typical toys have "high conversation value" and, in echoing the mother, they are likely to stimulate more conversation from her, and enter into a conversational relationship. Girls with language disorders always have a severely disturbed relationship with the mother. Boys' problems with language are intensified on entering school where a woman teacher, identified with the mother, awaits and pressures abound around language skills and competition with girls. [*See VIII-A.*]

IX. NONVERBAL ASPECTS OF COMMUNICATION

Findings of sex differences in nonverbal communication, in the literature of the several disciplines that investigate it, are not uncommon. However, they've largely been simply reported and left unexplored. Most of the articles cited below are ones that have focused in some way on sex differences, either through original research or theory, or through reviewing others' research. The subsections use some of the more common categories for dividing up the field, but it should be noted that this section might have many of the same divisions of the portion on language and speech. For instance, general ability in nonverbal communication, women's and men's nonverbal languages, and nonverbal conversational patterns are all possible topics at this stage of our knowledge, though the section concentrates on the nonverbal equivalent of "sex differences in word choice, syntactic usage, and language style" (section II-B). With further advances in research and theory, future topics could be the sexism in the nonverbal gesture system (e.g., the female-excluding handshake, obscene gestures), nonverbal language acquisition, nonverbal aspects of multilingual situations, and so on.

A. Comprehensive Sources

BIRDWHISTELL, RAY.
> "Masculinity and Femininity as Display." In *Kinesics and Context*. Philadelphia: Univ. of Pennsylvania Press, 1970, pp. 39-46.

Birdwhistell begins with a discussion of gender behavior, noting an increasing realization that "intragender and intergender behavior throughout the animal kingdom is not simply a response to instinctual mechanisms but is shaped, structured, and released both by the ontogenetic experience of the participating organisms and by the patterned circumstances of the relevant environment." When different animal species are rated on a spectrum by the extent of their sexual dimorphism, on the basis of secondary sexual characteristics human beings are relatively close to the unimorphic end. Such "weakly dimorphic species necessarily organize much of gender display and recognition at the level of position, movement, and expression." Informants from seven different societies could distinguish male movement from female movement, and interpreted the differences as instinctually and biologically based. Birdwhistell discusses "inappropriate" gender display, behavior in context (and the absence of any single message indicative of homosexuality), gender display in relation to division of labor, and the learning of gender display by the young in an age of rapid social change. [*See IX-D, IX-F.*]

FRIEZE, IRENE HANSON.
> "Nonverbal Aspects of Femininity and Masculinity Which Perpetuate Sex-Role Stereotypes." Paper presented at Eastern Psychological Association, 1974. (Frieze is at Dept. of Psychology, Univ. of Pittsburgh.)

Certain nonverbal behaviors are associated with dominance and status, others with liking and warmth; the same behaviors also differentiate men and women, in ways that perpetuate sex-role stereotypes. That is, males display more dominance and high status cues, and females indicate greater emotional warmth nonverbally. A behavior associated with dominance and high status, and with males, is control of greater territory and personal space, including a greater tendency to touch. Nonverbal behaviors associated with liking or warmth are also associated with women, and with lower status, suggesting that women's characteristic warmth and expressiveness are necessitated by their submissive roles. Higher status individuals show less direct eye contact, while women show more social eye contact. Women smile more than men; if the smiling is for other purposes than happiness or greetings, it would be another example of communication of low status. Women's greater receptivity to others' nonverbal cues, while supporting the stereotype of greater emotional warmth, may be necessary for their survival, as with other low status groups (blacks have been shown to be better than whites at interpreting others' nonverbal signals). "Clearly women communicate low status and submission, often unconsciously, through their use of 'feminine' nonverbal cues. Such behavior, although quite possibly caused originally by their lower status in our society, also serves to perpetuate sex-role stereotypes and lower status for women." The behaviors are difficult to confront since they are largely unconsciously emitted and interpreted. Women who are conscious of them are put in the position of having to choose between "feminine" and assertive behavior [*on this point, see also references to Lakoff, especially V*]. [*See IX-C.*]

HENLEY, NANCY M.
    "Power, Sex, and Nonverbal Communication." *Berkeley Journal of Sociology,* 18 (1973-74), 1-26. Reprinted in Barrie Thorne and Nancy Henley, *Language and Sex: Difference and Dominance.* Rowley, Mass.: Newbury House, 1975.

The minutiae of everyday life (e.g., personal space, eye contact, touching, interrupting) are examined in the context of their contribution to social control, as micropolitical acts serving to maintain and perpetuate hierarchical social structure and to intimidate those who would change it. Women are particularly affected by subtle verbal and nonverbal cues because of their socialization to docility, their physical integration around centers of power, and their greater sensitivity to nonverbal communication. Much nonverbal behavior is not innate but culturally learned and designed to emphasize sex differences. Some 30 studies, both empirical and analytical, using both observational and experimental techniques, are reviewed, as well as a number of essays, to support and illustrate the discussion. Sex differences in language usage tend to put women at a disadvantage; there is also misogyny in much linguistic convention. Men talk more and probably interrupt more. There are sex and status differences in self-disclosure, and status differences in terms of address, the structure of which serves as a model for discussion of several nonverbal behaviors. In the nonverbal realm all the following are associated with higher status and with men: freedom of demeanor, greater personal space, freedom to touch others, staring, and withholding of personal information (particularly about emotions). Men's greater touching of women cannot be explained by sexual attraction, because that explanation would require women to touch men equally. Touch is analogous to the use of first name: used reciprocally, it indicates intimacy; nonreciprocally, it indicates status. Staring, pointing, touching, and interrupting are dominance gestures; lowering or averting the eyes, hesitating or stopping action or speech, cuddling to the touch, allowing interruption, and smiling are submission gestures, all more common to women than to men. There is a pattern of reaction to women's appropriation of the correlates of status (male gestures) which attributes them to sexual invitation. Many of these gestures, e.g., touching, staring, proximity, and relaxed demeanor, have a dual nature in that they are used between intimates, and therefore lend themselves well to sexual interpretation that denies women's assertion of power. Though manipulating these status cues will not change fundamental power relationships in the society, knowledge of them will raise consciousness and help people change those relationships.

HENLEY, NANCY, and JO FREEMAN.
"The Sexual Politics of Interpersonal Behavior." In Jo Freeman, ed., *Women: A Feminist Perspective.* Palo Alto, Ca.: Mayfield, 1975.

This paper covers much of the same ground as "The Politics of Touch" (*see IX-E*) and "Power, Sex, and Nonverbal Communication" (above), in a less academic vein than the latter, with more detailed attention to the nitty gritty. Topics are: the sexist environment, initiation of sexual activity, demeanor, posture, clothing, self-disclosure, caring, personal space, touching, eye contact, verbal dominance, gestures of dominance and submission, language, and interpretation of women's violation of sex status norms.

JOHNSON, KENNETH R.
"Black Kinesics—Some Nonverbal Communication Patterns in the Black Culture." *Florida FL Reporter,* Spring/Fall, 1971, 17-20+.

The existence of Black English has been conclusively demonstrated and described, and it can be expected that nonverbal communication patterns in the black culture also differ from those in the dominant culture. Black dialect is believed to have been influenced by the former African languages of black speakers; similarly, black nonverbal communication patterns may be related to African origins, as well as to blacks' isolation from the dominant culture. Differences in eye behavior and posture are described in detail to illustrate Black-white differences, and male-female differences among blacks, particularly in encounters with authority or in courtship. [*See IX-D, IX-F.*]

MEHRABIAN, ALBERT.
Nonverbal Communication. Chicago: Aldine Atherton, 1972.

This book is a review of the extensive research of Mehrabian and his associates in identifying, describing, and classifying variables in nonverbal behavior. "Some of the most consistent findings about individual differences in implicit communication," he writes, "were related to sex differences" (p. 133), and he reports on these findings repeatedly in the book. He develops a three-dimensional framework which has the major factors of positiveness, potency (including dominance-submissiveness and status), and responsiveness, and interprets most of the findings relative to women in terms of the positiveness factor, relating them to other findings of greater affiliation and approval-seeking in females. Females are also seen to be more submissive in their nonverbal behaviors. [*See also IX-B, C, D, F, G.*]

O'CONNOR, LYNN.
   "Male Dominance: The Nitty-Gritty of Oppression." *It Ain't Me Babe,* June 11-July
   1, 1970, 9-11. Part of her essay, "Male Supremacy," reprint available from KNOW,
   Inc., P.O. Box 86031, Pittsburgh, Pa. 15221.

   O'Connor compares animal gestures of dominance and submission with gestures between
men and women, e.g., the direct stare, "presenting," effects of physical features. Submission
in women is conveyed by averting the eyes, lowering or turning the head, smiling. "Charm is
nothing more than a series of gestures (including vocalizations) indicating submission."
Dominance gestures used by women result in several outcomes: re-establishment of control
(through the use of depression or neuroticism) by the "submissive" man, heavy taming
campaigns by aggressive men (through tyranny or temporary admiration), labelling as
bitches and shrews, loss of job (domestic or paid), and general punishment. This analysis is
presented in the context of male supremacy in society, which establishes the economic
dependency of women on men and provides the backdrop against which the nitty-gritty of
oppression occurs in the one-to-one relationship.

B. General Nonverbal Behavior

MEHRABIAN, ALBERT.
   Nonverbal Communication. Chicago: Aldine Atherton, 1972.

   In an experiment where subjects were observed while waiting with a stranger of the same
sex, females were seen to be more affiliative (a composite measure), intimate (involving both
body orientation and distance) and submissive (judged from body relaxation) (p. 154). In
the matter of general ability in nonverbal communication, Mehrabian cites two studies that
found no sex differences in ability to encode or decode moods (pp. 136-137). He reports his
own study in which females were better able to convey and to interpret variations in
like/dislike than males were. Male encoders were better able to communicate positive
attitudes, and females were better at negative attitudes. A person's ability to communicate
variations in negative attitude largely accounted for overall attitude-communicating ability;
Mehrabian points out that our culture discourages explicit verbalization of negative feelings,
thus the greater importance of the "implicit" channels of communication to express them.
Furthermore, females' better encoding ability with negative attitudes is explained by males'
"greater latitude to express negative feelings explicitly" (pp. 141-146). [*See IX-A, C, D, F,
G.*]

ROSENTHAL, ROBERT, DANE ARCHER, JUDITH H. KOIVUMAKI, M. ROBIN
DiMATTEO, and PETER L. ROGERS.
   "Assessing Sensitivity to Nonverbal Communication: the PONS Test." *Division 8
   Newsletter* of the Division of Personality and Social Psychology of the American
   Psychological Association, January, 1974, 1-3. See also "Body Talk and Tone of
   Voice: the Language Without Words." *Psychology Today,* 1974 (Sept.), 8, No. 4,
   64-68.

   This is a continuation of the research by Rosenthal and his associates on effects of
experimenters' expectations on subjects' responses (and teachers' expectations on students'

performance), focussing more recently on nonverbal cues as the link between expectation and response. To develop a measure of nonverbal sensitivity (PONS = Profile of Nonverbal Sensitivity), they made film clips of 220 segments of acted-out performances. There were 20 different scenarios, with variations on the positive/negative affect dimension and the submissive/dominant dimension. The film visual portion showed face, torso, both, or neither (auditory portion only). The audio track was manipulated so that subjects heard no sound, or heard either randomly scrambled voice (acoustical properties retained) or content-filtered voice (acoustical properties and intonation patterns retained) with each of the four visual conditions. Subjects who saw and/or heard the film clips were asked to choose the best description of the scene portrayed, and were judged for their "accuracy" in matching the intent of the actor. These early findings report on nearly 100 samples of subjects from North America, Europe, the Middle East, Australia, New Guinea, and East Asia, varying widely in age, education, cultural background, professional training, and mental health. In 75-80% of the samples, females performed slightly better than males. Female superiority held at all seven grade levels tested (from grade five through college), though the difference decreased with age. (The original film clips were made with a female actor, but when a partial version of the test was made with a male actor, female subjects still performed better). Among Americans, subjects were inaccurate at estimating their own PONS scores, though their spouses were fairly accurate at judging their (the subjects') sensitivity. In one group of teachers it was found that those more sensitive to nonverbal communication scored as less authoritarian and more democratic in teaching orientation, on another scale. Females were relatively better than males at interpreting negative affect; Rosenthal, et al. acknowledge that this superiority "may have had survival value." (It's also interesting to note that subjects retained 68% accuracy even when the film was speeded up to 1/24 of a second, indicating the extreme alertness with which people respond to nonverbal cues.)

WEITZ, SHIRLEY.
    "Sex Role Attitudes and Nonverbal Communication in Same and Opposite-Sex Interactions." Paper presented at American Psychological Association, 1974.

    Videotapes were made of 24 dyadic interactions of same- and mixed-sex pairs, cameras focused on the full body of each interactant separately. The subjects also filled out scales measuring sex role attitudes, dominance, and affiliation. The first minute of each interaction was analyzed for interpersonal warmth and dominance, without sound and without knowledge of the other in the dyad, by ten raters, and correlated with the attitude scales and sex of subject and of partner. Liberalism in sex role attitudes was significantly correlated with rated nonverbal warmth for men in both same-sex and opposite-sex interaction, i.e., men with liberal sex role attitudes were seen as warmer nonverbally, with both men and women, compared with men with conservative attitudes. (Women's nonverbal warmth was not significantly related to sex role attitudes, though Weitz reports a nonsignificant negative correlation between females' nonverbal warmth and liberalism in sex role attitudes, in same-sex interaction.) The rated nonverbal dominance for females was significantly negatively related to male dominance scale scores and rated female nonverbal warmth was significantly negatively related to male affiliation scores. Weitz suggests "a monitoring mechanism by which women adjust their nonverbal responses to the personality of the male in the interaction," creating "an equilibrium in the interaction which would result in maximum interpersonal comfort (especially for the male)." There was no significant relationship between females' nonverbal behavior and *female* partner scale scores, nor between male nonverbal ratings and partner scale scores. Females elicited warmer nonverbal responses from partners of either sex than did males, but women's nonverbal behavior was not rated as warmer than men's, contradicting earlier findings. Weitz emphasizes that these findings are from the first minute of interaction, and the dynamics of later interaction may reveal a different pattern; but the findings do present "a considerably more complex picture of sex differences in nonverbal communication than previous work which relied on the dominance=male, affiliation=female equation."

C. Use of Space

FRIEZE, IRENE HANSON.
    "Nonverbal Aspects of Femininity and Masculinity Which Perpetuate Sex-Role Stereotypes." Paper presented at Eastern Psychological Association, 1974. (Frieze is at Dept. of Psychology, Univ. of Pittsburgh.)

Control of greater territory and personal space is a behavior associated with dominance and high status, and with males (and exhibits a similar pattern in animals). One study reports that women are less likely to have a special and unviolated room in the home, others show that people tend to stand closer to women than to men, or to disturb women's path in crossing a street. Frieze also suggests that fathers often have a "special chair," and that men take up disproportionately more space than women in a double bed. Touching is another violation of personal space; women tend to be touched more, and men to do more touching [See IX-E]. Since these space relationships are associated with both status and sex, "controlled studies are needed to test the proposition that even when occupational status is controlled for, women occupy smaller and/or less desirable space." [See IX-A.]

LOTT, DALE F., and ROBERT SOMMER.
    "Seating Arrangements and Status." *Journal of Personality and Social Psychology,* 7 (1967), 90-95.

This article reports four studies, three questionnaire and one experimental, of how a subject would locate her/himself with regard to a person of higher, lower, or equal status, and of either sex. The first two studies, having 224 male and female university students (exact numbers for each sex not controlled, and not reported), reported significant sex differences. Both studies, in which paper-and-pencil diagrams of rectangular tables were used, showed a clear association of the "head" position (either extreme) with the higher status figure. When subjects designated the seat they would take on arriving first, and the seat the other would then take, "Approximately twice as many females as males sat side by side, and this is more frequent vis-à-vis a low-status than a high-status person." When subjects were asked to name the seat the other would take on arriving first, they tended to place all others at an "end" (of long side) chair, and this tendency was significantly greater for a high-status *male* authority figure. The authors further report: "It is also interesting that 37 subjects chose the head chair for themselves vis-à-vis Professor Susan Smith while half that number chose it vis-à-vis Professor Henry Smith."

MEHRABIAN, ALBERT.
Nonverbal Communication. Chicago: Aldine Atherton, 1972.

Mehrabian cites studies with the findings that females assume closer positions to others than males do; that female pairs take closer positions to each other than male pairs do; and that others assume closer positions to females than to males (all these are interpreted as females' expression of positive attitudes, and others' reciprocation of them) (pp. 133-134). Another study found male/female pairs to sit closest, then female/female, then male/male (pp. 20-21). [*See IX-A, B, D, F, G.*]

PIERCY, MARGE.
Small Changes. New York: Doubleday, 1973.

In this novel, a female character is teaching movement to a theater group: "Wanda made them aware how they moved, how they rested, how they occupied space. She demonstrated how men sat and how women sat on the subway, on benches. Men expanded   into available space. They sprawled, or they sat with spread legs. They put their arms on the arms of chairs. They crossed their legs by putting a foot on the other knee. They dominated space expansively. Women condensed. Women crossed their legs by putting one leg over the other and alongside. Women kept their elbows to their sides, taking up as little space as possible. They behaved as if it were their duty not to rub against, not to touch, not to bump a man. If contact occurred, the woman shrank back. If a woman bumped a man, he might choose to interpret it as a come-on. Women sat protectively using elbows not to dominate space, not to mark territory, but to protect their soft tissues." (p. 438).

SILVEIRA, JEANETTE.
"Thoughts on the Politics of Touch." *Women's Press* (Eugene, Ore.), 1 (Feb., 1972), 13.

Silveira observes that women are expected to walk around men in passing on the street, and reports an observational study that supports it: in 12 out of 19 man-woman pairs approaching each other on the street, women moved out of men's way (in four cases both moved, and in three the man moved). She comments on touching and smiling, and discusses the importance of changing power signals between men and women. [*See IX-G.*]

WILLIS, FRANK N., JR.
"Initial Speaking Distance as a Function of the Speakers' Relationship." *Psychonomic Science,* 5 (1966), 221-222.

Forty experimenters (members of a course) carried tape measures and, when approached by anyone, remained still and measured the inter-nose distance when the approacher began speaking. Sex of the listener-experimenter was found to be the most influential variable: women were approached more closely than men, by both men and women. Relationship of the two (stranger, acquaintance, etc.) had different effects on the different-sex approachers: "women stand quite close to good friends when speaking but stand back from . . . friends." Women speakers approached closest to close friends, next closest to acquaintances, and stood farthest from friends, while men stood closest to friends and about equally distant from acquaintances and close friends.

D. Posture and Movement

ANONYMOUS.
"Exercises for Men." *Willamette Bridge* (date unknown). Reprinted in *Radical Therapist,* 1, No. 5 (1971), 15.

This is a short six-point piece, with illustrations, detailing some of the awkwardness of the prescribed public postures allowed to women: (1) "Sit down in a straight chair. Cross your legs at the ankles and keep your knees pressed together . . . " (2) "Bend down to pick up an object from the floor. Each time you bend remember to bend your knees so that your rear end doesn't stick up, and place one hand on your shirtfront to hold it to your chest. . . . " (3) "Run a short distance, keeping your knees together. You'll find you have to take short, high steps . . . " (4) "Sit comfortably on the floor. . . . Arrange your legs so that no one can see [your underwear]. Sit like this for a long time without changing position." (5) "Walk down a city street . . . Look straight ahead. Every time a man walks past you, avert your eyes and make your face expressionless. . . . " (6) "Walk around with your stomach pulled in tight, your shoulders thrown back, and your chest out. . . . Try to speak loudly and aggressively in this posture."

BIRDWHISTELL, RAY.
"Masculinity and Femininity as Display." In *Kinesics and Context.* Philadelphia: Univ. of Pennsylvania Press, 1970, pp. 39-46.

Birdwhistell gives some American examples of leg angle and arm-body angle, pelvic angle (roll) and facial expression. American females "when sending gender signals and/or as a reciprocal to male gender signals" bring the legs together; males typically separate the legs by a 10-15 degree angle. Female gender presentation has the upper arms close to the trunk, while male gender presentation moves the arms 5-10 degrees away from the body. Females may present the entire body from neck to ankles as a moving whole, whereas the male moves the arms independent of the trunk, and may subtly wag his hips. The male tends to carry his pelvis rolled slightly back, the female, slightly forward. [*See IX-A, IX-F.*]

JOHNSON, KENNETH R.
"Black Kinesics—Some Nonverbal Communication Patterns in the Black Culture." *Florida FL Reporter,* Spring/Fall, 1971, 17-20+.

The "black walk" of young black males—a slow stroll, casual and rhythmic, head slightly elevated and tipped to the side, one arm swinging with hand slightly cupped, the other arm limp or tucked in the pocket, thumb out—communicates the message of masculine authority (as does the young white males's walk). With the added message that "the young black male is beautiful," it beckons female attention to his sexual prowess, and communicates that he is "cool." In dealing with authority, when it's used in walking away from a reprimand it indicates the reprimand has been rejected. Young black females communicate rejection of authority by pivoting quickly on both feet, sometimes with a raising of the head and twitching of the nose, and walking briskly away. In courting, black males use a "rapping stance" which is a kind of stationary form of the "black walk"—at a slight angle to the female, head slightly elevated and tipped toward the female, eyes about ¾ open, weight of the body on the back heel, and arms as in the black walk. (The young white male rapping stance backs the female up against the wall, the YWM leaning toward her, one palm against the wall for support, and all his weight on the foot closest to the female; "sometimes, both arms are extended to support his weight, thus trapping the female between his two extended arms.") The young black female listens to the black male's rap nonchalantly, hand on hip. This stance in any situation communicates intense involvement, and in situations other than courtship communicates hostility and negative feelings toward the speaker. It is the black female's most aggressive stance, and is characterized by feet placed firmly in a stationary step, weight on the rear heel, buttocks protruded, one hand on the extended hip with fingers spread or in a fist. It may be accompanied by a slow rock, rolling the eyes, and twitching the nose. Chicano females communicate the same message with both hands on hips, feet spread wide, head slightly raised. [See IX-A, IX-F.]

MEHRABIAN, ALBERT.
    Nonverbal Communication. Chicago: Aldine Atherton, 1972.

Female communicators have more immediate orientation to the addressee than male communicators do (pp. 28, 65, 81); females oriented to face a liked addressee more directly than a disliked one, though males did the reverse when feelings were intense (p. 55). Males assumed more symmetric leg positions and more reclining positions, and had higher leg and foot movement rates than females (pp. 69-70). For females, but not males, a decrease in the trunk-swivel rate correlated with persuasiveness (p. 68). Males are generally more relaxed than females (pp. 14, 134), and communicators are more relaxed with females than with males (as communicators also are more relaxed with lower status addressees) (pp. 27-28). Females are said to "convey more submissive attitudes by characteristically assuming less relaxed postures in social situations" (p. 30). Males showed less body relaxation and greater vigilance toward an intensely disliked male addressee than did females (to the same), a finding Mehrabian attributes to the greater threat posed to the males (p. 101). [See IX-A, B, C, F, G.]

MEHRABIAN, ALBERT, and JOHN T. FRIAR.
    "Encoding of Attitude By a Seated Communicator Via Posture and Position Cues."
    Journal of Consulting and Clinical Psychology, 33 (1969), 330-336.

Subjects (24M, 24F) were asked to imagine themselves in situations involving different kinds of addressees (liked/disliked, higher/lower status, male/female), and to sit in ways in which they would if they were actually interacting with them. The most important variables for the communication of positive attitude were found to be small backward lean of torso, close distance, and more eye contact; there was less sideways lean and more eye contact in communications with high-status addressees; and for females, less arm openness is an indicator of higher status of the addressee. Orientation: Both male and female subjects oriented farther away from an addressee of the opposite sex; females' leg orientation was farther from the addressee than was males'. Openness: Females showed less arm openness to high-status addressees than to low-status ones (males didn't differentiate); the mean degree of leg openness of male encoders was greater than that of female encoders. Relaxation: Torso lean was more backward for disliked addressees than for liked, and torso lean of male subjects was farther back than that of females.

E. Touching

HENLEY, NANCY M.
   "The Politics of Touch." Paper presented at American Psychological Association, 1970. In Phil Brown, ed., *Radical Psychology*. New York: Harper & Row, 1973, pp. 421-433. Reprint available from KNOW, Inc., P.O. Box 86031, Pittsburgh, Pa. 15221.

Women are constantly kept in their place by many "little" reminders of their inferior status: the sexist environment, language, nonverbal communication. Verbal putdowns to halt a woman in intellectual discussion or anger are disguised as humor or compliments; veiled physical threats are similarly disguised. Anecdotal and descriptive analysis are offered suggesting that touching is a gesture of dominance often used by males on females. An observational study was made of who initiated touch among people in public: men touched women much more than vice versa, and touch between men and between women was about equal. That touch is a status sign is supported by findings that persons of higher socio-economic status more often touched those of lower status, and older persons more often touched younger, than vice versa. The few psychological studies that have been made on touch report females being touched more than males. The hypothesis that men's touching is sexually motivated is discussed and rejected. Touch has a dual nature (as do other behaviors, such as calling someone by first name) in that it can be used to indicate intimacy (in mutual usage) or status (nonmutual usage, toucher has higher status). Women's initiation of touching is often interpreted as a sexual advance. Men should guard against using touch to assert authority, especially with women, and change their reactions to being touched by women; women should refuse influence by touch, and become more assertive tactually when appropriate, though these actions themselves will not change the basic male chauvinist nature of male-female interaction.

HENLEY, NANCY M.
   "Status and Sex: Some Touching Observations." *Bulletin of the Psychonomic Society*, 2 (1973), 91-93.

This is a straighter version, with additional data, of "The Politics of Touch" (above). Among same-age white adults, women's *non*reciprocation of men's touch was significantly greater than men's nonreciprocation of women's, and nonreciprocation by younger persons of the touch of older ones was significantly greater. When public settings were categorized as either indoor or outdoor, the sex differences in touching showed up more clearly in the outdoor settings, with little difference indoors.

JOURARD, SIDNEY M.
   "An Exploratory Study of Body-Accessibility." *British Journal of Social and Clinical Psychology*, 5 (1966), 221-231.

A body-accessibility questionnaire was given to over 300 male and female unmarried students, asking what areas of the body were seen and/or touched by parents and closest friends of each sex, and what areas of the body of parents and friends the respondents saw and/or touched. Males reportedly touched fewer regions of their mothers' bodies than were touched by their mothers, and were not touched by mothers on as many regions as were females. Females exchanged physical contact on more areas of the body with their fathers than did males. The degree of accessibility of the different regions of the body was similar for the two sexes. Intercorrelations among the respondents' being-touched scores for different regions were higher for females than males, suggesting either more consistency about body accessibility, or "less discrimination . . . in accepting or spurning the extended hand of others."

JOURARD, SIDNEY, M., and JANE E. RUBIN.
    "Self-Disclosure and Touching: A Study of Two Modes of Interpersonal Encounter and Their Inter-Relation." *Journal of Humanistic Psychology,* 8 (1968), 39-48.

A body-contact questionnaire (see above) and self-disclosure questionnaire were given to 84 female and 54 male unmarried students, asking about parents, same-sex, and opposite-sex friends. Women and men showed similar patterns for physical contact except in relation to their fathers, whom the women touch more and are touched more by than the men. Women's mean total being-touched score was higher than men's. For women, opposite-sex friend reportedly touched them the most, but for the men, opposite-sex friend touched the least of the four target persons.

MONTAGU, ASHLEY.
    Touching: The Human Significance of the Skin. New York: Columbia Univ. Press, 1971. (New York, Harper & Row, 1972.)

"Sexual differences in cutaneous behavior," writes Montagu, "are very marked in probably all cultures" (p. 241). He states that females are "more apt to indulge in every sort of delicate tactile behavior than males," are more sensitive to tactile properties of objects, do more fondling and caressing, and are more gentle in approach on every level. "Backslapping and handshake crushing are specifically masculine forms of behavior," he (needlessly) informs us (p. 241).

TUAN, N.D., RICHARD HESLIN, and MICHELE L. NGUYEN.
    "The Meaning of Four Modes of Touch as a Function of Sex and Body Area." Available from Richard Heslin, Department of Psychological Sciences, Purdue University, W. Lafayette, IN 47907.

In this questionnaire study, students rated their agreement that certain meanings could be attributed to touch applied to certain areas of the body. The possible meanings assigned were playfulness, warmth/love, friendship/fellowship, sexual desire, and pleasantness. The touch modalities were pat, stroke, squeeze, or brush. The subjects, 41 male and 40 female unmarried undergraduates, were asked, "What does it mean when a (close) person of the opposite sex [not a relative] touches a certain area of my body in a certain manner?" They indicated their agreement on a four-point scale. Subjects were in general agreement that touch conveys warmth/love and is pleasant; "sexual desire" is the least likely interpretation given to touch, except that to "sexual" body areas (and males and females agreed on the areas associated with sexual desire). Analysis of variance for each meaning category showed an interaction of sex of subject and body area rated, indicating disagreement between the sexes about the meanings of touch to different areas. For males, pleasantness, sexual desire, and warmth/love formed a cluster; for females, touch that signified sexual desire was *opposed* to pleasantness, love/warmth, friendliness, and playfulness. The researchers compared their questionnaire responses to published reports on the skin sensitivity of various areas of the body, and found, in general, no significant relationship, except that body areas ranking high on sexual desire (and pleasantness, for males) also have high thresholds, i.e., are relatively insensitive. Females discriminate between their body areas more than males do, for touch; males, on the other hand, are more attuned to touch modalities than women. The authors interpret the differences only briefly, as a possible result of the sexual double standard and/or women's vulnerability to exploitation; and question whether the same results would be obtained from married women or non-college-student women (the women of this study are implicitly seen as the deviants).

F. Eye Behavior and Eye Contact

ARGYLE, MICHAEL, MANSUR LALLJEE, and MARK COOK.
"The Effects of Visibility on Interaction in a Dyad." *Human Relations,* 21 (1968), 3-17.

A series of three experiments was performed in which visibility was varied for both members of a dyad, and measures of speech production and reported comfort, knowledge of others' reactions, and desire for more information were made. Females were uncomfortable if they could not see the other person when invisible themselves, which was not the case with male subjects. With reduced visibility males talked more and females less in a male-female pair; regardless of concealment, males seemed motivated to dominate and did so largely by interrupting and talking more. Females, especially when talking to males, felt "observed." [*See IV-D, IV-E.*]

ARGYLE, MICHAEL, and ROGER INGHAM.
"Gaze, Mutual Gaze, and Proximity." *Semiotica,* 6 (1972), 32-49.

Three experiments are reported which examine the effect of distance on eye contact with relation to speaking, for males and females in both mixed- and same-sex dyads. Females seem to indicate intimacy by looking at the other when they themselves are talking; males indicate it by looking at the other while they are listening. There was less looking in male-female pairs than in either type of single-sex pairs. Also, when visibility was varied so that the subject saw the other through a one-way glass, females more than males tended to look more than in the normal, both-seeing condition; or, put another way, "females were more inhibited than males by the possibility of eye contact."

BIRDWHISTELL, RAY.
    "Masculinity and Femininity as Display." In *Kinesics and Context.* Philadelphia:
    Univ. of Pennsylvania Press, 1970, pp. 39-46.

According to Birdwhistell, males in American society are prohibited from moving the
eyeballs while the lids are closed, and generally should close and open their lids in a
relatively continuous movement. [*See IX-A, IX-D.*]

EXLINE, RALPH V.
    "Explorations in the Process of Person Perception: Visual Interaction in Relation to
    Competition, Sex, and Need for Affiliation." *Journal of Personality,* 31 (1963), 1-20.

Visual interaction was observed in 32 artificially-created three-person groups, half of
them all-male and half all-female. Women were found to engage in mutual visual interaction
(with each other) more than men, and sex was found to interact with affiliation need:
highly affiliative females look more at one another relative to less affiliative females than is
the case for males, who show the opposite tendency. Women's mutuality of looking was
greater when total looking was held constant. Competition seemed to inhibit mutual glances
among high affiliators and increase them among low affiliators, with women showing more
reaction to the situation than men. Women's visual activity is both more oriented toward
social stimuli than men's, and more affected by relevant social field conditions. Women have
also been found in some experiments to be more affected than men by visual cues in
establishing their bodily orientation in space, or in recognizing embedded figures; i.e., they
are "field dependent." Sex differences in eye contact may similarly be due to greater visual
dependence on objects in the social field.

EXLINE, RALPH, DAVID GRAY, and DOROTHY SHUETTE.
    "Visual Behavior in a Dyad as Affected by Interview Content and Sex of
    Respondent." *Journal of Personality and Social Psychology,* 1 (1965), 201-209.

Forty male and forty female college students were interviewed, half of each sex by a
male and half by a female interviewer. Women engaged in more mutual glances than did
men, and tended to look more at the interviewer while the latter was talking than did men,
particularly when instructed to conceal their feelings. Men, on the other hand, looked less
when told to conceal. All subjects gave much visual attention when the interviewer spoke
(more looking while listening than looking while speaking), regardless of other variables. The
data support an earlier finding of greater mutual glance among women than men, and
suggest also that women may maintain more eye contact regardless of the other's sex. The
data also suggest that sex differences in eye contact are a result of women's greater
orientation toward affectionate and inclusive relationships with others.

JOHNSON, KENNETH R.
    "Black Kinesics—Some Nonverbal Communication Patterns in the Black Culture."
    Florida FL Reporter, Spring/Fall 1971, 17-20+.

"Rolling the eyes," an expression of impudence and disapproval of someone in
authority, is more common among black females than among black males. It consists of

moving the eyes from one side of the socket to the other in a low arc (usually preceded by a stare at the other, but not an eye-to-eye stare), away from the other, with slightly lowered lids, and is very quick. The expression is mainly one of hostility, though it can also be used in general disapproval (as of another's uppity airs). [*See IX-A, IX-D.*]

MEHRABIAN, ALBERT.
   Nonverbal Communication. Chicago: Aldine Atherton, 1972.

Mehrabian cites his own and others' research with the following findings: females maintain more eye contact with others than males do; females tend to increase eye contact in positive interaction, while males decrease (both sexes decrease in aversive interaction) (p. 10). However, males showed more eye contact with extremely disliked males than with extremely disliked females (p. 101). In a persuasibility experiment, females speaking at the greater of two distances were more persuasive with greater eye contact than with less (90% vs. 50% contact), while males were more persuasive with less eye contact. [*See IX-A, B, C, D, G.*]

G. Smiling

Numerous feminists have made the observation that women engage in more smiling than men do, as appeasement and as a requirement of their social position, and perhaps further, out of fear and nervous habit. A survey of seven recent books on nonverbal communication (all of them by men), however, failed to uncover any statistics on the frequency of smiling or any recognitition of this difference which the women's movement regards as obvious and basic.

BUGENTAL, DAPHNE E., LEONORE R. LOVE, and ROBERT M. GIANETTO.
   "Perfidious Feminine Faces." *Journal of Personality and Social Psychology,* 17 (1971), 314-318.

Videotaped interactions of 20 families with "disturbed" children and 20 with "normal" ones, socioeconomically matched, were analyzed for parental facial expressions and verbal content: 81% of the children of the first group, and 86% of the second group, were boys. Fathers made more positive statements when smiling than when not smiling, but mothers' verbal messages were no more positive when smiling than when not. Mothers' verbal messages were more variable than fathers' verbal messages; there were no effects that were a function of child disturbance. Only 13% of the lower class mothers smiled more than once, whereas 75% of the middle class mothers smiled more than once (there was no significant difference between classes in fathers' smiling). Parents, particularly mothers, smiled often when observed, very little when supposedly unobserved. Earlier studies had found that children respond to women's smiles, in comparison with men's, as relatively neutral, and that they respond to contradictory messages (negative statement accompanied by a smile) as negative, and more so if the speaker is a woman. Since women use the smile as part of a culturally prescribed role, there may be little or no relationship between smiling and verbal message. The young child's response to a woman's smile is then seen as accurate, in the sense that her smile does not directly signal friendliness or approval.

CHESLER, PHYLLIS.
    Women and Madness. New York: Doubleday, 1972.

    "Women, as well as men, are deeply threatened by a female who does not smile often enough and, paradoxically, who is not very unhappy. Women mistrust and men destroy those women who are not interested in *sacrificing* at least something for someone for some reason" (pp. 278-279).

FIRESTONE, SHULAMITH.
    The Dialectic of Sex. New York: Bantam Books, 1970.

    "The smile is the child/woman of the shuffle; it indicates acquiescence of the victim to his own oppression. In my own case, I had to train myself out of that phony smile, which is like a nervous tic on every teenage girl. And this meant that I smiled rarely, for in truth, when it came down to real smiling, I had less to smile about. My 'dream' action for the women's liberation movement: *a smile boycott,* at which declaration all women would instantly abandon their 'pleasing' smiles, henceforth smiling only when something pleased *them*" (p. 90).

MEHRABIAN, ALBERT.
    Nonverbal Communication. Chicago: Aldine Atherton, 1972.

    In an experiment on persuasiveness, males' "facial pleasantness and activity" were judged to be less than those of females (p. 70). In a role-playing experiment, males increased their facial pleasantness when attempting to deceive, whereas females in the deception condition showed no more facial pleasantness than in the truthful condition (p. 88). [*See IX-A, B, C, D, F.*]

NIERENBERG, GERARD I., and HENRY H. CALERO.
    How to Read a Person Like a Book. New York: Hawthorn, 1971. (New York: Pocket Books, 1973.)

    Nierenberg and Calero cite a smile classification system of Ewan Grant (Birmingham University—reference not given), in which one of the five basic smiles is the "lip-in smile . . . often seen on the faces of coy girls." It is similar to another basic smile, the "upper, or how-do-you-do, smile," which has only the upper teeth showing and the mouth slightly open. In addition, in the lip-in smile, the lower lip is drawn in between the teeth. "It implies that the person feels in some way subordinate to the person she is meeting," quote the authors (Pocket edition, p. 32).

SILVEIRA, JEANETTE.
  "Thoughts on the Politics of Touch." *Women's Press* (Eugene, Ore.), 1 (Feb., 1972), 13.

  Silveira cites smiling as a signal of submission, particularly from women to men, and compares this with its similar use among monkeys and apes. Women seem more apt to smile especially (1) when a woman and man are greeting each other, and (2) when the two know each other only moderately well. The smile indicates assurance that no harm or aggression is intended, rather than pleasure and friendliness. [*See IX-C.*]

RELEVANT WOMEN'S GROUPS

Caucuses, Committees, and Independent Groups in Disciplines Related to the Study of Sex Differences in Language, Speech, and Nonverbal Communication

[This list is not meant to be complete, but should be able to put readers in touch with the main and most active groups in a given field.]

Language and Linguistics

Linguistic Society of America
    LSA Women's Caucus
        Correspondent: Lynette Hirschman
                      4709 Baltimore Avenue
                      Philadelphia, PA   19143

Modern Language Association
    Women's Caucus of the MLA
        President: Dolores Barracano Schmidt
                      R. D. 3
                      Slippery Rock, PA   16057

Committee on the Status of Women in the Profession
    c/o   Elaine Hedges
                  Towson State College
                  Baltimore, MD   21204

Sociology

Sociologists for Women in Society
        Chairperson: Arlene Kaplan Daniels
                      Department of Sociology
                      Northwestern University
                      Evanston, IL   60201

Psychology

Association for Women in Psychology
        Correspondent: Dorothy Camara
                      7012 Western Avenue
                      Chevy Chase, MD   20015

American Psychological Association
    Division of Psychology of Women
        c/o   American Psychological Association
                  1200 Seventeenth Street, N. W.
                  Washington, DC   20036

Anthropology
American Anthropological Association
Committee on the Status of Women in Anthropology
1703 New Hampshire Avenue, N. W.
Washington, DC   20009

New York Women's Anthroplogy Conference
c/o   Constance Sutton
                                 Department of Anthropology
                                 New York University
                                 25 Waverley Place
                                 New York, NY   10003

Philosophy
Society for Women in Philosophy
c/o   Philosophy Department
                                 University of Illinois, Chicago Circle
                                 P. O. Box 4348
                                 Chicago, IL   60680

American Philosophical Association
    Women's Caucus
        Chair: Mary Mothersill
                                 Department of Philosophy
                                 Barnard College
                                 New York, NY   10027

Writing
Feminist Writers Workshop
c/o   Ruth Todasco
                                 Loop Center YWCA
                                 37 South Wabash Avenue
                                 Chicago, Il   60603

Teachers of English
National Council of Teachers of English
    Committee on the Role and Image of Women in the Council and Profession
        Chair: Johanna S. DeStefano
                                 200 Ramseyer Hall
                                 The Ohio State University
                                 Columbus, Ohio 43210

AUTHOR INDEX TO THE BIBLIOGRAPHY